SHADOW GOVERNMENT

The Hidden World
of Public Authorities—
And How They Control Over
$1 Trillion of *Your* Money

DONALD AXELROD

John Wiley & Sons, Inc.
New York · Chichester · Brisbane
Toronto · Singapore

To Selma, Jonathan,
and Rosemary

In recognition of the importance of preserving what has been written,
it is a policy of John Wiley & Sons, Inc., to have books of enduring value
published in the United States printed on acid-free paper, and we exert
our best efforts to that end.

Copyright © 1992 by Donald Axelrod

Published by John Wiley & Sons, Inc.

All rights reserved. Published simultaneously in Canada.

Reproduction or translation of any part of this work beyond that permitted
by Section 107 or 108 of the 1976 United States Copyright Act without
the permission of the copyright owner is unlawful. Requests for permission
or further information should be addressed to the Permissions Department,
John Wiley & Sons, Inc.

Library of Congress Cataloging-in-Publication Data

Axelrod, Donald, 1916–
    Shadow government : the hidden world of public authorities and
how they control $1 trillion dollars of *your* money
/ Donald Axelrod.
    p. cm.
    Includes bibliographical references and index.
    ISBN 0-471-52767-X
    1. Corporations, Government—United States. I. Title.
HD3885.A94   1992
338.6'2'0973—dc20   91-44086

Printed in the United States of America

10 9 8 7 6 5 4 3 2 1

PREFACE

Mention public authorities, also known as government corporations and special districts, to most people and you draw a blank stare. They know virtually nothing about an obscure but powerful fourth branch of government that affects our lives for better and worse. Some 35,000 frequently free-wheeling and autonomous public authorities exist today and control some of the most vital services of the country: transportation, economic development, housing, water supply, sewage and waste disposal, power generation and distribution, urban redevelopment, higher education loans, and the construction of schools, universities, hospitals, and prisons.

In power, affluence, and assets, public authorities rival the largest state and local governments and commercial banks in the United States. They borrow more billions of dollars than state and local governments combined. They have run up a debt that is second only to that of the U.S. government itself. The annual operating expenditures of large public authorities exceed the budgets of many states and most countries in the world. Yet, in the main, public authorities don't answer to governors, mayors, legislatures or the voters. This amounts to a loss of the power of the purse and undermines the very constitutional foundations of government.

In what amounts to a quiet revolution, we now have two governments working side by side: the visible general government and the shadow government of public authorities. Freed of control and surveillance, and insulated from the voters, many public authorities are quagmires of political patronage, corruption, and mismanagement. Conversely, many stand out because of their considerable achievements and their response to public needs. Still, in the main, they are unaccountable.

Even though public authorities are the fastest growing form of government, shockingly, we know little about them. It is fairly easy to get vital data about the federal, state, and local governments. Conversely, information on public authorities is sparse, fragmentary, and scattered throughout the nation. They are the *terra incognita* of government.

This frustrating lack of information led to this book. For the last 10 years I have followed the explosion of public authorities, yet have been unable to size them up fully. Documentation is scarce, and gathering information for this book could not have been completed without the help and confidences of many individuals.

For a firsthand look at public authorities, it was necessary to crisscross the country and to conduct hundreds of interviews. More people than I can openly acknowledge were fruitful sources of information. Some preferred to remain anonymous. When they read this book, I hope they will appreciate the contributions they have made.

Several gifted financial specialists guided me in exploring the mysteries of tax-exempt bonds, which are the plastic credit cards of public authorities and governments. In particular, I should like to acknowledge the assistance of John W. Illyes of Nuveen and Co.; Hyman C. Grossman, managing director of the municipal finance department of Standard and Poor's; Jay Abrams, a vice president of Standard and Poor's; Claire G. Cohen, executive managing director of governmental finance, Fitch Investors Service; Joseph M. Giglio, senior vice president of Chase Securities Inc. and former chairman of the National Council on Public Works Improvement; Heather L. Ruth, president of the Public Securities Association; Natalie R. Cohen, vice president of Enhance Reinsurance Co.; and Richard Lehmann, president of the Bond Investors Association.

Investigative reporters and newspaper morgues proved to be invaluable. Among journalists who helped me ferret out the seamier side of public authorities were Diana B. Henriques of the *New York Times*; Steven Weinberg, executive director of Investigative Reporters and Editors (IRE) at the University of Missouri School of Journalism in Columbia; John Strahanich of *Boston Magazine*; and Ben Weberman of *Forbes*.

Many former and present senior government officials provided insights into the bright and dark sides of public authorities. I owe much to Peter C. Goldmark, Jr., president of the Rockefeller Foundation and former executive director of the Port Authority of New York and New Jersey; Alton G. Marshall, former chairman of Lincoln Savings Bank in New York City and former secretary of Governor Nelson A. Rockefeller; Alden Raine, former secretary of economic affairs in Governor Michael S. Dukakis' administration; Richard A. Skerry, Jr., general counsel of the Massachusetts Industrial Finance Agency; David McKenzie, a senior staffer with the ways and means committee of the Massachusetts state senate; the staff of Paul Levy, the then executive director of the Massachusetts Water Resources Authority; and Edward M. Kresky, former vice president of Wertheim and Co. and currently a member of the New York State Public Service Commission.

In California doors were opened for me by Elizabeth Hill, legislative analyst; Suzanne Burton of the treasurer's office; Richard R. Ray, assistant director of finance; Ralph Martinez, who monitors special districts in the comptroller's office; Dean Miseynzski of the state senate office of research; and Robert G. Potter and Lawrence Mullnix, deputy directors of the California Department of Water Resources. Thomas Pollard, executive director of the Texas Bond Review Board, brought me up to date on authority financing in that state. One of the national experts in debt financing is Merl Hackbart, budget director of Kentucky. He shared both his insights and data with me. I also benefited enormously from the assistance of several individuals in and out of government in Illinois: the staff of the Illinois Economic and Fiscal Commission; Douglas Whitley, president of the Illinois Taxpayers' Federation; Robert L. Mandeville, the then director of the state bureau of the budget; and Robert G. Cranson, auditor general of Illinois.

In nearby Wisconsin Robert W. Lang, director of the Legislative Fiscal Bureau, and Richard J. Longabaugh, executive director of the Wisconsin Housing and Economic Development Authority, explained why their state relies less on public authorities than other states. Richard Molloy of the governor's office, Edward P. Westreich of the legislative staff, and the senior staff of Douglas C. Berman, the state treasurer, in New Jersey familiarized me with the many public authorities in that state. For a national view of public authorities I am indebted to Barry Van Lare, deputy director of the National Governors Association, and Gerald Miller, former executive director of the National Association of State Budget offices.

Several federal agencies were also most generous in providing data to me: the U.S. Bureau of the Census, the Environmental Protection Agency, the Department of Transportation, the Department of Energy, and the General Accounting Office. Washington, D.C. is also the home of national organizations that represent public authorities in nearly every field. I am grateful for the assistance of Larry Hobart, executive director of the American Public Power Association; Rexford B. Sherman, director of research of the American Association of Port Authorities; Larry Pham, director of research of the American Public Transit Association; and Mary K. Nenno, associate director of the National Association of Housing and Redevelopment Officials.

Only a small band of scholars in academia recognize the significance of public authorities. I benefited from the assistance of several, including Annemarie Hauck Walsh, former president of the Institute of Public Administration; Jameson W. Doig of Princeton University; David C. Perry of the State University of New York at Buffalo; James Leigland of the University of Kentucky; and Ronald Forbes and David Andersen of the State University of New York at Albany. Harold Seidman, former assistant director of the U.S. Bureau of the Budget and a senior fellow at the National Academy of Public Administration, is the nation's premier expert on government corporations. He generously shared his views with me.

Such strength as the book has is due in large part to the perceptive editing of Roger W. Scholl and Judith N. McCarthy at John Wiley & Sons. My wife Selma not only supported my two-year commitment at the expense of a piece of our personal lives, but also unfailingly spotted rough patches in language and ambiguities in content.

Without two small but highly specialized libraries, my task would have been far more difficult. I am indebted to Richard D. Irving of the Thomas E. Dewey Library at the State University of New York at Albany and Janet Butlin of the library in the New York State Division of the Budget. With incredible patience, Lori Saba typed and retyped my field notes and manuscript.

In a book of this kind disclaimers are especially important. Such errors of fact that may exist are mine, and mine alone. The strong views on public authorities that lace the book are also mine and should not be attributed to the many individuals who helped me.

If the book will serve to bring public authorities out of the shadows, it will have achieved its purpose.

CONTENTS

1 The Rise of the Shadow Government   1

2 Always a Borrower or a Lender Be   35

3 A Fate Worse Than Debt   63

4 Who's Minding the Store?   92

5 The Law Be Damned!   118

6 The Public Authority Sweepstakes:
Winners and Losers   141

7 Bucking the Economic Tide   168

8 Housing Horrors   194

9 The Big Fix   220

10 The Big Cleanup   245

11 Power to the People   270

12 Public Authorities Join the Welfare State   290

13 Reclaiming the Shadow Government   310

Select Bibliography   *321*

Notes   *323*

Index   *341*

On Public Authorities

"The big advantage: free from the control the people have; the big disadvantage: free from the control people have."
Mario Cuomo

"For forms of government let fools contest; whate'er is best administered is best."
Alexander Pope (1688–1744) in Essay on Man

"But man, proud man, drest in a little brief authority."
William Shakespeare (1564–1616) in Measure for Measure

"When money speaks, the truth keeps silent."
Russian proverb

1

The Rise of the
Shadow Government

During the American Revolution against Britain, a stirring call to battle was the cry: "no taxation without representation!" Since then Americans have regarded popular control of public funds as a birthright. It would be unthinkable, says conventional wisdom, for government to tax, spend, and borrow funds without voter or legislative approval. It would be unthinkable to take any of these actions behind closed doors.

Yet the unthinkable is occurring today on a staggering scale.

The Washington, D.C. Shell Game

One of the greatest financial crises since the Great Depression is the failure of over 1,000 savings and loan associations—the so-called thrifts. Only superficially regulated during the lax years of the Reagan administration, they made indefensible investments and siphoned off billions of dollars of depositors' money through mismanagement, fraud, corruption, negligence, and outright theft. To protect depositors against such hazards, the Federal Savings and Loan Insurance Corporation (FSLIC), a federal government corporation, charged each savings and loan institution a premium that insured deposits up to $100,000. Ordinarily these premiums were sufficient to take care of occasional defaults and peccadilloes. In the 1980s they proved to be hopelessly inadequate. From 1984 to 1989, the FSLIC lost over $100 billion, the largest deficit reported by any

1

public or private corporation anywhere. Looming ahead were losses of $300 billion to $500 billion. No one had a precise figure. But the federal government had to make good on its guarantees.

In the greatest bailout in the history of the country, the Bush administration proposed in 1989 that the taxpayers cover the lion's share of the deposits. The thrifts would be responsible for a relatively small amount through increased premiums. Regardless of the wisdom of this policy, any proposed expenditure, large or small, would usually appear in the president's budget. Congressional committees would scrutinize it in detail. Voters would spell out their views in letters and calls to senators and representatives. In the end, Congress would pass an appropriations bill providing for a bailout. So one would assume.

Not this time! Under no circumstances did the president want the funds to appear in his official budget. That would swell an already large and intolerable deficit that was growing at the rate of over $200 billion a year. Instead, the president urged Congress to eliminate FSLIC and to create a new government corporation, the Resolution Trust Corporation (RTC), to sell off the assets of the failed thrifts. RTC would be under the direct supervision of the Federal Deposit Insurance Corporation (FDIC), still another government corporation, which insured deposits in commercial banks. It would get the authority to sell bonds in the capital markets, borrow directly from the U.S. Treasury, and use the proceeds to pay depositors. Like its parent, FDIC, RTC is off-budget—that is, its expenditures don't count as part of the official government budget. Only a small amount of its funds come from direct congressional appropriations. Of course, the government would be stuck with the payment of interest on the bonds over a 30-year period, but this would be spread over a long period of time and, commingled with payment of interest on the national debt, would confuse the already overwhelmed voters.

Holding its nose, in August 1989 Congress barely approved what Senator George Mitchell, the majority leader, called "a budget fraud." The stench, however, did not prevent Mitchell and other congressional leaders from agreeing in 1990 to keep the entire S&L bailout off budget except for an initial payment of $20 billion.

Through such fiscal legerdemain the administration and Congress removed extraordinary expenditures from the open budget and appropriation processes. They cooked the nation's books so that the deficit would appear to be smaller than it was. They set up a government corporation outside of the regular government with the authority to borrow funds. They left the voters hopelessly muddled about who does what. And they added still another pea to the Washington, D.C. shell game. So much for voter control of the power of the purse!

What Bush and Congress did was not new. Only the magnitude of the bailout by the RTC was record-breaking. In fact, several of the large federal corporations had been off-budget for years. The motivation then was the same: to make the federal budget look smaller than it was. Thus, in 1954 the Federal National Mortgage Association changed from an on-budget, wholly-owned federal corporation to an off-budget, public-private corporation (later it was wholly privatized). To extricate himself from budget problems, in 1955 President Eisenhower proposed the creation of an off-budget Federal Highway Corporation to build the national interstate highway system. He settled, however, for a highway trust fund financed with earmarked gasoline and tire taxes to do the job.

No federal schemes, however, even come close to the widespread conning of the voters by state governments when setting up off-budget public authorities—a term they prefer rather than "government corporations."

The Rockefeller Miracle

Nelson A. Rockefeller set the pace for such financial gimmickry when he was governor of New York State from 1959 to 1974. He dominated state politics as no governor had before. An activist, he had ambitious schemes to expand the state university, modernize mental health hospitals, build affordable housing, and improve the highway network. Only the voters and the state constitution stood in his way. Like most state constitutions, New York State's is studded with restrictions to control taxing, spending, and borrowing by state and local governments. One such roadblock is the stiff requirement of voter approval of all bond issues through referendums. Exercising their constitutional privilege, voters in New York State turned down several Rockefeller-initiated, multimillion-dollar and multi-billion-dollar bond issues for housing five times, for transportation two times, and for higher education four times.

Determined to give the voters what they wanted but refused to pay for, the frustrated governor turned to John A. Mitchell, then an eminent Wall Street bond counsel in the firm of Nixon, Rose, and Mudge (later a convicted felon because of his involvement in the Watergate coverup when he was President Nixon's attorney general).

Mitchell came up with a seductive formula: Establish a public authority off-budget and outside of the general government structure. He proposed giving the authority power to issue tax-exempt bonds that it could pay off with fees and rents charged for its services. Self-financed, the authority would be independent of the state government. No voter approval would be needed because the debt would not be state debt. No legislative approval of authority expenditures would be necessary since the authority would be off-budget. The state budget would not include its expenditures and revenues.

But how could investors be persuaded to buy the bonds of public authorities when they lacked state-backed constitutional guarantees of repayment? All state bonds approved by the voters in accordance with constitutional requirements have such guarantees and have the best security of all behind them: the full faith and credit of the state. This means that the entire tax system of the state is the security for the bondholders.

In addition, Mitchell had to contend with bond-rating organizations, like Moody's Investment Service and Standard and Poor's, which rate the risk of municipal bonds from C (risky) to BBB (passable) to AAA (the crème de la crème). These ratings influence both investment decisions and interest rates. Highest ratings go to bonds that enjoy the full faith and credit of the issuing government. These bonds command lower interest rates than nonguaranteed bonds.

Mitchell came up with a new fiscal invention—the "moral obligation" bond or what Alton G. Marshall, former secretary of Governor Rockefeller, calls a "no worry" bond. He proposed that legislation and bond covenants require public authorities to have on hand at all times a reserve sufficient to pay one year's principal and interest on their debt. Should the reserve fall short of the required amount of coverage, the governor would recommend to the legislature that it replenish the reserve.

This was unabashed chicanery. No legislature could bind future legislatures to appropriate funds for a debt service reserve. At best, authority bonds were no more than "moral obligations." As Marshall puts it, they were a "sop to bond buyers" because they looked like guarantees. Fundamentally, they were no more than informal pledges to appropriate funds for shortfalls in authority reserves. Marshall further describes the moral obligation bonds as "part deception, part honesty." They were honest in the sense that the authority's flow of revenue backed up the bonds and, seemingly, it would not be necessary to dip into the reserves. They were deceptive in the sense that Mitchell and the other insiders knew all along that some authorities lacked financial stability and that it would be necessary to tap state funds and replenish the reserves.

Mitchell later recalled Rockefeller's delight at his contrivance for bypassing the constitution and raising funds for cherished programs: "Old Nelson espoused my theory like it was the salvation of mankind. He treated the money like manna from heaven."[1]

Rockefeller was less colorful on the subject when he testified before Congress after President Ford had nominated him as vice president: "I was unable to obtain public approval of state bond issues. We therefore devised an innovative approach."[2]

To highlight the independence and autonomy of public authorities, Rockefeller and the legislature went further by placing them off-budget. They gave authority boards the power to run their own financial affairs and to dispose of their earnings as they saw fit. They could appoint their own chief executive officers. They were largely freed from the fetters that shackled regular state agencies. No governor or legislature would approve their budgets; no civil service agency would control the hiring and firing of their staff or their pay plans; and no state accountants would approve their contracts and purchases. Like any private corporation, they would be on their own.

Bedazzled by the sheer inventiveness and ingenuity of the Mitchell formula, Rockefeller, with legislative support, added 23 public authorities to the 26 already in existence in New York State. Some of the biggest among them financed their activities with moral obligation bonds. Emerging in short order were: the Urban Development Corporation to attack problems of housing and urban renewal; the Mental Health Facilities Construction Fund to build mental hospitals and community mental health clinics; the State University Construction Fund to build facilities for the burgeoning State University of New York; and the Housing Finance Agency to expand low-income and middle-income housing.

Pre-Rockefeller public authorities were given new life. The Metropolitan Transportation Authority took over the New York City subway system, bus lines, commuter railroads, and several major bridges. The New York State Power Authority became one of the largest utilities, public or private, in the country. The Dormitory Authority evolved into an investment bank that financed the construction of public and private college buildings, nonprofit hospitals, and nursing homes. What would become the multibillion-dollar authority-empire of the Empire State was well on its way.

Word of the Rockefeller miracle soon spread to all the states where governors and legislatures also confronted restrictive constitutions and testy taxpayers. They sent emissaries to Albany to observe firsthand the arcane art of spending money on projects and programs without increasing budgets or raising taxes, and without having to obtain voter approval. They found that authority finances conveniently don't count as part of state finances. They noted that citizens paid no taxes for the services of authorities. Instead they paid fees and, most fascinating, started no fee revolts.

What the envoys saw they liked and nearly every state hastened to follow the Rockefeller route. Hundreds of new authorities sprang up across the nation. In more than half the states, authorities issued moral obligation bonds. These bond issues became the darling of Wall Street. Delighted investors, consoled by the security blanket of moral obligations, bought billions of dollars of tax-exempt bonds.

The authority-financed building boom reached new heights. Seemingly, the only loser was the federal government, which annually lost nearly $40 billion in revenue since it couldn't tax the interest on authority and other state and local bonds.

Mayor Koch and the Big Apple

New York proudly proclaims itself "the state that has everything." It does, including the financial woes of New York City. In 1975 the city faced virtual bankruptcy when it couldn't pay the interest on bonds and notes issued lavishly by a succession of colorful but imprudent mayors. In an eleventh-hour rescue, New York State and the federal government had to bail out the city.

In 1977, and for the next 11 years, Mayor Edward Koch presided over the city's tangled finances. Few options were available. State aid from Albany was at a new high and recalcitrant upstate legislators balked at any significant increases. The city had pushed its taxing authority to the limit. Any further tax increases might hasten the exodus of business firms from the city. In the meantime, the antiquated 6,000-mile water system, with its nineteenth-century pipes, needed to be replaced. The city could no longer handle the thousands of tons of waste and garbage that piled up every day. It was running out of landfills, and old sewage plants no longer met environmental standards. The federal government flatly prohibited any further dumping of sludge in the Atlantic Ocean, while other states and third world countries made it clear that they would not welcome a garbage fleet bringing the city's waste to their shores.

Adding to the mayor's troubles, the city's 200 bridges and road network were deteriorating dangerously. Many of its 918 school buildings were obsolete and unsafe.

In the midst of this crisis the mayor heard the siren song of public authorities. Without raising budgets or taxes, he could provide pure water to the hapless residents, rid them of their waste, assure them a safe journey on the bridges, and transform the schools from blackboard jungles into palaces of learning. Of course the public would pay fees and charges for such delightful amenities. But poll after poll showed that voters preferred user charges rather than taxes.

Schools posed something of a problem because parents ordinarily don't pay tuition for public schools. Fortunately, though, another public authority, the Municipal Assistance Corporation (Big MAC), was restructuring the debt of New York City and had a tidy surplus that could be used for school construction.

The mayor campaigned aggressively to establish five new authorities in addition to the 10 already existing in the city. Albany met him part of the way. In 1984 the legislature and governor approved a Municipal Water Finance Authority. In 1988 they went along with a School Construction Authority funded in large part by Big MAC. In the face of union and banker opposition they stalled in setting up multibillion-dollar waste management, highway, and bridge authorities, but the city's perpetual fiscal crises made these actions inevitable.

Governor Dukakis Confronts Boston Harbor

For Michael Dukakis, governor of Massachusetts and unsuccessful Democratic candidate in the presidential election of 1988, a public authority was the way out of a painful dilemma. In an ugly campaign, the Republican candidate, George Bush, had blamed Dukakis for failing to act on the pollution of Boston Harbor, one of the filthiest bodies of water in the United States. The attack was only partly justified.

Indeed, 43 communities, including Boston, poured their waste into the harbor, but the State of Massachusetts did not have the political support to raise the billions of dollars necessary for the cleanup. It was already dubbed "Taxachusetts" for having one of the highest state tax rates in the country. No single local government could venture to attack a regional problem. Republican administrations had sharply cut back federal funds for sewage and wastewater treatment. In this impasse the Dukakis administration floundered.

Finally, court orders forced Dukakis and the legislature to act. In 1984 the legislature reluctantly accepted Dukakis' proposal to create the Massachusetts Water Resources Authority (MWRA) with the dual mission of restoring the harbor to a pristine state in 10 years, at an estimated, cost of $8.1 billion, and providing water to

46 communities. Fees and charges would support the entire operation. MWRA became the 24th state public authority in Massachusetts. Dukakis' administration had been responsible for creating half of them.

Governor "Big Jim" Thompson

In the heartland of America Governor "Big Jim" (James C.) Thompson of Illinois (1976–1990) seemingly had no need of public authorities. The electorate in 1970 had graciously expunged a constitutional amendment that limited state debt to $250,000. He merely required the support of three-fifths of the legislature for a bond issue. And that was easy to get. It looked as if the golden age of fiscal probity and openness had arrived in Illinois.

But the governor realized that debt service for state bond issues would have the effect of inflating the state budget. Rising budgets would tarnish Thompson's image as a tight-fisted, economy-minded, Republican chief executive. The answer, once again, was to establish public authorities whose debt and expenditures would not count as part of budget totals. Governor Thompson created 14 authorities, almost rivaling the record of Nelson Rockefeller. It didn't matter to Thompson that public authority debt, with its high interest rates, would eventually be more expensive for the state. The appearance of fiscal conservatism mattered more. But his conservative budget was something of a hoax since authority debt did not appear in it.

Robert G. Cranson, the auditor general of Illinois, described budgetary manipulation in Illinois this way in one of several interviews: "The real function of the [Thompson] Bureau of the Budget is to fund through indebtedness that which they can't fund through appropriations. It's the same situation that the federal government has except they don't have the privilege of printing money. The Governor and the Bureau of the Budget have a vested interest in seeing that the lack of a balanced budget does not get exposed."

Like Rockefeller, Thompson became a master builder on a vast scale and delighted in ribbon-cutting ceremonies that opened new facilities built by public authorities. The apple of his eye was a $1.5-billion expansion of the gigantic McCormick Place Convention Center.

Ploys in Other States and Cities

In the 1970s, public authorities became the center of a political storm in California. While tax revolts were commonplace in most states, none equaled the passion, the demagoguery, and the size of the uprising in California. In 1979 California voters approved Proposition 13, a constitutional amendment that cut real estate taxes by $2.5 billion and set tight ceilings on future tax increases. In short order local governments ran out of funds for schools, libraries, parks, recreational services, hospitals, fire protection, urban development, and street and road maintenance. At that time the state had a hefty surplus of some $6 billion. It used these funds to provide stopgap aid for two years. But once the quick fix was over, local governments had two options: cut services disastrously or get around Proposition 13 by establishing public authorities (usually termed "special districts" in California). Some communities took the first painful course; most opted for the latter. Supported by fees and special taxes, public authorities would not be subject to the tax limits of unlucky 13. They would be off-budget. Within a few years public authorities (special districts) in California reached a new high—some 6,000.

In the nearby State of Washington power shortages loomed as a dangerous possibility in the 1970s. For years the state had benefited from the hydroelectric power furnished by the federal Bonneville Power Administration, which had harnessed the energy of the turbulent Columbia River. But this and other energy sources proved to be inadequate in the wake of the industrial boom and population growth of the postwar years. Under a succession of governors the state responded by creating the largest public authority in the United States—the $8-billion Washington Public Power Supply System (WPPSS), known more familiarly and appropriately as WHOOPS. By selling tax-exempt bonds WHOOPS planned to build five nuclear plants to serve 88 communities. Utility charges were to pay the principal and interest of the bond issues. This was, of course, under the assumption that the project would run smoothly and utility charges would come rolling in.

In New Jersey and Pennsylvania deliberate and blatant circumvention of state constitutions led to the establishment of hundreds of public authorities. Troubled by the profligacy of local governments, the New Jersey state legislature in 1975 limited increases in local budgets to 6 percent annually. Localities quickly discovered the magic ability of public authorities to sidestep the legislative ceiling and to deceive the voters as to the size of the budget. By 1988 they had spawned over 500 public authorities/special districts. They made the authorities responsible for numerous activities that previously had been tax-supported. Now fees in large part fund these functions. In Pennsylvania, local governments hatched over 2,600 public authorities to evade clear-cut constitutional constraints.

A Pervasive Presence

Thanks to the Rockefellers, Dukakises, Thompsons, Koches, and governors, mayors, and legislatures past and present, public authorities reach into every nook and cranny in the nation. So addicted is the United States to them that they are with each of us from the womb to the tomb. Chances are that we enter and leave this life in hospitals financed and constructed by public authorities, not to mention visits for health crises along the way. We depend on them for pure water and the removal of waste and wastewater, and in many parts of the country they light and heat our homes and illuminate our streets.

Public authorities are as much a part of education as the three "Rs." They finance the construction of elementary and secondary schools for our children. Should our progeny go on to public or private colleges, they will use authority-financed academic buildings, libraries, and dormitories. If we require loans for higher education, a friendly public authority will likely provide or guarantee them.

As we drive to school or work or visit friends and relatives, we will probably travel on roads, bridges, and tunnels financed, constructed, and operated by authorities. When we arrive at our destinations, an authority stands ready to park our cars at a price. Should we forsake our cars for trains, buses, and trolleys, another public authority will see us through our trips. If we fly, we will in all likelihood depart from and arrive at airports operated by public authorities.

At the happy moment when we are ready to buy houses, public authorities may offer us mortgages at attractive, low-interest rates. They may even guarantee the payment of our mortgages. They will also buy mortgages from banks so that the banks will have more funds to lend our kin and friends for the purchase of houses. If we cannot afford our own homes, we may live in privately owned middle-income apartments with the rent directly or indirectly subsidized by a public authority. Should this prove to be too much for our pocketbooks, we may qualify for apartments in housing developments owned by public authorities. In our golden years we may opt for retirement homes or nursing homes financed by authorities.

The jobs we get may be in firms assisted by public authorities that dangle low-interest loans before companies in order to entice them to start, expand, or keep going. If we live in port cities, we see authorities developing attractive facilities to make sure our community gets its fair share of seaborne or airborne commerce. Should we work for government, our offices may be in buildings financed and constructed by public authorities. For those of us who must live and work in decaying parts of the city, urban renewal and community development authorities may assist us in rehabilitating the area and attracting industry to it. Once we prosper we may wish to move to a suburban haven—possibly even work there. Again the open arms of public authorities welcome us as they develop the roads and water and sewer systems that we need.

In our leisure moments we can relax in parks and wilderness areas controlled by authorities. Or we can watch our favorite baseball, basketball, and football teams in stadiums constructed or operated by public authorities. An exciting event may attract us to the nearby convention center. In all likelihood this too will be an authority enterprise.

Nor can we escape public authorities in the more traumatic episodes of our lives. If we run afoul of the law, we may end up in a jail financed by a public authority. Our children may spend some time in an authority-run youthful offender facility. Emotional illness may bring us to a mental clinic or a hospital built by an authority.

No, there's no hiding place from public authorities in modern America. They are with us everywhere.

How Many Are There?

No state is without tales of manipulation of public authorities to mislead the voters. Strapped by fiscal, legal, and political strait-jackets, the state and local governments, in a gross violation of their own constitutions and laws, have established frequently autono-mous and unaccountable public authorities on an unprecedented scale. In what amounts to a quiet revolution in American govern-ment, some 35,000 shadowy public authorities (special districts) now exist side by side with the visible general governments. This estimate may be low, because no one knows what the exact figure is—not the federal government and not the states. No agreement even exists as to what a public authority, a special district, and a government corporation is. Are they one and the same? If we cannot identify them, how can we count them? The striking result is that the fastest growing form of government in the United States is the least understood and the least countable.[3]

The U.S. Bureau of the Census, which is supposed to keep tabs on such things, is of only marginal help. Every five years it con-ducts a census of all governmental units in the United States. The last count took place in 1987; the data were released in 1989. Another one is due in 1992. In its enumeration the bureau uses the term "special district" instead of "public authority." This umbrella term covers public authorities with such titles as "agency" [the Texas Housing Agency]; "system" [Washington Public Power Sup-ply System]; "fund" [The Economic Revitalization Fund of Penn-sylvania]; "bank" [Vermont Bond Bank]; "trust" [New Jersey Wastewater Treatment Trust]; "district" [Omaha Public Power Dis-trict]; "board" [Kansas City Board of Public Utilities]; "commis-sion" [Washington Suburban Sanitary Commission], and "com-pany" [Massachusetts Municipal Wholesale Electric Company].

In the lexicon of the bureau special districts are "independent limited-purpose local governmental units that exist as separate legal entities with substantial administrative and fiscal independence from general purpose governments." Note that the word "state" does not appear. Also note that "substantial" is a slippery term.

A more precise and long-standing definition of public authorities comes from Luther Gulick, one of the small band of experts on public authorities/special districts: "An authority is a government business corporation set up outside of the normal structure of traditional government so that it can give continuity, business efficiency and elastic management to the construction or operation of a self-supporting or revenue-producing public enterprise."[4]

The bureau's litmus tests for identifying special districts compound the confusion. In its schema any public authority/special district subject to administrative or financial control by the state or local government is a subordinate agency and not a bona fide independent special district. If an authority/special district board includes any state or local officials, it is not "independent." By bureau alchemy it is transformed into a "dependent" or "subordinate" agency and folded into the general government. The bureau applies still other tests for independence. Too many government officials on the board? Obviously dependent. In the distant future is it likely that the special district/public authority will revert to the parent government once it has paid off its debt? Sorry—dependent. Does the state or local government participate in decision making? If so, the entity is dependent. Can the governor or mayor veto some actions of the authority? Truly a subordinate agency.

The outcome of this kind of semantical and statistical massaging is bizarre. In 1987 the bureau identified 29,632 special districts. This count excluded thousands of public authorities on the grounds of dependency, including some of the largest multibillion-dollar authorities in the United States. It found the self-financed and autonomous New York State Power Authority to be a dependent agency while the heavily subsidized Massachusetts Bay Transportation Authority was classified as an independent special district. The financially independent Massachusetts Turnpike Authority was, in the bureau's view, a subordinate agency, but the Chicago Transit Authority (which is part of the Regional Transportation Authority) was classified as independent. These are but a sprinkling of thousands of examples of misclassification.

Startling differences appear between state and bureau data. What the states regard as independent frequently signifies dependency to the bureau. This is especially true in the larger states. For example, in 1987 the bureau found 2,734 special districts in California; only

Illinois had more (2,783). Using his own definitions of independence, the state comptroller spotted about 6,000 special districts. Henry Wulf, a senior official in the Bureau of the Census, explains discrepancies this way: "When it comes down to it, we're pigeon-holing things. Sometimes we're faced with conflicting evidence and we just have to make what we feel is the best decision."[5]

Many of the states are no better. A New York State legislative committee inventoried 100 state public authorities. The comptroller and the budget office counted about 50. In Illinois the precise number of special districts/public authorities is anybody's guess. The information is locked away in a massive computer file in Chicago. In the last few years the comptroller's office has failed to extricate any useful information from this file.

At best, under the circumstances, we can only guesstimate the number of public authorities/special districts/government corporations in the United States. We can accept as a base the Bureau of the Census total of 29,532 special districts and try to reconcile that with an estimated 8,000 to 10,000 state and local public authorities. Since the bureau's figures include an unknown number of state and local public authorities, there is a real danger of double counting. A safe estimate, then, might be 35,000 public authorities. This excludes 50 massive federal corporations that are outside the scope of this book.

But what are these quasi-governmental creations called public authorities? It is clear by now that a public authority cannot be identified by name since it appears under more than a dozen different labels. But regardless of title we can spot our quarry unfailingly if it meets the duck test. If a creature waddles like a duck, quacks like a duck, and swims like a duck, *ergo* it must be a duck. Similarly, if any quasi-public entity displays these features, it must be a public authority no matter what it may be called:

- A public benefit corporation created by a special law or a general law
- A distinct corporate entity legally separated from the state or local government
- A corporate management that includes a board appointed by a governor or mayor or local government council (at times

elected by the voters) and a chief executive officer and staff responsible to the board

- Power to issue tax-exempt bonds and notes to finance its operations
- Authority to finance, construct, and operate capital projects
- Freedom to perform all authorized functions to carry out its mission
- Power to set fees, charges, and rents for its services, but no power to tax unless the legislature permits assessments for its services
- Freedom to enter into contracts and to own and dispose of property, to sue and be sued
- Exempt (in most cases) from state and local government control over staff appointments, salaries, budgets, contracts, and procurement of supplies
- Power of eminent domain (in some cases)
- Flexibility to create subsidiaries
- Power to contract with federal, state, and local governments and other public authorities

A quasi-public entity that meets these tests is a public authority. It becomes a vehicle to accomplish a public purpose that state and local governments cannot or will not do.

Some caveats are in order. Not all public authorities enjoy complete exemption from the controls that fetter regular governmental agencies. They may get partial exemptions. Not all public authorities finance their operations completely. Some, especially in housing and transportation, are heavily subsidized. About 43 percent of the special districts can levy some property and sales taxes if the voters approve. Most of their revenue, however, comes from user fees such as fares, tolls, and water and sewer charges. A public authority often depends on a mix of sources for its revenue: fees, charges, rents, taxes, subsidies, loans, and grants. What counts in the last analysis is legal autonomy and independence from state and local governments. This is the link among public authorities regardless of titles and slight differences.

The result of the existence of 35,000 or so public authorities has been an unchecked borrowing spree. They have become the plastic credit cards of hard-pressed governments.

Shadow Governments around the World

The United States has about 35,000 public authorities, which is the highest figure in the free-enterprise world. Japan has some 3,000 public enterprises neatly relegated to off-budget status so as to limit the size of the official budget. Some 5,000 public enterprises exist in former West Germany. Hundreds of public enterprises in France and Britain perform some of the most critical economic functions, such as banking, insurance, transportation, and manufacturing, although the numbers are being reduced sharply by growing "privatization" policies. In Italy, two giant holding companies control hundreds of public enterprises in every economic sector. Over 400 government-owned crown corporations in Canada include such public enterprises as Air Canada and the Bank of Canada. In Australia, Brazil, Israel, and Ireland more people work for public enterprises than for national, state, and local governments.

Public enterprises have been especially crucial in developing countries, where few large private firms exist. They engage in virtually every form of economic activity. On the whole their performance has been dismal and most of them suffer from waste, mismanagement, and inefficiency. They are responsible in large part for the debt crises in South America and Africa.

The United States thus does not stand not alone in its reliance on public authorities. But it is unique in having the most and some of the biggest. Dozens of public authorities are multibillion-dollar firms that in power, assets, and debt rival the largest private corporations in the United States. Among the giants in terms of their outstanding debt are the $4.2-billion Municipal Electric Authority of Georgia; the $6.2-billion New Jersey Economic Development Authority; the $8-billion State of Washington Public Power Supply System; the $7.3-billion New York State Municipal Assistance Corporation (Big MAC) that is refinancing the debt of New York City; and the $3.2-billion California Housing Finance Agency that is pumping money into low-income and moderate-income housing. Multimillion-dollar transportation authorities provide mass transportation in California, Texas, Georgia, New York, and Illinois. In urban areas alone public mass transit has become a $14-billion industry.

Not to be overlooked are thousands of smaller public authorities with assets running from a few million dollars to over a billion dollars. Regardless of size, they dominate major programs in states, cities, counties, and towns all over the United States. For example, the Solid Waste Disposal Authority of Delaware, with an annual budget of $21 million, processes solid waste through landfills and recycling and incineration plants. It has quickly become a model for other states. The New Jersey Wastewater Treatment Trust (a public authority) is a major investment bank that lends money to local governments for the construction or upgrading of wastewater treatment plants. With a broader portfolio, the Economic Revitalization Fund of Pennsylvania (also a public authority), with assets of $190 million, finances local infrastructure projects such as transportation, water supply, and the generation of electricity. In Florida 450 special districts (public authorities) provide water, build roads, develop parks, and process waste. The 6,000 special districts in California perform similar functions. In Pennsylvania, the roughly 2,600 public authorities support virtually every significant local program.

The vast explosion of public authorities in all fields has changed the political, economic, and financial landscape of the United States almost beyond recognition. No longer are state and local governments the biggest borrowers outside of the federal government. Public authorities are now in second place. The outstanding long-term state and local debt was $893.6 billion in the 1990 fiscal year. Most of this is authority debt. This enormous amount equals about one-fourth of the national debt of roughly $3.7 trillion as of September 1991.

Dangerous Debt

One of the best kept secrets in the United States is that public authority debt is an explosive mixture waiting for a destructive spark. Before public authorities mushroomed, government debt enjoyed a constitutional guarantee of repayment. Bonds had behind them "the full faith and credit of the state." This meant that guaranteed debt had the second lien on the resources of the state, no matter what. The first lien was to fight insurrections, and none are expected in the foreseeable future. The chief debt instrument backed by the taxes of the state is the GO (general obligation) bond.

Before the 1960s two-thirds of all state and local debt was guaranteed in this fashion and consisted mainly of GO bonds. With the rise of public authorities and "innovative" financing like moral obligation bonds the reverse occurred. GO debt is now merely one-third of all debt. As of 1990, $601.9 billion—mainly authority debt—carries no binding constitutional guarantees of repayment. The chief debt instrument is the revenue bond backed up by fees, charges, subsidies, and special taxes. These are IOUs that may or may not be honored even though the record of repayment has been good so far. But the threat of default is not idle speculation. So far $9 billion worth of defaults have occurred in the last decade, largely at the expense of the bondholders. In 1991 alone defaults totaled nearly $5 billion. Should recessions deepen and persist, defaults would likely skyrocket and U.S. public authorities may join developing countries in pleading for debt cancellations, extension of debt repayment, and lower interest rates.

Until the 1980s public authorities could issue tax-exempt revenue bonds without restrictions. This meant that all taxpayers subsidized bondholders who paid no taxes on the bond interest. It also meant large revenue losses for the U.S. Treasury. For example, tax-exempt funds with low interest rates were loaned to private firms and real estate developers who were fully able to borrow money from banks at standard market rates. Those free and easy days of tax-exempt financing are over. In a series of tough laws ending with the Tax Reform Act of 1986, Congress clamped down on the unrestricted use of tax-exempt bonds. Jolted by these setbacks, public authorities are still exploring imaginative ways of continuing to enjoy the benefits of tax-free financing.

First in borrowing among state and local governments, many public authorities are second in operating budgets. Their annual expenditures are now about one-third of the operating expenses of several state governments. This is a new high and every sign points to even larger budgets in the years to come. In New York State alone the combined budgets of 40 public authorities—about $11.5 billion in 1990—exceeded the budgets of 39 state governments and most countries in the world.

The fees and charges of public authorities are growing faster than state and local sales, property, and income taxes. Taxpayers who up until now have accepted authority charges without a murmur are beginning to revolt as in Massachusetts, California, and New Jersey.

Public authorities have become the fastest growing part of the public sector and will continue to proliferate at an astonishing rate. Their vast powers show no signs of abating. As matters stand now, they have taken over some of the most vital functions of state and local governments. This is just the beginning. Frustrated governors and legislatures will add to their portfolio as budget crises deepen, federal aid to state and local governments diminishes, and obsolete constitutions stand in the way of change.

The new mandarins that run public authorities are above the battle. Wrapped up in their golden cocoons, they are insulated from voters, governors, and legislatures. Normal checks and balances, accountability, and control do not apply. Not for them the muck of budget and appropriation battles. In these extraordinary arrangements the benefits are obvious, but the costs are heavy. Public authorities have both a bright and a dark side, and for every savior among them there may also be a Frankenstein.

In the meantime, in their sleek corporate headquarters public authorities enjoy the best of both private and public worlds. They have all the appurtenances of a private corporation: a board of directors appointed by governors and mayors and a chief executive officer. Like any private corporation, they have a broad charter to borrow money, raise their own revenues, and manage their financial and administrative affairs. In a "heads I win, tails you lose" game, they retain their earnings and are free to dispose of their surpluses. When they incur operating losses they can usually count on the parent government to come to the rescue. However, this delightful fiscal paradise may soon fade as deficit-ridden governments begin to dip into authority reserves and become increasingly loath to make up their losses. Bondholders may be stuck once again.

The unfolding story will show that governors and legislatures generally follow a hands-off policy with regard to public authorities. They are pleased to leave them in their privileged sanctuaries so long as they avoid scandals and heavy financial losses. But the price of autonomy and independence is a solid balance sheet. Blessed with such virtues authorities can—and do—write their own financial tickets. Shedding their simple corporate structures, some have become large conglomerates and holding companies with subsidiary corporations. The subsidiary corporations are twice removed from their parent state and local governments and practically unreachable by those who cherish old-fashioned notions of accountability.

Beating the System

For governors like Rockefeller, Dukakis, and Thompson, public authorities were marvelous tools for getting around the system. By exempting them from bureaucratic controls over budgets, contracts, construction, salaries, and the purchase of supplies and equipment, they were able to put their cherished programs and projects in the fast lane and move them along at a rapid clip. As they saw it, they also got the added plus of more businesslike and efficient practices in an autonomous public authority than they found in sluggish state and local bureaucracies.

Public authorities also serve as political bomb shelters. Unable to take the heat of tough and unpopular decisions on transportation, the environment, housing, and the like, politicians frequently insulate themselves in public authorities. Not subject to control by the voters, these quasi-public agencies act as a buffer between outraged citizens and their elected leaders.

Paul Levy, former head of the beleaguered and controversial Massachusetts Water Resources Authority, saw his role this way: "We were created to do unpopular things because the legislature couldn't do them . . . to site unpleasant facilities and to raise rates for improvements to invisible water and sewer pipes."[6]

Through public authorities it is also possible to skirt around constitutional prohibitions against lending money to private interests. Industrial and economic development authorities stand ready to lend money to private firms at below-market interest rates. So do housing finance agencies that advance funds to real estate developers; student loan authorities that work with banks in initiating, guaranteeing, or subsidizing loans for higher education; health facility authorities that borrow money in behalf of private, nonprofit hospitals; educational facility authorities that lend money at attractive interest rates to private nonprofit colleges and universities; and transportation and power authorities that take over failing private railroads, bus lines, and utilities. All may be worthy causes. But they make a mockery of constitutional clauses.

Still all is not negative. At least a minority of public authorities have a more noble lineage. The only feasible way to cope with regional problems such as pollution, transportation, waste disposal, and water supply is to set up regional authorities that may encompass several governmental jurisdictions. This was the reasoning behind the genesis of the bistate Port Authority of New York and New Jersey; the Bay Area Rapid Transit (BART) in the San Francisco area; the Dallas–Fort Worth International Airport Board; the Solid Waste Disposal Authority of Delaware; the Pawtuxet River Authority in Rhode Island; the Laurens County Water Resources Commission in South Carolina; the Quad Cities Regional Economic Development Authority in Illinois; the Seattle Metro that provides water, transportation, and waste disposal in a multicity area; and hundreds more.

Like private utilities, many public authorities charge the beneficiaries of their services directly rather than burden the general taxpayer. This is true of toll roads and bridges, publicly owned power authorities like the Texas Municipal Power Agency, and many other water, sewer, and waste disposal authorities. When it comes to mass transportation and housing, those who benefit cannot in most cases afford the full cost of the services. Hence, their payments cover about one-third of the cost. Federal and state subsidies make up the difference.

Public Authorities from the Old World to the New World

While the growth and powers of public authorities are unparalleled in the United States in this century, authorities themselves are not new. In fact, their roots go back at least 500 years. For centuries

British, French, and other European monarchs relied on them to keep royalty living in high style. They set up crown corporations (essentially public enterprises) to manufacture tobacco, matches, liquor, textiles, and weapons. The French court led the way in the number of state-owned enterprises. No historians, however, have even intimated that this alone triggered the storming of the Bastille.

As the Industrial Revolution dawned, England issued revenue bonds for toll highways and bridges in the late 1700s and early 1800s. Similar forces were at work in the United States. Buoyed up by economic expansion and the inexorable movement to the West, the states went on an investment spree in the early part of the nineteenth century. They chartered private corporations to start banks and to build railroads and canals. They invested heavily in these new enterprises—more heavily than did private interests. Except for some shining examples such as the Erie Canal, most of the corporations went bankrupt in the depression of 1837–1843 and defaulted on the payment of their debt to the states. More than 50 percent of state government debt was in default in all parts of the country. Equally traumatic was evidence on all sides of corruption, chicanery, special privilege, and fiscal mismanagement in building railroads and canals and chartering banks, a prototype of the savings and loan scandals to come in the 1980s.

The defaults of the 1840s led outraged voters to demand the first set of constitutional limits on state borrowing: debt limits, referendum requirements, and prohibitions of loans or credits to private individuals and corporations. With the states temporarily paralyzed, local governments eagerly jumped into the breach and took the lead in stimulating economic development through loans to and investments in corporations. By the 1860s they had more outstanding debt than the states. They suffered the same fate. Financial manipulation and the depression of 1873–1879 resulted in major bankruptcies and defaults. Nearly 25 percent of all local government debt was in default. This time local governments too were put in a constitutional vise of debt ceilings and prohibitions against lending money or giving credit to private corporations and individuals.

As the West developed, special districts, especially in the Pacific and Mountain states, issued bonds for irrigation, levee construction, and drainage. Many of them also defaulted on the payment of debt, especially during another depression—that of 1893–1899. Again the constitutional noose tightened.[7]

Some determined state and local governments soon found ways to chip away at these constitutional restraints. Spokane, Chicago, and New Orleans were among the first to float nonvoter-approved revenue bonds for capital projects in the 1890s. The Port of New Orleans, funded with these bonds, had all the earmarks of a modern public authority. In 1894 the Boston Transit Commission, a public authority, built the first subway system in the United States (the precursor of the Massachusetts Bay Transportation Authority) and leased it to a corporation controlled by J. P. Morgan—the Boston Elevated Railroad Company. In 1897 *Harper's Weekly* enthusiastically applauded this move: "The whole undertaking will not cost the municipality a dollar." During the next 90 years governors, mayors, and legislatures were to echo the same "cost-free" advantage of public authorities. (Incidentally, the company failed in 1918 and the subway with its debt reverted to the City of Boston, costing the taxpayers rather more than a dollar.[8])

During World War I the federal government relied on public authorities to construct and operate the merchant fleet, to buy and sell sugar and grain, and to build, rent, and sell houses. Among them were the U.S. Grain Corporation, the U.S. Housing Corporation, and the U.S. Sugar Equalization Board. All were self-financed and none were a drain on the Treasury. At the end of the war the government hastily liquidated them.

By 1920 only a few public authorities were scattered around the country. Their resurgence did not begin in earnest until 1921 when the states of New York and New Jersey created the Port Authority of New York and New Jersey and Congress blessed the union by approving an interstate compact. Ten years later New York State established the Power Authority, the prototype for the TVA (Tennessee Valley Authority). These dramatic events were watersheds that led to momentous changes in the United States.

At the beginning of the twentieth century transportation, shipping, and stevedoring in New York Harbor were chaotic. Transcontinental railroads terminated in New Jersey. Cargo and passengers headed for New York City had to be transferred from trains to lighters or ferries. On the return trip the same delays occurred. Piers were congested and uncoordinated. On the west side of the Hudson River, Newark, Hoboken, Jersey City, and Elizabeth owned piers as did several railroads; on the east side of the river New York City operated piers. No one benefited from the competition as the entire transportation system bogged down in high costs, delays, and inefficiency.

At the same time economic competition between New York and New Jersey intensified. To the chagrin of New Jersey, New York City handled nearly half of all international cargo and railroads paid one price for shipments to New Jersey or New York despite the high costs of the trip across the Hudson. In 1916 New Jersey filed a complaint of freight rate discrimination with the Interstate Commerce Commission but lost.

After many abortive attempts to solve these problems, it became clear that the only feasible solution was a bistate public authority that would be responsible for improving and coordinating the transportation systems. One of the early supporters of the authority was Democratic Governor Alfred E. Smith of New York State. He was a towering political figure whose achievements have never received their just due. If the general public remembers him at all, it is as a failed presidential candidate who became an embittered reactionary in his late years.

Especially influential in the formation of the Port Authority was Julius Henry Cohen, a quiet, self-effacing, methodical attorney who advised several New York State governors. Rather than the flamboyant, self-advertising, pugnacious Robert Moses who at one time headed a dozen authorities and other agencies in New York State, Cohen was truly the founder of the modern public authority. Cohen drafted the legislation that created the Port Authority of New York and New Jersey.

Over the opposition of entrenched Democratic political machines in New York and New Jersey both states approved the legislation and gave the Port Authority the mission of developing the port area within 25 miles of the Statue of Liberty. They made it financially independent by authorizing it to levy fees and charges for its services, and gave it complete autonomy in running its own affairs without having to look to Trenton or Albany to approve its budgets,

financial plans, personnel system, construction programs, and purchases. As a precaution, however, the governors insisted on the
right to approve the authority's policies as reflected in its minutes,
in effect giving them veto power.[9]

For the first time in the twentieth century the legislation provided
a significant alternative to competing, sluggish, and inflexible state
and local bureaucracies. What made the authority especially irresistible as a model was the superb management that developed after
some halting starts. In 1942 the governing board appointed by both
governors had the good sense to select Austin I. Tobin as executive
director, a post he held until he retired in 1972. Tobin recruited the
brightest and the best no matter where they worked and paid them
salaries no governments could match. More important, he inspired
them with the sense of an urgent mission. The authority's airports,
bridges, tunnels, and piers bear Tobin's stamp (although he does not
merit similar encomiums for railroads and mass transportation).

A bitter struggle preceded the creation of the New York State
Power Authority in 1931. In his annual message to the legislature in
1924 Governor Smith urged the establishment of a state-owned
public authority that would develop the hydroelectric potential of
the St. Lawrence River at low cost and in behalf of the people. He
described it as "a public corporation, municipal in character, having
no stockholders, deriving its power from the State, and having
duties specifically imposed upon it to take over and develop the
power resources of the State." With this approach there would be no
"need to burden the taxpayers either through the issuance of State
bonds or by appropriations from current revenues." At the governor's elbow, every step of the way, was Julius Henry Cohen.

In the political storm that followed, the Republican-controlled
legislature turned down the proposal. They wanted private utilities
to control hydroelectric power, and castigated the plan as "socialis-
tic." Smith made this the leading issue in the next two gubernatorial
campaigns and won. When Smith persuaded Franklin D. Roosevelt
to run for the governorship in 1928, Roosevelt too campaigned for
public power and also won handily. By 1931 a chastened legislature, under public pressure, reluctantly agreed to the creation of the
Power Authority.[10]

It took over 20 years for the Power Authority to become operational. Roosevelt was too preoccupied with the Great Depression and World War II to give priority to his own creation, and Truman favored federally owned power. Finally, in 1953 the Federal Power Commission gave the Power Authority the license to proceed and Governor Thomas E. Dewey appointed Robert Moses as head of the authority. With the concurrence of several governors Moses subverted the mission of the authority by giving preference in the allocation of electricity to private utilities rather than to municipal systems.

The First Wave

From these beginnings, public authorities inundated the United States in five waves. The first was during the Great Depression of the 1930s. In 1933 newly elected President Roosevelt not only found the country in economic shambles, but governmental agencies paralyzed and ill-equipped to cope with failing businesses, mass unemployment, bankrupt farms, home foreclosures, and closed banks. Under the banner of the New Deal, Congress and the president targeted major pieces of legislation directly at these problems. Few Americans are aware, however, that they selected government corporations rather than federal agencies to attack the most urgent issues. Roosevelt had two vivid models before him: the Port Authority of New York and New Jersey and the New York State Power Authority.

In short order dozens of government corporations rolled off the drawing boards of the New Deal. The Federal Deposit Insurance Corporation (FDIC) and the Federal Savings and Loan Insurance Corporation (FSLIC) insured bank deposits. The Home Owners Loan Corporation (HOLC) staved off home foreclosures. The Commodity Credit Corporation (CCC) and the Farm Mortgage Corporation (FMC) provided loans to hard-pressed farmers. The Government National Mortgage Association (GNMA) and the Federal Housing Administration (FHA) insured mortgages. The refurbished Reconstruction Finance Corporation (RFC), actually a Hoover creation, channeled loans to businesses. The Tennessee Valley Authority (TVA) pumped new life into one of the most depressed regions of the country by providing electricity, constructing navigable waterways, manufacturing fertilizer, and promoting advanced agricultural practices.

Roosevelt described TVA as "a corporation clothed with the power of government but possessed of the flexibility and initiative of private enterprise." This view guided the creation of other government corporations as well. The accent was on the corporate structure, businesslike practices, self-sustaining operations, and a large measure of freedom from government red tape and controls.

The states lagged far behind the federal government in repairing the ravages of the Depression. Short of funds, stuck with constitutional requirements to balance budgets, and hemmed in by debt limits, they were impotent. If state government was at the nadir, local government with depressed property values and severe debt limits was virtually irrelevant. As a former governor of New York State, Roosevelt recognized the predicament of the states. In a message to all the governors he bluntly advised them to bypass their obsolete constitutions and to set up public authorities as vehicles for public works projects. Such changes in municipal financing, he wrote, were "absolutely essential at least for the duration of the existing emergency." He described the proposed public authorities as nonprofit benefit corporations "without the power to tax, but with power to issue bonds payable solely from the revenue producing improvements such as water, sewer, and electric light and power systems."[11]

As a lure to the besieged governors and local officials, Roosevelt dangled before them the commitment to buy the authority revenue bonds through RFC and the newly created Public Works Administration (PWA). He also promised federal grants to the new authorities and provided additional incentives to state and local governments to create local public housing authorities for slum clearance and low-cost housing. During the 1930s hundreds of these quasi-public entities sprang up all over the United States.

These turbulent times provided unusual opportunities for the entrepreneurial skills of Robert Moses.[12] Overawing governors and state legislatures as well as other elected officials in New York, he soon became the unrivaled czar of public authorities in New York State. At the height of his influence, he ruled authorities and agencies in transportation, parks, recreation, power generation, housing, and urban renewal. His crown jewels were the Triborough Bridge and Tunnel Authority (TBTA) and the Power Authority of the State of New York (PASNY).

Through TBTA (originally TBA before it acquired tunnels under the East River in New York City) Moses discovered the path to power and the immortality of public authorities. Originally TBA was a temporary means of escaping the fiscal trap of debt limits in New York City and New York State. Its goal was to build bridges connecting the boroughs of Manhattan, Queens, and the Bronx; it was supposed to go out of business once it paid off its bonds. To Moses' amazement the tolls poured in so quickly that he was in a position to retire the bonds seven to 12 years prior to their maturity date. That would also mean the retirement of Moses and the end of TBA.

Moses, however, was not ready to give up his money machine. He found that he could refund bonds by issuing new bonds. In this way TBA would live forever. With the only deep pockets in the Depression-ridden town, TBA was in a position to finance the construction of the Bronx-Whitestone Bridge, other bridges, tunnels, parks, and roads. State and city officials readily assented to an expansion of the functions of TBA to engage in these activities. As a hedge against fickle politicians, Moses inserted language in bond covenants that legally protected his already formidable powers. Now no legislature could challenge them unless it was ready to break what in effect was a contract between bondholders and TBA. Moses knew that no court would sanction that. In the process TBA evolved into an autonomous multipurpose construction agency linked to a network of intertwined public authorities and state and city governments.

With TBA as the cornerstone, Moses fashioned a political bastion that would last until 1967, when Governor Nelson A. Rockefeller determined that New York State had room for only one master. He forced Moses out of his long-time and cherished position as chairman of the Council of Parks and appointed his brother Laurence Rockefeller instead. He combined the Triborough Bridge and Tunnel Authority with the newly formed Metropolitan Transportation Authority, directed by his former secretary William Ronan (dubbed by unkind critics as "the emperor of the Wholly Ronan

Empire"). Rockefeller quickly accepted Moses' resignation as head of the Power Authority. All the other posts fell by the wayside as well.

Moses' legacy is controversial. Every plaudit of his role as a master builder is matched by charges that he destroyed communities in the name of slum clearance and manipulated bond funds in the Power Authority and TBA to escape accountability. What is certain is that he used public authorities on an unprecedented scale.

The Second Wave

The second wave splashed on governments during World War II. It mainly covered the federal government, which found that private firms were distressingly slow in shifting from a peacetime to a wartime economy. To expedite the manufacture of war materials, the Roosevelt administration created several giant holding companies. One of them, the Defense Plant Corporation, owned over 2,000 factories. Managed by private contractors, the plants churned out hundreds of items required by the war machine. Roosevelt also put the Reconstruction Finance Corporation on a war footing. RFC promptly organized subsidiary corporations to distribute rubber, metals, and petroleum. Once the war was over, the administration quickly terminated the public enterprises, leaving a clear field to private enterprise.

The Third Wave

In state and local governments the war also came first. Because of lack of materials and man and woman power, they shelved hundreds of thousands of projects, large and small. By the end of the war the backlog of deferred construction and maintenance of schools, roads, bridges, waterways, hospitals, sewers, and water supply systems had reached monumental, if not crisis, proportions. At the same time millions of demobilized veterans returned home to resume their peacetime lives. They wanted jobs, education, marriages, and homes. They looked to the states especially to meet their needs for housing and higher education.

What saved the day in the beginning were the billions of dollars state and local governments had accumulated in their treasuries during the war. Taxes had rolled in merrily and the governments could not spend what they received. The nest egg seemed large enough to take care of deferred construction as well as the demands of the veterans. But the money soon ran out and governments faced the tough political choices of raising taxes and borrowing or sidestepping the pain altogether by spawning still more public authorities.

Enter the third wave running strong from about 1946 to 1960. Hundreds of new public authorities arose to satisfy the pent-up demands for the construction of essential public works and for housing and schooling for veterans. This was the heyday of toll roads such as the New Jersey Turnpike and the Florida Sunshine Parkway, running from sea to shining sea. This was the period when university campuses mushroomed as never before. Standing ready to finance the new centers of learning were dormitory authorities, school building authorities, university construction funds, and government bond banks. Public authorities steered veterans and others to their friendly bankers to borrow funds at low interest rates for higher education with repayment guaranteed by the authorities. Pushed by the veterans, housing authorities and newly crafted housing finance agencies broadened housing programs to take care of moderate-income as well as low-income groups. Sewer and water authorities flourished. The federal government was a ready partner in all these activities and initiated hundreds of grant programs to provide federal aid to state and local governments and to public authorities.

An unexpected eddy in the third wave was the rise of public authorities to take over vital private firms that were failing. As the age of the automobile came into its own, the public deserted railroads and subways in favor of toll roads, the Eisenhower interstate highway system, and new state roads funded by gasoline taxes. Many privately owned bus lines, subways, commuter railroads, and passenger and freight railroads soon went bankrupt. To avoid a dangerous collapse of the transportation network, federal government corporations and state public authorities acquired the failed systems with a handsome profit to shrewd investors. Amtrak ran passenger lines and Conrail ran freight lines. Conrail did so well that the federal government later sold it to private investors.

These takeovers brought about the genesis of the Massachusetts Bay Transportation Authority (MBTA), the Bay Area Rapid Transit (BART) in the San Francisco area, the New York State Metropolitan Transportation Authority (MTA); the Metropolitan Atlanta Rapid Transit Authority (MARTA) in Atlanta, the Metropolitan Transit Authority (MTA) in Houston, and hundreds of others.

The Fourth Wave

As the 1960s dawned vast social changes transformed the United States. The baby boomers were crowding elementary and secondary schools in record numbers. Suburbia was on the march, and large and small Levittowns rose on grounds where corn, peas, and potatoes had grown. Shopping malls emerged to serve the new suburbs. As the white middle classes fled the cities, their places were taken by blacks and Hispanics migrating from the South and Puerto Rico. Without affluent taxpayers, the central cities soon deteriorated.

Taken together, these forces led to unprecedented demands for education, housing, roads, medical care, drinkable water, utility services, mass transportation, pollution control, and adequate systems of waste disposal. The federal, state, and local governments responded quickly by offering a large menu of programs. The price tag was enormous. The state governments were especially hard hit as their spending rose at a faster clip than federal and local expenditures. Larger cities were squeezed between the needs of their poor residents and a tax structure weakened by the exodus of industry and the affluent. To shore up state and local finances President Johnson's Great Society stepped up federal aid sharply to the point where it amounted to about 15 percent of state and local budgets. And it continued to grow until 1980.

Quick to take advantage of and to expect government services, taxpayers, nevertheless, balked at steadily rising taxes. Tax revolts soon spread throughout the land and left in their wake even more constitutional and statutory ceilings on taxing, spending, and borrowing. In referendum after referendum voters consistently turned down bond issues for a variety of projects.

In this climate, impatient and aggressive legislatures, governors, and mayors deliberately created thousands of public authorities to bypass constitutional restraints. This was the fourth big wave. It was a ploy "to beat the system." And it worked. By the time the wave petered out in 1980, it had left behind authorities engaged in the major functions of government, a variety of revenue bonds, "innovative financing" like moral obligation bonds, and a monumental debt.

The Fifth Wave

In the 1980s state and local budgets became even leaner in real dollars, taking inflation into account. Reaganomics was the chief culprit. After eight years as the biggest spender and borrower in the history of the United States, the Reagan administration left a bare-bone legacy: a national debt of about $3.0 trillion and an annual deficit of over $200 billion with no end in sight; IOUs of $300 billion to $500 billion or more to bail out savings and loans associations; $150 billion to clean up polluted nuclear weapons plants; and untold billions to rescue banks holding "nonperforming" domestic real estate loans and the debt of developing countries. The Reagan and Bush administrations refused to increase taxes except for marginal changes. Hence, claimants on the federal purse competed fiercely for shrinking federal dollars. In this competition state and local governments stood last in line. Federal aid dropped precipitously with no prospect of relief.

Baffled by the complexity of federal finances, irate voters vented their frustrations on the states once again. In their continuing revolt against taxes, they left most states with sizable deficits. Yet the states had to cope with collapsing bridges, deteriorating highways, a poisoned environment, mountains of waste, polluted water supplies, crime, drug addiction, and thousands of homeless people. Even conservative estimates suggested that it would take about $3 trillion by the end of the century to salvage an "America in ruins."

Their treasuries virtually empty, state and local governments floundered in the great recession of the late 1980s and early 1990s.

This was as much a government recession as an economic recession. Paradoxically, it came at a time when the United States was the wealthiest country in the world with a GNP of nearly $6 trillion. Next to Japan it was the most undertaxed country among so-called advanced industrialized countries. Unemployment was relatively low. By any standard the United States was economically rich, but its governments were budgetarily poor. In 1958 John Kenneth Galbraith contrasted "the opulence of our private consumption" with "the poverty of our schools, the unloveliness and congestion of our cities."[13] In the 1990s the contrast has sharpened as public squalor has become more widespread.

Predictably, in a fiscal and legal crunch, governments once again turned to public authorities for salvation. Thus, the fifth wave of authorities, a recession-induced wave, swept upon the United States. The crest is not yet in sight and the wave may not peak until the year 2000. By then we can expect well over 40,000 public authorities.

This use of public authorities signals a breakdown in the traditional political, fiscal, administrative, and legal structures of state and local governments. As the old forms of government have crumbled, the shadow government of public authorities has taken their place. Unlike general government, it is, in most cases, safely outside of the reach of voters and elected officials. This means that ordinary citizens have little say about governmental functions that affect them most. Most are virtually unaware of the existence of the autonomous fourth branch of government.

The consequences are most serious. Public authorities have unalterably changed the political and economic landscape for better and for worse.

2

Always a Borrower or a Lender Be

Before Polonius was impaled on Hamlet's sword, he uttered the famous words: "Neither a borrower nor a lender be." Modern political leaders would offer contrary advice: "Always a borrower or a lender be."

This is their current theme although it defies nearly every state constitution in the United States. When it comes to borrowing, spending, and taxing, constitutions are replete with "thou shalts" and "thou shalt nots." They carry long lists of prohibitions and taboos that come out of the long night of greed, corruption, and mismanagement in the nineteenth century.

The constitution of the State of Texas is typical. Distrustful of legislatures and governors, it warns sternly: "No debt will be created by or on behalf of the state, except to supply casual deficiencies of revenue, repel invasion, suppress insurrection, defend the state in war, or pay existing debt; and the debt created to supply deficiencies in revenue, shall never exceed in the aggregate at any one time two hundred thousand dollars."

Short of another Alamo, there is only legal means of getting around this barrier. Two-thirds of the legislature must approve a bond issue and the majority of voters must concur in a general election.

In New York State the constitution is even tougher: "No debts shall be hereafter contracted by or in behalf of the State, unless such debt shall be authorized by law for some single work or purpose, to be distinctly specified therein. No such law shall take effect until it shall, at a general election, have been submitted to the people, and have received a majority of all the votes cast."

It then goes on to prohibit any financial assistance to public corporations (read public authorities): "Neither the State nor any political subdivision thereof shall at any time be liable for the payment of any obligations issued by such a public corporation heretofore or hereafter created, nor may the legislature accept, authorize acceptance of or impose such liability upon the State or any political subdivision thereof."

The warm sun in Florida has not thawed out these chilly words in its constitution: "State bonds pledging the full faith and credit of the state may be issued only to finance or refinance the cost of fixed capital outlay projects upon approval by a vote of the electors. . . . The total outstanding principal of state bonds issued pursuant to this subsection shall never exceed fifty percent of the total tax revenues of the state for the two proceeding fiscal years."

Relenting somewhat, the constitution permits the issuance of revenue bonds without a referendum for roads, bridges, air and pollution control, solid waste disposal, and water facilities. But it warns that these bonds "shall be payable from sources other than state tax revenues."

With more controls over the government purse than most other states, the California constitution lays out these ground rules on debt: "No such law [creating debt] shall take effect until at a general election it shall have been submitted to the people and shall have received a majority of all votes cast for and against it at such election, and all moneys raised by authority of such law shall be applied only to the specific object therein stated or to the payment of the debt thereby created."

All 50 state constitutions contain fiscal straitjackets in every size, shape, and form. Nineteen require direct voter approval to go into debt in the first place or to override debt limits (usually expressed in dollar terms or as a percent of revenue collections or property values). The big states that borrow the most fall in this category. Eleven state constitutions impose tight borrowing limits but dispense with debt referenda. Especially extreme are 10 constitutions that bar debt altogether except for a few safety valves in times of crisis. Taken together, 40 states are in constitutional debt shackles.

Bucking the tide, 10 constitutions, mainly in the smaller states, continue to demonstrate a touching faith in their legislatures. Six insist solely on extraordinary majorities (usually two-thirds) to approve a bond issue. And four—Maryland, New Hampshire, Tennessee, and Vermont—make do with a simple majority vote by legislators.[1]

Not content with debt limits alone, the voters in 22 states have tightened constitutional screws on taxing and spending. Typically, budgets and revenue cannot rise faster than inflation, population growth, and personal income. In some states the ceiling on increases is a percent of the total personal income in the state. These limits are the fruits of tax revolts of the last 15 years. Still more are in the wings.

Unlike the federal Constitution, state constitutions compel governors and legislatures to produce balanced budgets. Only Vermont escapes this restriction because of its traditional frugality.

As creatures of the state, local governments are in a special fiscal bind. Their debt may not exceed a fixed percent of the value of their property, usually ranging from 5 percent to 10 percent. In most states they need voter approval to borrow money. High property taxes are anathema everywhere. In extreme cases, as with Proposition 13 in California and Initiative 2 1/2 in Massachusetts, voters have rolled property taxes back and imposed ceilings on future tax increases. Most states have similar roadblocks—smaller, perhaps, but still tough barriers.

These constitutional walls have turned out not to be deterrents but challenges to imaginative politicians who vault over them easily. Except for a handful of governments that follow the letter of the law, most political leaders employ their talents in devising canny and obscure ways of bypassing constitutions, especially to borrow money. They have two choices: They can take the high road of openness, voter approval, and compliance with the constitution. This they consistently reject as politically risky. Given a chance, voters will regularly turn down many bond issues as they did in the November 1990 election when they rejected over 41 percent of the issues. Or politicians can take the low road of conning the voters through obfuscation and evasion—that is, through what they euphemistically call "creative" and "innovative" financing. This is the preferred course.

This is what the "politics of debt" is all about, to use David Perry's phrase. The chosen instrument for such politicking is the public authority.

So far the political leaders have been smashingly successful in launching the biggest state and local borrowing spree in the history of the country. At their side are highly paid "merchants of debt"—bond counsel, brokerage houses, and financial advisers—ever eager to fashion dozens of intricate and complex debt mechanisms that go over the heads of most voters. Calling these maneuvers "deliberate obfuscation," Auditor General Cranson of Illinois puts the issue this way: "So complex have these financial instruments become that even legislators fail to understand them. Increasingly, it becomes difficult for voters and many members of the legislature to influence policies with multibillion-dollar price tags."

Two gimmicks underlie even the most labyrinthine financial schemes: (1) Borrow by all means, but never call your debt state or local debt; call it authority debt; or (2) Borrow, but never call your debt at all; call it something else. Astonishingly these work. And the constitutional walls come tumbling down.

Revenue Bonds: The Savior of Public Authorities

To unravel this web of debt and deceit, let's remember that bonds issued in accordance with constitutional procedures are usually general obligation (GO) bonds backed by the taxing power of the state or city. These are a precious few. All other bonds carry no such guarantees. They are generally labeled "revenue bonds," bonds that presumably are secured by a fixed source of revenue. Let's recall, too, that in 1990 the outstanding long-term debt of state and local governments was over $893.6 billion. About one-third of this debt was guaranteed and two-thirds had no guarantees. Most of this was the debt of public authorities.

How do public authorities pay off revenue bonds? The security for these bonds is a mix of fees, charges, grants, earmarked taxes (such as a percentage of the sales tax allocated to public transportation), and subsidies. As public authorities have proliferated, the use of revenue bonds has exploded. In 1950 they represented only 20 percent of all tax-exempt bonds. By the late 1980s and early 1990s they hovered around 70 percent.

In the intervening years revenue bonds have become chameleons with changing shapes and colors designed to deceive the onlookers. At first they were fairly straightforward. Public authorities that operated roads, bridges, utility plants, ports, water and sewer systems, airports, and transportation systems charged fees for their services. As security, the bonds they issued had behind them a steady stream of revenue. They were simple, understandable, unequivocal revenue bonds.

The Lease-Purchase Shell Game

Then the shell game started. As governments searched for inventive ways to bypass constitutions, they pulled out of their fiscal bag of tricks something new, the "shell authority." This species of public authority operates nothing and manages nothing. Its sole reason for existence is to sell revenue bonds to construct public buildings, schools, universities, hospitals, and jails. The authority then leases the facility to the government. And the grateful government pays "rent" for the shining new building. Under a lease-purchase plan the government owns the facility at the end of 20 or 30 years. In the fiction of this transaction, this is not constitutional debt. It is merely rent money that comes out of the regular operating budget and is paid for by taxes. Through this transparent device elected officials finance buildings without voter approval and in the face of voter rejection of bond issues.

For investors who always wanted to own a jail or a hospital or a university campus, the shell authority satisfies their fondest dreams. It sells them a revenue bond. The security for the bond? Rent money, that is, tax dollars. In this setup, the bond issue has all the earmarks of a revenue bond. Never mind that lease payments are ploys to escape debt limits. Never mind that through shell authorities governments raise billions of dollars by violating their own constitutions. Never mind that the whole scheme makes a mockery of bona fide revenue bonds.

In short order the shell game became a national sport and was popular even in a state like Wisconsin that is known for its open and progressive government. Prior to 1969 Wisconsin could not incur debt at all under its constitution except to repel invasion, suppress insurrection, defend the state in wartime, and defray extraordinary expenditures up to $100,000. Happily, only tourists invade Wisconsin every summer. Yet the state desperately needed funds for college campuses and office buildings. In a fiscal charade, beginning in 1923, it created four "private," nonprofit building corporations and authorized them to sell tax-exempt bonds for a variety of facilities. The state would pay off the "revenue" bonds through annual rents that covered the debt service and then eventually own the buildings. By 1969 the state that couldn't borrow money for capital construction had run up a debt of nearly $500 million through clever subterfuge.

But the voters by then had enough of the devious and cumbersome mechanism for evading the constitution. They approved an amendment empowering the state to issue bonds directly so long as the governor and legislature agreed. They placed a fairly generous ceiling on the annual amount of debt and outlawed the use of dummy authorities after January 1, 1971. In fact, they revolted against public authorities altogether. As a result, Wisconsin has the smallest number of state public authorities—only three. Government services are first-rate and the state prospers. Unfortunately, the fervor for open and accountable government stops at the Wisconsin border.

In the shell game sweepstakes Pennsylvania is the all-time winner. Confronted by a forbidding constitution and voter resistance to bond issues, local governments and school districts spawned over 738 paper authorities for school construction, beginning in 1935. These were part of a chain of over 2,600 local public authorities set up for a variety of purposes. The usual devious routine followed. The authorities issued over $5 billion in bonds and the school districts bought the new buildings on the installment plan. In this arrangement the lease neatly equaled the term of the bonds and the annual rental equaled the annual payment of principal and interest. A constitutional change in 1972 eased the debt limits for local governments. Nevertheless, all financing of school construction is lease-backed financing.

A neighbor, New Jersey, goes through fiscal contortions to sidestep its constitution. To put up new office buildings former Governor Thomas Kean and his predecessors manipulated three public authorities. One is the New Jersey Building Authority, a shell authority established solely for lease-financing schemes. The second is the New Jersey Economic Development Authority, designed to lend money to industrial and commercial firms. Yet it diverted $110 million of its funds to put up an office building complex for the state under the customary lease-purchase plan. Finally, the state leases two large office buildings from a local public authority, the Mercer County Improvement Authority. Coincidentally, the annual rental equals the debt service necessary to pay off $103 million in bonds issued by the authority. In appreciation the state also makes an annual contribution to the county in lieu of paying real estate taxes.

With some $8.5 billion in lease-purchase plans in effect as of 1990, New York State leads the country in this new form of "creative" financing. Governors Nelson Rockefeller, Hugh Carey, and Mario Cuomo have seen to that. Through a network of public authorities the state employs leasing mechanisms to finance the construction of State University and City University buildings, health and mental health facilities, prisons, highways, and office buildings.

A prime example of the misuse of these authorities is their role in constructing prisons. In 1981 the voters spurned a $500-million bond issue for prisons. Undaunted, Governor Cuomo and the legislature authorized a most unlikely public authority, the Urban Development Corporation (UDC), to issue bonds precisely for prison construction. UDC turned the money over to a state agency, the Office of General Services, which supervised the project in behalf of the Department of Correctional Services. Through the lease-purchase plan New York State annually appropriates funds to pay its debt to UDC. What it couldn't do through the front door, it accomplished through the back door.

While admitting some doubts about the entire transaction, a legislative leader argued that the legislature had no choice but to approve the bonds, given the acute shortage of prison space. "When you're talking about prisons, that's a crisis situation. We cannot turn criminals out into the street, because we can't put them any place," he said. A colleague agreed. "To put out for a referendum the construction of prisons, and other minor borrowings would slow down the state's ability to get things done."[2]

So convoluted are New York State's lease-purchase schemes that it would take the wizardry of the legendary Rube Goldberg merely to chart them on paper. Like other states New York was in a hurry to erect university buildings and hospitals during the hectic 1960s. It decided to allow one authority, the Housing Finance Agency (HFA), to sell bonds for these purposes. Despite its name, HFA has become a multi-purpose investment banker for the state. Once investors snapped up the tax-exempt bonds, HFA turned the proceeds over to two additional authorities: the State University Construction Fund and the Mental Health Facilities Construction Fund. The first constructed academic buildings in behalf of the State University; the second built hospitals in behalf of the Mental Hygiene Department.

To pay the debt service on the bonds the State University turned over tuition payments and a variety of fees to the State University Construction Fund. The fund in turn channeled the money to HFA for payment of principal and interest to the bondholders. Similarly, the Mental Hygiene Department transferred patients' fees and Medicare and Medicaid payments to the Mental Health Facilities Construction Fund. And the fund forwarded the appropriate amounts to HFA. All of this was backdoor debt; none of it had constitutional guarantees.

This elaborate and difficult-to-follow hocus-pocus is meant to be confusing. The point is to keep the voters in the dark about the deliberate defiance of the constitution through backdoor financing and through a string of public authorities.

To construct prisons, Texas has its own style of lease-financing schemes. It created a Public Finance Authority that sells bonds in behalf of correctional, mental health, and mental retardation facilities. In 1989, the largest bond issue ever floated in Texas was for building 16 new prisons. The state now leases the facilities from the authority.

California and Florida almost match New York State in the misuse of lease-purchase plans. For California, lease financing is the preferred way of circumventing Proposition 13. Florida has achieved its eminence through sheer ingenuity. Prior to April 1990 two obstacles blocked lease financing especially at the local level: the requirement for voter approval and a flat prohibition on the use of taxes to pay lease rentals. No problem for some imaginative bond counsel who devised a complex legal fiction to break the impasse. To the delight of everyone concerned, the Florida Supreme Court endorsed the formula without blinking a collective judicial eye. Now leases no longer require voter approval, *provided they can be cancelled annually by the lessee*, say the local government or the school district. Now taxes can be used to pay rent *so long as they are not pledged for such purpose*. Judicial hairsplitting sanctioned a detour around the constitution.

What happens if the local government refuses to appropriate funds for rent or cancels the lease? In that unhappy event, investors, acting through bond trustees, would take possession of the schoolhouse or jail and would be free to let it to anyone in the market for such a facility. But they wouldn't be able to sell it. Broad winks all around assured investors that defaults could never happen.

At this sudden legal revelation the floodgates for lease financing in Florida opened. In 1989 Florida ranked ninth among the states in new issues of lease-backed security bonds. The sudden surge in investments will surely catapult it into the top ranks.[3]

Nationally, lease-backed bonds have taken off in what appears to be explosive growth. In 1988 they represented 9 percent of all tax-exempt bonds sold. In the next five to 10 years this figure should easily triple. At least 41 states have discovered the virtues of lease financing and four—Colorado, Kentucky, South Dakota, and Idaho—depend on them almost exclusively to borrow money. As vehicles for lease financing, virtually all states have clones of building and financing authorities.

Despite the Byzantine complexity and seeming risks of lease financing, investors gobble up the bonds as soon as they are issued. Brokerage houses and mutual funds peddle them eagerly. One of the largest mutual funds, Nuveen, assures its investors that "Leases are popular with issuers because they bypass voter approval requirements and debt limits which constrain states and localities in providing services." In 1989 Moody's Investment Service allayed the fears of investors who were worried about a possible default in a lease-backed bond in Kentucky: "the likelihood of a true default appears limited barring economic recession."[4]

COPs—A Lucrative Form of Lease Financing

The latest twist in lease financing are certificates of participation (COPs). Pioneered in California as a bypass around Proposition 13 and sundry debt limits, then avidly taken up by New Jersey, COPs are sweeping the country. Like other forms of lease financing this debt instrument is designed to borrow money without calling it debt.

This is how it works. Acting frequently through a public authority, a state or local government invites a private firm to construct a jail, hospital, or convention center for it or to sell it major pieces of equipment such as computer systems, fire trucks, power systems, or telecommunication networks. A lease-purchase plan covers the entire arrangement. The go-between the lessor (the private firm) and the lessee (the public authority or government) is typically a commercial or investment bank. The bank carves up the lease into "certificates of participation," usually in units of $5,000. Investors who buy the certificates get periodic rental payments covering principal and interest from the bank with the funds coming from annual appropriations by the government. In this topsy-turvy financing world the Internal Revenue Service regards the COPs as tantamount to municipal bonds and exempts the interest from taxation. So does the state. To circumvent the constitution, though, the government calls its payment for COPs "operating expenses" even though lessees are borrowing under another name.[5]

In 1985 when Oxnard, California, a city 65 miles north of Los Angeles, wanted a sports facility and hotel for spring training for the Los Angeles Raiders football team, it turned to COPs. A delicately orchestrated and complex financial ballet followed. The Oxnard Public Facilities Corporation (PFC), a public authority, issued COPs amounting to $16 million. With these funds a developer built the sports-hotel complex. PFC leased it to the city and the city, in turn, subleased it to the hotel operator. The city gets lease payments based on room rents and food and beverage sales from the hotel. It turns the proceeds over to PFC for eventual payment to the investors. In the event of a shortfall in hotel receipts, the city backs up the lease payments with its own revenue.[6]

Starting in a small way, tax-free lease issues via COPs now run to about $5 billion annually with about $50 billion outstanding in 1990. While this is a small part of the nearly $128 billion in municipal bonds sold in 1990, it is one of the fastest growing instruments of hidden debt. Forty-five states now resort to COPs for a variety of facilities. Only five are holdouts: North Dakota, Wyoming, Hawaii, Vermont, and New Hampshire.

Everyone seems to benefit except the taxpayers and the federal government. The state or local government acquires a needed facility. But it pays higher interest—up to 1 percent more—than it would pay for a GO or revenue bond. In Illinois, a legislative fiscal agency estimated that the additional burden was about 3 percent. Investors avoid taxes on the interest to the federal government. Banks get big fees for their services. Finally, taxpayers pay more for the facility than they would have paid through traditional and straightforward borrowing via general obligation bonds.

A senior official in California who prefers to remain anonymous blew up at the very thought of COPs: "The rules about it are so slippery that in many cases you can't identify it. It will merely show up as a lease expenditure in the budget. You don't know whether it's a five-year or 20-year obligation or not unless you can dig up the contract. It represents a huge potential liability. At best it's intellectually dishonest if nothing else."

Even investors are at risk as they are seduced by high interest rates. At any time a legislature can refuse to appropriate funds for lease rentals. Unlike bonds, COPs usually have no valid security behind them, just the word of honor of the government. Should the government default, it may not be possible to repossess the property, depending on the terms of the contract. Even if lenders can take over the facility, they are stymied. As Ben Weberman, a highly respected and long-time bond watcher and columnist in *Forbes* put it, "If it [the government] decides it can do without the jail, the payments stop and you and other investors get the jail back . . . and try to turn it into a shopping mall. Lots of luck."[7]

In a 1990 official statement (prospectus) on a COPs issue, New Jersey waves the red flag of caveat emptor and warns investors: "The State's obligation to make lease payments does not constitute a debt or liability of the state within the meaning of any constitutional or statutory limitation and neither the faith and credit nor the taxing power of the state is pledged to make such payments." So protesting, it goes on to make an offer investors can't refuse.

Should defaults become significant, COPs and robbers may become the name of the game.

Moral Obligations and Some New Wrinkles: Contractual Obligations

Lease-financing ploys and moral obligation bonds are the preferred tools in the kit of "creative" financing. The John Mitchell invention, the moral obligation bond, has captured the imagination of governments intent on gutting their constitutions. With New York, Illinois, and Massachusetts in the lead, nearly half the states attempt to reassure investors by attaching "moral obligations" to many of their bond issues (about $11 billion in New York and $8 billion in Illinois). At best this is an overly clever gimmick to confer pseudolegality on what is tacitly understood to be an unconstitutional transaction.

Ever inventive, bond counsel (lawyers hired to give legal opinions on bonds) and financial advisers have come up with a variation of the moral obligation bond that appears to have a solid ring to it. It is called a contractual obligation bond and is a cross between a moral obligation bond and a lease-financing bond. Under this stratagem the state contracts with a public authority and commits itself to pay the authority's debt service in whole or in part. On the surface the contractual obligation bond is a revenue bond, but much of the revenue comes from state appropriations that can be cut off any time and not from fees collected by authorities. Once again the state assumes a debt burden without calling it debt. The figures merely appear in the operating budget as annual installments to pay off a contract.

New York, Massachusetts, and Illinois are in the vanguard of this latest financial maneuver. So far the main beneficiaries have been public authorities responsible for mass transportation, convention centers, and public housing. In 1990 New York State had contractual obligations amounting to nearly $2.5 billion. One of its beneficiaries is the monumental and scandal-ridden Jacob K. Javits Convention Center in New York City. In a complicated transaction the state persuaded the Triborough Bridge and Tunnel Authority (TBTA) to float bonds for the construction of the center. None of TBTA's tolls will be used to pay the bondholders. Instead the state makes an annual payment to TBTA for debt service. This fools none of the insiders— only the voters who never got a chance to object.

An especially tortuous example of contractual assistance is a $1.25-billion program for constructing and renovating court buildings in New York State. The New York State Dormitory Authority issues tax-exempt bonds to finance the projects and then leases the facilities to various cities and counties. Under a lease-purchase plan the local governments pay annual installments to the authority and, when the bonds are paid off, take title to the new hall of justice. Should they fail to pay, the state comptroller withholds a proportionate share of state aid that would otherwise be due them. The lease is carried on the books as a "contractual liability." In this deft move the local government does not require voter approval of the project and its payments are not subject to constitutional and statutory limits on debt and taxes.

Illinois and Massachusetts have devised similar schemes for convention centers in Chicago and Boston. In Massachusetts, though, this is small potatoes compared with a commitment to pay 90 percent of the debt service on nearly $1 billion in bonds issued by the Massachusetts Bay Transportation Authority (MBTA). With this form of contractual assistance the state pays over $1 billion annually to authorities.

New York, Massachusetts, Illinois, New Jersey, and other states display their financial ingenuity mainly at the state level. None, however, equals California in overcoming constitutional barriers to debt at the local level. After two thirds of the voters approved Proposition 13 in 1979, local revenues in California plummeted by 52 percent. Another blow to local governments was a later constitutional restriction requiring the approval of two-thirds of the voters for a local bond issue. The results disheartened local officials. From 1986 to 1990 California held 130 local bond elections. Sixty-three bond issues passed while 67 failed to get the required two-thirds vote.[8]

Clearly, the constitutional route was not the way to go. Within a few years local governments devised at least 15 different ways to bypass the constitution, including lease financing, COPs, and the creation of special districts (public authorities). The number of special districts reached a new high (some 6,000 in 1989) and encompassed nearly every governmental function. Fees and charges soared 21 percent and their climb has continued to the point where special districts depend more on such revenue than on taxes and special assessments.

Tax Increment Financing

One of the potent fiscal weapons in the California armory, and now adopted by some 37 states, which takes direct aim at the constitution is tax increment financing (TIF), otherwise known as tax allocation bonds. Say a city wants to redevelop a blighted and decayed area for economic development. To attract industry, commercial firms, and shopping centers, it is necessary to reconstruct road, water, sewer, and lighting systems. The first step is to set up a development or redevelopment district and authorize it to issue revenue bonds. But where does it get the revenue to back up the bonds? Should the project become a smashing success, the value of the property and property taxes will increase. The difference between taxes before and after development is the tax increment. This increment is the revenue that backs the bonds. In many cases the formula works. But the landscape also includes white elephants that ultimately drain city funds.

By the beginning of 1989 California local governments had created 343 redevelopment districts to launch nearly 600 projects. Together with other special districts designed to improve the infrastructure, they accounted for nearly 12 percent of all local debt. At first Proposition 13 curtailed TIFs in 1978 by rolling back assessed values of real estate, thus sharply reducing tax increments. But they clearly recovered and are now flourishing.

TIF didn't fare as well in Illinois. Started in 1977, it had only indifferent success with about 50 districts under way by 1985. To entice more communities into the fold, the state made an irresistible offer. It agreed to supplement increases in property taxes with increases in state and local sales taxes attributable to economic development. With this inducement, 100 new TIF districts were created in 1986 in what local observers described as a "land rush" atmosphere. Upon close examination some three years later the state found that 45 percent of 137 districts receiving additional sales taxes had failed to comply with state standards for eradicating blight and stimulating economic development. Abuses were rampant; even some affluent areas pleaded poverty to take advantage of the state's largess. In the meantime the state was committed to a $2 billion expenditure over a 23-year period. It quickly closed the program to districts created after January 1, 1987, no matter how deserving of state support they were.

Like Proposition 13 in California, Initiative 2 1/2 in Massachusetts became the hobgoblin of politicians. Under its tough strictures local taxes cannot increase by more than 2.5 percent unless the taxpayers choose to override the ceiling by a two-thirds vote in a special election. But water and sewage don't mix with this political brew. Hence, regardless of 2 1/2, the Massachusetts Water Resources Authority collects its fees from local governments for furnishing water and collecting waste. In fact, the legislature exempted such charges from 2 1/2. If a local government balks at paying the fees, the state comptroller can intercept state aid otherwise owed to the community.

In the fastest growing states such as Florida, Texas, New Mexico, Colorado, and California public authorities/special districts are the key to the rapid development of the infrastructure, often from scratch, in new communities. In a typical practice, the land owners (usually the real estate developer, kin, and associates at the start) vote to create water, sewer, road, and lighting districts or they get a friendly legislator to do it for them. These districts are then free to issue bonds and to impose the burden of paying for the bonds on all future residents. This is big business with over 1,000 water districts in Texas, over 1,000 special districts in Colorado, and 500 with several functions in Florida.

In Texas alone the debt of these districts exceeds the debt of all general local governments. No debt limits get in the way since these transactions take place outside of the constitution. But two troubling problems exist. If the development fails, the bondholders lose their investment. No guarantees exist other than the possible repossession of the properties. Or unscrupulous developers may pocket the proceeds of the bond issue without completing the infrastructure. In *Shadow on the Alamo* Harvey Katz documents such lurid tales. He quotes a Houston contractor who described in the early 1970s how he started one of the profitable utility districts:

> At one point I was thinking of getting a utility district for an area. I went to a lawyer here—I can't tell you his name—and he told me right off that it would cost me two thousand bucks just to get the bill passed. Half for him and half for the representative who would sponsor the bill. And that [the token payment] didn't include other legal work he'd probably have to do.[9]

Burned by scandals and under financial pressure, some local governments have become wary of quick development schemes and the misuse of special districts. Increasingly, they require developers to pay impact fees to relieve the strain new residential communities and commercial ventures impose on the local infrastructure and services. The payments can be in kind or in money. If in kind, the developers turn over land and completed phases of the infrastructure to the government. If in money, they follow intricate formulas to pay their fair share for fire, police, school, library, and recreational services. This is the way communities like Corpus Christi (Texas), Orlando (Florida), Loveland (Colorado), and Upper Merion Township (Pennsylvania) handle the financial squeeze of development.

Public Authorities Take On Social Programs

Since the 1920s state and local public authorities had mainly been engines for capital construction. A quiet revolution took place in the 1960s during the free-wheeling Rockefeller era in New York with repercussions that reached throughout the country. New forms of public authorities emerged, essentially multibillion-dollar investment banks, which focused not so much on self-financed capital projects as on social objectives like housing, health, education, and job creation. In a few short years they changed the nature of debt financing. Outpacing the traditional public authorities, they sold tax-exempt bonds in the capital markets and loaned the proceeds at low interest rates to real estate developers, industrial and commercial firms, banks, nonprofit hospitals, private universities, and college students.

The results have been dramatic. Housing finance agencies blossomed in every state to stimulate the construction of low-income and middle-income housing by private developers. Mortgage finance agencies also sprang up to pump money into banks for low-interest home mortgages and to take over existing mortgages in order to enlarge the banks' lending pool. Urban development corporations multiplied to rehabilitate the decaying, crime-ridden areas of cities.

As college enrollments soared, higher education financing authorities borrowed and guaranteed funds for low-interest loans to students in public and private colleges. Commercial banks processed loan applications with repayment guaranteed by state and federal governments and interest rates subsidized by both. Dormitory authorities channeled low-interest loans to private colleges. Health-financing authorities did the same for private hospitals, nursing homes, and retirement communities for senior citizens.

Nothing, though, topped the proliferation of state and local industrial development and economic development authorities. With the avowed goal of creating jobs they floated the largest amount of tax-exempt debt in American history for such a purpose. They eagerly lent this money at below-market interest rates to private firms for the purchase of land and equipment and the construction of commercial and industrial facilities. This was part of a cornucopia of benefits that included property tax abatements and exemption from sales taxes. The formula was simple: provide or retain jobs to get the benefits.

Many took the government up on this offer. Even profitable firms that could easily afford commercial loans dipped into this largess. Turned away by their unfriendly local banks, many risky and marginal firms found a sympathetic ear and a deep pocketbook in the new authorities. But the public authorities had nothing to lose because they did not stand behind their loans. In the event of a default, the private firm alone was ultimately responsible for repayment of the debt. If necessary, investors could seize the property or get relief from a bankruptcy court. Since the public authority was no more than a conveyor belt passing tax-exempt funds to private firms for private purposes, the industrial bonds it issued were labeled "pass-through," "conduit," "no-commitment," or "nonrecourse" bonds. In the words of Hyman Grossman, vice president of Standard and Poor's, these hybrids were "nonmunicipal municipal bonds."

The tax-exempt bonds for private not-for-profit hospitals, universities, and nursing homes were also "pass-through" bonds. Again the state public authorities that issued these bonds assumed no responsibility for repayment of the debt. This troubled a legislative leader in Massachusetts who fretted: "These authorities seem to forget that they were created by a public body to serve a public purpose and, while the money may be private, it is private money handled by an arm of the public." His worries turned out to be justified. Among hundreds of defaults, the travails of LTV, a steel manufacturer, stand out. In 1986 it defaulted on the payment of $550 million, primarily in industrial development bonds.[10]

Among the thousands of bonds issued by authorities for social objectives rather than capital projects, only housing and student loan bonds enjoyed the backing of state and federal governments. This was done through a series of interlocking "moral obligations" and guarantees.

This, then, is the anatomy of state and local debt in the United States. It is a rattling skeleton in the closet. Coupled with ploys to evade state and local limits on taxing and spending, many of the debt-financing schemes are an open and monumental conspiracy to subvert state constitutions. Why don't our elected officials end it once and for all? Sadly enough, they are the prime co-conspirators. It would seem that the courts, then, would be defenders of state constitutions. Unfortunately, their records are no better. As Chapter 5 reveals, they have largely turned a blind eye to blatant violations.

Without avid buyers of bonds who relish the tax-free interest, the municipal bond market would collapse. Are these investors conscious of the risks they take in buying bonds lacking the security of the full faith and credit of the government or a sure and steady source of revenue? Up to a point. Before they plunge ahead, they generally look for bond ratings, guarantees, insurance, or a combination of all three.

The Bond-Rating Game

Ratings come first. The most influential raters are Standard and Poor's Inc., Moody's Investment Service, and Fitch Investment Service. For a handsome fee paid by the authority they rate the bond issue for quality and safety. The top rating is a triple A and the lowest rating of investment grade is a triple B. In between are numerous gradations of ratings with each rating service using its own classification system. Anything below BBB is a scarlet letter—a junk bond. Some momentous decisions ride on these ratings. They determine investor acceptance of the bonds, the price of the bonds, and the amount of interest paid. The higher the rating, the higher the price and the lower the interest rate. The lower the rating, the lower the price and the higher the interest rate. These grades affect the expenditures of hundreds of millions of dollars.

The rating game is competitive. Eager for a good rating, a public authority or government may retain one or more bond-rating firms and get different results. For example, in December 1990 Moody's rated a Massachusetts bond issue Baa while Standard and Poor's gave it a BBB and Fitch an A.

Paul Levy, former executive director of the Massachusetts Water Resources Authority, laid out the financial stakes this way: "The biggest variation in the cost of the harbor cleanup is the cost of money. A 1 percent increase in interest rates on the bonds is worth $430 million over the next thirty years. So we want to get a good bond rating. Every quarter percent is worth $100 million. No other single thing we're doing will affect the cost of the project as much as the bond rating we're going to get."[11]

Only eight states get the coveted triple A, primarily for their GO bonds: California, Georgia, Maryland, New Jersey, North Carolina, South Carolina, Utah, and Virginia. Some though are teetering at the edge of a lower rating. Their public authority bonds merit the slightly less favorable AA or A. At the bottom are Massachusetts and Louisiana with barely passable variations of B ratings. In January 1992, New York State joined Louisiana by getting a Baa rating from Moody's, a notch above a junk bond category. This was a comedown from AA ratings in the 1980s. Only Massachusetts was lower. The fall from grace is worth millions of dollars since interest rates will rise. Among cities Philadelphia and some of its public authorities hit the bottom in 1990 with a CCC rating that means serious risk. As the recession compounds the deficits of state and local governments and their authorities, bond ratings will skid everywhere in the United States.

By no means are the bond-rating agencies infallible. They have not always alerted investors in time to looming defaults in the payment of principal and interest. This is what occurred with the $2.25-billion default of the Washington Public Power Supply System and the $135-million default of the New York State Urban Development Corporation.

Although not entirely foolproof, one way to get a triple A rating is to insure the bond issue against default or to get a letter of credit, also in effect insurance, from a domestic or foreign commercial bank. Several bond insurance companies and a few dozen banks stand ready to provide this service at a very substantial cost. For example, in 1990 Massachusetts faced the dilemma of selling $300 million of bonds with or without insurance. Insured bonds would yield an interest rate of about 7 percent, uninsured bonds 7.5 percent to 8 percent because of the state's low bond rating. Massachusetts chose the former route and paid a premium of $4.4 million or about 1.5 percent of the value of the bond issue.

Three bond insurance companies dominate the field and insure the principal and interest of about 28 percent of all municipal bonds issued: American Municipal Bond Assurance Corporation (AMBAC Indemnity Corporation), owned by Citibank and with over $700 million in capital; Municipal Bond Investors Assurance (MBIA), with about $700 million in capital; and Finance Guaranty Insurance Company (FGIC), owned by General Electric and with $531 million in capital. All enjoy a triple A rating by Moody's Investors Service and Standard and Poor's. To spread their risks in the event of catastrophic defaults some are reinsured by other companies such as the Enhance Reinsurance Company.

On the surface this looks like gilt-edged protection against wayward or bankrupt public authorities and their parent governments. But a hard look at the figures dispels this optimism. Should a major recession trigger far-flung defaults, the capital reserves of the insurance companies may fall far short of covering their liabilities. For example, MBIA has about $700 million in capital resources to cover $137 billion of insurance, giving it, in the jargon of the experts, a risk to capital ratio of 190 to 1. This means it has $1 in the till for every $190 in potential losses. The average in the industry is 121 to 1. For business regulators in California a 200 to 1 ratio is an alarm bell that signals the possible collapse of a private business and is enough to stop the business from operating.[12]

The bond insurance industry turns apoplectic at the mere hint that it may be "too leveraged in terms of exposure to capital ratios." Kenneth J. Ferrara, senior vice president of FGIC, argues that "general obligation bonds are backed by the full faith and credit of a municipality. Should a municipality fail to make a debt service payment, it is . . . required by law to raise taxes, if necessary, to cover its obligations. Therefore, should FGIC advance funds to ensure the timely payment of principal and interest to bondholders, the company could expect full eventual recovery of any debt—service payments."

These soothing words apply only to a minority of bonds—GO bonds.

Heather L. Ruth, president of the Public Securities Association, the trade organization of dealers in municipal bonds, takes a more global view: "Despite recent well-publicized problems of some municipal issuers, the vast majority of the more than 50,000 state and local governments that issue bonds are on a solid financial footing and worthy of investment. Indeed, some credits in the South and Southwest are improving as economies recover from depressed oil prices in the 1980s."[13]

For the rest of the decade the issue is how many more problems will become "well publicized." A look at the recent past in the next chapter hardly leads one to bubble over with optimism.

Letters of credit (LOCs) are a distant second to bond insurance in "credit enhancement" although their use has become extensive. In 1990 U.S., German, Japanese, and Swiss banks guaranteed the payment of about $13 billion in public authority bonds for higher education, housing, transportation, pollution control, and other functions. LOCs cover over 10 percent of all new bond issues. But LOCs are no better than the creditworthiness of the individual banks. While the record of repayment has been good, some troubling signs appeared in 1990 and 1991 as the bond-rating organizations placed several large banks on a "credit watch" and downgraded bond issues backed by LOCs from such banks as Citicorp, Manufacturers Hanover, and Sumitomo Bank of Japan. Should banks issuing LOCs fail, the guarantees to bondholders will be meaningless.

In a crunch the state itself may bail out failing authorities by invoking its "moral obligation." Even without any commitments, it may rush to the rescue lest it and its creatures are shut out of the capital markets because of low bond ratings. Several states go further, however, by actually guaranteeing the payment of the principal and interest of the bonds even though they are not GO bonds. Used sparingly, such guarantees generally require voter approval. This type of protection is in effect in New Hampshire, where the state backs up $190 million of water pollution control bonds; in Massachusetts, with guarantees of $260 million for local public housing authority bonds; in New York State, with a guarantee of $900 million for the Job Development Authority; and in Oklahoma, with state guarantees of the debt of local water authorities. These are but a few of many examples.

The Shock of Advance Refunding

Sheltered by guarantees, letters of credit, and bond insurance and fully aware of the risks, conservative investors can now presumably entrust their hard-earned money to public authorities. Well—not quite yet. Pitfalls still lurk ahead. After a few years the high tax-exempt interest rates that attracted the investor in the first place may vanish. How? The authorities may suddenly call the bonds in and return the principal and any interest that is due to investors. The device for shattering the dreams of high interest rates that go on and on is called "advance refunding."

Typically, two dates stand out in bond issues: the callable date and the maturity date. The callable date usually occurs 10 years after the bonds are issued. At that time the bond issuer has the option of paying off the bonds at a slight premium of $2 to $3 per $100. The maturity date represents the life of the bond, say 20 to 30 years. At the end of that period the public authority must redeem the bonds no matter what. Should investors have 30-year bonds that pay 11 percent interest, they lose that attractive return for 20 years if the bonds are called in at the end of 10 years. At least they are consoled by the slight premium and the knowledge that they were warned in advance of such contingency. Still, when all this happens, the money they get back can now earn no more than 7 percent interest.

Especially galling are bonds that are "prematurely redeemed" even before the callable date. This has been the fate of many housing and mortgage bonds and defaulted bonds covered by bond insurance and LOCs. With virtually no warning, investors may find that cherished high-yielding bonds have slipped out of their hands. It's little consolation to find out later that fine print, invisible to all but the sharpest eyes, on bond documents and in bond covenants deal with such an event. In the end the investor discovers that what has happened is usually quite legal although obscure and seemingly unethical.

Advance refunding has become a big business. Of $128 billion in bonds issued in 1990, $22.5 billion or about 18 percent were refunding issues.[14] Although this may be devastating to investors, the bond issuers usually find a way to reduce their interest payments. In 1982 bonds paid 11 percent to 14 percent; in 1991 they paid less than 7 percent. Refunding, then, can save millions of dollars. Or a public authority may be eager to change restrictive bond covenants. The covenant is a contract that lays out the terms of payment, specifies the sources of revenue, and fixes the ways in which money can be spent. To change any of this, it is necessary to refund the bond issue and start over again. Frequently, state and local governments cast covetous eyes on the surpluses of public authorities. The only way to capture this largess is to change the bond covenant in a new bond issue. As Robert Moses discovered, refunding can be a ticket to immortality. Keep on refunding bond issues and the authority lives forever.

"Tax Reform" Shrivels Tax-Exempt Bonds

After the 1980s a more serious threat emerged for investors, public authorities, and state and local governments. Choked with mounting deficits, Congress and President Reagan were eager to get their hands on the nearly $40 billion in taxes they lost every year because interest on municipal bonds was exempt from taxes. Only one obstacle stood in the way. From the earliest days of the Republic, federal, state, and local governments had followed the principle of reciprocal immunity, which meant that state and local governments didn't tax federal securities and the federal government didn't tax state and local bonds. Four federal acts and a U.S. Supreme Court decision ended this hands-off relationship and wiped out total tax exemption for many municipal bonds.

The federal onslaught began in a small way, then gradually accelerated. For the first time three federal acts imposed unprecedented controls over tax-exempt bonds issued by public authorities: the Mortgage Subsidy Bond Act of 1980, the Tax Equity and Fiscal Responsibility Act (TEFRA) of 1982, and the Deficit Reduction Act (DEFRA) of 1984. They limited the amount of mortgage subsidy bonds that could be used for owner-occupied housing, and capped the volume of tax-exempt bonds for "private purposes," especially industrial bonds and student loan bonds.

These changes were but the opening salvo. Finally, the Tax Reform Act of 1986 demolished the existing structure of tax-exempt bonds almost beyond recognition. It divided municipal bonds into two classes: "public purpose" and "private purpose" bonds. So-called public purpose bonds still enjoyed tax exemption provided that no more than 10 percent of the proceeds benefited private parties and that no more than 10 percent of the debt service could be paid by private firms and individuals.

Private purpose bonds, especially complex, were subdivided further into three categories. One category lost tax exemption altogether. These are bonds for private pollution control facilities, sports centers, convention centers, and "small issue" industrial bonds for nonmanufacturing firms like hotels, motels, and fast-food chains. A second category lumped mortgage revenue, housing, industrial development, and student loan bonds. Congress imposed on this group a unified volume cap in each state that ultimately amounted to $50 per capita or $150 million, whichever was greater. Unless the state government made other provisions, this bounty was to be split 50–50 between state and local governments.

The third "private purpose" category continued to enjoy tax exemption. This consisted of bonds issued for private not-for-profit institutions, especially universities, hospitals, and nursing homes. The only strings on these bonds are a $150-million ceiling on the total amount of tax-exempt debt each institution can have (hospitals have no such limit); a 2 percent cap on bond issuance costs; and a 5 percent limit on private participation.

In further qualifications and technicalities running into hundreds of pages, the Tax Reform Act clamped many additional restrictions on tax-exempt bonds. The following, in particular, hit public authorities especially hard:

Alternative minimum tax. Determined to tax individuals and corporations that paid little or no federal taxes because of heavy investments in municipal bonds, Congress imposed an alternative minimum tax that in effect wiped out tax exemptions of interest "on private purpose" bonds for incomes of $200,000 or more.

Bank investments. Prior to 1986 commercial banks held 35 percent of all municipal bonds. There was every incentive to do so. For tax purposes they could deduct 80 percent of the interest costs incurred in buying or holding tax-exempt bonds. This privilege vanished except for investments up to $10 million.

Arbitrage. Before the tax axe fell, public authorities and general government could invest bond proceeds for which they had no immediate use in U.S. Treasury bills and notes. Since the Treasury paid higher interest than the tax-exempt bonds, the public authorities earned a tidy profit. In the lexicon of Wall Street they benefited from arbitrage, the difference between the two interest rates. Now, they must rebate any "profits" to the Treasury except for money earned on a small reserve.

Limits on bond issuance costs. Outraged by the high fees paid to the merchants of debt, Congress placed a 2 percent ceiling on the cost of issuing industrial revenue bonds and, as noted, bonds for nonprofit institutions. It lacked the political will to extend the cap to all tax-exempt bonds.

Advance refunding. To control the churning market of advance refunding, Congress limited new bond issues to one refunding and old ones to two refundings.

Tax increment financing (TIF). The abuses in TIF for the redevelopment of blighted areas led to severe restrictions. New criteria defined blighted areas narrowly and mandated the investment of 95 percent or more of the bond proceeds in redevelopment projects.

Qualified versus non-qualified bonds. Intricate formulas spelled out those bonds that were qualified for tax exemption and those that were not. To qualify, 90 percent to 95 percent of the bond proceeds for housing, industrial development, student loans, and nonprofit corporations had to go directly to the beneficiaries and not to private interests. Other formulas governed the use of bond proceeds for housing veterans and low-income groups.

The final blow came two years later in April 1988 when the U.S. Supreme Court ruled in *South Carolina* v. *Baker* that Congress could tax interest income from municipal bonds. Tossing out the time-honored doctrine of reciprocal immunity, the Court stated flatly that the Constitution does not prohibit federal taxing of state and local bonds. Panic-stricken bond dealers, governors, and mayors quickly lobbied congressional leaders, who reassured them that they would take no further action to restrict the use of tax-exempt bonds. Dan Rostenkowski, chairman of the House Ways and Means Committee, and Senator Daniel Patrick Moynihan of New York vowed, in particular, that Congress would never tax municipal bonds issued for "true public purposes." No one bothered to define a "true public purpose."[15]

Between the chopping block of the Tax Reform Act and the axe of the Supreme Court decision the tax-exempt bond market dropped precipitously. From a high of $204.3 billion in long-term bonds issued in 1985, the volume plummeted to $151 billion in 1986 and $105.4 billion in 1987. Then it picked up slightly in 1990 to $128 billion. The surge in 1985 had been in anticipation of the passage of the Tax Reform Act. So-called private purpose bonds were especially hard hit. From a pre-tax reform volume of $41.6 billion in 1984, they fell 70 percent to about $13 billion in 1989.

Much of the bond market dried up because of the alternative minimum tax and the loss of tax advantages by banks and insurance companies, previously heavy buyers of municipal bonds. Individual bond buyers and mutual funds specializing in tax-exempt bonds became the largest single group of investors. But even individuals balked at buying bonds after the top marginal tax rate dropped from 50 percent to 28 percent in the Tax Reform Act. This made municipal bonds a less inviting tax shelter. Another damper on investment was the complexity of the rules governing public and private purpose bonds and qualifying and nonqualifying bonds.

Only the federal government, accountants, and attorneys profited from the restrictions on tax-exempt bonds in the Tax Reform Act of

1986. The federal revenue loss attributed to these bonds dropped sharply from about $40 billion in 1985 to $22.6 billion in 1990, a gain of $17.4 billion for the federal government. Because of the complexity of the act, it turned out to be the "Full Employment Act for Attorneys and Accountants" as they alone were able to delve into the arcane statutory language governing the alternative minimum tax, private and public purpose bonds, and qualifying and nonqualifying bonds.

For state and local governments bent on providing affordable housing and improving the infrastructure, the environment, and mass transportation, the act turned out to be a disaster at least in the short term. Like it or not, in the United States these projects cannot succeed without a close public-private partnership. By imposing volume caps on so-called private purpose bonds and taxing the interest on other bonds such as pollution control bonds, the act set back hundreds of projects. In 1987 27 states deferred vital projects because of the new restrictions.

The act introduced unprecedented complexity into debt financing. Now public authorities and their parent governments must carefully dole out bond proceeds lest they run into limits on arbitrage. They must time any advance refunding precisely. They must monitor volume caps lest they run afoul of the law. And they must keep the Internal Revenue Service informed every step of the way on all of these transactions.

The volume caps triggered fierce competition among public authorities responsible for housing, economic development, student loans, and assistance to nonprofit institutions. Each authority that issued tax-exempt private purpose bonds attempted to get its fair share of the caps. Some authorities even invaded the fiscal turf of other authorities to increase their bonding capacity. In Massachusetts a skirmish flared between the Massachusetts Industrial Financing Authority (MIFA) and the Higher Education Facilities Authority (HEFA). Having lost much of its power to issue industrial bonds, MIFA tried to finance the construction of buildings for private colleges, a HEFA prerogative. Governor Dukakis temporarily declared a cease fire. In turn, HEFA began to take over the financing of public colleges from several college-building authorities.

Ever entrepreneurial, public authorities began to experiment with the use of taxable bonds. Given an attractive interest rate and solid security, investors might prefer a taxable bond to a long-term Treasury bond or corporate bond. So far taxable municipal bonds account for only about 3 percent of the bonds issued in recent years. They finance programs for housing, electric power, telephone communications, industrial development, and student loans.

One of the pioneers in the use of taxable bonds is MIFA. Richard A. Skerry, Jr., general counsel, said defiantly and with much bravado: "Each time there has been a change in the tax law, the agency has looked upon that as a challenge to go in other directions. We're not going to let a change in the law get us down. . . . I don't have to worry about arbitrage. I don't have to worry about capital spending limitations. I don't have to worry about tax opinions."

Paradoxically, despite the bleak scenario, the future has never looked brighter for public authorities. In the early stages of the 1990 recession at least 30 states were deficit-ridden, their worst plight since the 1982 recession. They had little prospect of federal relief and no appetite for squeezing their citizens for more taxes. All signs point, then, to a sharp expansion of public purpose bonds and ever more inventive forms of lease financing, COPs, moral and contractual obligations, and even taxable bonds. Rather than shrinking, the number of state and local public authorities will grow and the borrowing spree will continue.

3

A Fate Worse
Than Debt

The accomplishments of many public authorities are stunning; thousands of successful projects and programs stand as monuments to their achievements. Other public authorities, however, offer nothing but grim tales of mismanagement, financial chicanery, and default. Every part of the country has its share of runaway and uncontrolled authorities. Perhaps none stand out more than the failures of the Washington Public Power Supply System (WPPSS, also called WHOOPS) in the state of Washington; the Urban Development Corporation (UDC) of New York State; the Massachusetts Housing Finance Agency (MHFA) and the Massachusetts Bay Transportation Authority (MBTA); the New Jersey Turnpike; industrial development authorities in Ohio, Minnesota, and Illinois; and health-financing authorities in several states. On a smaller scale, accounts of the financial skullduggery of public authorities abound nearly everywhere.

The repercussions of the failures have been far-reaching, shaking up capital markets, undermining the confidence of investors, and in the case of WHOOPS, leading to losses running into billions of dollars. Some of the punitive measures in the Tax Reform Act of 1986 were spawned by such failures and have started a movement for federal regulation of the tax-exempt bond market.

WHOOPS

By any measure WPPSS (WHOOPS) was the biggest and most spectacular loser. Climaxing a series of financial and management fiascos, WPPSS, one of the largest public authorities in the United States, defaulted in 1983 on the payment of interest on $2.25 billion of tax-exempt bonds. The money had been raised for the construction of two of five nuclear plants for generating electricity in the Northwest. The default was the single largest of any public agency in the United States, unmatched even by the governmental financial disasters of the Great Depression. Up to 1983 the $2.25-billion bond issue was the largest tax-exempt bond issue on record and part of a record total of over $8 billion of bonds sold for the construction of the five plants. Except for the Tennessee Valley Authority (TVA), the project was the largest public nuclear power project in the history of the United States.

The results were drastic. Thousands of investors lost most of their money while the ambitious program to build five nuclear plants collapsed. Out of the wreckage one plant became operational, two were mothballed, and two were shut down for good. These failures set back the economy of the Northwest for at least 50 years. Bitter law suits engulfed all of the participants: the investors, banks, WPPSS, the State of Washington, financial advisers, bond counsel, brokerage firms, engineering firms, and the Bonneville Power Administration (BPA), a federal agency responsible for marketing hydroelectric power in the Northwest, principally from the Columbia River.

Only 20 years before the default, the future had never looked brighter for the development of public nuclear power in the region. On a crisp autumn day in September 1963, President John F. Kennedy opened the ground-breaking ceremony for WPPSS' first nuclear power electric generating facility at the Federal Hanford Nuclear Reservation. He sketched a vision of a new frontier blessed with abundant low-cost energy: "As it is well known here at Hanford, we must hasten the development of low cost atomic power. I think we should lead the world in this."[1]

The ceremony culminated more than 10 years of planning for the expansion of power resources. Up to that point the chief provider of electrical power in the Northwest was the Bonneville Power Administration (BPA), now part of the Department of Energy. A New Deal creation, BPA was supposed to be the cornerstone of economic development in the Northwest, just as the Tennessee Valley Authority (TVA) had been in a multistate area around Tennessee. President Roosevelt had originally proposed the establishment of a Columbia Valley Authority (CVA) with broad functions similar to TVA's to develop, generate, and distribute electric power. The power would be generated by dams along the Columbia River. A coalition of private utilities, coal mine operators, and railroads fought this proposal and succeeded in killing it in Congress. Instead of CVA, the government created BPA with the sole responsibility of selling power wholesale to public and private utilities from 30 hydroelectric dams built and owned by the Army Corps of Engineers and the U.S. Bureau of Reclamation. By the early 1970s BPA was distributing half of the power in the region with preference given to publicly owned utilities.

As early as the 1950s it was clear that hydroelectric resources were limited and could not possibly keep up with the demands for power that were growing at an estimated rate of 5 percent to 7 percent a year. The Northwest had become a mecca for migrants from the Northeast and the Midwest. Along with the population boom, new aerospace, aluminum, and forest product industries had developed and required dramatic increases in energy. Not only was BPA reaching the limits of its capacity, but its authorizing statute prohibited it from purchasing nonfederal power. One obvious solution was to tap the nuclear power at the Hanford Nuclear Reservation in the State of Washington.

Hanford had been built during World War II to produce plutonium for nuclear weapons, but the wasted heat of the reactors could be used to generate electricity as well. With the support of President Kennedy, Senators Henry M. Jackson and Warren Magnuson of Washington promoted federal funding of an electrical generating facility at HNR. At first they failed when, once again, private interests blocked the expansion of public power.

To break this impasse, the governor and the legislature created WPPSS in 1957 and gave the new public authority the power to finance, build, own, and operate electrical generating and transmitting facilities. The state itself had no direct role in the authority. It was run by a board of directors designated by members of different public utility districts (PUDs) in the state. Because of a strong populist tradition in the state, the residents, in the main, preferred public ownership of power systems. PUDs—in effect small public authorities—were their chosen vehicle. Most PUDs bought their power from BPA. Under the new arrangements they would sell power to BPA as part of the regional grid.

WPPSS started modestly enough with the construction of a relatively small hydroelectric facility, with power transmitted by the BPA system. Only 16 PUDs participated in the project. Then WPPSS entered the nuclear age when Senator Jackson and President Kennedy finally succeeded in getting congressional approval to generate electricity at Hanford. By 1966 the new system was operational and served 71 publicly owned utilities and several investor-owned utilities in the Northwest.

Considering the burgeoning demands for power, public and private power utilities and BPA regarded these steps as temporary palliatives. They set up a joint planning council that in the early 1970s developed a Ten Year Hydro-Thermal Power Program. The council envisaged the need for at least 20 nuclear plants costing about $16 billion by the year 2000. In the meantime, WPPSS and BPA settled on building five reactors at an estimated cost of $6.7 billion. Eighty-eight PUDs, cities, and private utilities joined WPPSS in this venture. In 1974 construction planning for this massive project began.

From the start the financial arrangements were intricate and in later years would haunt all the participants. In effect BPA guaranteed the financing of three plants—projects 1, 2, and 3—through net billing arrangements. Under this system BPA agreed to pay WPPSS and its participating members for all the costs they incurred in building the plants, including debt service. It deducted from the costs charges for BPA power. If BPA bills were less than WPPSS costs, BPA made up the difference (hence the term "net billing"). BPA melded in or averaged these costs with the cost of producing hydroelectric power. It passed on the combined costs to the utilities and ultimately to the consumers in the form of higher rates. Indirectly, then, the credit of the federal government backed the first three projects even though no explicit federal guarantees or subsidies existed.

Because of limits on its credit and growing congressional opposition, BPA did not extend the net billing agreement to projects 4 and 5. Nevertheless, it encouraged WPPSS to build the new plants on its own. With visions of a golden nuclear age before it, WPPSS enthusiastically agreed to undertake the new construction. As is typical in the power industry, the 88 participating utilities signed "take-or-pay" or "come-hell-or-high-water" contracts with WPPSS. These committed them to pay their share of the costs, including debt service, whether or not the plants were completed or operating.

At that point the atmosphere was heady with optimism. No whiff of any problems was in the air. In this spirit Wall Street embraced the five projects warmly as prospects of high fees danced before the eyes of brokerage houses, bond counsel, financial advisers, bond-rating organizations, management consultants, and engineering firms. Brokerage houses recommended the bonds enthusiastically and sold over $8 billion of them. The highest ratings went to projects 1, 2, and 3 because of federal support. Projects 4 and 5 commanded at least A ratings that held up to the time of default. Only two dissenters questioned the need for projects 4 and 5— Wertheim and Company, an investment banking firm, and Drexel, Burnham, and Lambert, the ill-fated brokerage firm. In general, euphoria on Wall Street far outweighed any concerns.

In the late 1970s and early 1980s a veritable plague of problems engulfed the five projects. It seemed that anything that could go wrong did indeed go wrong. Costs escalated, rising from the original estimate of $6.7 billion to well over $24 billion, due in part to raging inflation and high interest rates. Without federal backing, WPPSS had to pay interest rates as high as 15 percent for bonds for projects 4 and 5 despite the A rating. For most of the sharp jumps in costs, WPPSS had only itself to blame. Mismanagement dogged the projects from the beginning while major delays set back all the projects by years. Cost plus contracts accelerated expenditures. Changes in design and cost overruns were commonplace, some due to faulty planning, some due to changing federal regulations. A small army of poorly supervised contractors worked on the projects because state laws required bidding on all contracts over $10,000. Because of the fiscal and management chaos that ensued, WPPSS' costs were 42 percent higher than the average for the entire nuclear power industry.

Relatively unsophisticated, the board of directors of WPPSS proved to be incapable of monitoring the simultaneous construction of five plants. Their only experience had been with small public utility districts (PUDs) that had elected them to office. They were part of an old boy network connected more by political skill than technical knowledge. The executives they appointed came from similar backgrounds. This didn't prove to be a problem in the early 1970s when WPPSS had only 88 employees. In 1981, with over 2,000 employees and 14,000 construction workers in the field, WPPSS was overwhelmed. It was unable to cope with the confusion, overspending on projects, overly high salaries, and the purchase of gilt-edged materials.

The board stubbornly stuck to its original plans even as evidence mounted that the original projections of the demands for power had been grossly exaggerated. At a time when dozens of private utilities were cancelling or deferring over 100 nuclear power projects, the board persisted in going ahead with projects 4 and 5. It ignored the disillusionment with nuclear power that swept the country and the crises in plants like Seabrook in New Hampshire, Shoreham on Long Island in New York, and TVA, where serious management problems dogged the operation of newly constructed nuclear plants.

As its woes multiplied, WPPSS tinkered with its management systems and retained outside engineering and management consulting firms to unravel its organizational, systems, and fiscal problems. Few significant changes resulted from these expensive efforts. No helpful oversight came from allies outside of WPPSS. Despite its heavy financial stake because of the net billing arrangements, BPA kept WPPSS at arm's length and interceded unsuccessfully only at the eleventh hour as the crisis deepened. Once it created WPPSS, the state government paid no further attention to it. No state auditors or state budget officers probed its finances. No attorney general pondered its contracts. The legislature launched an investigation only after the fact.

Wall Street maintained its conspiracy of optimism in the face of known WPPSS failures. Federal backing of projects 1, 2, and 3 and take-or-pay contracts for projects 4 and 5 assuaged any doubts about the evidence of mismanagement. Brokerage houses eagerly continued to sell WPPSS bonds without advising investors of WPPSS problems, and several tax-exempt mutual funds invested heavily in them. What appeared to be adequate security for payment of principal and interest satisfied Moody's and Standard and Poor's, whose analysis of the creditworthiness of the bonds was at best superficial and who maintained their high bond ratings.

Investigative reporter Howard Gleckman, who plumbed the failures of WPPSS, marveled at the lack of disclosure by Wall Street underwriters: "During this period," he wrote, "investors in WPPSS bonds consistently received less information about the true state of the Supply System's construction program than did investors in four private utilities which owned shares in the WPPSS units."[2]

Finally, a consumer revolt brought the crisis to a head. In the early 1980s all that WPPSS had to show for its vast efforts were five incomplete projects, heavy costs, and no additional electricity. Consequently, electricity rates shot up sharply. Residents of Washington, Idaho, and Oregon started recall elections to fire commissioners of PUDs that participated in WPPSS. In their place they elected dissidents who withheld payments from PUDs and boycotted banks acting as trustees for WPPSS. In November 1981 voters in the State of Washington approved an initiative requiring a public vote on WPPSS bond sales, only to be overturned by the federal courts. Voter hostility to take-or-pay contracts stiffened. Most PUDs refused to pay interest on bonds for projects 4 and 5 and sued WPPSS to challenge the legality of take-or-pay contracts, and to prevent WPPSS from pressuring them to pay for power they didn't get.

The end came on June 15, 1983, when the elected, politicized Supreme Court of Washington voided take-or-pay contracts altogether. In a highly controversial opinion it stated flatly that the PUDs had no statutory authorization to make such contracts in the first place:

> From reading the record, it is clear that the monumental crisis brought on by WPPSS was created by the simultaneous construction of five nuclear plants, as well as mismanagement. To save itself, WPPSS has asked us to approve a plan to mortgage the futures of ratepayers by requiring huge increases in electricity rates, in exchange for nothing, in violation of our statutes and state constitution. This we cannot do.[3]

The Oregon and Idaho courts took the reverse position, but decided that the PUDs in their states should abide by the Washington ruling.

With this decision the security for $2.25 billion of bonds for projects 4 and 5 vanished. Including interest, the debt at that time came to $3.3 billion. During the life of the bonds interest alone would amount to $5 billion. As trustees of the bondholders, the Chemical Bank of New York in August 1983 insisted on immediate repayment of the debt. Virtually bankrupt, WPPSS defaulted on the payment of principal and interest. It terminated projects 4 (24 percent complete) and 5 (16 percent complete) altogether, mothballed projects 1 and 3 for activation in later years, and completed only project 2. Subsidized by the taxpayers, BPA has continued to pay for projects 1, 2, and 3 and to pass the costs on to utilities. Because of an unaccountable public authority, public power policy in the Northwest was a failure.

Outraged bondholders refused to take the ruling of the Washington Supreme Court as the last word. To salvage their investments they turned to federal district courts in Washington and Arizona for relief and sued WPPSS, PUDs, the State of Washington, BPA, brokerage houses, financial advisers, and engineering firms. They also took another tack in federal and state courts by charging negligence, misrepresentation, fraud, and violation of federal and state securities laws in connection with the WPPSS sale of projects 4 and 5 bonds.

As the legal machinery creaked on, many of the defendants decided to settle the cases with the approval of the federal courts. BPA agreed to pay $35 million; the State of Washington $10 million; the PUDs of Seattle and Tacoma $50 million and $40 million, respectively; 53 public and private utilities about $250 million; Paine Webber $20 million; Wertheim and Company, investment bankers, $1 million; Merrill, Lynch and other underwriters $10 million; and the bond counsel for WPPSS, Wood, Dawson, Smith, and Hillman, $500,000—just a tender slap on the wrist. With other bits and pieces of settlements a figure short of $800 million was reached in early 1990—just about one-fourth of the total debt of $3.3 billion. Legal fees consumed over $100 million of the settlement.

The recovery rate for investors who settled ranged from 9.4 cents to 50.3 cents on the dollar depending on when they had bought the bonds. Under these circumstances the Chemical Bank as a trustee for bondholders decided to continue its suit against WPPSS and

BPA. Investors who bought WPPSS bonds after the default for about 12 cents to 14 cents on the dollar, in the hope of reaping sizable awards through settlements, formed a national committee to press their claims through a class action suit. In the meantime, court actions charging fraud, misrepresentation, negligence, breach of duty, and violation of the laws accelerated in various parts of the country.

Only investors who had bought bonds for projects 1, 2, and 3 remained smug throughout this ordeal. Shielded by BPA guarantees, they continued to receive tax-exempt interest averaging about 8 percent. As investors learned the hard way, all WPPSS securities were not equal.

To the astonishment of bondholders still clutching their near-worthless securities, WPPSS came back to the market in August 1989 with the approval of the state and BPA. This time they sold $450 million of refunding revenue bonds for mothballed projects 1 and 3, even though only project 2 was operational. Some of the underwriters who touted the new bonds were the same firms that had eagerly sold the bonds for projects 4 and 5. A warm welcome also came from the rating services that prior to default had given an A to 4 and 5 bonds. Moody's rated the new issue A while Standard and Poor's and Fitch went somewhat higher with AA- ratings. Such are the wonders of federal backing through BPA![4]

Investors gobbled up the issue that yielded 7.5 percent to 7.75 percent interest. There was apparently no end to investor gullibility.

Predictably, the plaintiffs in the law suits were bitter at this latest insult. In an emotional letter to WPPSS and Robert Abrams, the attorney general of New York State, their counsel played up the moral issues: "Issuing new bonds for the ultimate benefit of the Supply System, the Bonneville Power Administration and other entities deeply involved with the projects 4 and 5 debacle, without any benefit to holders of defaulted projects 4 and 5 bonds, affronts common sense notions of good faith and fair dealing."[5]

The Securities Exchange Commission was a paper tiger throughout this long and traumatic episode. It spent nearly five years investigating the many dubious transactions and finally released a staff report in September 1988. That was the end of its role. It made no attempt to take any enforcement action, arguing that disciplinary measures by the SEC might duplicate ongoing litigation. It merely questioned the adequacy of disclosure in the official statement (prospectus) on project 4 and 5 bonds. Rather than focusing on this alone, the SEC proclaimed its intention to implement new regulations covering all municipal securities.

From the start Wall Street's role was ignominious. Summarizing a series of investigative reports for *The Bond Buyer* in 1984, Howard Gleckman concluded:

> Paid millions of dollars to raise money to build massive projects. Wall Street failed to do its job. It started what it could not finish. It let short-term greed overcome longer-range concerns. It ignored evidence that the projects might not be feasible. Later, its desperate effort to salvage the projects cost WPPSS and its investors billions more in wasted money. To many, the story of WPPSS is as much the failure of Wall Street as it is of the supply system, Bonneville, and the region's utilities and contractors.
>
> Yet to some, there was no failure at all. Asked what went wrong with WPPSS, one investment banker replied, after being promised anonymity: "Nothing went wrong. We all made money, didn't we?"[6]

New York State Urban Development Corporation

Compared to the colossal WPPSS failure, the default of the New York State Urban Development Corporation (UDC) was relatively minor. It amounted to a mere $135 million in short-term notes issued for the construction of low-income and moderate-income housing. The default was temporary and quickly contained by the swift intervention of New York State. Yet it proved to be an explosive event that rocked the financial markets, barred New York State and its public authorities from those markets for several months, and led to unprecedented controls over public authorities.

UDC's fate was to become an involuntary symbol of the fiscal shenanigans of New York State and New York City and the failure of the most ambitious housing policy in the nation. At the time of its collapse UDC was the largest developer of subsidized housing in the United States, having a construction program of over $1 billion well under way. UDC had already successfully marketed $1 billion in tax-exempt bonds and had the authority to borrow an additional $1 billion.

From the time of its creation in 1968 UDC was a keystone of the Rockefeller administration's housing program. No sooner had Rockefeller assumed office as governor in 1959 than he singled out the lack of affordable housing for low-income families as a festering state problem. For 10 years the state had subsidized housing for middle-income groups through low-interest loans and tax abatements to developers. Barely adequate, it still met obvious needs. Aside from local public housing authorities that had existed since the 1930s, no significant programs expanded housing for low-income and moderate-income groups.

At this time the flight of the middle class to the suburbs was in full swing, leaving ghettos behind. Urban planning as practiced after World War II had produced a wasteland. In the name of slum clearance, many square miles of housing had been leveled and the central part of cities razed as in New York, Detroit, Chicago, and Houston. Such development that came was too little and too late. Both state and cities lacked the authority and the money to take effective remedial action while at the local level obsolete building codes and discriminatory zoning discouraged low-cost housing. Antagonistic and apathetic voters systematically rejected bond issues for housing.

At Rockefeller's bidding the legislature created three public authorities to solve these problems: the Housing Finance Agency (HFA), the State of New York Mortgage Agency (SONYMA), and the Urban Development Corporation (UDC). HFA loaned money to developers at low interest rates and insured mortgages. A conservative organization averse to risk, it quickly became an investment banker for housing, health, and education programs. SONYMA bought mortgages from banks to expand the lending pool and also lent money to qualified individuals for the purchase of homes. The tough task was left to UDC: to build low-cost housing, wipe out urban blight, and provide jobs.

As envisaged by Rockefeller, UDC, with the combined mission of housing and economic development, was to be the most powerful agency of its kind in the nation. To stimulate building it would have the unusual authority to override local zoning laws and building codes and other restrictions that kept the poor safely locked away in the ghetto. It would be the closest thing to an overall state planning agency. Money would not stand in the way as it would have the authority to issue $2 billion in bonds backed by the "moral obligation" of the state; to borrow money and receive grants from the state; and to draw on federal rent subsidies under Section 236 of the Great Society Federal Housing and Urban Development Act of 1968. Instead of high-rise warehouses for the poor, it would build attractive facilities with a mix of residents to achieve racial and economic balance: 70 percent with middle and moderate incomes, 20 percent with low incomes, and 10 percent hard-pressed senior citizens.

The vision was both noble and risky. For most private developers it was simply not feasible. Rockefeller had no illusions about the risks. "Let's not forget we are not running a bank here," he testified later. "We are running a social institution trying to help people. We were trying to build houses for people who needed them and our objective was to do every thing we could to achieve that objective. . . . Therefore, I was always ready to err on the side of achieving social objectives, feeling that, sure, we ran some risks here, that the moral obligation might be called upon, but that the bulk of the money would come on a self-liquidation basis and that this was a better than a straight on government expenditure."[7]

The state legislature and local mayors headed by John V. Lindsay of New York City fought UDC from the start. As they saw it, the legislation threatened local powers to regulate land use and building construction. To conservatives the entire scheme smacked of socialism. Yet the Rockefeller juggernaut was seemingly invincible as the governor applied his charm, political clout, and money.

Then an unexpected opportunity arose to scuttle UDC. After the assassination of Martin Luther King, Rockefeller flew to Atlanta on April 9, 1968, to attend the funeral. He took with him liberal black legislators. In their absence the legislative leaders chose this moment to call up the bill creating UDC and to kill it in the assembly, the lower house. A furious Rockefeller called his secretary, Alton G. Marshall, and ordered him to "turn them around, whatever it takes."

Sitting in the speaker's office, Marshall called in the recalcitrant legislators, one by one, to find out what it would take to approve the bill. Amazingly enough, the price was small. A traffic circle here; weed control in the lake there; assistance to a hospital; and other cherished local projects. What started out as an ideological debate turned quickly into an oriental bazaar with votes bartered for projects. Reflecting on the intense bargaining some 22 years later, Marshall observed, "The legislators were not so philosophically opposed that they could not tell me what they wanted and, if they got it, could be persuaded to rethink their vote."

On the evening of the same day Rockefeller returned from Atlanta and intensified the pressure on the legislators. Two days later the bill passed. But the political price was high. Embittered legislators, local officials, and building contractors never forgot the incident and were looking for the first opportunity to knife UDC. The appointment of Edward J. Logue as the first president and chief executive officer of UDC did not help matters. His domineering, abrasive, and arrogant management style chilled even would-be supporters.

By no means was Edward Logue Rockefeller's preferred choice. He first offered the appointment to George D. Woods, former head of the World Bank and in 1968 a director of the First Boston Corporation, but Woods refused. It was then that Rockefeller turned to Logue who by all accounts had accomplished miracles of urban planning in New Haven and Boston where he had directed urban redevelopment offices. At that very moment Logue was considering an offer by Mayor Lindsay to run the New York City Housing and Development Administration. In the end Rockefeller's counteroffer could not be matched. Not only would Logue get a high salary and many perquisites of office as the CEO of UDC, but he would also receive over $200,000 in personal loans and gifts from the governor to help him meet the high living costs of New York City.

At a news conference Rockefeller introduced Logue as "the ablest young creative imaginative developer in the country. I would say he was successful in Boston the same way Bob Moses was successful in New York, because of a tremendous personality and drive and the ability to break through red tape."[8]

Rockefeller still wanted Woods as part of UDC and offered him the position of chairman of the board of directors. Woods agreed only on the condition that his firm, the First Boston Corporation, would be the senior managing underwriter for UDC bonds. Fearful of an obvious conflict of interest, Rockefeller asked Louis Lefkowitz, the attorney general, to rule on Woods' conditions. Lefkowitz found no problem so long as Woods personally did not vote on any bond issues affecting the First Boston Corporation.[9]

These were the birthing pains of UDC. Once they were behind him, Logue started a fast-paced construction program, with 80 percent of the funds allocated to housing and 20 percent to industrial and commercial development. In less than a year UDC had planned 50 projects in 23 cities. By December 1970, less than three years after its creation, UDC had 45,438 housing units in various stages of completion. Several commercial and industrial projects dotted the state. UDC developed three new towns through subsidiary corporations: Audubon outside of Buffalo; Radisson near Syracuse; and Roosevelt Island (formerly Welfare Island) in Manhattan. It also built a state office building and community center in Harlem.

Virtually from the start doubts arose as to Logue's financial policies and project management. Under pressure from Rockefeller, HFA reluctantly provided the initial financing of UDC's first two projects. Allowing for the rivalry between HFA as New York's first state housing authority and the upstart UDC, HFA was deeply troubled by Logue's mode of operation. It questioned the choice of project sites; the economic viability of projects; construction commitments without money on hand to back them up; expensive gilt-edged architectural design; and a "fast-track" method of operation that brooked no delay. Several projects failed to meet HFA's feasibility standards. Finally, both public authorities agreed to a divorce when UDC successfully issued $250 million in long-term bonds and no longer needed HFA. Now UDC was on its own.

Even with later bond issues UDC was not self-supporting. Not enough revenue came in to support operating costs of $1 million a day. Logue resorted to short-term borrowing by issuing one-year bond anticipation notes (BANs) two or three times a year in amounts up to $100 million each. Worried about the shaky finances of UDC, Logue's highly regarded treasurer and business manager, Robert S. Moss, had advised him as early as December 1971 to "seek a reliable judgment as soon as possible as to UDC's effective borrowing capabilities for 1972 and 1973, before committing beyond the point of no return in 1972 construction starts."

Logue's reply was curt: "I don't believe there is any evidence to support your conclusion and I do not propose to go looking for any. We are going to build as much as we can. The need is here now." When Moss persisted in calling attention to UDC's negative cash flow, Logue fired the messenger who had brought him the bad news. [10]

Moss turned out to be prophetic. In 1973 Moody's lowered UDC's bond rating from A to Baa because of growing doubts as to its ability to repay its debts without state assistance. Other problems beset UDC. First Boston Corporation, Morgan Guaranty, Chase Manhattan, and other investment firms expressed reservations about underwriting future bond issues. Interest rates soared in a nation dogged by stagflation. President Nixon impounded funds for subsidy payments. Of nearly 31,000 housing units constructed by or with the assistance of UDC, over 90 percent depended on federal subsidies. In a meeting at the White House Rockefeller persuaded John Ehrlichman to unfreeze New York State's share of the funds for FY1973. He could, however, exact no future commitments as to one of UDC's major sources of funding.

Climaxing a year of troubles for Logue, Rockefeller resigned as governor in December 1973 after 15 years in office and a fruitless quest for the presidency of the United States. An exposed Logue found himself without his chief patron and no political base. Lieutenant Governor Malcolm Wilson succeeded Rockefeller as governor and braced himself for the November 1974 elections. He soon learned about the sinking fortunes of UDC and appointed a task force headed by Budget Director Richard L. Dunham to develop possible solutions. The task force urged a contraction of UDC activities; implementation of existing contractual commitments; cancellation of $400 million worth of projects; a cap of $1.6 billion on UDC's borrowing authorization; and a $50-million state appropriation for a loss reserve.

The proposed changes were fiscal bandaids and not long-term solutions. Their aim was to improve UDC's immediate financial position and to restore investor confidence. They were more or less in line with the views of the Wall Street banks. Eager for a Republican victory, some of the banks and investment houses, spearheaded by David Rockefeller who was chairman of Chase Manhattan, were determined to rescue UDC from insolvency. As David Rockefeller put it, UDC "should be treated on a different level from a normal request, because of UDC's critical importance to the State of New York." In a last ditch effort 28 banks, in a private placement, bought $100 million worth of bonds and First Boston sold a $125-million issue of long-term bonds. Simultaneously, UDC made an unsuccessful effort to get HFA to take over some of its projects at an estimated cost of $190 million.

On November 5, 1974 Congressman Hugh L. Carey defeated Malcolm Wilson for the governorship. A power vacuum now developed. As a lame duck incumbent, Governor Wilson was impotent. As governor-elect, Carey was wary of UDC problems and kept them at arm's length. What he found appalled him. "In New York State we haven't found only backdoor financing. We got side-door financing, . . . we got money going out of the doors, the windows and the portholes," he noted tartly.[11]

When it became clear that UDC was still short of cash and unable to gain reentry into the bond market, Carey, on the eve of his inauguration, stressed that "the financial viability of the UDC is important." He committed himself "to support the direct and indirect obligations of the State of New York, even though the method of financing is open to serious and valid criticism . . . my administration will neither condone nor continue the apparent fiscal irresponsibility and mismanagement which led to this crisis."[12]

After he assumed office in January 1975, Carey found that UDC needed nearly $700 million to pay off short-term notes, cover debt service and operating expenses for 1975 and 1976, and complete projects under way. This was in addition to the $1.1 billion UDC had previously raised through bond issues. With UDC shut out of the market, only bank loans or state appropriations could provide the necessary financing. Despite intensive efforts the banks and the Carey administration were unable to reach agreement on the appropriate mix of state and private funding. On February 25, 1975, UDC failed to repay approximately $135 million in short-term loans. Now it was in default.

Carey quickly took three major steps. He asked for Logue's resignation, appointed a commission to investigate the debacle, and sent a package of emergency measures to the legislature. The heart of his proposals was the creation of still another public authority, the Project Finance Agency, which would issue notes and bonds and receive state appropriations to buy UDC mortgages at their face value. A compliant legislature endorsed this method of refinancing and provided additional funds for debt service and operations. Commercial and savings banks also agreed to additional loans up to about $400 million. All sides agreed that UDC should complete projects under way, but not undertake any new ventures. With these steps the UDC fiscal crisis ended, but the aftermath for UDC was serious. No longer did Carey and his successor Mario Cuomo want to assume the risk of funding housing programs. Instead they converted UDC almost exclusively into a safe economic development agency. They shattered Rockefeller's vision of UDC as an agency that, in the words of Alton G. Marshall, "was intended to walk on the razor's edge. Its mission was to build housing and commercial facilities that no private developer would undertake. At best they were marginal, at worst probably not economically viable."

New York City's Troubles and UDC

Ordinarily the state could have taken the UDC default in its stride. But three extraneous events occurred that blew the crisis out of all proportion to the relatively small amounts involved. In 1974 the states of New York and New Jersey attempted to repeal bond covenants of the Port Authority of New York and New Jersey that barred the use of authority revenues for mass transportation (aside from the PATH line between New York and New Jersey). While the courts ultimately rebuffed the states, the attack on the "sanctity" of bond covenants sent shudders through investors. Coupled with UDC's problems, the bonds of New York State and its authorities were suddenly suspect.

The final blow that made UDC bonds even more suspect came in May 1975 when New York City could not pay over $2.4 billion in short-term notes due by December. These were part of a package of $8 billion in notes that the city had issued in 1974 to cope with its chronic defaults. The Securities Exchange Commission reported that 546 banks in 26 states held about $4.2 billion in city, State, and state public authority bonds. As the impact of the city's virtual bankruptcy began to sink in, municipal bonds all over the United States lost about $12 billion of their value.[13] Suddenly Governor Carey confronted the converging crises of UDC, the Port Authority, and New York City. The fearful financial markets dried up and did not distinguish among New York State, UDC, and New York City bonds. The three had become pariahs and plummeted in value.

Big MAC to the Rescue

At this critical juncture Carey displayed extraordinary and imaginative leadership. Working closely with Felix G. Rohatyn, a senior partner at Lazard Freres, Inc., investment bankers (and probable secretary of the Treasury if Dukakis had been elected president in 1988), and Budget Director Peter C. Goldmark (later head of the Rockefeller Foundation), Carey came up with a trio of unprecedented solutions: a three-year moratorium on the payment of New York City debt; the creation of an Emergency Financial Control Board (EFCB) to supervise the city's finances; and the creation of the Municipal Assistance Corporation (Big MAC) to restructure the city's debt.

The moratorium was especially controversial since it meant the abrogation of a contract between the city and its bondholders. Reluctantly, the state legislature approved it, even the conservative Republican senate that found it a difficult pill to swallow. A year later the highest state court, the Court of Appeals, outlawed the moratorium as unconstitutional. Nevertheless, it had stalled long enough to give Big MAC and EFCB a chance to clean up the city's augean fiscal stable. EFCB was an unusual agency and virtually crafted the city's budget. Chaired by the governor, it consisted of the mayor, the state comptroller, the city comptroller, and three members appointed by the governor. It was a symbol of a city on its knees and in receivership.

Big MAC became the city's savior and converted the city's short-term debt into long-term debt. No sooner had the legislature approved the new public authority than Governor Carey appointed

Rohatyn as chairman. With the city, UDC, and the state ostracized by the capital markets, Big MAC had the authority to borrow up to $10 billion and lend the money to the city for the repayment of its debt. As security the state diverted to MAC the city's share of the sales tax, the stock transfer tax, and state aid intended for the city. Whatever MAC didn't need for debt service would be turned over to the city.

Even with these pledged securities, the skittish capital markets rejected MAC bonds. It became clear that the key to Wall Street were federal guarantees of the repayment of much of the city's debt as well as temporary loans to tide the city over. At first President Gerald Ford and Secretary of the Treasury William Simon refused to help. The *New York City Daily News* immortalized the incident in an unforgettable headline: "Ford: N.Y. Drop Dead." However, Congressman Barber Conable, Jr. from Rochester (later president of the World Bank) and Melvin Laird, secretary of defense, persuaded Ford to reverse himself. The loans turned out to be one of the better investments of the federal government. The city not only repaid the loan, but paid the government a premium of $90 million for loan guarantees. With federal backing assured, Rohatyn and Goldmark carefully cobbled a financial package that included state loans, small bank loans, and investments by the state and city pension funds.

These steps overcame Wall Street resistance. In subsequent years MAC easily issued $9.5 billion in bonds and turned the proceeds over to the city. Counting new issues and refundings, it sold over $20 billion in bonds from 1975 to 1990. Because of their security the bonds were of premium quality and received an AA rating. More important, MAC restored the credit of the city and enabled it to return to the capital markets. Gradually, New York State, UDC, and other state public authorities regained the confidence of investors.

Since its creation in 1975 MAC had developed a surplus of over $4 billion as a result of skillful investment policies. Under carefully controlled conditions MAC channeled this largess to the city for capital investments in school construction, mass transportation, and law enforcement. With the strong support of two governors (Carey and Cuomo) Rohatyn and Rohatyn alone set the terms of transfer.

Not the city and not the legislature and certainly not the voters. For example, Rohatyn insisted that the state and city should establish a School Construction Authority as a prerequisite for obtaining MAC funds. Early in his administration, New York City's Mayor Koch raised no objections about Rohatyn's role. But as the city's finances improved and Mayor Koch's already sizable ego swelled, he challenged MAC's funding as a usurpation of his powers. In one of his frequent colorful exchanges Koch castigated Rohatyn as "the Bob Moses" of municipal finance and accused him of "inappropriate discretion in disposing of billions of dollars of City tax revenues." Rohatyn rejoined, "I could argue that if Ed Koch had been more austere . . . in squirreling away in some of the good times money to deal with what was coming—then we wouldn't be in the shape we're in today."[14]

MBTA and MHFA

The tale of Massachusetts is equally disheartening and centers on two public authorities: the Massachusetts Bay Transportation Authority (MBTA, known popularly as the "T") and the Massachusetts Housing Finance Agency (MHFA). One of the largest mass transit systems in the United States, MBTA serves 78 towns and cities in the Massachusetts Bay area, including Boston and its suburbs. No one expects a public transportation system to be self-sufficient. All are losers. All depend on heavy state, local, and federal subsidies since fares alone rarely cover more than one-third of the costs.

Even allowing for these built-in constraints, few transportation authorities can match MBTA's high costs, mismanagement, inefficiency, and shoddy patronage practices. It has become a runaway and uncontrolled authority, and a chronic drain on the resources of the state. The Massachusetts state senate fiscal committee called it the center of a "silent crisis."

With a budget of more than $600 million MBTA runs a yearly deficit of about $464 million, or three-fourths of its budget. Fares and incidental income account for only 23 percent of its revenue. For the rest of its income MBTA relies on the state for about 50 percent, participating communities 22 percent, and the federal government about 5 percent. In this arrangement the state is the "big daddy" in compensating MBTA for the difference between its income and expenditures. This is just the beginning of the state's burdens. In 1990 MBTA's outstanding debt exceeded $1 billion. The state pays 90 percent of the debt service—a figure reflected in its 50 percent share. Furthermore, the state subsidies will rise steadily above the 50 percent mark. Under Initiative 2 1/2, the increase in local subsidies cannot exceed 2.5 percent a year. To the extent that costs are greater, the state will have to make up the difference.

Despite the high stakes, MBTA is not subject to the control of the state government or the state legislature. It has a blank check. At the end of the calendar year it bills the state and member communities for the net cost of its service. Without advance approval it spends the money and, after the fact, presents the bill to the state. The state's fiscal year does not begin until July 1. Until then it cannot cover the deficits. In the interim MBTA issues short-term notes that cost the taxpayers an unnecessary $30 million a year. The senate ways and means committee compares this method of financ ing to "a profligate son living off his credit cards and relying upon his parents to pay the bill."[15]

In 1970 Governor Francis Sargent and in 1975 Governor Michael Dukakis attempted to leash the politically influential runaway authority. Their efforts came to nought in 1980 when Edward J. King became governor. He ousted a first-rate management team and restored the iron grip of powerful unions on MBTA.[16]

In the late 1980s, during his last term, Governor Dukakis tried another gambit. He appointed Frederick P. Salvucci, his secretary of transportation, as chairman of the MBTA board. Hailed as the "little Bob Moses of Massachusetts" and the "czar of transportation," Salvucci not only nominally controlled MBTA, but also sat on the boards of the Massachusetts Turnpike Authority and Massport (the operator of Logan Airport among other facilities). "No one in the country is even close to him in power and he's invisible, you don't see him. . . . He's harder to see than the governor," said a watcher of public authorities in Massachusetts. Stephen Coyle, director of the Boston Redevelopment Authority (Logue's erstwhile preserve), agreed. "Salvucci, because of his extraordinary ability and willpower, has centralized control to an extent never seen before," he added.[17]

Salvucci quickly discovered that even his power had limits at MBTA. As chairman of a seven-member board that represented local interests, he had only one vote and was unable to control the budget and a staff of over 6,700 employees. The board as a whole and a powerful advisory board, composed of influential local politicians, made the important decisions and could easily overrule Salvucci. Thus was MBTA effectively insulated from the state government that paid the bill.

A frustrated legislature tried to subject MBTA to the budget and appropriation processes in effect for all state agencies. With the governor's approval it adopted a set of elementary controls: Change the budget process from a retrospective to a prospective system so that the legislature would review MBTA's budget in advance; strengthen management to cut costs; and cap the assistance of MBTA communities. Except for the last, the new law was dead on arrival. One practical factor explained this failure. To fund MBTA on a current basis would require a transitional cost of $500 million—the cost of the last calendar year; the cost of six months from January 1 to the beginning of the state fiscal year on July 1; and the cost of a new fiscal year running from July 1 to June 30. With a nearly $2-billion deficit Massachusetts was in no position to take on this additional burden. As a senior budget official commented sadly, "we will continue to have a curious after-the-fact relationship with MBTA . . . and an expensive one at that."

Thus, Massachusetts continues to absorb uncontrolled MBTA deficits at a time when it is least able to do so. So much for the state's oversight of public authorities!

Another $500-million-plus fiasco resulted from the troubled programs of the Massachusetts Housing Finance Agency (MHFA) and local public housing authorities. MHFA financed low-cost housing throughout the state with tax-exempt bonds backed by the "moral obligation" of the state. In August 1975 the shockwaves triggered by the UDC collapse in New York State reached Massachusetts. Suddenly the MHFA could not sell its bonds to nervous investors who were suspicious of moral obligations and preferred more solid security. To avert a default, the legislature reluctantly backed up $500 million in debt with the full faith and credit of the state—a commitment it had never contemplated when it created MHFA. The new burden damaged the state's bond rating, but enabled the authority to sell its bonds and escape default.

But all these maneuvers were only a temporary reprieve from crisis. A year later $543 million in short-term notes of local public housing authorities became due. In a moment of optimism the state had guaranteed these notes even though it exercised no effective control over local housing authorities. After the UDC default, the local authorities could not roll over the notes into other short-term notes. Wall Street flatly rejected any further stopgap financing. Faced with the distressing prospect of still another default, the state converted the short-term notes into long-term debt. It did this by issuing $535 million in new state bonds—one of the largest bond offerings up to that time. Even then the state could lure investors only by paying the highest interest rates in its history. It avoided a financial catastrophe only temporarily and at enormous cost. In doing so, it planted the seeds for still greater crises to come in the late 1980s, in large part because of fiscal mismanagement in MHFA, MBTA, and other public authorities.[18]

The New Jersey Turnpike Authority

Despite its growing urban sprawl, New Jersey nostalgically still calls itself the "garden state." One of its richest harvests in recent years, however, was not agricultural but fiscal. It was a $2-billion bond issue sold in 1985 by the New Jersey Turnpike with an unexpected economic and political fallout.

The Turnpike is one of the earliest post-World War II highway public authorities. A long corridor that links the New York State Thruway in the north and the Pennsylvania Turnpike in the south, the Turnpike has been financially successful since it started operations in 1950. As it became the busiest toll road in the United States, truck and car traffic quickly outpaced even the most optimistic estimates. Time-consuming and dangerous congestion developed in critical areas.

By the mid-1980s it was clear that the Turnpike required many miles of widening and reconstruction. At that time Joseph "Bo" Sullivan was chairman of the Turnpike board. A successful politician, he hoped to use the Turnpike as a springboard for catapulting himself into the governor's chair in Trenton. In 1985 he had sudden visions of reaching his goal through an extensive program of highway modernization that would be virtually cost-free except for some minor toll increases in the distant future.

Sullivan attempted to accomplish this financial miracle through arbitrage—investing the proceeds of a low-interest bond issue in high-yield Treasury notes and bills and other securities to reap a handsome profit. Up to that point the Turnpike had borrowed money in stages as needed and as is customary in large-scale public works projects. This time the Wall Street brokerage firm of Smith, Barney, Harris, Upham, and Co. persuaded Sullivan to issue a $2-billion tax-exempt bond offering in one fell swoop, making it one of the largest issues in the history of the country. Sold at a low interest rate of 7.2 percent, the bonds, so claimed the brokerage house, would pay for themselves. It would be easy to invest the proceeds to get a higher rate of return with profits running into hundreds of millions of dollars. The restless taxpayers of the state would gain these benefits without any significant fee increases and be everlastingly grateful to Sullivan.

But it was necessary to act quickly. Looming ahead was the Tax Reform Act of 1986 that would outlaw arbitrage for tax-exempt bonds. In planning his financial coup, Sullivan consulted no one except his own staff and the brokerage firm. He didn't take up his proposal with the Department of Transportation that was responsible for statewide transportation planning, the governor's office, the budget office, the state treasurer, or the legislature. No definitive plans existed as to the timing, specifications, length, and cost of the project, or its effect on the environment.

Sullivan's timing was carefully calculated. In November 1985 Governor Thomas Kean, a popular Republican chief executive, easily won a second term in office. After relaxing from the rigors of the campaign, he returned to Trenton to find that Sullivan was one of his early callers. Sullivan advised him for the first time that the Turnpike was ready to release the bond offering in two weeks and requested his approval. Unlike most governors, the governor of New Jersey has veto power over the policies of nearly all public authorities in the state, but what Kean had before him was nothing less than a completed deal. Approve the issue now or lose millions of dollars in arbitrage profits and the opportunity to end turnpike congestion.

Kean's commissioner of transportation Roger Bodman urged a veto, arguing that "the authority's publicized schedule for advancing its plans appears to be unrealistic." Briefly, but only briefly, Kean contemplated this action. Resentful of Sullivan's eleventh-hour pressure, he complained, "My question was why can't we take a step back, take our time, do it in a different way. They said it was so far along, it would jeopardize our financial reputation on Wall Street."

Finally, convinced of the hazards in turning down a bonanza, Kean reluctantly approved the bond issue. Financial and transportation specialists were appalled. Barbara L. Lawrence of the prestigious nonprofit Regional Planning Association called it "a classic case of an authority run wild. This independent authority has driven public policy in New Jersey. Nobody looked closely at the plan because it was presented to all of us as a fait accompli." Joseph M. Giglio, senior vice president of Chase Manhattan and chairman of the National Council on Public Works Improvement during the Reagan administration, characterized the Turnpike board as a "loose cannon" and a "rogue elephant."

A defiant Bo Sullivan invoked the spirit of Bob Moses to defend his actions. "The purpose of an independent authority is to work on its own to get the job done. Doing great public works is always complicated. It didn't deter Robert Moses."

When Governor Kean's second term ended in 1988 (two terms are the limit for New Jersey governors), Sullivan resigned as chairman of the Turnpike board in 1988 to advance his own candidacy. Frank A. Loveys succeeded him as chairman.

In the spring of 1989 the rosy estimates of Wall Street blew up and with them Sullivan's chances for the governorship. Standard and Poor's found that the highway reconstruction project would cost at least $1 billion more than Sullivan had forecast. While arbitrage profits were indeed tidy and paid a good part of the debt service, they weren't enough. A toll increase of 40 percent to 70 percent appeared to be inevitable. Unexpected engineering and environmental problems developed. The new chairman proposed cutting back the scale of the project envisaged by Sullivan. Sullivan blamed everyone but himself for the fiasco. He lashed out at the Environmental Protection Agency, the Army Corps of Engineers, and the foot dragging of the state bureaucracy.

This was the crisis that Democrat Jim Florio inherited when he was elected governor in November 1989. Three gloomy options faced him: raise the toll rates to avoid a default in debt service; risk a default although the bondholders could be paid out of reserve funds; or call in $1.3 billion in outstanding bonds ($700 million had been spent by January 1990). Castigating the Turnpike board as irresponsible, he charged in February 1990: "You don't go out and take out a mortgage for the thrill of taking out a mortgage. Before I raise tolls I want to look New Jersey drivers straight in the eye and say what we are going to do with their money is sensible. Today quite frankly I can't say that."

Florio rebuffed the overtures of Loveys and refused to meet with him. Loveys promptly resigned. At the same time Douglas C. Berman, state treasurer and close adviser to Florio, advised him that at best the Turnpike could not delay a toll increase of about 60 percent beyond 1991.

From Florio's perspective, the Turnpike's financial problems couldn't have occurred at a worse time. The state government had a deficit of over $2 billion and in his first year in office Florio, at the height of his popularity, had pushed through combined sales and income tax increases of $2.8 billion, the largest one-time tax increase in the history of the state. Infuriated voters stormed the statehouse and besieged their legislators to cut taxes and change the new formulas for state aid to education that transferred funds from wealthy to poor school districts.

As the recession deepened, it brought more bad news for Florio. Despite the tax rise another deficit of over $800 million was likely in 1991. With no new taxes available, Florio pondered the unthinkable: a hike in Turnpike tolls and approval together with Governor Cuomo of New York of a $1 increase in Hudson River bridge and tunnel crossings operated by the Port Authority of New York and New Jersey. He assured the voters that the additional revenue would create about 7,000 new jobs through an expanded program of highway construction, improvements at Newark Airport, and expansion of mass transit. Despite the wrath of motorists, Florio in January

1991 approved a 70 percent increase in Turnpike tolls for cars and 100 percent for trucks. He also planned to sell state roads worth $400 million to the Turnpike to lighten the state's budget. Now the scorned Turnpike was to become a super-public authority.[19]

Like New York and Massachusetts, New Jersey has a long history of independent authorities that have become just a little too independent. In 1983, seven years before Florio became governor, the State of New Jersey Commission of Investigation (SCI) reported on the results of its inquiry into malpractice by local sewerage and utility authorities. It unearthed

> (1) inadequate monitoring of grant funds, (2) widespread lack of oversight of plant construction, (3) a serious potential for collusion in bond financing, (4) costly overuse of bond anticipation notes, (5) questionable practices in the appraisals and acquisitions of treatment plant sites, (6) shoddy management of facilities by authority members and employees, (7) numerous incidents of conflicts of interest, (8) political influence in the appointments of authority members and executives, and (9) a serious lack of specialized expertise among authority members and plant personnel.[20]

In the wake of the investigation, several heads of utility authorities went to jail.

Shady Practices Elsewhere in the United States

New Jersey is not unique. Dubious practices have occurred in other states in the sale of tax-exempt industrial bonds and bonds for nonprofit institutions such as hospitals, nursing homes, and retirement centers. While public authorities issue these bonds, they do not stand behind them. Private firms and nonprofit organizations alone are responsible for repayment of the debt. Between 1980 and 1988 some 300 "nonrecourse" bond issues were in default according to the Bond Investors Association, which routinely collects information on such dismal happenings. About half were industrial revenue bonds and one-third bonds for retirement centers and nursing homes.[21]

One of the largest defaults resulted from the $4-billion bankruptcy of LTV, a steel manufacturer, in 1986 because of mismanagement and inability to compete in a global market. When it collapsed LTV defaulted on the payment of $550 million in tax-exempt industrial development and pollution control bonds. Twenty-seven state and local public authorities in Ohio, Minnesota, and Illinois had sold these bonds to unsuspecting investors. The industrial development authority in Silver Bay, Minnesota, had the dubious distinction of being the largest issuer, with $205 million loaned to LTV. The security behind these bonds were LTV's plants and mines. So low was the value of these assets that bondholders lost most of their investments.

Even the Tax Reform Act of 1986 turned out to be a poor defense against bond scams directed at nonprofit hospitals, nursing homes, and retirement centers. From 1986 to 1989 public authorities had raised some $67 billion in tax-exempt funds in behalf of such nonprofit institutions. Most of these enterprises were legitimate and successful. A large number, however, fell into the hands of fly-by-night companies that defaulted on the payment of hundreds of millions of dollars of bonds.

An early victim was the Faith Evangelistic Mission Corporation, established in 1983 in Kansas City, Missouri, to engage "in religious, charitable and educational activities." Shortly after its creation, it came under the control of Lee F. Sutliffe, a real estate developer. Sutliffe changed the name of the organization to First Humanics and persuaded 21 local public authorities, including the economic development corporations of the cities of Detroit and Terre Haute, to issue $82 million in tax-exempt bonds for nonprofit nursing homes. With financing assured, he bought nursing homes with his own funds at bargain-basement prices and sold them to First Humanics at a handsome profit, ranging from $100,000 to $450,000 per nursing home. First Humanics was able to do this because it was flush with authority money. Sutliffe's companion, Carol Zandlo, also benefited from these lucrative transactions, earning many thousands of dollars in fees for decorating and renovating nursing homes. The bubble burst in 1988 when First Humanics failed to make its heavy interest payments and went bankrupt. Only the bond investors lost. Sutliffe not only retained his hefty profits, but went on to look for other investment opportunities in retirement homes.

Matthew Schifrin of *Forbes* who had investigated Sutliffe's deals also found that nonprofit organizations were "a handy vehicle for unloading less profitable nursing homes." He cited a windfall by Beverly Enterprises, a national chain of private nursing homes with $2 billion in sales in 1988. In attempting to shrink its $800-million debt, much of it in junk bonds, Beverly sold some 300 marginal nursing homes. A nonprofit enterprise, Mercy Health Initiatives, bought 41 of these facilities with the proceeds of an $86-million tax-exempt bond issue yielding 10 percent. Public authorities were at the center of these transactions. The guiding spirit behind Mercy Health was Bruce H. Whitehead, a Dallas entrepreneur, who owned 30 small companies including a bank holding company in Amarillo.

In shaping the deal Whitehead won twice. An up-front payment of $6.5 million for his efforts was likely. In addition, another Whitehead company, Britwell, managed the 41 facilities for $2.3 million a year plus up to 2.5 percent of gross operating revenues. Such are the opportunities of tax-exempt bond financing even in the shadow of tax reform.

These tales highlight the results of the lack of oversight and control of public authorities. They reminded Schrifin of Mae West's confession, "When I'm good I'm good, but when I'm bad I'm better."[22]

4

Who's Minding
the Store?

When public authorities collapse, the elected officials who created them to beat the system scurry for cover and follow predictable scenarios, assuming outraged postures of surprise, shock, and anger. Venting their choicest cliches about the breakdown of accountability and control, they mount time-consuming, expensive, and futile investigations. They slap a few obvious culprits on the wrist and go through the motions of controlling authorities. Then they hunker down until the storm blows over. Once the media and the public turn to other diversions, they cheerfully create more public authorities, or they continue to bail out failing authorities to save face and foster even more irresponsibility.

Taxpayer tolerance for such hocus-pocus seems to be unending. No sooner is one debacle behind them, than their political leaders suggest still another scheme of "free" financing through the use of authority revenue bonds. No one bothers to raise the obvious point that revenue bonds, aside from the dubious constitutionality of many of them, are more expensive than general obligation bonds now and in the future. This is especially worrisome to Claire Cohen, vice president of Fitch Investors Service and one of the most knowledgeable bond analysts in the country. "Government officials have gotten away from the people. They don't tell them that things cost money," she stresses. Joseph Giglio, vice president of Chase Manhattan, puts the problem this way: "One way they [political leaders] have to evade their responsibility is to create authorities. . . . They're a convenient instrument for elected officials to slide by the accountability issue."

The erosion of accountability is painfully commonplace in state after state. Who's minding the store? Certainly not governors, legislatures, and mayors, except to serve their immediate and narrow interests. Annemarie Hauck Walsh, a leading specialist in public authorities, reminds us that they "have been very tightly controlled by one group or another, either by the governor's office or whichever group they happen to be responsive to."[1] But not by the voters. State comptrollers and auditors usually turn out to be toothless watchdogs, while part-time authority boards regularly abdicate their power in favor of strong chairmen and chief executive officers.

Can we look for oversight and objective analysis outside of the government structure, say, by bond underwriters, bond counsel, financial advisers? With eyes focused more on profits than on project feasibility, they have turned out to be weak reeds. Bond-rating organizations, with their reputations and profits at stake, offer a slight flicker of hope. Bond insurance companies, wary of risks, tend to be more objective, but they insure only a small fraction of the bonds. What about the Securities Exchange Commission (SEC)? Under pressure from state and local governments and the brokerage firms, Congress has given only negligible power to the SEC to regulate municipal bonds.

Oversight? Accountability? Control? The true story is one of pretense, lip service, impotence, blurring of lines of responsibility, and hollow and deceptive rhetoric.

The New York State Fiasco

New York State played out this melodrama to the hilt when it staged the UDC (Urban Development Corporation) follies. The legislative leaders who pride themselves on running the most powerful state legislature in the country were by turns "surprised," "shocked," and "dismayed" by the UDC default. Senator Warren Anderson, majority leader of the state senate, pondered a blunt question about legislative oversight of UDC put to him by an attorney of the commission that investigated the debacle: "But I take it, nobody ever sat down and said, 'What are we going to do if this doesn't pay off?.'" His answer: "No, that's true . . . it was a question of getting something built if it was needed." Stanley Steingut, speaker of the assembly, also confessed to minimal scrutiny of UDC when the commission asked him: "Do you recall any discussion of the problems of the kinds of practices that UDC had undertaken or the problems of the rapid rate of growth during the discussion at any of these appropriations?" Steingut replied, "Not to my recollection."

Governor Rockefeller agreed that Edward Logue's "forte" as head of the UDC was not "fiscal management." Nevertheless, he argued that public authorities should be independent of the executive branch to keep them out of politics. Rockefeller's secretary, Alton G. Marshall, frequently attended meetings between Logue and Rockefeller and recalled that Logue kept the administration fully informed of UDC's activities and problems.

The Budget Division, one of the most powerful staff agencies in the country and the right arm of the governor, was caught short by UDC's plight. The commission that investigated UDC questioned the former budget director about the division's role in monitoring UDC's finances. "Is it correct to say that up until the time that it became apparent that UDC was running about $1 billion short and the state should have to protect its credit in that order of magnitude, that absolutely nothing was done in the Division of the Budget to your knowledge to develop any contingency plans, reserves or any other provision for this type of risk that the state had apparently undertaken by standing behind these moral obligation bonds?" The official's reply was laconic: "No reserve funds were set aside. No."

The elected and independent state comptroller has the statutory power to approve the sale and terms of public authority bonds, including UDC's. Nonetheless, Arthur Levitt, the state comptroller during the years of UDC's troubles, didn't regard his powers as "a significant control." Asked directly, "Didn't you at any time feel that you could restrict the activities of the executive office?" he defended his narrow view of his role. "Is the comptroller expected to exercise a veto over legislative action? I think no. I think he is expected to be vigilant, to inform the press, to inform the media and inform members of the legislature, to go about making speeches, but to say that the comptroller is empowered by any reason to override an act of the legislature I think goes too far. That is not what the people elect a comptroller for."

All he had to do was to use his approval authority to say "no" to a questionable bond issue. He didn't.

One by one, in a domino effect, every institutional check and balance against UDC's free-wheeling management failed and those responsible explained away the failure with yards of dubious rationalization.

No wonder that the Moreland Act Commission appointed by Governor Hugh L. Carey in 1975 to investigate UDC and other public authorities concluded: "Public authorities in New York have been allowed to create debt obligations without adequate consideration, supervision or control by the executive and legislative branches of government."[2]

The commission proposed unprecedented controls over public authorities. The centerpiece of its recommendations was the creation of a Public Authorities Control Commission in the executive branch to oversee public authorities and their bond financing in behalf of the governor and the legislature. The commission also urged honest-to-goodness accountability by boards of directors, termination of all moral obligation bonds, and a constitutional amendment to discontinue public referenda on state debt.

All that the commission had to show for its efforts was a hard-hitting report that was doomed to gather dust from the start. The legislature and the governor turned down their recommendations, which would have had the effect of upsetting a well-established patronage system and cozy relationships with private groups that thrived on authorities. Instead they provided token oversight by creating a Public Authority Control Board in 1976, chaired by the budget director and composed of representatives of the executive and legislative branches. The title is a deliberate misnomer. PACB does not control public authorities in New York State, but it merely monitors 10 of 50 state public authorities. These are primarily authorities financed by "moral obligation" debt. PACB approves bond issues and limits the total indebtedness of each of the 10 authorities. It does not review the feasibility of projects or the performance of the authorities.

From this low point the state of affairs deteriorated still further. In 1982, the Dormitory Authority (DA) erupted. With a broad portfolio to finance the construction of facilities at public and private colleges and at hospitals, DA had temporary cash balances of hundreds of millions of dollars. It invested $305 million, 60 percent of its holdings, with Lombard-Wall, a dealer in government securities.

Of this amount $55 million was unsecured. When the firm went bankrupt, DA desperately attempted to avert a potential loss of the $55 million. After intricate legal maneuvers, it cut the loss to $21 million.

The usual legislative investigation followed with this solemn pronouncement: "This bankruptcy reverberated throughout New York State and raised serious questions about the investment practices of various state agencies and authorities involving billions of dollars of public funds. The governor's office professed ignorance about these transactions. . . . Oversight agencies, i.e., the State Department of Audit and Control, Public Authorities Control Board, New York State Division of the Budget, Legislative Commission on Expenditure Review, and privately retained certified public-accounting firms, failed to exercise meaningful oversight of investment activities."[3]

In the wake of the inquiry some ritualistic firings took place, and Governor Mario M. Cuomo successfully proposed "tough legislation" requiring public authorities to adopt guidelines for investments, contracts, and financial reporting.

As the old French proverb has it, things change but remain the same. William J. Stern, former chairman of the Urban Development Corporation, demonstrated the accuracy of this adage when, for reasons still obscure, he broke with Governor Cuomo and in 1986 unleashed a broadside against public authorities:

> Two arguments have always been given for establishing authorities: They insulate public activities from overt political pressures and they can issue tax-exempt securities and thus circumvent the borrowing constraints placed on the regular state government. In recent years, the credibility of these arguments has been shattered.
>
> Management of public authorities is rife with inefficiency and patronage without the accountability required of elected officials. Moreover, the ability of public authorities to circumvent borrowing constraints led directly to the state's fiscal crisis in 1975. Currently, the debt of the public authorities is 6½ times the size of the state's general fund debt. Is it any wonder New York has the lowest credit rating of any state?
>
> Authorities are all vehicles for the redistribution of income.

They shift wealth from the average taxpayer to those who are best at accessing and manipulating government—usually more affluent New Yorkers. The worst aspect of this "upward redistribution" is that it tackles state problems in an indirect and ultimately ineffective fashion.[4]

With this bait, the press, notoriously indifferent to and ignorant about authorities (but for some shining exceptions), went into a feeding frenzy. Uncommon headlines like these suddenly sprang up across the state:

"Untamed Authorities Running Wild"
"Closer Controls Urged for Public Authorities"
"New York State Must Rein in Runaway Public Authorities"
"Public Authorities Hide Millions"

Even the hitherto quiescent state Assembly Committee on Public Authorities swung into action in 1987. It revealed that 108 and not 50 public authorities ran virtually uncontrolled around New York State and operated with "no rhyme or reason." It singled out as targets the high salaries of authority executives (some 62 authority officials received more than Governor Cuomo's salary of $100,000 a year); hiring of consultants; political patronage; and noncompliance with guidelines on debt financing and contracts. Oliver Koppel, chairman of the committee, added some strong personal views: "Public authorities have taken on a character and life of their own. Sometimes they become fiefdoms of individuals. They also transcend individuals because of self-perpetuating entities that try to insulate themselves from political influences and people."[5]

Public interest groups such as the League of Woman Voters and the City Club of New York joined in bashing the authorities. In a letter to Governor Cuomo in 1987, the City Club claimed that public authorities serve

as a shield to protect elected officials from being held accountable and provide limitless patronage opportunities. . . . There are strong political and private interests which oppose all efforts to improve oversight and control of public authorities and corporations. The Moreland Act Commission Report in 1975, after the

UDC disaster, contained excellent recommendations for reform. None of these were fully implemented. . . . We cannot allow private interests to dictate the future of our state and our counties and cities by out-of-sight, out-of-control privately operated public corporations. . . . We cannot accept the danger that the major policy decisions of the authority will fail to run parallel with the democratically determined decisions of other agencies affecting the same area, or actually run counter to those decisions.

The City Club, in consultation with specialists, developed several thoughtful recommendations to strengthen the Public Authority Control Board: control authority borrowing, improve financial reporting, reduce the number of authorities, curb patronage, prohibit the use of subsidiary organizations, and open the records of authorities to public scrutiny.[6] Like others before them, these, too, were "shot down by the Assembly leadership or the Senate or the Governor." Instead of being hampered, public authorities and their subsidiaries became even more powerful during the Cuomo administration. And the most powerful of all was the Urban Development Corporation, which rose like a phoenix from its own ashes and multiplied through subsidiaries and affiliates.

Undaunted by these rebuffs, the New York State Commission on Government Integrity revisited public authorities in 1990, 15 years after the Moreland Commission investigation. Nothing had changed. Calling public authorities an "insiders' game," the commission complained, "It's difficult to get at the most rudimentary information. No one has even an approximate count of how many of these organizations exist and where they are." It found that oversight is "fragmented, weak or nonexistent . . . we now have two governmental systems—one is accountable; the other is not." The commission also charged that public authorities frequently escape controls over favoritism, political influence, corruption, fraud, waste, and misuse of government funds. To its astonishment it learned that the "underground government" still survives.[7]

Colorado and Its Public Authorities

Those who don't know Colorado may think that its chief problems are the depth of the snow base for skiers, smog over Denver, and mining. Now the accountability of public authorities has joined the list of worries.

Debt is anathema to the state constitution. Consequently, the state literally has no general obligation debt whatsoever. Instead it depends exclusively on a mix of lease-financing schemes, including certificates of participation and moral obligation bonds. In recent years the use of these debt mechanisms to finance prison construction and the Denver Convention Center has been very much in the public eye. Seven independent state public authorities and nearly 1,100 special districts (public authorities) are the main issuers of tax-exempt bonds. By the standards of New York State this is small potatoes, but in Colorado nearly $2 billion in state public authority debt and $2.3 billion in "special district" debt is big money.

Concerned about the autonomy and growing debt of public authorities, the state legislature in 1989 created a Committee on Independent Governmental Authorities and directed it to probe their affairs. The committee focused on "the citizens' ability to influence policies of the governing boards of authorities and the extent of accountability of boards" and the "responsibility of the state or any of its political subdivisions" for "the financial difficulties of the authorities."

The committee took its assignment seriously and developed several useful proposals to control authorities, consolidate some of them, and root out conflicts of interest. Its major contribution was a recommendation to create a state debt management commission that for the first time would oversee all state debt, including the financing of public authorities, lease-purchase agreements, and certificates of participation. The overseers on the commission would be officials of the executive and legislative branches, chaired by the state treasurer.[8]

This was an idea whose time had finally come. In May 1990, impatient with legislative delays, Governor Ray Romer issued an executive order establishing a state coordinating committee on debt management. He stressed the need "to protect the credit rating of the state and the state's debt issuing entities." It's too early to judge the results of this venture into accountability, but only state public authorities are covered—not local ones. If the state cannot muster political power to control local public authorities, it may fail to bring state authorities to heel.

Illinois Looks the Other Way

In Illinois the stakes are bigger in terms of both the size of public authority debt and the number of public authorities. One official who has displayed unusual candor and courage in grappling with public authorities is Robert G. Cranson, the auditor general of Illinois. Much of the time, however, his has been a lone voice in the wilderness. Finally, in 1989 he launched an investigation that finally could not be overlooked or whitewashed. This is what he found:

- A potential state liability of about $17 billion of debt of public authorities with negligible de facto or legal oversight by the state
- A sharp rise in the number of bond-issuing authorities even though the voters lifted constitutional restrictions against general obligation debt
- An uncoordinated issuance of debt by 22 government entities, including public authorities and the Bureau of the Budget
- Lack of planning, monitoring, and control of state debt, primarily public authority debt
- A growing use of moral obligation bonds that rose to over $8 billion in early 1990
- State financial backing of questionable authority projects
- The development of complex debt instruments to guarantee or subsidize private projects
- Overlapping responsibility between state and local public authorities that issue bonds

Considering the political realities in Illinois, the auditor general merely suggested the consolidation of four authorities, the elimination of one, strengthened oversight by the governor and legislature, and improved financial reporting.[9] With Governor James Thompson intent on creating more authorities, a budget office bent on concealing the amount of state debt, and a legislature given more to rhetoric than action, the auditor general held out little hope that his modest proposals would be adopted. But the record remains, should future elected officials become serious about controlling public authorities.

Douglas L. Whitley, the highly respected president of the Tax-payers' Federation of Illinois, has a ready explanation for the breakdown of accountability in Illinois: "Many beneficiaries feed on the bond financing trough. This is insider patronage. And the insiders are the bond houses, the banks, the law firms, the con-struction firms and the labor unions. The more bonds you can sell, the more you can help your friends. It's big money to be made fast. The fact of the matter is that $26 billion is going to be spent in the state. And a lot of people have a stake in seeing that it is spent their way. Bond issues allow you to do a lot politically when you could not necessarily do it within your own budget. You can reward the law firms and the bond houses and the banks. You can reward the capital construction industry because some-body has got to build these things. And you can reward the labor unions because you're going to get people to work. Somebody will pay for it later."

The State of Washington and Its Blind Eye

In the State of Washington not even a pretense of accountability existed when the Washington State Public Power Supply System (WPPSS) defaulted on the payment of a $2.25-billion bond issue. From the moment of its creation the governor and the legislature imposed no outside controls on WPPSS. In the authorizing legisla-tion they ducked all the hard questions: net billing; take-or-pay contracts; the role of state government; the nature of oversight; the responsibilities of public utility districts; and the handling of de-faults. Oddly enough, they deliberately excluded themselves from decision making affecting the largest project and the most signifi-cant program in the state.

The legislature belatedly launched an investigation of the WPPSS scandal in 1980. To the surprise of no one but itself, the state senate concluded that "WPPSS management has been the most significant cause of cost overruns and schedule delays in the WPPSS projects." Long after the fact it discovered the failure of the board of directors to address project issues "adequately," the "apparent" lack of "any

realistic discipline in budget and schedule processes," and "duplicate efforts . . . of the many contractors on the same site."

Not to be outdone, Governor John Spellman of Washington State
also came out of hibernation at about the same time and asked
Governor Victor Atiyeh of Oregon to join him in investigating
WPPSS. Together they appointed a "blue ribbon" panel of business
leaders to ferret out the causes of the debacle.[10]

What emerged from both inquiries was too little, too late. Adding
to the heap of dozens of reports, the legislature asked the University
of Washington to undertake still another comprehensive analysis of
the failings and prospects of WPPSS. The governor and the legislature changed the composition of the board to include three outside
directors and at long last sought independent audit reports. They
were delighted to approve a state contribution of $10 million as part
of the overall settlement, provided all further claims against the
state were dropped. Indeed, the state got away cheap.

One can hardly accuse the state of a breakdown of oversight and
accountability when there was none to begin with. So diffuse was
responsibility for the system that no one person or body seemed
responsible. Yet ultimately all the participants shared the blame: the
state government, Bonneville Power Administration, private and
public utilities, and the rate payers who, late in the day, began to
question the actions of the members of public utility districts they
elected to office. In the power vacuum, bond underwriters, bond
counsel financial advisers, and consultants in dozens of specialties
fed unchecked on the public trough.[11]

The Massachusetts Story

An equally dismal tale unfolded in Massachusetts, where elected
officials abdicated from the oversight of public authorities even
in the face of known expensive failures. One woman, Patricia
McGovern, chair of the powerful senate ways and means committee, stood in their way as in report after report she skewered the
activities and finances of public authorities. But she could not
budge Governor Dukakis and the legislative leadership, especially
Billy Bulger, majority leader of the senate. In the crunch they
protected the administrative creatures they had spawned.

Considering this political climate, the committee's 1985 report, *State Authorities: The Fourth Branch of Government*, was a bombshell. Senator McGovern castigated state authorities that "constitute a fourth branch of government which operates with little understanding, oversight, or control by elected officials and the general public. A greater understanding of the workings of authorities is in the public interest, as authorities are simultaneously independent of normal governmental controls while representing actual or potential costs to Massachusetts taxpayers. . . . The continued creation of authorities may constitute a threat to general purpose government in the Commonwealth. The present and future . . . the financial stability of the state is largely in the hands of organizations which are subject to little oversight and control by elected officials and by the taxpayers themselves. . . . While each authority may have been justified on its own merits, the combined effect of these efforts has been to place the state in a precarious situation where many of its critical functions are performed by autonomous, non-elected governmental units."[12]

Senator McGovern laid out the damning evidence in public for the first time: an authority debt that exceeded state debt by many billions; the profligate and deficit-ridden Massachusetts Bay Transportation Authority (MBTA); heavy subsidies not only to MBTA but also to the Massachusetts Convention Center Authority, the Massachusetts Housing Finance Agency, and college-building authorities; the near default of the Massachusetts Housing Finance Agency and local housing authorities that cost the state over $1 billion; the red balance sheet of the Massachusetts Municipal Wholesale Electric Company that had unwisely contracted to buy nearly 12 percent of the power of the Seabrook nuclear plant, constructed by the Public Service Company of New Hampshire; and the Government Land Bank that was financing private development.

Not out to find scapegoats, the committee proposed several modest and workable changes. Develop guidelines for the creation, consolidation, and dissolution of public authorities. Declare a one-year moratorium on the creation of new authorities to permit a closer examination of the issues of accountability and control. Restrict through constitutional amendment the establishment of new authorities. Require uniform and timely financial reporting. Single out several named authorities for termination and/or consolidation. Disclose authority finances in the state budget.

Somewhat sadly the committee admitted four years later, in 1989, that "the record on authorities has not improved much."[13] It managed to get a moratorium on the creation of new authorities, to scuttle Governor Dukakis' proposal for an Infrastructure Bank, and to exact more detailed financial reporting although much of it was, in the view of a senior budget official, "fairly worthless." The governor and legislature ignored all the recommendations on accountability and financial control since all the authorities were after all "their babies." From then on the course was predictable. Subsidies to authorities increased while controls weakened. The drain on state finances led in large part to the state's fiscal crisis.

Patricia McGovern lost the battle, but never stopped fighting and prodding the legislature and governor about public authorities. "They think they're above government and the people," she said. "They are not overseen by the legislature, the public or the media. In the end if we don't scrutinize them, the public loses . . . they are hidden from public view. People don't understand they are there."[14]

Unlike the indifferent press in other states, Boston newspapers and magazines rarely relaxed their vigilance over public authorities. In a week-long series of front-page reports beginning in October 1989, the *Boston Globe* exposed the machinations of 30 state authorities and 477 local authorities. A banner headline captured the theme of the series: "Mass. Authorities Enjoy Autonomy Without Oversight." The *Globe* exposed heavy state subsidies to 10 authorities that originally were supposed to be self-supporting. Conversely, it shed light on tidy profits and hefty reserves by such authorities as the Massachusetts Turnpike, the Massachusetts Industrial Financing Authority, and the Health and Education Facilities Authority. The authorities were free to use the surpluses any way they saw fit. There were uncontrolled rises in authority fees and charges, erosion of state control, exemption from competitive bidding for contracts and supplies, and excessive salaries. The *Globe* uncovered public authorities as patronage machines with Senate President William Bulger and Transportation Secretary Frederick P. Salvucci exercising "raw political muscle" and told of high fees and commissions to favored bond underwriters, lawyers, banks, and insurance agents.

In delving into this last point, the *Globe* cited $1.1 million in commissions by Massport to four underwriters for a 1988 bond issue: Merrill Lynch, Morgan Stanley, Dean Witter, and Grigsby Brandford. At the same time it paid $1.9 million in legal fees to Ropes and Gray and Palmer and Dodge. It spent over $3 million in insurance premiums, with Robert Pike Insurance and Johnson and Higgins getting the lion's share. Massport's chosen bank, State Street Bank, where it deposited its operating funds, got fees of over $63,000. The beneficiaries of other public authorities included Goldman Sachs and Co., Paine Webber Inc., Lazard Freres Inc., the Bank of New England, the Bank of Boston, the Shawmut Bank, and the law firm of Mintz, Levin, Cohn, Ferris, Blovsky, and Popeo. They stand to gain another $6 million to $12 million from bond issues of the Massachusetts Water Resources Authority. So influential were these firms that the *Globe* concluded: "There are powerful forces aligned alongside authorities, led by the state's largest banks and investment houses, that have a vested interest in protecting the status quo."

Calling public authorities "sleek vehicles of patronage and power," the *Globe* found it ironic that it was under "Governor Dukakis—who perhaps more than any other Massachusetts chief executive has considered patronage anathema—that authorities have made their greatest spurt. In his three terms eight of the state's major authorities have been created, most of them involved in the financing of economic development."

Senator Bulger, a close ally of Governor Dukakis, had a special interest in the John B. Hynes Auditorium Convention Center. When Boston had one of its frequent spells of deep financial trouble, Bulger bailed out his good friend Mayor Kevin White by arranging for a state takeover of the convention center from the city. The price was steep. The state floated a $200-million bond issue, paid 100 percent of the debt service, and covered all deficits in operating costs. Never self-sufficient, the center quickly became a patronage pool. And the good citizens of Boston paid twice: once for the city's development of the center and again for the state's costs.

The *Globe* discovered virtues in some authorities, stressing the efficiency and professionalism of the Massachusetts Water Resources Authority that was constructing the largest public works project in the country. Without Salvucci's control over the state department of public works and three transportation authorities, it doubted whether the "Big Dig" (a new central highway artery in Boston) and a third tunnel under Boston Harbor to Logan Airport could be built. One of the defenders of authorities cited by the *Globe* was Frank Keefe, Dukakis' secretary of administration and finance and a top-flight professional administrator. "To tear them [authorities] asunder and make them the creatures of the hurly-burly of everyday politics would be a large mistake," argued Keefe. "They serve public interests, they are accountable, they do planning and look to the long term; they pay attention to a logical series of steps to implement a plan."

The *Boston Magazine* rejected this rosy view. Culminating a four-month investigation, John Strahinich hurled even more barbs at authorities in his article "Inside the Shadow Government" in the November 1989 issue. One of the first investigators to piece together the full fiscal, political, and economic impact of public authorities on Massachusetts, Strahinich estimated that a middle-class family paid authority fees and charges equal to about one-third of its state tax bill. No legislative body responsible to the voters levied this "tax." Strahinich found that authorities at times "behave like a rogue government, placing their own survival above the public policy of an elected administration. . . . Authorities constitute a permanent, expansionist government, collecting and spending more and more public money, running up more and more public debt, and making more and more critical decisions on the public's behalf with each passing day. And because authorities do all this out of sight and beyond the control of the general public, they constitute finally a shadow government."

New Jersey Loses Controls over Public Authorities

Substitute New Jersey for Massachusetts in the above recital and the results would be the same even though on paper New Jersey now has more controls over public authorities. The breakdown of accountability in New Jersey permeated every level of local and state public authorities. After a detailed criminal inquiry in 1983, the State Commission of Investigation singled out the absence of oversight as the chief corrosive flaw:

> A principal finding of the Commission's investigation was a lack of accountability by New Jersey's county and local authorities to the governmental agencies whose grant funds enable their facilities to be financed and to the public such facilities were designed to serve. Shielded by an autonomy which insulated them from public scrutiny, many authorities were found in violation of a state law requiring submission of annual fiscal audits to the state. Although there may be more than 250 county and local authorities in New Jersey, no state official was found who could provide a precise count of them. No single state agency had any statutorily definitive oversight over county and local authority financing, budgets, operational and maintenance expenditures, or reserves—if any—for future expansion or replacement. In fact, the Commission's inquiry determined that most authorities were beholden only to themselves as—behind closed doors—they made extremely costly contractual commitments for plant design, engineering and construction plans, for raising required cash in the bond market, for selecting personnel to operate and maintain facilities, for establishing rate charges that are supposed to put their sewerage systems on a self-supporting basis. Nobody— including the taxpaying citizens who are an authority's captive customers—was sharing in these actions in any substantial manner. Little or no opportunity was made available for community access or reaction to matters so vital to its wellbeing. The SCI probe also revealed the absence of any consistent pattern of oversight of the various complex phases of a sewerage plant development—no adequate review of plant design, no viable inspection of plant construction, no external review of bond financing, no controls over rollover interim financing, no monitoring of performance of plant management or staff, no enforcement of the statutory bidding process.[15]

In *Machinery of Greed*, a book that will shock even jaded readers, Diana B. Henriques documents the corruption that led up to the commission's indictment. What she found was based not only on the commission's investigation, but also on her own probes as an investigative reporter. She discovered the approval of a low-interest loan by the New Jersey Economic Development Authority to a contractor who had been a "bag man" in a local housing authority scandal. She reported extortion, bribery, and kickbacks by the executive director of the New Jersey Highway Authority that operates the Garden State Parkway, and two former members of Governor Richard J. Hughes' cabinet; the award of lucrative contracts by the chairman of the Delaware River Port Authority to his relatives; convictions of officials of the Lindenwold, New Jersey Municipal Utility Authority for corruption; and guilty pleas by other officials. In addition, officials of the Newark, New Jersey Watershed Authority and city officials were indicted for conspiracy and misconduct. The executive director, the finance director, and two staff members of the Newark Development and Housing Authority were charged with racketeering and extortion. The list goes on *ad nauseam*.

Henriques cast her net to cover other states as well and came up with a "rap sheet" of criminal practices in the 1970s and early 1980s by housing, electric, transportation, and water authorities in Texas, Connecticut, Tennessee, Utah, New Mexico, New York, Massachusetts, Washington, Alabama, Oklahoma, Missouri, Pennsylvania, Florida, California, and Illinois. Omission from the list does not necessarily testify to the purity of the other states. More likely, it merely reflects incomplete coverage.[16]

In the wake of the well-publicized hearings and recommendations by the Commission of Investigation, a reluctant New Jersey legislature imposed the most severe controls in the nation over the nearly 500 local public authorities/special districts. No new authority can be created without the approval of a county or city local finance board, while the governing body that establishes the authority can now dissolve it. The State Department of Community Affairs reviews and approves all local authority budgets, and a state local finance board analyzes all bond issues by local public authorities. While its recommendations are not legally binding, nevertheless, they constitute de facto approval or disapproval. Bond-rating organizations follow them closely. All authorities must submit detailed financial reports to the Department of Community Affairs. No bonds can be issued for water and waste disposal facilities without the endorsement of the State Department of Environmental Affairs.

Still, some troubling omissions stand out. Local public housing authorities are exempt from the controls even though they are plagued by scandals because they are largely financed by the federal government. Local governments lack veto power over the actions of public authorities that affect them. The Department of Community Affairs lacks adequate funds for auditing local authorities. Instead of anticipating problems, it often reacts to them after the fact. Still pending are proposals to require disclosure of financial affairs by senior officials, standards for personnel systems, and policies governing relations with bond underwriters and financial advisers.

When Governor Jim Florio assumed office in 1990, he inherited not only the financial miscalculations of the New Jersey Turnpike, but nagging problems in the other 39 independent state authorities. Together they had an outstanding debt of $15 billion, five times the official state debt. They generated fees and charges running into hundreds of millions of dollars. They operated as separate governments virtually free of checks and balances. "You have autonomous somehow being synonymous with irresponsible, not accountable to," he noted during his third month as governor. "We just can't continue to allow these agencies to conduct themselves free from any perceived sense of responsibility to the state public interest goals. We hope for the best that their perception of their interests is the same as the public interest. Rarely is that the case. In the last eight years or ten years the country and this state have been working from the premise we should have minimal government not doing a heck of a lot. That has resulted in the savings and loan situation. It has resulted in a whole lot of things not being monitored very well. It has resulted in public dollars being wasted."[17]

To exert overdue control, Governor Florio had one weapon envied by all other governors—the right to veto the actions of 27 of the 40 state authorities. To his amazement he found that his four predecessors had rarely exercised this option. He had a ready explanation for such self-inflicted impotence. It gave the governors the "option of deniability" so that they could deny any knowledge of authority plans to increase fees or take any other controversial actions. Florio declared himself ready to strip himself of such camouflage by using his veto power as part of the decision-making process. "Not only am I willing to give it up, but I am anxious to give it up," he stated. "Because, in fact, if something is going to come home to roost back here in my office at some point because of someone's less-than-diligent monitoring of these systems, give me that authority, and I will be happy to take the praise and the black eye from time to time. But I am not going to do that unless I have the ability to monitor what is happening out there."[18]

Matching actions to words, Florio took a series of swift steps to enforce his will on public authorities. He used his appointment powers to take majority control of authority boards. His state treasurer, as is true in a minority of states, became a key member of most of the boards so as to harmonize the fiscal policies of the authorities with the state's policies. As in Massachusetts, his transportation commissioner also had an appointment as a member of transportation authorities; his commissioner for economic development represented the governor on several economic development authorities; and his environmental protection commissioner had a major role in water, wastewater, and solid waste disposal authorities. The governor breathed new life into a dormant unit in his own office that monitored the activities of all authorities. He made it clear that state policy in housing, transportation, economic development, and environmental protection came first. Whether they liked it or not, the authorities were going to conform to these policies and stop, in the governor's words, "doing their own thing." No longer would he accept authority spending plans and priorities on a take-it-or-leave-it basis with only 10 days to veto or accept them. Whatever he got would bear Florio's stamp from the start.

Several interstate public authorities such as the Delaware River Port Authority were still beyond his reach. To fill this power vacuum he consulted with Governor Mario M. Cuomo of New York and Governor Robert P. Casey of Pennsylvania on ways and means to control them. He was also determined to impose his will on 13 public authorities in New Jersey over which he had no statutory veto power.

So fast did Florio make his moves that a breathless senior official in his administration knew exactly who ran authorities in New Jersey. "It's not the executive director, not the chairman. The boss is the Governor of New Jersey," he said.[19]

But even this aggressive governor soon learned the limits of his power. He could not by fiat dismiss the moral obligation bonds of authorities. Like a Damocles' sword they hovered over the finances of the state. Default on these bonds was tantamount to a default by the state. Long-standing bond covenants locked in fees, policies, and levels of service that the governor could not change. The bondholders' rights reigned supreme, as numerous court decisions reminded ambitious governors and legislatures. One of Florio's financial advisers on Wall Street claimed that the veto power "is a feeble way of controlling authorities." Yet, this was the only tool available. Inventing other mechanisms of oversight would require wholesale amendments of the many separate statutes governing authorities. With his plate full, Florio was not ready to engage in more legislative battles. As the financial crisis of New Jersey deepened, only authorities with their fees and charges had the means to take on cherished programs. Otherwise taxes, already burdensome, would have to be increased. For these reasons, Florio like Cuomo, Dukakis, and Thompson, could not kick the authority habit. He, too, became addicted and relied especially on the Turnpike Authority to raise money for the state.

Local Public Authorities/Special Districts

Because of their size and importance state public authorities stand out. Relatively obscure are the many thousands of local public authorities/special districts that are truly the invisible government. Yet they have the power to collect fees, raise taxes, and sell bonds for one or more functions. Unless scandals pop up (as in New Jersey) or fees suddenly skyrocket, taxpayers are oblivious to their existence.

Ironically, because voters in some states elect members of local authority boards, they suffer under the illusion that authorities are accountable to them. Nothing could be further from the truth as consumers of electricity in the State of Washington learned. What intensifies these problems is that local public authorities are now the "alternative method of funding government services."

If you live in Chicago, you may pay taxes and fees to 13 different public authorities/special districts. In nearby DuPage County, 262 tax-collecting and fee-collecting units stand ready to dip into your pocketbook. You're fortunate if only the charges of 15 authorities appear on your tax bill. Chances are that you will join other tax-payers in aiming your fire at mayors and local councils rather than on the real culprits—the well-hidden local authorities and the citizens who create them.

"No one ever blames the Metropolitan Water Reclamation District or the Library District," noted Jeffrey Esser, executive director of the Government Finance Officers Association. "In fact," he added, "most taxpayers don't have the faintest idea who sits on authority boards. They even forget that they elected these officials in the first place."[20]

Small wonder "the deck is stacked against the taxpayer," commented Douglas Whitley, president of the Illinois Taxpayers Federation. "There are no uniform fiscal years, few coterminous boundaries and no uniform accounting methods. The first people a taxpayer approaches about a high tax bill—the mayor or the legislature—actually have very little influence on the final bill."[21] Whitley worries about the growth and influence of local authorities. "The biggest lobby in Springfield is not labor. The biggest lobby is not big business. The biggest lobby is governments [local authorities] lobbying government." This leaves the taxpayer out in the cold.

Illinois, California, Texas, and Colorado lead the nation in the number of local public authorities/special districts. Their controls are sparse and accountability is largely a fiction. What a fertile breeding ground for scandals, misuse of funds, and marginal enterprises! Texas is a prize example, with an outstanding debt of over $18 billion. Texas road, water, river, hospital, navigation, power, and transit authorities borrow and spend as much as all local governments combined. In their trail-blazing reports on larger-than-life Texas scandals, Virginia M. Perrenod and Harvey Katz reveal how many hundreds of millions of dollars have fallen into the hands of unscrupulous real estate developers, legislators, attorneys, and bond houses.[22]

"Never use your own money to make money" was the motto of several Texas developers who easily created municipal utility districts and, through the districts, sold tax-exempt bonds for water and sewer projects. Some local authority boards were merely facades for private interests that readily exploited the fiscal powers of authorities. Once they got the money, they took off and saddled future residents with debt.[23]

Obviously, this is not the whole picture. Side by side with the shady exploits are public authorities that run efficient and professional systems such as the mass transit authority in Houston, the Greater Tacoma Utility Authority in northeast Texas that provides water and treats sewage and solid waste, the Red River Authority that controls navigation in 39 counties, and the Gulf Coast Waste Disposal Authority that checks pollution in the heavily industrialized Houston Ship Channel/Galveston Bay area.

The spate of scandals in Texas led to some tightening of controls over local public authorities, but hardly enough. None of the controls even come close to those in New Jersey, where the Department of Community Affairs approves budgets and analyzes bond issues; in North Carolina, where a Local Government Commission approves all borrowing by local authorities; and in Florida, where a Division of Bond Finance sells bonds in behalf of authorities and local governments. If the state and local governments cannot monitor the local authorities, some have found they can at least provide comprehensive information. In this respect, California, Texas, and Colorado have done a notable job. In Illinois data about local authorities are so sparse as to be almost a classified secret.

Public Authorities as Cash Cows

In the recession of the early 1990s state and local public authorities have taken on a new life with their relatively easy access to resources. Where once some states bailed out authorities, now some authorities involuntarily open their treasuries to the states, blurring accountability even more. To use a worn Wall Street cliche, they have become the "cash cows" of several states. No state milks these cows more than New York and no governor more vigorously than Mario Cuomo. Facing chronic deficits, he diverted about $2 billion in authority reserves and surpluses to the general fund of the state over a four-year period. In a reverse twist he also billed the authorities for services rendered by the state for bond issuance, budgeting, auditing, and other forms of oversight. His latest proposal in

1991 was to have the Thruway Authority take over the 71 miles and 99 bridges of the deteriorating Interstate 84. This would relieve the state of $10 million in annual maintenance costs and at least nearly $43 million to $100 million in renovation projects. By taking on this new burden, the Thruway Authority would assume additional debt. And the day that it would be debt-free and toll-free, once optimistically estimated to be in the early 1990s, receded even more into the hazy future. Instead, drivers may find themselves paying tolls on the erstwhile free I84.

In another gambit Cuomo sold Attica prison to the Urban Development Corporation (UDC) for $200 million. This meant one-time revenue for the state and more debt for UDC for which taxpayers would be responsible.

No authority in New York has demonstrated more generosity than the Municipal Assistance Corporation, which transferred over $4 billion in surpluses to an ailing New York City. Even the smaller Battery Park Authority that is redeveloping the lower Manhattan area for housing and commercial purposes has done its bit by shifting about $40 million to the city for low-income housing. None of this redistribution of authority largess takes place under the umbrella of open budgeting and appropriation processes. Behind the scenes the main players are the governor, the mayor, and the heads of the authorities.

Across the Hudson River the State of New Jersey has exacted regular annual tribute from the New Jersey Turnpike, the Garden State Parkway, and the New Jersey Sports and Exposition Authority, the operator of the Meadowlands sports complex. This turned out to be only token payments when compared with Governor Florio's latest plan for the purchase of $400 million of state roads by the New Jersey Turnpike.

In coping with their $1-billion deficit in 1990, Massachusetts legislators eyed enviously New York's and New Jersey's preemption of authority surpluses. They attempted to capture some of the reserves of affluent authorities such as the Massachusetts Turnpike and the Massachusetts Industrial Financing Authority. At the very least they insisted that the turnpike should remove snow and ice on all state roads at very significant savings to the state. Governor Dukakis rebuffed these raids on authority funds, arguing they would violate bond covenants and undermine the capability of authorities to achieve public purposes.

Hundreds of small cities in the United States have dipped into the surpluses of electric power, water, and sewer authorities. To the great pleasure of the voters these transfers have made it possible in South Carolina, Florida, and other states to contain property taxes and expand services. Of course the voters pay for the transfers through higher rates, but find this less painful than hikes in property taxes.

Some large issues are at stake here. When governments seize authority funds, the burden of running government shifts from the general taxpayer to the user of authority services. Since everyone pays the same fees and charges to authorities regardless of income, these fees hit lower-income groups harder than anyone else. Like the sales tax they are a regressive burden. But why have surpluses in the first place? Public authorities are not profit-making ventures. If the fees are too high, why not lower them? Why not pay off the bonds earlier to reduce the debt load? Better yet, why not eliminate fees altogether once the bonds are paid off? Why use indirect back-door methods of financing rather than an appropriation process visible to everyone?

Generally, though, governments would rather force feed their cash cows by switching more functions to public authorities.

Debt Watchers

In the complex relationships between states and authorities, accountability is a sometime thing. To be sure, the appurtenances of oversight and accountability exist, but frequently atrophy through disuse and misuse.

Some states have invented different instruments of oversight, including the veto power over authority policies as in New Jersey and New York. Clustered in governors' and mayors' offices, program and political advisers maintain their own lines to public authorities on a day-to-day basis.

Some more elaborate structures exist to guard against profligate borrowing by authorities. After some well-publicized scandals Texas created a bond review board that can veto bond issues and lease-purchase financing schemes by public authorities and state agencies. In Kentucky an office for investment and debt management approves and markets bond issues for all authorities and state departments. A state treasury board in Virginia has a more limited role. It controls only borrowing by authorities subsidized by the state.

As befits the most populous and wealthy state, California has a constellation of debt watchers in the elective state treasurer's office that reached the zenith of its powers under the popular and controversial politician, Jesse Unruh. A finance committee composed of the treasurer, the controller, and the director of finance approves the issuance of general obligation bonds subject to a voter referendum. A debt advisory commission tracks state and local debt. A debt limit allocation committee apportions among competing authorities the state's share of tax-exempt private purpose bonds. A district securities advisory commission checks the financial, economic, and technical feasibility of projects undertaken by local public authorities/special districts. The accent is on the word "advisory." A mortgage bond tax credit allocation committee authorizes the issuance of mortgage bonds and tax credits for low-income and moderate-income housing. As a monument to these far-reaching powers, at least on paper, the state now calls the office complex housing the state treasurer's staff the Jesse Unruh Building. The entire superstructure provides information and advice, but few controls.

All states have treasurers, some elected, some appointed. None can flex their financial muscles like the California state treasurer. All states have elected or appointed comptrollers and auditors, but most are glorified accountants and data crunchers. Their impact on public authorities is minimal. To be sure, they often issue hard-hitting audit reports that view with alarm and point to the dangers of the "fourth branch of government." As a senior official in the Massachusetts audit office stresses, "As an auditor, you cannot command. You can only recommend. And we hope that management will follow our recommendations." With some exceptions, attorneys general are no better despite their power to interpret statutes authorizing bond issues. Central budget offices have the potential to control public authorities. But rarely do governors use them for this purpose.

Can we look to the legislature, the tribune of the people, to rein in public authorities? Available to state legislatures is the largest legislative bureaucracy in history with unparalleled analytic and investigative capability. Fiscal committees, special committees on authorities, and standing committees monitor public authorities as never before. For all the sound, fury, hoopla, and hyperbole, the results of this collective oversight are not especially meaningful.

Not for a moment will elected officials dismember their own creatures when they serve political and policy ends and are the only means of leapfrogging over constitutions, laws, and voter resistance.

Bond counsel, financial advisers, and bond underwriting houses cannot be counted on as mechanisms of oversight. Because of self-interest they can no more serve as overseers than foxes in a chicken coop. Bond-rating and bond insurance companies, however, exert some discipline over public authorities and their parent governments—in fact, the only significant source of control.

After the financial collapse of New York City and the New York State Urban Development Corporation in 1975, Congress attempted to give the Securities Exchange Commission (SEC) the power to regulate municipal bonds just as it does with regard to corporate securities. Under pressure from state and local governments, public authorities, and the municipal bond industry, Congress caved in. As a weak compromise, it created the Municipal Securities Rulemaking Board (MSRB), which regulates brokers and dealers in municipal bonds but does not control official statements (prospectuses) and the bond offerings of public authorities and state and local governments. Composed of representatives of the security industry, MSRB is essentially a self-regulating body. Such full financial disclosure as exists is entirely voluntary on the part of authorities and governments. Even timid federal attempts to improve financial reporting have failed.

The courts, then, would be the next place to turn as the protectors of constitutions.

5

The Law Be Damned!

Contrary to their purpose, the highest state courts have a dismal record in defending state constitutions against subversion of debt limits and in checking the rampant growth of unaccountable public authorities. They draw the line only at attempts to tamper with the rights of holders of tax-exempt bonds. The sanctity of a bond covenant is held supreme.

One of the few exceptions to this bleak state of affairs is the Supreme Court of New Mexico. Confronted by one of the 57 varieties of lease-financing schemes, it had the courage, lacking in other courts, to state explicitly that lease obligations are debt. As such, they are subject to constitutional controls on debt. With this judgment, it found the emperor naked despite the pretense that he was wearing new clothes.

Leading to the decision was a squabble at the local level in Valencia County, New Mexico, in 1988. There a county commissioner had the temerity to challenge his colleagues about a lease-purchase agreement they had arranged with a private contractor to build a county jail with certificates of participation as the financing vehicle. What upset the commissioner was that the county took this action after the voters had twice rejected bond issues for jail construction. He sued in the courts, claiming that the lease was a ploy to evade constitutional debt limits. Turned down by the lower court, he found a sympathetic ear in the state's Supreme Court.

The court explicitly ruled that a lease was debt within the meaning of the constitution and no debt could be created without voter approval. Cutting through the hypocrisy of the lease-purchase arrangement, it said sharply, "We find the lease purchase agreement to be a lease in form only. The arrangement is in essence an installment-purchase agreement for the acquisition of a public building, with actual financing and payments spread over twenty years, and, as such, it requires voter approval."[1]

Getting around State Constitutions

This straightforward stand of the New Mexico court contrasts sharply with the mealymouthed position of other courts as in the adjoining State of Texas. In 1984, Jim Mattox, the attorney general, refused to approve the issuance of $10.5 million in revenue bonds by the Texas Building Authority to construct a state office building. Once again, at issue was a lease-purchase plan. The agencies using the building would pay "rent" to the authority with the rent money coming from state appropriations. To Mattox this was a transparent device to sidestep the constitution, which required voter approval of debt. And the lease-purchase plan was clearly debt.

The Building Authority sued in the state Supreme Court and requested a writ of mandamus to force Mattox to approve the bond issue. Of course the lease was not debt, according to the court. The legislature had said so in the act authorizing the bond issue. Even the fine print on the bonds denied that the faith and credit of the state stood behind them. "While such provisions are not conclusive in and of themselves," opined the court, "they do indicate that the legislature's interest in authorizing the issuance of the bonds was to avoid conflict" with the constitution. What counted to the court, apparently, were intentions, not deeds.

To allay the fears of any doubting Thomases, the court boldly declared that state debt was not the issue: "The bonds would create no debt against the State of Texas . . . such bonds would be payable solely from the rents and profits to be derived from the operations of the . . . building, unless the legislature in the exercise of its power and discretion should see fit when making the biennial appropriations, to include therein a sufficient sum of money to pay such bonds."

This language dripped with guile. The court knew full well that the building could be financed only with state appropriations. Nevertheless, it continued the hoax that this would not be the case and that the authority was self-sufficient. It then directed Mattox to approve the bond issue.[2]

Under another set of circumstances the Wisconsin Supreme Court also caved in under political pressures. Following the lead of New York State and other states, Wisconsin created a Housing Finance Authority in 1971 and gave it the power to sell tax-exempt bonds for low-income and moderate-income housing. As is customary in the program, the funds would be lent at low interest rates to contractors and real estate developers. Fearing a possible constitutional conflict, the legislature inserted the usual disclaimer in the act that the bonds would not be the debt of the state.

The brokerage firm of Blyth, Eastman, and Dillon was ready to buy and market the bonds when Joseph Nusbaum, the state's powerful secretary of administration, jolted it by refusing to allocate a small $250,000 appropriation for a capital reserve for the bond issue. Nusbaum suddenly had qualms about the constitutionality of this step. Other troubling questions surfaced as well. Would the authority incur state debt contrary to constitutional provisions? Could it defy the ban on the transfer of state money and credits to private interests, namely, the construction industry? Would the bond issue serve a public purpose as required by the constitution since private groups would benefit?

Called upon to settle these nagging issues, the Supreme Court quickly dismissed them. Of course the legislature can "create separate entities to carry on a public purpose." In amazingly frank language, the court agreed that "the obvious purpose behind the creation of many such entities [public authorities] has been the indirect achievement of some purpose that the state can not achieve directly because of various constitutional limitations placed upon the state." It even recognized that public authorities could be regarded as "subterfuges" to evade constitutional provisions, but none of this disturbed the court. Instead it gave the legislature the green light to create even more "entities": "It is never an illegal evasion to accomplish a desired result, lawful in itself, by discovering a legal way to do it."

Machiavelli couldn't have done better! Authority borrowing was not an issue since this is not "a legally enforceable obligation" against the state. As for state subsidies to the authority, the state may choose to do this voluntarily, but is not compelled to do it legally. What about loans to private firms and individuals? Fine, as long as they serve a public purpose. Besides other states were doing it, such as North Carolina, Michigan, Massachusetts, Maine, and New York. In any event the state itself is not responsible for the loans. And so the State of Wisconsin launched the Housing Finance Authority anointed with judicial blessings even though the language of the decision was less than compelling.[3]

In the early 1960s private railroads and bus lines failed in Massachusetts and other states and led to a mass transportation crisis. Each state grappled with the problem in its own way. Massachusetts' solution was to create the Massachusetts Bay Transportation Authority (MBTA) and give it a broad portfolio: buy private transportation systems as needed; issue tax-exempt bonds to raise money; operate the far-flung system; and rely on the state and 78 municipalities of the greater Boston area to subsidize its operations. Again a sticky state constitution with debt restrictions and bans on the transfer of state money to private interests was a roadblock. A syndicate of banks was reluctant to buy the bonds unless the Supreme Judicial Court of Massachusetts gave them the official seal of approval.

As hard as the court looked, it could not find a trace of unconstitutionality. So long as the legislature decided that the purchase of private facilities serves a public need, the court had no problem with public funds being paid to private companies. A state contract with MBTA to subsidize its debt service and operating cost was not debt in the court's view. Hence, the state need not obtain a two-thirds vote in the legislature, ordinarily applicable to all new debt, for annual expenditures. Even though the state finances most of MBTA costs, MBTA and not the state is the principal borrower. The court discovered that the heavily subsidized MBTA "has a substantial, independent existence; a substantial business, and substantial business income. It is the Authority that borrows and for its own independent purposes." Court alchemy had taken a dependent authority with empty pockets and transformed it into an independent entity.[4]

Through similar fanciful interpretations of the constitution, the Florida Supreme Court in 1990 opened the floodgates of lease financing. Until then, in several landmark cases, it had followed the constitution to the letter, requiring that voters approve long-term borrowing and insisting that property taxes could not be used to pay lease rentals. Brokerage firms and banks champed at the bit since 41 states, led by California, New York, and New Jersey, allowed tax-exempt leasing. But the big bonanza in Florida still eluded them.

Suddenly and abruptly the Supreme Court reversed previous decisions that had blocked lease financing. Suddenly lease-purchase bonds and certificates of participation, hitherto banned without voter approval, were no longer debt in the constitutional sense. So long as leases could be terminated at any time and property taxes were not earmarked for lease rentals, a local government, school district, and public authority were free to engage in lease-purchase plans without burdening the taxpayers with referenda.

No one doubted that government units would rely on taxes and fees to pay for the leases. What, then, was the difference? Splitting hairs meticulously, the court cautioned that holders of bonds and certificates of participation would have no right to compel the collection of taxes to repay debt through judicial action. Satisfied with this fine distinction, the court still distanced itself from the effects of its own decision: "Our approval of these financing arrangements does not constitute an endorsement of the bonds and certificates of indebtedness to be issued. Questions of business policy and judgment are beyond the scope of judicial interference and are the responsibility of the issuing governmental units."[5]

At this sudden legal insight, lease bond financing surged, approximating $1 billion in 1990. And 1991 looked even brighter.

Perhaps no court stretches the constitution more than the New York State Court of Appeals. Several judicial quagmires highlight the imaginative proclivities of this court. In November 1981 voters in New York State, as previously noted, rejected a $500-million bond issue for the construction of new prisons. Ordinarily, that would be the last word on the subject. The constitution requires a referendum on long-term debt and the state held a referendum.

For Governor Cuomo and the legislature this was a mere technicality. Dismissing the referendum, they authorized the Urban Development Corporation (UDC) to finance prison construction. For UDC this was a new venture. It had financed the building of housing, hotels, convention centers, factories, and assorted projects designed to further economic development, but it had never built a prison. This time it issued tax-exempt bonds to build prison cells. It leased the prisons to the Department of Correctional Services with the Office of General Services as an intermediary. Through appropriations the department receives funds to pay the "rent." Once the bonds are paid, the state and the UDC will own the prisons.

The ritualistic expressions of outrage for public consumption followed. "Gimmicky," said the head of a taxpayers' organization. "A circumvention of the constitution," said a legislator who headed the assembly committee on public authorities. "An abuse of UDC," said a secretary of the powerful senate finance committee.

One group went further and challenged the entire dubious transaction in the courts as unconstitutional. Considering the circumstances, its case looked like a winner. But the New York State Coalition for Criminal Justice, as the group called itself, did not reckon with the New York courts. In brief decisions, unusual for state courts given to long philosophical disputations, the lower court (the Supreme Court), the middle court (the Appellate Division), and the highest court (the Court of Appeals) in turn curtly dismissed the complaint.

Without exploring the issues, the courts ruled that the plaintiffs as a private interest group and as taxpayers had no standing to sue. To do this they would have to demonstrate that they were injured. Depriving them of the right to vote on a bond issue did not constitute an injury. Furthermore, they had waited too long in starting legal action, thus violating "the doctrine of laches" (unreasonable delays in law suits). This was just window dressing. What really bothered the courts was that UDC had already sold nearly $300 million in bonds for prison construction. Any adverse judicial action at this point would "cause unacceptable disorder and confusion." Rather than disrupt these projects, the courts rationalized an obvious violation of the constitution, in these words: "Where, as here, we are called upon to deal with an intricate scheme of public financing or for public expenditures designed to meet a public interest, the court must proceed in its review with much caution. It is the legislature which is mandated to make policy decisions in such areas and the court may not invalidate its decision, enacted into law, out of a mere preference for a different or more restrained approach."[6]

A long trail of similar decisions reveals a court bending before political pressures. With benign neglect, it permitted the state government and its public authorities to violate at least four constitutional provisions: the requirement for a referendum before contracting debt; the prohibition against state loans and credits to private interests; exemption of the state from liability for the debt of public authorities; and prohibitions against guarantees of the repayment of authority debt. Thus, the Court of Appeals subverted the state constitution, aiding and abetting disturbing antidemocratic trends in the state.[7]

During the financial travails of New York City in 1974 and 1975, the court reached an especially low point in explaining away unconstitutional actions. Boycotted by the capital markets and with no Municipal Assistance Corporations (MACs) available to bail it out, the city desperately needed funds. As a stopgap measure it persuaded the state to create a Stabilization Reserve Corporation (SRC) in 1974. SRC could sell up to $580 million in bonds and turn the money over to the city. Through annual appropriations the city would repay the SRC loans. Should it fail to pay, the state comptroller would divert to SRC state aid funds intended for the city.

Immediately public interest groups attacked the new financial scheme as unconstitutional. They raised by now similar arguments: the city cannot contract debt without pledging its full faith and credit and repaying the debt through taxes (this was not done); it cannot advance funds to public or private corporations; it cannot assume liability for the debt of a public authority; and it cannot use a subterfuge to exceed its debt limit.

By a narrow 4 to 3 vote the Court of Appeals supported the creation of SRC. Had the city lost, no SRC or MAC could have become its fiscal savior. The court minority dissented in biting language far more persuasive than the tortured reasoning of the majority:

> The Stabilization Reserve Corporation Act violates the letter and the spirit of article VIII of the State Constitution. No amount

of words can disguise the simple fact that while liability of the city is disavowed, it effectively commits its sources of revenue from the State to the discharge of the obligations of the Stabilization Reserve Corporation. It is, therefore, indistinguishable from a commitment of its credit. . . . As a consequence, the act is unconstitutional.

However we might empathize with the plight of local governments in general and the City of New York in particular at this time of unprecedented fiscal crisis, the constitutional limitations upon local finance cannot and should not be blinked. Indeed, judicial condonation of constitutional evasion only prolongs the agony of the cities by postponing to the indefinite future a sensible reappraisal, by those charged with the responsibility, of the need and the form of constitutional limits upon local finance. . . .

From what has been said, it should be clear that SRC is a barely disguised technique for debt ceiling avoidance and subverts in varying degrees the constitutional limits upon local finance. . . . The SRC and other techniques for debt ceiling avoidance erode the principle of constitutional supremacy.[8]

More concerned with a city on the brink of bankruptcy than constitutional niceties, state and local officials were delighted with the decision. Peter Goldmark, the state budget director at that time and one of the architects of SRC and MAC, minced no words about the "close call." "Had the Court of Appeals turned down the SRC, the situation would have been chaotic."

The decision hit at the very heart of the issue that troubles state and local governments. Without SRC and, later, MAC, the city might have fallen into fiscal chaos. Under the pressure of events, the court legitimatized a patently unconstitutional action, highlighting the dilemma faced by governments: Change the constitution if it stands in the way; if change is impossible, evade it.

A perpetual gadfly of elected officials was Louis E. Wein, an attorney and legal scholar, who challenged the stream of questionable financial schemes that poured out of Albany and New York City. He was the guiding spirit behind the SRC case. When the state created MAC, Wein launched additional legal attacks. By refinancing the city's debt, he charged, MAC violated the contract between the city and its bondholders. By intercepting state aid due to New York City, MAC was depriving creditors of the security behind the city's bonds. By forcing the State Insurance Fund (in effect a public authority) to buy MAC bonds, the state was creating an unconstitutional debt. Again he lost in the Court of Appeals because the court decided that debt was not debt if it was repaid from current appropriations that could be cut off any time.[9] But Wein's arguments reverberated through Wall Street. As much as any other factor, they had the effect of shutting MAC out of the market in its early days.

One of the judges who participated in decisions affecting MAC was Associate Judge Jacob D. Fuchsberg of the Court of Appeals. To the embarrassment of the court, it turned out that he had some $3.4 million in New York City notes that would be refinanced by MAC. Because of this apparent conflict of interest, the court set up a special Court on the Judiciary to probe Fuchsberg's financial dealings. By a 2 to 1 vote this court held that Fuchsberg's conduct, while reprehensible in some respects, did not warrant removal from the bench. The court found no evidence of deliberate fraudulent conduct or corrupt actions inspired by financial interests. It agreed, however, that the transactions raised "difficult questions of propriety" and "were ill-advised." While the transgressions didn't violate the letter of judicial canons, they definitely "violated the spirit."[10]

In less dramatic decisions, large and small, the New York State courts have demonstrated a touching solicitude for public authorities that does not permit the constitution to stand in the way. From the early 1930s to the early 1990s they rarely wavered in their support of the authorities, even under trying circumstances. In 1935 the Court of Appeals dismissed a contention that the creation of a Buffalo Sewer Authority was a deliberate evasion of the city's debt limit. As a separate entity, the authority was free of "normal government restrictions on debt creation, referendum and local debt limits according to the court."[11] When the Elmira Parking Authority ran up deficits, the city turned over to it revenue from parking meters. Was this a blatant defiance of a constitutional prohibition against city loans to public or private corporations? By a 5 to 2 vote the Court of Appeals termed it merely a justifiable switch of money from one public corporation (the city) to another (the authority).[12]

After rejecting attempts to control the Thruway Authority that operates a nearly 500 mile toll road, the court gave it a blank check. "However close such relationship [between the State and the Authority] may be, though, it is abundantly clear that the authority stands on its own feet, transacts its business affairs through its own personnel and on its own initiative and is not subject to the strict requirements imposed upon a board or department of the state."[13]

Like other bedroom communities, Nassau County on Long Island had to pay its share of the costs of the Metropolitan Transportation Authority for maintaining the commuter railroad and stations. When it refused to pay this high annual tribute that its voters had not approved, the state comptroller withheld an appropriate amount of state aid otherwise due to the county and transferred it to MTA. Sorry, said the court, but MTA comes first. Without fees and cost sharing MTA cannot pay off the bondholders. This was the legislature's intent and, according to the court, was constitutional.[14]

Thanks to the court, the Jones Beach State Park Authority, also on Long Island, once part of Moses' empire, had the untrammeled power in 1975 to raise tolls on the Southern State Parkway. Despite local opposition the court found this was a reasonable exercise of the authority's discretion.[15] Irked by the increase, Governor Carey pressured the authority to reduce the tolls. In censorious tones the court lectured the governor: "Since the toll is the sole source of funds for bond repayment, any limitations on the authority's power to collect a toll sufficient to pay the bonds deprives the bondholders of an essential attribute of their contract."[16]

Playing its usual fiscal sleight of hand, New York City, with the approval of the legislature, switched the responsibility for supplying water from the city to the Municipal Water Finance Authority in 1984. This deft move cut the city's budget by hundreds of millions of dollars and let the authority take the onus for sharp increases in charges. After the authority issued nearly $2 billion in tax-exempt revenue bonds, five state legislators, in 1989, challenged the constitutionality of this method of financing. Under the constitution, the city could sell only general obligation bonds and not revenue bonds, they argued. Predictably, the court ruled that the city and the authority are separate entities and not subject to the same restrictions. Hence, the bond issue was legal.[17]

Before the Urban Development Corporation (UDC) defaulted on

the payment of its notes, a taxpayer in 1971 contended that a $250-million issue of moral obligation bonds was unconstitutional. The state could not guarantee the repayment of the bonds without a referendum, so he argued. Once again the court found no problem. After all the bonds were not the "money of the state," nor was the "money under its control."[18] Even when the state bailed out UDC in 1975, a divided Court of Appeals endorsed the advance of state funds to a public corporation, notwithstanding the constitution.[19] In a minority opinion, a normally placid judge sputtered about the "very magnitude of the illegality."

If the courts in New York State coddled public authorities and investors, the highest court in the State of Washington was cavalier in its treatment of investors who had bought $2.25 billion of WPPSS bonds. In 1982 a lower court had found valid so-called dry-hole, take-or-pay or hell-or-high-water contracts. Whether or not projects 4 and 5 were completed and generated electricity, the 88 participants in WPPSS (mainly publicly owned utility districts) still had to pay their share of the debt service. This was standard practice in the industry. In other states courts had consistently upheld such contracts. And the legislature had acquiesced to the well-publicized contracts by not taking any action against them. After all, this was the legislature that had created WPPSS.

Nevertheless, the Supreme Court, in an opinion more slanted to the political winds than to the constitution, ruled in 1983 that the participants lacked authority to sign take-or-pay contracts. Thus it kicked over the props supporting debt service and forced WPPSS to default on the payment of principal and interest on the $2.25-billion bond issue. This was the court's chief argument:

> In the present case, the participants lacked substantive authority to enter into this type of contract because they constructed an elaborate financing arrangement that required the participants to guarantee bond payments irrespective of whether the plant was ever completed; to surrender ownership interest and considerable control to WPPSS; and to assume the obligations of defaulting participants. As such these contracts failed to protect unsuspecting individuals, the ratepayers, represented by the partici-

pants. . . . The agreement is not a standard contract for the purchase of power because the payments are due irrespective of whether any electric current is delivered. . . . Therefore, we hold that the Washington PUDs [public utility districts] and Washington municipal participants lacked authority to enter into the agreement. . . . Because the plants are unfinished there is no electricity to sell, and hence no revenues. There is no obligation to pay revenue bonds when there is no revenue.

Only two of the nine justices dissented and subsequent events were to attach more importance to their views than to the opinions of the majority. Calling the decision "narrow," they supported the authority of municipalities to "provide electric power to their citizens by all advisable means. Their determinations of advisability are not subject to judicial review, except to the extent that they are arbitrary and capricious." What the minority was saying was that a deal is a deal. If economic and management factors made it impossible to complete plants 4 and 5, then the participants were no more entitled to relief from bond guarantees than they would be entitled to a refund for the purchase of oil when the price fell below a contracted price. Had the projects succeeded, they would have enjoyed the benefits of cheap electricity. This was not a heads-I-win-tails-you-lose proposition.[20]

In the face of a later partial settlement of bondholders' claims approved by federal district courts in Arizona and Washington in 1989, the effect of the majority decision slowly withered. The Arizona court was "stirred" by the moving letters it received from investors. "Almost universally," the court wrote, "they complained about buying a highly rated and recommended security only to find it to be essentially valueless. The Court does not have boundless power to rectify such grievances, however, even though they may be legitimate." Unable to overturn the Washington State Supreme Court decision, the federal courts approved or modified each of the many settlements. These actions closed "the story of the largest municipal bond default on record."[21]

Even the Washington court could not turn a deaf ear to charges of fraud and negligence brought against state officials. When lower courts dismissed those charges, the Supreme Court insisted on pursuing them, but to no avail. Whether or not this represents second thoughts on the part of the court is difficult to say.

Like most state constitutions, the New Jersey constitution is tough in its restrictions on debt. One would never suspect this from the soft heart of its state Supreme Court. As early as 1949 the court turned back an attack on the creation of the Turnpike Authority. Despite a constitutional ban on state debt without voter approval in a referendum, the court stated flatly that authority debt is not state debt. In its ruling it leaned on the statute that created the authority. The act explicitly specifies that turnpike bonds "shall not be deemed to constitute a debt or liability of the State . . . or a pledge of the faith and credit of the state." In other words, no problem of constitutionality arises because the statute says there is no problem. The court could also point to existing independent authorities all around the country. For example, look at the Port Authority of New York and New Jersey or the California Toll Bridge Authority. They demonstrate that the independence and autonomy of public authorities are "long established principles."[22]

With the blessings of its highest court, the state proceeded to create even more public authorities. Again the court wilted when a taxpayer in 1953 protested the state's $255-million guarantee of the punctual payment of revenue bonds issued by the Highway Authority that operates the Garden State Parkway. This was tantamount to an unconstitutional loan of the state's credit to a public corporation, complained the taxpayer. In a tortuous opinion the court observed that a changing economy and society call for "new applications" of constitutional principles. With this flexible approach, the court decided that the guarantee was not a loan or pledge of the state's credit. What was involved was "rather the state's own debt or liability incurred in the service of an essential public need through the instrumentality of the authority." It was quite an admission to regard the authority debt as state debt. Ordinarily, the constitution required that the state could not borrow money without a referendum. But neither the taxpayer nor the court raised this nettling issue.[23]

True to form, the court upheld a special high fee imposed by the Turnpike Authority and the Highway Authority on interstate buses.[24] It exempted the Turnpike Authority from the state's bidding and procurement requirements because it was a separate entity. In this regard the appellate court stressed that the authority had "broad discretion."[25] Without any difficulty, the Turnpike Authority brushed aside an attempt by the City of Newark to prevent the construction of two interchanges in the city. Once again the Supreme Court played up the authority's role as an "independent public corporation." So long as the authority operated within its statutory powers and demonstrated no bad faith, fraud, corruption, and abuse of discretion, the court would not interfere with its management and policies.[26]

When an operator of a lunch-wagon was convicted of selling food at Newark Airport without authorization of the Port Authority of New York and New Jersey, an appellate court rebuffed his defense: lack of norms or standards with regard to the sale of merchandise and denial of equal protection of the law. The incident is less important than the court's sweeping comments on the autonomy of the authority. With the widest range of managerial latitude, the authority has "sole discretion . . . over all details of financing, construction, leasing, charges, rates, tolls, contracts and the operation of air terminals. . . . Its decision in connection with any and all matters concerning such air terminals shall be controlling and conclusive."[27]

At the local level public authorities in New Jersey are equally independent. Once cities create them, they lose control over them and their hiring, financing, purchasing, and contracting practices. So the cities of Bayonne, Trenton, and Camden learned to their sorrow after they established parking authorities. Nothing can be clearer than this judicial edict: "A parking authority created pursuant to the Parkway Authorities Law is not an authority or agency of the municipality creating it."[28]

From the early 1950s California has been a citadel of lease financing with the enthusiastic support of its Supreme Court. Like courts in other states it has indulged in semantical contortions to justify this form of "creative" finance.[29]

In this spirit the court looked benignly at the use of a special state fund by the state port authority in San Francisco to supplement its revenue. This type of debt does not require a voter referendum, ruled the court. Had the authority dipped into the general fund of the state, then and only then would a constitutional problem arise.

Needless to say, special funds sprouted in California and elsewhere in the wake of this and similar rulings, leading to even more voter confusion on sources of funding and who was responsible for what.[30]

So contagious were these opinions that they seduced the Supreme Court of Colorado as well. In the usual travesty used to bypass the constitution, the City of Lakewood created a building authority to construct a city hall. Over a 29-year period it would issue over $6 million in bonds and would pay for the building through a lease-purchase plan. Several crotchety taxpayers protested that the authority was merely the city's alter ego and was an obvious subterfuge to get around debt limits and voter referenda. Not so, concluded the court. It then propounded a novel doctrine that some may find ingenious, others disturbing. The constitution prohibits debt without a referendum, but it does not require a referendum to build a city hall. Let the court's words speak for themselves:

> The premise of the plaintiffs' argument that the plan for financing and construction of a city hall is a fraud or works an injustice upon the city's taxpayers is that it is a device to accomplish, by change of form with no change of substance, the same result which has been rejected by the voters. This premise is faulty. It is not the construction of a city hall for which voter approval is required under Colo. Const. Art. XI, § 6. Rather, it is the creation of a general obligation debt of the city which requires the assent of the voters. The plan submitted to and rejected by the voters would have created such a general obligation debt. The plan now proposed does not. This difference is constitutionally significant.

Anyway, the court claimed somewhat defensively, "Other states which have considered similar questions under their own constitutions have concluded that utilization of a building authority as a vehicle for financing governmental buildings does not violate state constitutional constraints on creation of governmental debt."[31]

Equally quick to embrace public authorities has been the Supreme Court of Illinois. As early as 1945 the court approved the establishment of the Chicago Transit Authority, arguing that the bonds of the new authority did not create a governmental debt.[32] In

1989 it neatly disposed of another problem affecting public corporations, including authorities and school districts. Bucking a tide of rising interest rates, the legislature in 1983 had imposed a 7 percent interest ceiling on bond issues. Look as hard as it might, the Allendale school district could not find such attractive rates. Reluctantly, it sold a bond issue with a 9.75 percent interest rate. Immediately several taxpayers brought suit because the district had pierced the statutory ceiling. In the meantime the legislature had retroactively recognized its error and passed another bill that, in effect, waived the ceiling. Somewhat troubled, the court still rationalized these intricate maneuvers. "Since the bonds in question are not void instruments but defective ones, we find that the legislature has the power to validate them through a curative act."[33]

Far more was at stake here than the interest rates of one school district. Before the Supreme Court found it could accept "defective" bonds, the appellate court had declared that the excess interest rate was illegal. By this ruling it jeopardized hundreds of high-interest bonds issued by public authorities, school districts, and local governments. This decision literally froze the bond market in Illinois. The prestigious Chicago law firm of Chapman and Cutler, which acted as bond counsel to many governmental units, cautioned: "until this matter is resolved either in the legislature or in the courts, we are unable to deliver our usual form of approving opinion with respect to financing falling within the broad scope of the Bates decision." It then rallied the financial community with these consoling words: "We are confident that with your cooperation and assistance, this troubling situation will be satisfactorily resolved and political subdivisions in Illinois will again have free access to the bond markets."[34]

The Supreme Court was pleased to break this logjam, notwithstanding "defective" bonds.

Rarely have the courts rejected fees and charges set by public authorities. So long as the fees are uniform, consistent, and not arbitrary, they are as good as gold. In this spirit the court turned down a challenge by Donald Trump, the real estate promoter, to water connection fees for his Atlantic City casinos.[35] In Illinois the Supreme Court upheld a flexible fee structure of the Aurora Sanitary District despite residents' complaints that fees unfairly ranged from

$15 to $160.[36] Whether in Tennessee, New York, Utah, California, Arizona, or many other states, the courts are one in supporting authority fees required to repay revenue bonds.[37]

The Courts Look at Bond Covenants

Above all the courts zealously defend the rights of bondholders and the sanctity of bond covenants, the one significant exception being the default by WPPSS in the State of Washington. As the courts see it, two provisions in the U.S. Constitution make authority bond issues tamper-proof. One is the contract clause: "No state shall pass any . . . law impairing the obligations of contracts" (Art. 1, Sec. 16). The other is the "due process" clause (Art. 14): "nor shall any state deprive any person of life, liberty or property without due process of law."

Beginning with Robert Moses, public authorities have been quick to draft bond covenants that, under the protection of the U.S. Constitution, free them from legislative and executive meddling. The formula is deceptively simple. The authority board approves a resolution to issue bonds and in the resolution spells out the purpose of the bonds; the fees pledged to support specific projects; the activities in which the authority can engage; the uses to which all funds will be put; and the disposition of surpluses, if any. Locked in the bond covenant that is an integral part of the bond issue, the restrictions stand as long as the bonds are outstanding. This can be as long as 30 to 40 years. The bond covenant is a contract between the authority and the bondholders and has been held as nearly inviolable by the courts.

Three rarely used safety valves do exist to change bond covenants. If the covenant provides for alteration, the way is open. If two-thirds of the bondholders approve a change, no problem arises, but it is difficult to track down so many investors. Finally, under certain conditions, the authority can pay off the bond issue in advance. However, it cannot reduce the promised payments of principal and interest. In this event, the authority is free to write another bond covenant.

The Bob Moses-inspired bond covenants have turned out to be effective devices for insulating public authorities from political control. Yet rarely have political leaders challenged the usurpation of their powers. Rarely have they made even timid overtures to regulate bond covenants.

In 1962, an unprecedented event occurred in the annals of bond covenants. The Port Authority of New York and New Jersey and both states joined in demolishing a bond covenant that restricted the use of authority fees. Under pressure from both states, the authority agreed to acquire the bankrupt Hudson and Manhattan Railroad that ran from New Jersey to Manhattan and to build and operate the World Trade Center, one of the world's largest skyscrapers. To mollify the bondholders who protested that the bond covenant didn't permit these massive ventures, the Port Authority promised that no other revenues and reserves would be used for mass transportation. In special legislation both states approved the breach of the covenant with a firm commitment not to fund any other mass transit projects and skyscrapers. Their fears temporarily allayed, the bondholders took no further action.

By the early 1970s both state governments regretted the statutory straitjacket they had placed on the use of Port Authority revenues for mass transportation. On both sides of the Hudson River legislatures and governors complained bitterly that the Port Authority had reneged on its original mission of providing railroad transportation. The issue became even more acute in 1974 when OPEC started the oil embargo. At the same time, Brendan T. Byrne won the governorship in New Jersey after campaigning for a more energetic role by the Port Authority in mass transit. Because of the confluence of these pressures, the legislatures in both states repealed the 1962 covenant retroactively. The way was now open for a diversion of Port Authority surpluses to mass transportation.

Crying "impairment of contracts" and "violation of federal and state constitutions," the United States Trust Company in behalf of bondholders sued in the New Jersey courts in 1975. The New Jersey Supreme Court upheld the repeal of the bond covenant as a valid exercise of the state's police power. Furthermore, it emphasized that bondholders still had ample security and would not lose a penny. For relief the trustees turned to the U.S. Supreme Court. By a 4 to 3 vote the Court reinstated the covenant and struck down the repeal as a violation of a binding contract. While mass transportation was a major problem, the Court ruled, the states could deal with it in ways other than an unconstitutional shredding of a contract.[38]

Wall Street applauded the Supreme Court's reaffirmation of the untouchability of bond covenants. A municipal bond specialist emphasized, "The ruling affirms that a covenant is a covenant, no matter what the politicians say. And that is extremely important for the municipal bond market." A long-time proponent of mass transit, Theodore Kheel, denounced the decision as "the worst blow to New York City, since President Ford told us to drop dead."[39] Governor Byrne vented his frustration with the Port Authority by vetoing its minutes on several occasions, in effect preventing it from embarking on new projects.[40]

Even the Port Authority's subsidy of the commuter railroad (now called PATH [Port Authority Trans-Hudson]) was too much for the American Automobile Association in New York and New Jersey. When the Port Authority increased tolls from $2 to $3 on bridges and tunnels in 1987 to finance a large-scale capital program including improvements of the PATH system, AAA sued in the federal courts, charging that the use of automobile tolls for mass transit was illegal. The U.S. Court of Appeals ruled that subsidies were justified since "the bridges, tunnels, bus terminals . . . and PATH constitute an integrated, interdependent transportation system." Without PATH 70,000 riders a day would jam the already congested bridges and tunnels. On appeal, the U.S. Supreme Court concurred.[41]

Ignoring long-standing court decisions on bondholders' rights, New York State and New York City deliberately violated them in 1975 during the city's fiscal crisis. With the city in desperate straits and unable to pay its bills, Governor Hugh L. Carey and the state legislature approved a three-year moratorium on the repayment of $2.6 billion in short-term notes. The legislation offered bondholders, mainly small investors, one of two difficult choices. Accept the moratorium and receive in exchange for short-term notes an equal amount of long-term bonds issued by Big MAC. Reject it and receive annual interest of at least 6 percent, lower than the interest due on the notes. No matter what the legislature called it, this was a thinly disguised default.

In behalf of itself and other holders of the city's notes, the Flush-

ing National Bank led the charge against the constitutionality of the
Emergency Moratorium Act. The lower state courts supported the
act as a legitimate exercise of the state's police power in an emergency. Reversing these courts, the Court of Appeals upset the moratorium as unconstitutional:

> The act violates the State Constitution in denying faith and
> credit to the short-term anticipation notes of the city. The State
> Constitution prohibits the city from contracting any indebtedness
> unless it pledges its "faith and credit" for the payment of the
> principal of the indebtedness (N.Y. Const. art. VIII, § 2). Thus,
> the Moratorium Act, by depriving short-term noteholders of judi-
> cial remedies for at least three years, makes meaningless the
> verbal pledge of faith and credit.[42]

For all the sharp tones of the decision, the Court of Appeals gave
the state and city what they needed—a one-year period of grace to
get their financial house in order. It was just enough time to have
Big MAC take over the refinancing of the city's debt.

In an echo of the decision, a disgruntled bondholder in 1977
claimed that the diversion of the city's tax revenues to MAC was
unconstitutional and damaged his contractual rights. Not so, argued
the Court of Appeals. The city was going to get the money anyway
even though it was first routed through MAC. And the bondholders
would still enjoy their constitutional protection.[43]

The highest court in Massachusetts—the Supreme Judicial
Court—proved to be equally sensitive to the claims of bondholders.
In an advisory opinion it ruled out any attempt by the state legislature to curb the power of Massport to adjust tolls for the Callahan
and Sumner tunnels under Boston Harbor. The court warned that
the proposed statute "would impose an arbitrary restriction of toll
revisions which would seriously affect the Authority's contractual
arrangements with its bondholders." It would repudiate "the essence of the bond contract" and reduce "the attractiveness of the
revenue security."[44]

When the same authority gave its employees a more attractive
pension package, investors worried about the impact of the increased costs on the security behind the bonds. Not to worry, consoled the court: "This increase does not effect any substantial or

constitutional impairment of the security behind MPA's revenue bonds." What the authority did was to exercise its statutory power without impairing "the obligation of the contract" or violating "due process of law."[45]

The court also got embroiled in a local boat service controversy. For years the Steamship Authority had served Woods Hole, Nantucket, and Martha's Vineyard. During the summer it also took on passengers in New Bedford. But, in the view of bondholders, the legislature went too far in mandating rather than merely allowing the New Bedford service. Without corresponding revenue, the additional cost would damage their contractual rights. The court dismissed these fears: "We do not think the changes . . . materially affect the value of the bonds or the certainty of payment of principal or interest."[46] Besides, the court suggested, the state and local communities would cover any deficit.

Before Governor Dukakis vetoed a 1989 bill that would require the Massachusetts Turnpike Authority to assume an annual cost of $50 million for snow and ice removal on all state roads, he pondered the attempted repeal of the bond covenant affecting the Port Authority of New York and New Jersey. In the end he concluded that the bill was unconstitutional and impaired the authority's contracts with its bondholders.

Public Authority Autonomy

So long as they protect bondholders, public authorities can take on a life of their own and escape legislative control. This is the essence of major court decisions all over the country. In Wisconsin, for example, the court blocked an attempt by the legislature to regain control over an authority it had created. Following practices in most states, the legislature in 1967 had established the Wisconsin Higher Education Corporation (WHEC) to operate a $250-million state-guaranteed student loan program. Legally, it was a private, non-profit corporation. As the authority prospered, the legislature was dismayed to find that it had virtually no say in hiring practices, building construction, and financial policies. Determined to reassert itself, it passed a bill in 1985 that would regulate WHEC like any other state agency. Governor Anthony Earl vetoed the bill in challenging words: "This current governance structure is sufficient for public accountability . . . and I have therefore vetoed the legislative changes that unduly interfere in the governance and operation of a private corporation."

A furious legislature overrode the governor's veto. WHEC then turned to the state court for relief. There it found a sympathetic ally. In a far-reaching opinion in 1987 a county circuit judge not only found the act unconstitutional, but reaffirmed the unfettered autonomy of WHEC. Since the state created the authority as a private nonprofit corporation rather than as a government agency, it limited its "options to regulate the corporation freely," the judge wrote. "A mere governmental interest in regulation for the sake of regulation . . . is not sufficient justification for the infringement of contract . . . legislative ire is not synonymous with a valid public purpose."[47]

This firm language deterred the legislative leaders from appealing the decision to higher courts. And WHEC has continued to grow even larger without any legislative accountability whatsoever.

Similarly, the New York State Metropolitan Transportation Authority (MTA) evolved into a larger and more powerful public corporation than the legislature had originally intended. In the 1960s the deficit-ridden MTA cast covetous eyes on the surplus-swollen Triborough and Tunnel Bridge Authority (TBTA), the erstwhile crown jewel of the Moses fiefdom. In a power grab in 1967 Governor Rockefeller persuaded the legislature to merge TBTA with MTA so that its surplus revenues would offset MTA losses. This action openly and explicitly violated TBTA bond covenants and state laws. Just when bondholders were about to sue in the courts and charge breach of contract, Governor Rockefeller sweetened the arrangements. If bondholders would agree to modify the bond covenants and transfer surplus funds to MTA, TBTA would raise its interest rate by one-fourth of 1 percent. At this prospect of material gain, the bondholders quickly overlooked constitutional "technicalities" and decided not to sue.

This zigzag journey through the states has merely skimmed the cream off hundreds of cases upholding the autonomy of public authorities except when bondholders' rights are threatened. What is clear is that the courts, like governors and legislatures, fail to check the untrammeled powers of authorities and their misuse by governments. But the voters, in theory, can hold elected officials to account at the next general election (although not judges, necessarily, for many of them are appointed).

Similar developments at the federal level have troubled Harold Seidman, an astute and knowledgeable observer of federal public corporations. His concerns about the role of the federal courts hold for the state courts as well.

> Rampant delegation of legislative power and the expansion of third party government [government corporations and public authorities] compound enormously the accountability problem. As national governmental power has increased, so has it moved to the margins of the system where democratic control and responsiveness are already attenuated. In this shift, the judiciary has been cast as the arbiters between official government and their constituents or their unofficial proxies and surrogates. Inevitably, power attaches to such a role. As a result, the judiciary are now more involved in governance and less accountable to the governed than ever before.[48]

Many centuries ago the ancient Romans asked: Who watches the watchers? Who guards the guards? In contemporary America the question is even more urgent.

6

The Public Authority Sweepstakes: Winners and Losers

When public authorities and their parent governments issued about $128 billion in long-term bonds in 1990, a motley lot of private interests competed fiercely to steer the money their way. As Douglas Whitley of Illinois reminds us, "many beneficiaries feed on the bond financing trough." In this contest a few big winners and many losers emerge.

Towering in the winners' circle are the brokerage houses, law firms, financial advisers, and banks that reap enormous profits from the sale of bonds. Bond-rating organizations and bond insurance firms also continue to do well regardless of the ups and downs of the business cycle. Tidy fees pour in steadily. Nor is this a one-time event, for they monitor up to $1 trillion in outstanding bonds. For investors the results are mixed. While they enjoy tax-free interest, defaults and advance refunding of bond issues may jeopardize their holdings or cut their gains.

Other clear beneficiaries are building contractors, real estate developers, engineering and architectural firms, insurance companies, and labor unions that engage in large-scale construction projects. Understandably, they are among the most fervent supporters of public authorities and cater to the edifice complex of a Rockefeller or a Thompson or a Dukakis. For elected officials, authority-financed projects are a double boon. Isolated from the hurly-burly of checks and balances, they turn many public authorities into beehives of political patronage. They also have the additional advantage of hiding the truth about state and local finances by erecting a facade of public authorities.

But the losers are legion. State and local taxpayers pay three times. Through taxes they subsidize some of the biggest authorities in the country and through fees they pay for the burgeoning costs of all authorities. They also subsidize bondholders who avoid state and local taxes on their interest. As federal taxpayers, all citizens shoulder the costs of authorities by exempting interest on municipal bonds from U.S. taxes. While the Tax Reform Act of 1986 cut the amount of tax exemption, it still adds up to losses of billions of dollars a year.

The biggest losers of the public authority game by far are the poor and the near poor. User fees and charges cut into their incomes more deeply than into the incomes of the more affluent. When politicians shift functions from general government to public authorities, they force those with low and moderate incomes to bear a disproportionate share of governmental costs. The fees hurt the poor while tax reduction benefits the well-to-do. As William Stern emphasized earlier, this smacks of upward income redistribution and as such raises troubling questions of equity and fair play.

This, then, is what the toteboard shows as the overall results of the public authority sweepstakes. But the details are even more startling than the big picture.

Bond Underwriters

Compared with the lush years of the Reagan era, 1989 to 1990 were relatively poor years for underwriters, with major staff cutbacks, a sharp reduction in bond issues because of tax reform, and shriveled profits. Yet in 1990 they still managed over 11,000 long-term and short-term bond issues with a face value of $162 billion ($128 billion long term and $34 billion short term). Leading all the rest were the Big Five that, according to *The Bond Buyer*, sold nearly $50 billion in long-term bonds:[1]

Rank	Underwriter	Billions Sold	Issues Sold
1	Merrill Lynch Capital Markets	$14.3	285
2	Goldman Sachs and Co.	13.8	243
3	First Boston Corporation	7.7	94
4	Smith Barney, Harris, Upham, and Co.	6.7	169
5	Lehman Brothers	6.7	298
	Total	49.2	1089

The 1,089 bond issues managed by the Big Five represented only 12.5 percent of the 8,684 long-term bond issues that came to market that year, but, in dollar volume, they accounted for 38.4 percent.

Three of the Big Five, joined by two other megafirms, dominated the market in short-term notes (usually under one year):

Rank	Underwriter	Billions Sold	Issues Sold
1	Lehman Brothers	$ 8.3	194
2	Bank of America	5.3	28
3	Goldman Sachs and Co.	3.0	16
4	Merrill Lynch	1.8	16
5	Morgan Stanley	1.7	10
	Total	20.1	264

Again the big brokerage houses swept the field even though short-term notes are not as lucrative as long-term bonds. Of $34 billion in short-term notes sold in 1988, the five firms marketed 59.1 percent. The 264 issues they sold amounted to only 9.4 percent of all issues. In this case small was indeed beautiful.

The underwriters reap their profits from the "spread" between the amount they pay the public authorities and governments for the bond issue and the price they charge the public for the bonds. Through competitive bidding or negotiation a syndicate of underwriters buys the bond issue from, say, a public authority. It then resells the bonds to mutual funds, institutions, and individuals. The spread can be profitable, ranging from 2.2 percent for bond issues over $75 million to 4.1 percent for bond issues between $10 million and $25 million.[2] For straightforward general obligation bonds the spread is at the lower end. For more complex revenue bonds and private purpose tax-exempt bonds the spread can exceed 4 percent. On this basis the Big Five probably gained $1 billion to $3 billion in underwriting fees in 1990. This is quite apart from their brisk business in selling bonds in a secondary market (the resale of old bonds).

Both the underwriters and the public authorities run into risks in marketing bonds. If the bond issuance costs (the spreads) are excessive, the public authorities lose funds that could be devoted to projects. If interest rates go up between the time the underwriters buy the bonds and the time they sell them, they may experience heavy losses.

That brokerage houses incur significant costs is beyond question. But what is a fair rate of compensation for these costs and what is a fair profit? When fees in California ranged up to 3 percent of the amount of a bond issue, the state senate office of research investigated the costs of underwriting practices. It found that structuring and managing an intricate bond issue can cost as much as $4 per $1,000 bond. At $3 the management fee for a $100-million bond issue would be $300,000. For legal advice on tax exemption and bond covenants the underwriters and public authorities depend on bond counsel, whose fees may range up to $100,000. Finally, selling expenses are high, amounting to at least $8.50 per a $1,000 bond. For a $100-million bond issue this translates into a cost of $850,000. Combine all three cost factors and the illustrative underwriting fee for a $100-million bond issue could be roughly $1.5 million or 1.5 percent. Add a percentage for profit, and the overall spread could run from 2 percent to 4 percent. The study concluded that spreads around 2 percent are the fairest of all.[3] The Tax Reform Act of 1986 places a 2 percent limit on many revenue bonds.

The spread is the smallest part of the costs paid by a public authority or a state or local government. The largest single expense is interest to bondholders. Then the public authority hires a small platoon of costly specialists: its own bond counsel; financial advisers; bond raters; bond insurance firms; printers to churn out bond documents; paying agents to serve the bondholders; and trustee banks to hold funds and protect the rights of bondholders.

As the Texas Housing Agency learned, these costs can be appreciable, ranging from 1 percent to 3.5 percent, depending on the size of the bond issue. In 1987–1988 the authority marketed two issues of residential mortgage revenue bonds and multifamily housing revenue bonds with these results:

Issuance Costs	*Fees for $149 million residential mortgage revenue bond (8.86%)*	*Fees for $9.6 million multifamily housing revenue bond (6.58%)*
Underwriting spread	$1,117,500	$142,542
Bond counsel fees	105,863	68,054
Rating agency fees	65,000	5,000
Printing costs	28,397	4,560
Paying agent fee	—	18,972
Miscellaneous costs	65,693	96,900
	$1,370,453 (1%)	$336,028 (3.5%)

Actually, the Texas authority got away cheaply. It retained no financial adviser and required no bond insurance to enhance its ratings. In contrast the Texas Water Development Board paid $25,000 to its financial advisers for a $50-million bond issue, and the independent Texas A&M University System paid $306,294 for bond insurance covering a $72-million bond issue and a $35-million bond issue.[4]

With fierce competition in the capital markets, the ordinary citizen, with a naive faith in good government, would expect public authorities and governments to solicit bids for bond issues just as they require competitive bidding for construction contracts and supplies. Under this old-fashioned concept, the underwriters who offered the lowest interest rates and the lowest spreads would manage the bond issue. Alas, this is not what happens in the marketplace. Negotiated deals rather than competitive bidding are the rule of the day. In 1990 negotiated bonds accounted for nearly 75 percent of all long-term bond issues, virtually doubling the 40 percent rate in 1976.[5]

The extraordinary reliance on negotiated deals rather than competitive bidding has raised charges of undue political pressure, unnecessary high costs, and unfairness. In its report on bonding practices the state senate office of research in California highlighted these concerns:

> If the bonds are sold by negotiation, as are most revenue bonds, the Treasurer selects an underwriter or group of underwriters and works out a deal with them. The choice of underwriter is subjective, without any competitive process or any public explanation as to why a particular firm or group of firms was chosen. A remarkable number of things may be up for negotiation, beginning with the interest cost of the bonds, but also including which firms are to be part of the group of underwriters doing the deal, conceivably what share of the deal each firm will have, what proportion of the profits of the deal will go to the "management team" that is responsible for setting up the deal, and how losses will be apportioned if the bonds cannot be sold for the anticipated price and interest rate. Also, the underwriter will employ another bond counsel to do various legal chores for the underwriter. Preparing the official statement that explains the bond issue to prospective buyers is the most important of these chores. The choice of underwriter's counsel may also be up for negotiation. The negotiation of all these terms is done in private.[6]

In California the state treasurer, without even a pretense of competition, distributes largess to underwriters, bond counsel, and other specialists. This is a patronage pool par excellence. In 1987, a slow year, Treasurer Jesse Unruh spread around $56 million in private contracts to process $3.7 billion in bonds. When business was brisk as in 1986, various firms received $120 million for their services in connection with $7.5 billion in bonds. These practices piqued the interest of the *Los Angeles Times* and the *Wall Street Journal*, which ran articles in 1986 documenting the ways in which Treasurer Unruh used his "discretion to exact both campaign and personal contributions."[7]

In 1991 the Municipal Securities Rulemaking Board, the body

that regulates dealers in municipal bonds, jolted underwriters by suggesting that they disclose any contributions to the campaigns of elected officials. This would make it easier to finger public officials who rewarded contributions with bond business.[8] In the face of bitter industry resistance, Christopher Taylor, director of the board, downplayed the need for regulations, but indicated he would air the issue in "informal planning sessions" with underwriters, bond counsel, and bond issuers. Nothing came of it.

Edward Alter, the elected treasurer of Utah, faces no such dilemma. He prefers to pick bond underwriters the "old fashioned way," by written competitive bids "that pit one investment banking firm's price against another." His standard repartee is: "When investment bankers ask me 'when are we going to get to do business with the state of Utah?' I tell them, 'I'd love to do business with you. Be the low bidder on our next offering.'"

Florida's secretary of state, Jim Smith, who participates in bond decisions together with public authorities and other state agencies, described to *Governing* the feverish lobbying that took place on the eve of a $220-million transportation bond issue: "I could hardly take a shower at home for the phone ringing with someone wanting to talk about it. . . . A phone call saying, 'I'm your friend, vote for me now, is not the way we should do business.'"[9]

As in other states, bond business has been brisk in Massachusetts for underwriters deft in negotiations. From 1985 to late 1989 bond houses received $61 million from 12 major Massachusetts authorities. Three firms—Goldman Sachs, Merrill Lynch, and Paine Webber—garnered about 58 percent of the business. Currently, the high stakes are in bonds issued by the Massachusetts Water Resources Authority (MWRA). A $600-million bond issue could mean $3 million to $6 million for underwriters and as much for bond counsel, attorneys, and banks.

One of the stars in the bond firmament is Mark S. Ferber, former staff director of the state senate ways and means committee and former financial adviser to Mayor Raymond Flynn of Boston. Ferber left state government to become an executive vice president of First Boston Inc. and later a senior vice president of Lazard Freres and Co. where Felix Rohatyn is a senior partner. Ferber's contacts proved to be invaluable. Wearing two hats, he simultaneously acted as bond counsel and/or bond salesman for two of the largest state authorities, MWRA and MIFA. As bond counsel to both authorities, his fees totaled about $800,000 annually. As bond salesman, he steered multimillion-dollar bond issues to First Boston. In the municipal bond industry a bond counsel usually serves the bond issuer (e.g., the public authority) and the bond salesman protects the underwriter. Questioned about a possible conflict of interest, Ferber said, "That's baloney. MIFA is like a department store with several different products. I act as counsel for one department. I underwrite bonds for a department that has no connection to the one I am counsel for."[10]

An investment banker who chose to remain anonymous envied Ferber's clout: "To be in control of the Massachusetts Water Resources Authority, which will be the biggest issuer in the country, gives him incredible power. Every investment banker has to make peace with Ferber, because he'll be dealing out the business."

A competitor who also preferred anonymity agreed: "He's a politician, and politics is clearly his life and love. Of course he's bright, he's hard working, he's hardly a lackey. He wasn't appointed because he was somebody's brother-in-law. But still, the basis of his power has come out those days in the powerful Senate ways and means committee."

Ferber dismissed the innuendos: "I don't get clients from my connections in government. I get them as a result of what I learned in government. . . . As far as why my clients come with me when I leave one firm for another, look at it this way: If a doctor you had grown to respect and trust left one hospital to go to another, would you stick with the hospital or would you follow the doctor?"

Between skilled negotiators and bidders there is no contest. Austin V. Koenan, managing director of Morgan Stanley's municipal finance division, and many public authority and state officials defend negotiated bond issues as a desirable practice. Admittedly the spreads may be higher with negotiation, but they claim that you get what you pay for, insisting that many bond issues are so complex that they require unusual expertise and unique approaches. Numerous technical issues of fees and charges, reserves, interest payments, back up security, and wording of bond covenants arise.

Because of all this, they argue that it saves a lot of time to negotiate directly with the most qualified firm rather than opening a bidding process to all comers.[11]

Frank Hoadley of the Wisconsin budget office agrees. He recommends a negotiated sale for unusually complex offerings when it is essential to tap the expertise of specialized underwriters and investment banks. So does Mark Bonsall, treasurer of the Salt River Project in Phoenix that issues up to $350 million worth of revenue bonds a year, 60 percent of them negotiated. A negotiated sale makes it possible to change the terms of the bond issue quickly as conditions change. "You can cut and fit as you go along," he emphasizes. Jeff Green, deputy general counsel of the Port Authority of New York and New Jersey, recommends a negotiated sale only "if someone brings a truly unique idea to us."

Koenen of Morgan Stanley is impatient with critics who decry lack of competition and the high costs of upfront spreads in negotiated sales: "A lower spread with a higher coupon [interest rate] is worse than a higher spread with a lower coupon. . . . People are trying to make black and white what's gray. Gray is judgment and people are trying to make it a mechanical process. But service by definition is judgmental. Issuers have to make complicated decisions in a complicated world. . . . This is not a totally objective process. It concerns judgment about abilities. If you [as an issuer] are responsible for a big mass transit program, you're going to tend to rely on people you know and trust. People you don't know are, generally, going to lose. That's human nature."[12]

Contrast these persuasive words with one of Chicago's many "gray" areas. In 1983 the independent Park District of Chicago (a public authority) sold $66 million of bonds in a negotiated offering to a syndicate headed by the First National Bank of Chicago, Rodman and Renshaw of Chicago, and Blyth Eastman Paine Webber Inc. of New York. The comptroller of the Park District was Joseph M. Fratto and the head of the municipal department of Rodman and Renshaw was, coincidentally, Fratto's brother Anthony. Anthony Fratto had been Chicago's comptroller under Mayor Jane M. Byrne, but joined the brokerage firm after Mayor Byrne lost her bid for reelection to Harold Washington. Rodman and Renshaw had a minority share in this deal; they sold only $10 million of the bonds and received a fee of $140,000. In a front-page story the *Chicago Sun Times* alleged a conflict of interest.

The Fratto brothers denied the charge indignantly. However, Comptroller Fratto admitted that Rodman and Renshaw had never managed a park bond issue before and that their participation was not even mentioned at a public board meeting. "The decision to go with those underwriters was reached by First Chicago and the Park District," he explained. It turned out that First Chicago had pressured the district for a negotiated offering and finally suggested Rodman and Renshaw and other firms as possible participants.

Given the lack of experience of Rodman and Renshaw, it was difficult to see what expertise they could bring to the management team. First Chicago declined to comment on their role. The president of Rodman and Renshaw said his firm's participation was "coincidental" and described the *Sun Times* story as a "teapot without a tempest." The deputy director of the Municipal Securities Rulemaking Board said, "there aren't any specific rules in that situation." Only the *Sun Times* had a ready explanation for the favoritism shown to Anthony Fratto's firm by Joseph Fratto's Park District.[13]

Oklahoma, too, has its gray areas. It doesn't require a bond issuer to pick the lowest bidder, but permits the issuer to select an underwriter "which best meets its needs." Ostensibly complying with these procedures, the Oklahoma Housing Finance Agency in 1988 held a negotiated sale and chose the same underwriter it had used in the past. Other brokerage firms charged that the selection process was rigged, that no discussion was held with underwriters prior to the sale, and that the state's bond adviser had not monitored the sale as required by law. Reluctantly, the authority conducted a second round of selections. Again the favored underwriter won. But this time the authority had complied with the letter if not the spirit of the law.[14]

Excluding the federal government, New York City issues more bonds than any public authority or state and local government in the United States. In July 1990 the city selected five underwriters from a field of 53 companies to sell $6 billion in bonds: Bear, Stearns; Goldman Sachs; First Boston; Shearson Lehman Hutton; and Merrill Lynch. To no one's surprise, the *New York Times* revealed that all five had contributed $233,000 to the campaigns of Mayor David N. Dinkins and Comptroller Elizabeth Holtzman.

Defending their actions, senior officers of the companies claimed that the contributions were motivated only by good citizenship. Alan Greenberg, chief executive officer of Bear, Stearns, characterized the donations as "an extension of our philanthropy." One of his more candid colleagues who preferred to remain anonymous admitted "it's fair to say that the perception exists in the industry that since my competitors are making large contributions, I better make them too." Of course Dinkins and Holtzman denied any wrongdoing through their press secretaries who called the selection process "competitive and merit-based."

None of this was new in the city or state. Previously the State Commission on Government Integrity had reported that State Comptroller Edward V. Regan and former City Comptroller Harrison J. Golden had received sizable contributions from underwriters and investment banks. Both officials had played a key role in selecting brokerage firms.[15]

For good reason, the suspicious public cannot distinguish between a rigged deal and one that clearly serves the public interest. Sensitive to charges of favoritism, several states such as Florida, Louisiana, Mississippi, Oklahoma, and Texas have begun to require written and open justification for negotiated sales. Koenen does not fear public scrutiny: "Let the light of day shine on and let the political process deal with the issue. I have no problem with disclosing information elected officials believe is valuable to their decision. That's part of the rules of the game."[16]

In most states the light still remains hidden under mammoth bushels. And elected officials dole out only fragmentary information about behind-the-scenes negotiations over bond issues.

At the margin of the bond industry are scavengers that prey on naive state and local officials and public authorities/special districts. They dangle before hard-pressed governments the bait of public authorities as a way out of their financial squeeze. Like snake oil salesmen they offer a magic cure-all for whatever ails the body politic.

In 1988, Buchanan and Co., an underwriter of Jackson, Mississippi, established a dubious record by pulling out of 10 states in the wake of law suits and investigations. At least 50 bond issues underwritten by Buchanan from 1980 to 1988 had defaulted. Totaling about $300 million, the bonds had been issued mainly by small public authorities/special districts for retirement centers. As the investigation spread, the firm shut down and the bondholders lost much of their investments.[17]

In another malodorous case poor judgment rather than outright guile led to a fiasco for the Washington, D.C. firm of Johnston, Lemon. In the fall of 1988 the Portsmouth Virginia Development and Housing Authority had selected the firm to sell bonds for a variety of projects. One of the beneficiaries was a real estate developer who, unbeknownst to the authority and the underwriter, had gone bankrupt early that year. Nevertheless, he received a $600,000 loan that he could not repay. Under threat of a law suit by investors, the chastened underwriter paid over $600,000 to the authority.[18]

An obscure Wall Street bond house, Matthews and Wright, suddenly prospered by specializing in bond issues that were too small, too risky, or too geographically remote for other underwriters. From 1984 to 1986 it managed over $2 billion in tax-exempt bond issues for such distant entities as Guam, the U.S. territory of Palau, Lenaxa (Kansas), and other faraway governments and public authorities. The Guam venture, in particular, led to a federal indictment of the firm and its officials. In the indictment the federal grand jury found that Matthews and Wright had marketed hundreds of millions of dollars of fraudulent bonds, and cited it for fraud, bribery, and obstruction of justice. Guam's chief motive was to raise money through arbitrage, that is, to sell bonds at a low interest rate and invest the proceeds in high-yield Treasury bonds contrary to the Tax Reform Act of 1986. It did not use the money for multifamily housing as advertised.

Because of this flagrant violation of the law, the Internal Revenue Service ruled that Guam's housing bonds were taxable. This meant that bondholders owed taxes on interest they had assumed to be tax-free. Guam's co-conspirators, the officers of Matthews and Wright, pleaded not guilty.

As the mills of justice continued to grind away slowly, the unrepentant underwriters hoodwinked East St. Louis, Illinois, into selling a $224-million bond issue for a port project on the Mississippi River. After another indictment, they pleaded guilty to conspiracy and fraud Later the SEC barred one of the senior officers of the firm from the securities business for life.[19]

Even a respected firm like Bear, Stearns could not resist the temptation of high-yield municipal junk bonds. These are risky bonds that are not rated by Moody's, Standard and Poor's, and Fitch, and pay 2 percent to 3 percent more interest than safer tax-exempt bonds. From 1985 to 1987 Bear, Stearns managed some $2.2 billion in bond issues for public authorities and local governments including industrial development authorities that financed retirement homes, motels, and textile mills. Many of the bonds defaulted or plummeted in value, leaving in their wake disgruntled and threatening investors and mutual funds that had bought the bonds.

With its reputation hanging in the balance, Bear, Stearns pulled out of the "junk bond" market in 1987. Whatever doubts it may have had, it was consoled by at least $70 million in fees and markups.

E. F. Hutton and Co. and First Investment Securities Inc. found themselves on the defendant's dock in January 1988 when two public authorities and four cities in southern California charged them with fraud, violation of federal and state securities laws, breach of fiduciary duty, intentional misrepresentation, and violation of federal racketeering laws. As minimum compensation for these offenses the plaintiffs demanded over $22 million to cover losses and punitive damages. They were particularly incensed because the brokers had "initiated . . . trading in highly speculative securities inappropriate for public entities." Pending the resolution of the court case or a settlement, E. F. Hutton made a token payment of over $300,000 to two cities and a water district. The firm termed the payment merely a return of brokerage fees and not an admission of guilt, attributing the losses to a sagging bond market. All this was the opening gun in a protracted legal proceeding.[20]

At the same time San Jose, California, sued E. F. Hutton, seven other brokerage firms, two banks, and an accounting firm because of $60 million in losses resulting from "speculative" and "unsuitable" investments. Without admitting wrongdoing, three firms reached out-of-court settlements with San Jose. A battered E. F. Hutton displayed an eleventh-hour willingness to compromise.[21]

Alarmed by the ravages of the debt merchants in North Carolina, the treasurer broadcast the following alert to officials of public authorities and local governments in October 1988:

> An additional issue of concern is an investor's lack of knowl-edge of the security or of the dealer from whom the security is being purchased. Local officials should never invest in invest-ment instruments that they do not fully understand. Likewise, public moneys should not be placed with a firm unless the firm's history and reputation are known and its financial condition has been analyzed. It is essential that a unit knows with whom it is dealing. Officials of units of government should always feel se-cure about the future of the firm as well as the relationship with the individual broker or dealer. Lately, a number of out-of-state brokers have become very aggressive in North Carolina. The problem is that they may not be familiar with North Carolina law, and it may be difficult to establish a strong working relationship with someone who is not located in the area. If public officials do not feel comfortable with a broker or feel that they are being pressured into a commitment they are not ready to make, it is advisable to refrain from investing in a security.

Bond Counsel

Bond counsel are clearly among the winners. For handsome fees they prepare the necessary documents and advise both the bond issuer (the public authority or the government) and the underwriter. The fees are indeed eye-catching. In 1990 the Big Five among the bond counsel received the following multimillion-dollar fees for long-term bond issues, according to *The Bond Buyer*, which keeps an annual score:[22]

Orrick, Herrington, and Sutcliffe	$10,070,100
Brown and Wood	7,508,100
Mudge, Rose, Guthrie, Alexander, and Ferdon	7,147,500

| Chapman and Cutler | 5,840,900 |
| Mintz, Levin, Conn, Ferris, Glovsky, and Popeo | 5,374,900 |

These are quite apart from multimillion-dollar fees for short-term bond issues.

Mudge, Rose et al. was the erstwhile law firm of John Mitchell, the inventor of the moral obligation bond and, in his pre-Nixon days, probably the most outstanding bond counsel in the country. The firm still gets a substantial amount of its business from New York State public authorities and the state itself. For the last 10 years the State of California has been one of the major clients of Orrick et al., the top fee earner.

Without competition the bond issuer—the public authority or the state or local government—selects the bond counsel. The choice takes place behind closed doors and no elected official need justify or explain the basis of the selection. Compounding the secrecy, the fees are paid out of the bond proceeds so that it is difficult to track them down in public records. Depending on the size and complexity of a bond issue, the fees can range up to $100,000 and more. In 1985 alone several law firms collected $3.5 million in bond counsel fees from New York State and its authorities.

For these fees the bond counsel are expected to protect the financial interests of the bond issuers and the bondholders. Their main product is a legal opinion designed to assuage the doubts of the most suspicious investors and bond-rating organizations. The opinion certifies that the interest on the bond issue is tax-exempt and immune to any challenges by the Internal Revenue Service. It confirms that the debt of the public authority is legal and valid and complies fully with all relevant federal and state laws and court decisions. It assures investors that the finances of the authority are as solid as the proverbial Rock and that a sure and steady stream of revenue exists to pay the debt service. It stipulates that the revenue will be earmarked for specific projects and will not be diverted by the whims of politicians to extracurricular activities or arbitrage. It cites backup security like state guarantees and moral obligations that will protect the investor in a financial pinch.

The official statement (the prospectus) and the bond covenant incorporate the legal opinion and the binding guarantees. Going further, bond counsel also develop imaginative debt-financing schemes to sidestep constitutional roadblocks and entice investors. This presents a possible ethical dilemma to them. If they propose questionable financial ploys to public authorities, are they still acting as an advocate of the bondholders whom they are also supposed to serve? Yet no bond counsel will be retained unless they remain in the good graces of public authorities, state and local governments, and underwriters. Perhaps Goethe showed uncanny insight into this practice when he wrote in the eighteenth century: "Whose bread I eat, his song I sing."

Without the convincing opinion of bond counsel, bond ratings would plummet and interest rates would soar. In troubled times public authorities and governments seek the approval of bond counsel for possibly dubious courses of action. When Governor Cuomo was trying to capture public authority reserves through complex refinancing schemes, his office urged the Dormitory Authority to seek an opinion from Mudge, Rose et al. The firm assured the authority that it was perfectly proper for it to finance facilities of the State University of New York, thus easing the burden on Cuomo's official budget. In a reverse twist, Governor Dukakis leaned on an opinion of Gaston and Snow of Boston that it would be unconstitutional for him to divert the surpluses of the Massachusetts Turnpike Authority to sundry state purposes.

In most instances the opinions of bond counsel are professional and solid and withstand legal attack. But their record is not without major blemishes. Perhaps the most outstanding flaws are the opinions of Wood, Dawson, Smith, and Hillman that led, in part, to the default of the State of Washington Public Power Supply System. They conceded their poor professional judgment by contributing $500,000 to an overall settlement for bondholders.

In numerous defaults, large and small, bond counsel played an ignominious role in failing to protect the interests of bondholders. Where were the bond counsel in the five worst municipal defaults of 1989: the $7.1-million California cogeneration facility at Lassen Community College; the $3.5-million bankruptcy of two large Kansas restaurants financed by an industrial development authority; the $9-million Parkhurst Manor retirement home in Tennessee, again an authority—financed venture; the $5.5-million Bowling

Green, Kentucky Retirement Village; and the $2.6-million Ambassador Motor Inn in Decatur, Illinois? The latter two also drew their funds from friendly public authorities.[23]

In Polk County, Florida, bondholders sued three bond counsel in 1988 after the default of a $53-million bond issue sold by the county Industrial Development Agency for a health care facility. Furious that they retrieved only slightly more than 50 cents on the dollar, they accused the bond counsel of misrepresentation of facts. Reluctantly the law firms agreed to a $2.5-million settlement that they said implied no liability on their part. They merely wanted to avoid the time and expense of continued litigation.

Every profession has its share of shady entrepreneurs, and bond counsel are no exceptions. For example, an attorney in California thought he had the best of all possible worlds by serving as city attorney for two small local governments: Industry and Hawaiian Gardens. In that capacity he recommended the selection of an underwriting firm in which he had a heavy financial stake. When his dealings aroused the curiosity of the Los Angeles County district attorney, he quickly decided to settle for $300,000 to quash possible charges of conflict of interest.

Conversely, ethical bond counsel may find that the truth can hurt them in their pocketbooks. In 1979 the mismanaged Chicago board of education tried to borrow $225 million in the bond market. Because of its low ratings, it was shut out of the market. As a stopgap measure it suggested that state aid payments for education should guarantee the loan. For years the prestigious law firm of Chapman and Cutler had been bond counsel to the board. This time the firm stated categorically that the board had no authority to undertake the financing scheme. Nevertheless, exploiting its strong political connections, the board turned to the legislature, which obligingly created a Chicago School Finance Authority to bail out the school system. And it fired Chapman and Cutler, the harbingers of bad news.[24]

With the quantum jump in legal fees, some public authorities and state governments have revolted and developed new ways to shave costs. Mississippi took a timid step by clamping a lid on charges for general obligation bonds, but not the more lucrative and more common revenue bonds. Using a sliding scale, it pays $3 per $1,000 on the first $5 million of a bond issue and, at the other extreme, 50 cents per $1,000 on bond issues over $50 million.

Even these generous limits disturbed John Hampton Stennis, a bond counsel in Jackson, Mississippi. "Public finance even for G.O. bonds is getting more complex," he complained. "Each issue usually requires a considerable amount of creative drafting. It's important to make allowances for bond counsel who do a total tax analysis or other additional work."[25]

To control legal fees the attorney general in five states serves as co-bond counsel or provides an accompanying opinion (Louisiana, Massachusetts, New Jersey, New Mexico, and Pennsylvania). Judging by the lack of general protest by the legal profession, these steps appear to be token measures. In New York State the best contracts still go to prestigious law firms via negotiations. In 1987 Governor Cuomo astonished these firms by suggesting that the attorney general should serve as bond counsel since that official already acts as bond counsel for the state's short-term debt. Somewhat flabbergasted by these additional burdens, the attorney general's office agreed to serve as co-counsel with private firms as an experiment to give "its lawyers experience and reassure the market."[26] The suspicious *Long Island News* questioned the governor's motives and editorialized that "the Governor has saved himself a few potentially embarrassing questions about the propriety of a system that upon close examination looks a lot like an up-market pork-barrel scheme."[27]

After experimenting with the use of in-house counsel for tax opinions on bond sales, the Port Authority of New York and New Jersey decided to open the process of attorney selection to public exposure. It asked 19 investment firms to rank 24 bond counsel located in New York and New Jersey. The highest-ranked firm would be selected by the authority to provide an opinion on tax exemption to the winning bond underwriter, and the authority would pay $50,000 as its share of the legal costs. At the very next bond sale in April 1988 the authority's counsel joined the private law firm in writing the opinion on tax exemption. The results were gratifying as underwriters vied for the new business and investors snapped up the bonds beribboned with an opinion providing consoling reassurance about the tax-exempt features.

Working hand in hand with the bond counsel are the new breed of financial advisers like Mark Ferber and Austin Koenen. What they and their counterparts in investment banks and brokerage houses offer are expertise in the intricacies of state and local government, the capability to structure financial arrangements that dodge constitutional and legal barriers, "creative" debt-financing schemes, and keen insight into the bond market. Above all they work solely for a fee and, in many cases, to avoid a conflict of interest, divorce themselves from more lucrative bond underwriting. Not that the fees are small. In Texas they range up to $30,000 per bond issue. One hundred such issues can bring in $3 million. In addition, financial advisers draw handsome annual retainer fees.

In 1990, *The Bond Buyer* found that the Big Five among financial advisers had collected fees ranging from $2.7 million to $6.5 million. They were Public Financial Management Inc.; Public Resources Advisory group; Lazard Freres and Co.; and Security Pacific Securities Inc.[28]

Bond Raters

Capping the entire bond issuance exercise are credit ratings by the leading bond-rating services: Moody's, Standard and Poor's, and Fitch. These ratings for investment grade bonds, ranging from BBB to AAA, determine the interest rates, the largest single cost of a bond issue. Of course, economic conditions and monetary policy also control interest rates. But the ratings ultimately influence the amount of interest that bond issuers will pay. In their analysis the rating services ferret out creditworthiness, the capacity to pay principal and interest on time, the likelihood of default, the adequacy of the security behind the bonds, the availability of bond insurance, and the financial structure of the public authority.

For these services in early 1989 Moody's charged bond issuers in California $15,000 to $30,000 per issue, Standard and Poor's $10,000 to $20,000, and Fitch $5,000 to $15,000. Just about the same time the cost of credit ratings in Texas ranged from $5,000 to $55,000. For lifetime monitoring of a bond issue the charges increase.

The fees for rating services don't buy infallibility. Moody's and Standard and Poor's still have a lot of explaining to do for their upbeat ratings of the New York State Urban Development Corporation and the Washington Public Power Supply System in the face of obvious fiscal mismanagement.

More Winners

As investors scramble for safe bonds they increasingly insist on bond insurance or, in the euphemism of governments, "credit enhancement." In recent years over one-fourth of all bond issues carried such insurance. For this additional cachet of safety, the premium may run to hundreds of thousands of dollars. But lower interest rates may offset the additional cost in part.

Among the clear winners are building contractors, unions, and real estate developers. For them public authorities have been saviors. Federal outlays for nondefense capital construction peaked in the late 1970s. After 1972 state and local capital investment dropped precipitously. Looked at as a constant share of the gross national product (GNP), capital spending fell from 2 percent to 3 percent in 1960 to 1.1 percent in 1988. Yet enormous needs existed for affordable housing, repairs of a rotting infrastructure, and cleanup of the environment. Between 1990 and 2000 at least $1 trillion to $3 trillion will be required for these purposes, depending on the plausibility of the estimates one follows. Neither state nor local governments will be able to raise these funds through taxes. Only public authorities can do most of the job and for this they will need a basket of user fees. No wonder the builders, the workers, and the developers jumped with glee on the authority band wagon. As enormous profits and high wages poured in, they made icons of Robert Moses, Nelson Rockefeller, Jim Thompson, Michael Dukakis, and Felix Rohatyn, those individuals who fostered the hothouse growth of public authorities. They wined and dined with the heads of authorities who could easily contract for large and lucrative projects without governmental red tape and delays.

For politicians, many public authorities remain friendly sources of patronage. In many of the large authorities patronage really counts. It means lots of dollars and votes. But playful elected officials enjoy toying with small authorities as well. One such official was Thomas Whalen, a new-style, reform-minded mayor in Albany,

New York. The mayor soon discovered the advantages of authorities whose members he appointed and who were politically beholden to him. Moreover, he found that he could legally appoint himself as chairman of several authorities and expand his power base even more. In short order he headed an Industrial Development Authority, a Local Development Corporation, and a Parking Authority. Like Poobah in the *Mikado* he was a man of many hats. Incidentally, he also had a thriving law practice.

These strands came together when private interests were eager to redevelop a profitable downtown area. As mayor, Whalen approved the transfer of city-owned property to the Local Development Corporation (LDC). As chairman of LDC, he solicited proposals from developers. As chairman of the Industrial Development Authority (IDA), he approved a tax-exempt bond issue in behalf of the chosen developer. At the same time his law firm invested substantial sums in the project only to find that this practice violated federal regulations. It also negotiated a favorable lease for space in one of the newly developed buildings.

Except for his firm's investment, everything was of course perfectly legal and merely demonstrated the flexibility of the mayoralty. Equally legal was the mayor's participation in other loans of IDA while he was chairman from 1982 to 1985. During this period his law firm represented four clients who received loans ranging from $500,000 to $9 million. Not only did the mayor approve the loans, but, as a member of the law firm representing the applicants, he shared in the fees paid to the firm.

As head of the Parking Authority from 1983 to 1987 the mayor and his board rejected a low bid for the management of parking facilities and awarded the contract to a client of the mayor's firm. Apparently seeing no conflict of interest, the mayor participated in the vote.

These were some of the choice items examined by the New York State Commission on Integrity in Government in 1990. The commission found that existing laws did not bar such transactions, however questionable they may appear to be. So full of loopholes and ambiguities were the statutes that they fed rather than controlled the appetite for patronage.

Even more blatant was the easy-going style of Mayor Joseph

Alioto of San Francisco in the late 1970s. In 1976 the State of California had turned over the Port of San Francisco, an autonomous public enterprise, to the City of San Francisco. The mayor soon established firm control over the port by appointing the senior officials and treating it as an extension of city government. He persuaded the port to build a container terminal at its own expense for the Pacific Far East Line. What the mayor didn't disclose was that the Alioto family owned the steamship line. In a "sweetheart deal" the port charged the line below-market dockage rates, so low in fact that the new modern facility quickly ran up huge annual deficits. Despite this help from the city, the line went bankrupt in the late 1970s and owed the port more than $2.5 million in dockage fees. Alioto's political fortunes were damaged, but not his pocketbook.

The Port of Los Angeles competed vigorously for cargo with the Port of San Francisco. For years the L.A. port had been the personal fiefdom of Mayor Samuel Yorty even though the board members of the port were ostensibly independent. In mayoralty races of the late 1960s and early 1970, the challenger, Tom Bradley, charged Yorty with political manipulation of the port. During the Yorty regime two port commissioners had been convicted for bribery and one had drowned under suspicious circumstances. More than any other factor, the scandal led to Bradley's victory. Once he was safely ensconced in the mayor's seat, Bradley, too, began to intervene in every significant phase of the port's operation.[29]

The Losers of the Authority Game

So much for the winners and their handsome rewards. Last but most numerous are the losers.

At the bottom of the pyramid of public authority financing are those who pay: the users of authority services. And they pay and pay. Excluding federal aid, liquor store revenue, and untouchable trust revenue like retirement systems, state and local governments raise their own money from taxes, fees, and charges. Taxes are climbing, but fees are soaring even faster. In 1989–1990 fees and charges rose to 23.2 percent of the "own source" revenue of state governments ($85.8 billion of a total collection of $370 billion). For local governments fees came to 46 percent of combined taxes and fees ($184.5 billion of total collections of $343 billion). For every 54 cents in taxes, the local citizen pays 46 cents in charges. And fees and charges are beginning to overtake taxes at a rapid clip.[30]

Public authorities/special districts generate most of the fees and charges. According to the Bureau of the Census special districts alone raised nearly $51 billion in revenue in 1987 (the latest year for which data are available). And this figure, as we have stressed, may be a serious undercount. Even accepting it, note that over two-thirds of the revenues came from tolls, charges, and fees.[31]

Without these fees, capital construction and the repairs and replacement of the decaying infrastructure would screech to a halt. Fees and not taxes support about three-fourths of all capital financing in the United States.[32]

The hundreds of existing fees and charges are just the beginning as federal and state aid declines and the tax revolt intensifies. In the aftermath of Proposition 13, Sunnyvale, California, the pride of Silicon Valley, imposed over 400 user fees through special districts and public authorities. Now the fees account for over 40 percent of the city's revenue. Three-fourths of all local governments in the United States have followed Sunnyvale's example. Only their imagination limits likely sources of fees—and so far no one has accused them of a lack of inventiveness. Besides obvious charges for services, drunk drivers pay for processing their arrests; accident-prone drivers defray the cost of emergency services; developers pay impact fees; fire departments charge home owners for pumping water out of their basements; students pay fees for higher education loans as do would-be home owners looking for mortgages from public authorities. There are fees for pollution control, recreation, trash removal, fire inspections, misdemeanor convictions, new water systems, new sewer systems, ambulance services, libraries, and on and on. America has become the land of the fee.

How do fees affect individuals: the old, low-income and moderate-income groups, those on fixed incomes? No one knows. No one has yet taken on the massive task of analyzing the impact of pseudo-taxes—and that is what fees are. The shelves are full of sophisticated studies of the effects of personal income taxes, sales taxes, corporation taxes, payroll taxes, excise taxes on the poor, the middle class, the wealthy, businesses, and the economy. But no comprehensive analyses exist anywhere of the fastest growing source of revenue.

John Strahinich of *Boston Magazine* tried to fill this gap through shrewd estimates and anecdotage. Unfortunately, his example focused on a upscale family of four living in a bedroom community in Massachusetts and earning over $75,000 a year—hardly a typical family. The state tax bill for this family in 1989 came to $3,260; the assorted fees to public authorities totaled $1,288, or nearly 40 percent of the tax bill, as follows:[33]

State subsidies to authorities	$ 148
Massachusetts Water Resources Authority	201
Massachusetts Turnpike	461
Massport	51
Steamship Authority	68
Convention Center Authority	6
Lottery Commission	10
Victim and witness board	15
U Massachusetts Building Authority	266
MBTA	62
Total fees and charges	$1,288

Even so the authority fee bite is understated. The figures overlook the tax-free interest on bonds issued by industrial development, health-financing authorities, and educational-financing authorities. Whatever taxes the state and federal government lose must somehow be made up by the cozy family of four.

For blue-collar and white-collar families with an income of $25,000, authority fees and charges become a stifling burden. They get no special breaks and pay the same fees as their affluent suburban neighbors. Assume that these hardworking families owe a state tax of $1,000. Assume further that they have fewer luxuries, travel less, and cannot send their children to state colleges. Even in these straightened circumstances, their fees as a minimum would cost them about $825 or over 80 percent of their tax bill. Like the sales tax, the fees and charges of public authorities hit the working poor and the lower middle class disproportionately harder than they do the upper middle class and the wealthy.

As fees and charges increase and new fees spread, the burden on the poor and those with fixed incomes becomes even heavier. Now a dip in the swimming pool, a picnic in the park, a tennis game, or a visit to the zoo or museum costs money—a trifle for the middle class but a painful sum for the poor. Even worse, this becomes a deterrent to the use of recreational and cultural facilities by those who need them most.

For the first time the fairness and equity of authority fees and charges have become a hotly contested issue. Signs of a backlash by fee payers are appearing throughout the land. The battlelines are forming between those who would have general progressive taxes pay for the cost of nearly all government programs and those who view the services of public authorities as a special benefit for which only beneficiaries should pay. Between these extremes the compromisers are testing ways of lightening the burden on the poor through rebates, subsidies, special rates, and free tickets. Like tax reform, fee reform may soon reach the top of the political agenda.

Paradoxically, most voters prefer fees to taxes. Confused by taxes, they treasure the illusion that fees give them "a feeling of control They know where their money is going." John Shannon, former executive director of the Advisory Commission on Intergovernmental Relations, has tracked voter sentiment on taxes and fees over the years. "All of our public opinion polls indicate that when you confront citizens with their preference for raising revenue—user fees, property tax, local sales tax, local income tax—user fees win hands down, and that's what's kept this movement skipping right along," muses Shannon.

Yet Assistant City Manager John Shirey of Long Beach, California, has a "gut feeling" of a "coming backlash." Although he lacks empirical evidence, he suggests that the use of fees has peaked.[34]

For such evidence he could look to Boston and Denver. Just as Boston had the first tea party, so did it have the first fee party. In 1989 Barbara Anderson, executive director of Citizens for Limited Taxation (CLT) in Massachusetts, sounded the tocsin for the first fee revolt in the United States. A conservative, rabble-rousing anti-tax group, CLT collected enough signatures to place an initiative petition on the November 1990 ballot that would roll back fees and taxes to 1988 levels. From 1991 to 1993 public authority and state fees would drop by over $500 million dollars, and only the legislature would be able to approve any future fee increases.[35]

At this climactic moment the authority bond market was virtually paralyzed. No investors would buy bonds backed by a shaky and politically manipulated fee structure. While the fee rollback appeared to be patently unconstitutional as a breach of contract, bondholders had no stomach for time-consuming court challenges. In the 1990 election, the voters solved their dilemma by rejecting the rollbacks, albeit by a small margin.

The Colorado fee revolt was part of a complex and baffling initiative labeled "Amendment One." The brainchild of a veteran of California tax revolts and a migrant to Colorado, Douglas Bruce, the amendment would require a voter referendum for all fee, tax, and debt increases above the rate of inflation. Immediately tough questions surfaced. The new Denver Airport will cost about $2.3 billion. Would it be necessary to get voter approval for fee increases covering debt service and operating costs? Should library districts increase their fees above the rate of inflation, would they require consent of the electorate? Like its simpler Massachusetts counterpart, this initiative also failed in the November 1990 election.[36]

In this climate, governors have become queasy about approving fee increases even when they have the rare discretion to do so. For example, in 1990 the Port Authority of New York and New Jersey proposed an increase in round-trip tolls on its bridges and tunnels from $3 to $4 and a fare rise on the PATH train that runs between New York and New Jersey from $1 to $1.25. The increased revenue would fund some $300 million in essential projects. At this point Governor Jim Florio of New Jersey and Governor Mario Cuomo of New York became coy about endorsing the toll and fare hikes. Both men were still wincing from the backlash of budget deficits and higher taxes. Suddenly the new charges became the last straw. Governor Florio argued that higher fares would hurt poor commuters, and Governor Cuomo, uncharacteristically silent, stalled. In an Alphonse and Gaston act each governor waited for the other to move first.[37] Eventually, hand in hand, both governors simultaneously and quietly accepted the increase. Still the Port Authority held off on increasing the PATH fare.

When fare increases for subways and commuter railroads loom ahead, a delicately orchestrated political minuet starts. In Massachusetts the legislature and the governor blame the Massachusetts Bay Transportation Authority (MBTA). The MBTA cites rising costs, much of it patronage-driven. The passengers blame everyone. So do the local communities. Everybody's business becomes nobody's business, and the fares go up. In New York City, the Metropolitan Transportation Authority (MTA) takes the heat for fare increases. Indignant legislators check its books while a furious governor and mayor stand ready to draw a line in the sand. Civic groups and riders' organizations vent their spleen on slipshod management. After a customary catharsis lasting a few months and some feeble compromises, fares stagger upwards.

Once again the users are the losers. This is the dreary refrain not only in transportation, but also in economic development, housing, cleanup of the environment, power generation, repair of the infrastructure, health, and education. The succeeding chapters tell the stories, some edifying, some gory.

7

Bucking the
Economic Tide

The Massachusetts Miracle

For Governor Michael S. Dukakis the "Massachusetts economic miracle" was to be the launching pad for the presidency in 1988. His campaign staff invited opinion makers and columnists like David Broder to see firsthand what Dukakis had wrought. High on the itinerary was a trip to Lowell to observe how a dying milltown had become a dynamic high-tech center, with Wang Laboratories as the anchor. Next came the complex of bio-tech, computer, and financial service firms on Route 128 near Boston that rivaled Silicon Valley in California and the Triangle Research Park in North Carolina. Finally, the trip included obligatory stops in Taunton, Worcester, and other cities to gaze at the economic revival of decayed textile, paper and shoe towns.

The message was clear. Massachusetts had the know-how. As Alden S. Raine, Dukakis' former secretary of economic affairs, put it, "The slogan was, we know how to do it." Once he was president, Dukakis would export the Massachusetts miracle to the rest of the country.

As Dukakis loyalists tell the tale, Massachusetts was at death's door—a veritable Appalachia—when he first became governor in 1974. In the deepest recession since 1933, unemployment had soared to over 12 percent compared with a national average of 8.5 percent. In the inner cities it had reached 20 percent. Approximately one of five jobs had vanished. By 1986, in Dukakis' third term, the state economy had turned around dramatically. Unemployment dropped to 3.8 percent in contrast to a national average of 7 percent. The number of jobs climbed to a new high. Per capita income topped the national average by 15 percent. And Dukakis made the difference, according to his partisans.

In the Dukakis legend the turning point came when he appointed a Capital Formation Task Force in 1976. Composed of influential administrators, legislators, and academics, the task force spelled out the ingredients of the economic miracle. A statewide strategy of economic development targeted at specific distressed areas. A package of loans, loan guarantees, subsidies, tax incentives, technical assistance, and regulatory relief, primarily for small firms. The creation of 10 public authorities as the engines of economic development. Taken together, these aggressive measures would lure new business to the state, retain and expand existing firms, and encourage the startup of new small firms. They would jumpstart a sick economy, create new jobs, and accelerate private investment.

Above all the new public authorities would be the key to economic development. With their access to tax-free bond financing, they would have resources that dwarfed state and local grants, subsidies, and tax concessions. In short order the Dukakis brain trust completed blueprints for the following public authorities:

- The Massachusetts Industrial Financing Authority (MIFA), a state investment bank with the capability of issuing billions of dollars of tax-exempt and taxable bonds for manufacturing and commercial firms and nonprofit organizations.
- The Massachusetts Community Development Finance Corporation (CDFC), a state-owned venture capital company seeded with $12.5 million in state appropriations. Working with local community development corporations (CDCs) and the Community Economic Development Assistance Corporation (CEDAC), CDFC would finance real estate development and other projects that commercial lenders would not touch.
- The Massachusetts Capital Resource Corporation (MCRC), with $100 million in risk capital for marginal firms provided by eight private insurance companies that would get an equivalent amount of tax breaks from the state.

- The Massachusetts Land Bank (MLB) that could issue up to $40 million in state-backed debt for the commercial and industrial development of surplus federal and state land.

- The Massachusetts Product Development Corporation (MPDC) that, with state funds, would encourage "mature" industries, on the verge of extinction, to develop new and improved products.

- The Massachusetts Technology Development Corporation (MTDC), with $2.2 million in state funds, $7.7 million in private funds, and grants by the U.S. Economic Development Administration for loans to small high-tech firms.

- The Massachusetts Technology Park Corporation (MTPC), with state-guaranteed short-term notes of $3.5 million for the development of high-tech industrial parks.

- The Massachusetts Centers of Excellence Corporation (MCEC) for the distribution of state grants mainly to universities for applied research.

- The Bay State Skills Corporation (BSSC), with state appropriations for job training of displaced workers.

- The Massachusetts Thrift Fund, with a pool of $100 million of private bank funds for direct loans to small businesses.

- The Massachusetts Business Development Corporation that pooled state and private funds for loans to small and medium-sized businesses unable to borrow money from conventional sources.

- The Massachusetts Convention Center Authority (MCCA), financed by $200 million of state-backed bonds, to attract trade conventions and tourists to the Boston area.

In this constellation of economic development authorities no star blazed more brightly than MIFA. By 1990 it boasted that it had issued over $5.3 billion in tax-exempt and taxable bonds to finance about 2,400 manufacturing, commercial, and nonprofit institution projects that created nearly 80,000 jobs. Among its prize catches were Reebok International, Cape Cod Potato Chips, the Crane Paper Company, the Coppus Engineering Corp., the Olektron Corp., and the Magnesium Casting Company. The default rate on loans was 2 percent to 3 percent until 1990, when it crept up to nearly 5 percent. But no state money was at risk.

Ever entrepreneurial, MIFA survived the severe federal cutback in the issuance of industrial revenue bonds in 1986. In a power grab, it persuaded the legislature in 1988 to let it finance nonprofit educational and cultural institutions. Previously, the use of tax-exempt bonds for this purpose had been the exclusive turf of the Massachusetts Health and Educational Facilities Authority (HEFA). Capitalizing quickly on its new power, MIFA issued over $1.2 billion in tax-exempt bonds by 1990, mainly for private colleges, research centers, theaters, and museums. It pioneered in the use of taxable bonds and built up a reserve of about $30 million to guarantee bank loans to private firms. It expanded the use of taxable short-term debt for small firms. To encourage investors to buy such "commercial paper," it backed up the notes with letters of credit from foreign banks. It steered Massachusetts companies to the U.S. Export-Import Bank for guarantees of the repayment of exports. It persuaded state pension funds to buy taxable bonds.

MIFA was a money maker and didn't cost the state a penny. In contrast, the state paid the debt service for the Government Land Bank and the Convention Center Authority. From the start the Community Development Finance Corporation was a loser and dissipated nearly 38 percent of the state's investment in small companies. The other economic development authorities were far smaller than MIFA and depended on state and private funding.

Despite the best efforts of the state and the public authorities, the Massachusetts miracle evaporated by 1990. In a severe economic recession that afflicted all of New England, Massachusetts was hit especially hard. The high-tech firms dotting Route 128 suffered heavy losses. Banks failed and the financial services industry was in the doldrums. Retail sales plummeted while the peace dividend that was supposed to follow the end of the cold war brought no peace to Massachusetts. In fact, it resulted in the loss of $8 billion in primary defense contracts, not to mention heavy losses of secondary and tertiary contracts. State tax collections fell drastically. In 1989 and 1990 the budget deficit rose to nearly $2 billion and, in a bitter political battle, Dukakis and the legislature increased taxes by $1 billion a year.

In the declining days of his administration in 1990, Dukakis once again turned to public authorities as a savior to "get them through the next ten years." Before he left office, he attempted to initiate some $14.2 billion in authority-financed massive public works projects including the $8-billion cleanup of Boston Harbor by the Massachusetts Water Resources Authority; the $5-billion "Big Dig" by the Massachusetts Turnpike to construct a third tunnel to Logan Airport and a new artery to replace the congested downtown expressway; a $200-million expansion of Logan Airport by the Massachusetts Port Authority; and a $2-billion capital program for the Massachusetts Bay Transportation Authority. These would stimulate the state economy and lead to a second Massachusetts miracle according to the lame duck Dukakis cabinet.

But the days of the miracle maker were over. So low had Dukakis fallen in public esteem that he was now demonized. The ballyhoo, hyperbole, and inflated claims about the Massachusetts miracle backfired. More objective critics realized that Dukakis was no more responsible for the state's superb economic performance in the 1980s during his administration than he was for the deepening recession of 1989 and 1990. Like all other governors he was at the mercy of economic and political forces at both the national and global level that were beyond his control. Even in his heyday the state government played at best a marginal role through the public authorities in the resurgence of the economy. Here and there they tipped the balance in retaining old firms and attracting new ones by fostering a climate more beneficial to business. They were part of a coordinated approach to economic development.[1] These were useful incremental steps, but they were not the stuff that turns an economy around at the state level.

The Dukakis story is not much different from the story of Governor George Deukmejian in California, Governor Thomas Kean in New Jersey, Governor Robert P. Casey in Pennsylvania, Governor James Thompson in Illinois, Governor Robert Martinez in Florida, and Governor Mario Cuomo in New York. All ran for the governorship with stirring slogans about controlling crime and creating jobs. They could do neither any more than King Canute could roll back the sea tides. Yet they deluded themselves into thinking that the economic development authorities would revitalize state economies. Politically, they had no choice. They had to present an image of dynamic job creators, no matter what.

The State Economic Development Apparatus

To perpetuate the illusion of state leadership in economic development, political leaders offer multibillion-dollar bonanzas to industrial and commercial firms. Now all states have industrial development authorities like MIFA in Massachusetts, the Urban Development Corporation in New York State, the Economic Development Authority in New Jersey, the Illinois Development Finance Authority, the Utah Technology Finance Corporation, the Kentucky Development Finance Authority, and the State of Washington Economic Assistance Authority. Through tax-exempt (and, to a minor extent, taxable) industrial revenue bonds they provide loans to private firms at below-market interest rates. Nearly all states have hundreds of local industrial development authorities that use low-cost loans to lure firms to start or expand a business. While the Tax Reform Act of 1986 clipped their wings by curtailing sharply the issuance of tax-exempt industrial bonds for private purposes, they still dispense hundreds of millions of dollars of tax-exempt bonds. Even if the interest on a bond issue is taxable by the federal government, invariably the state or local government softens the blow by exempting the recipients of loans from sales and property taxes.

These inducements top a long gift list, full of sugar plums, offered by public authorities and state and local governments to industrial and commercial firms:[2]

- Direct loans in 28 states
- Loan guarantees in 31 states to coax banks to lend money to private firms
- Grants in 14 states
- Venture capital provided by public authorities and nonprofit private corporations in 38 states
- Export assistance in 33 states
- Enterprise zones in the inner cities of 31 states that attempt to attract entrepreneurs through tax breaks and job training programs

- Loans and loan guarantees to farmers and agribusiness in farm-belt states like Illinois, Wisconsin, and Kentucky
- Tax incentives that cut income taxes for business in 45 states, sales taxes in 50 states, and property taxes in 49 states
- Grants for research and development in 39 states
- "Incubators" (some 450) that provide low-cost space and services to budding businesses in 39 states
- Investments by state pension bonds in industrial development bonds in several states
- Nonfinancial attractions such as job training programs; technical assistance in arranging loans and starting businesses; a steady flow of business and economic data; marketing programs; and "regulatory relief" from "burdensome" state controls over the environment, pollution, and conditions at the workplace. (All states offer combinations of such noncash incentives.)

Alluring as this is, it is not enough. Without affordable and abundant energy, a reliable water supply, a trained workforce, and a solid infrastructure in place, entrepreneurs will resist such blandishments. Consequently, public authorities and governments in all states are feverishly rebuilding and expanding their highways, bridges, public transit, wastewater and solid waste treatment plants, airports, seaports, and industrial parks.

For many states tourism is still one of the magic keys to economic development. Besides exploiting their natural wonders, the states use public authorities to develop civic centers, exposition halls, convention centers, sports stadiums, and historic sites. The rush of tourists, it is hoped, will more than offset the heavy development costs in New York, Illinois, Massachusetts, California, and other states.

Dragging its feet every step of the way, the federal government reluctantly assists the states in economic development. After blossoming in the 1960s and 1970s, economic development program funds were shredded by the Reagan and Bush administrations. The key sources of direct loans and loan guarantees for small businesses had been the Small Business Administration (SBA), the Economic Development Administration (EDA), and the Export-Import

Bank (EIB), the latter a federal government corporation. In addition, the Department of Housing and Urban Development had channeled Urban Development Action Grants (UDAGs) to local authorities for the revitalization of the inner city.

Most of these agencies were early targets for termination by the Reagan administration. UDAG expired. Unable to eliminate the Small Business Administration, the Economic Development Administration, and the Appalachian Regional Commission, President Reagan gutted them.

The effects were swift and traumatic. From 1980 to 1989 the budget of the Small Business Administration skidded from $16.2 billion to $100 million. Direct loans fell by 76 percent to some $90 million. Loan guarantees plummeted to $2.4 billion. A venture capital loan program approximated $600 million a year. EDA loans and grants withered. Although considerably shrunk, the Export-Import Bank makes some loans to small business, but mainly guarantees and insures commercial bank loans for exports against business and political risks. The guarantees total less than $1 billion a year.[3]

For the states the keystone in the arch of economic development is the tax-exempt industrial revenue bond. Compared to the billions of dollars of bond funds channeled to small firms, all other state contributions are paltry, amounting to less than $1 billion a year. But the keystone is crumbling against the onslaughts of a Congress and president haunted by budget deficits.

From small beginnings in the 1930s industrial development bonds soared to a new high of nearly $58 billion in 1985, the year before tax reform.[4] Eager state and local economic development authorities raised these billions and turned them over to private manufacturing and commercial firms, real estate developers, operators of airports and docks, sewage and waste disposal systems, and companies forced to adopt pollution control equipment. In the jargon of Congress, these were "private activity" bonds.

The recipients of these loans knew a good thing when they saw it. None could resist borrowing funds at an interest rate 2 percent to 3 percent below that of taxable corporate bonds. Everyone seemed to benefit. Seemingly, it was an operation without risk—a free lunch. Although a public authority loaned funds to private entrepreneurs, it was not responsible for repayment of the bond debt. With nothing at stake, the public authorities in most states were relaxed about the loans they made.

Now and then the U.S. Treasury and members of Congress grumbled about the billions of dollars of revenue that were lost because interest on the bonds was tax exempt. The bond users countered by pointing to the new jobs they had created and to the federal taxes generated by those jobs. What the federal government lost in taxes on interest, it more than made up in income taxes from the new jobs, the public authorities claimed.

Soon the bubble burst. Large and profitable commercial, industrial, and retail firms that could easily borrow money from banks at market rates of interest found to their delight that they, too, were eligible for low-interest loans from industrial development authorities. Companies such as K Mart, McDonalds, Wendy's, Proctor and Gamble, Friendly, and motel chains became avid users of industrial revenue bonds and tapped them to build stores in shopping centers outside of the cities. These moves snared jobs from the downtown business district, the very jobs public authorities vowed to protect. Large utilities that could afford conventional bank loans also turned to tax-exempt bonds to finance pollution control equipment.

Waving the banner of economic development, local public authorities lent $5 million to a breeder of thoroughbred horses in Long Island, New York, $400,000 to an "adult" bookstore and topless bar in Philadelphia, and about $2 million to an entertainment center in Tennessee.[5] Imaginative ventures of this type flourished. Mismanaged, many of the enterprises failed and defaulted on the payment of their debt; between 1980 and 1988 some 300 defaults occurred. Nearly half were industrial development bonds and about one-third bonds for retirement centers and nursing homes.[6] At the same time the federal government lost about $20 billion in revenue annually because of "private purpose" tax-exempt bonds.

Finally, Congress had enough. In 1986 it approved the Tax Reform Act of 1986 that, among other measures, outlawed tax exemption altogether for some private activity bonds such as those for hotels, motels, retail stores, and pollution control and imposed a ceiling or volume cap on the rest. For each state the ceiling is $50 per capita or $150 million, whichever is greater. As of 1989 the national ceiling totaled $15.2 billion. California's volume cap was $1.5 billion, New York's $898 million, Texas' $850 million, Pennsylvania's $602 million. Most of the less populated states had $150-million limits. How the states carve up the volume cap is entirely up to them. Unless the states act otherwise, the cap is divided between the state and local governments. Each government picks its own formula for allocating tax-exempt bonds under the ceiling: the percent that goes for small manufacturing and commercial firms, housing, solid waste disposal, energy, and student loans.[7] For example, California favors small manufacturing firms and low-income housing. Georgia divides the bonds between economic development and housing. The unused portion of the volume cap can be carried forward three years.

Predictably, the volume of tax-exempt private activity bonds for manufacturing, housing, airports, student loans, sewage and waste disposal, and pollution control contracted. From the high of $58 billion in 1985, it fell to nearly $12 billion in 1986 and about $18 billion in 1988. Industrial development bonds limited solely to small manufacturing and commercial firms dropped from about $5.8 billion in 1986 to $4.4 billion in 1990.[8]

To what extent did "tax reform" set back economic development? Oddly enough, no one knows even though industrial development bonds are the heart of the strategy for job creation in all states. To what extent does the entire cornucopia of financial, tax, and nonfinancial incentives stimulate state economies? At best marginally according to studies all over the country. In struggling with this question, Marianne K. Clarke of the National Governors' Association concluded: "Hard data documenting job generation results is scant. Evaluation tools are sparsely used and the result is that currently it is difficult to assess what works best."[9] Roger Wilson of the Council of State Governments agrees: "Business incentives have little influence over industrial location decisions." He cites surveys in New England and Ohio that found that "Taxes and financial inducements seem to be at best tie-breakers acting between otherwise 'equal' towns or sites. These traditional linchpins of state and local industrial development simply cannot be relied on by themselves to attract new plants that would otherwise locate somewhere else."[10]

John Herbers, a highly respected economist, arrived at the same dismal conclusion: "In the long history of these efforts, disappointment has often overshadowed success. . . . Little is known about which kinds of public investment bring the best return in economic development."[11]

Contrary to conventional wisdom, tax breaks and low-cost capital are at the bottom of any list of incentives that lure businesses to a specific area. Yet, these are the very items that governors and legislatures favor. What private firms look for primarily are a skilled workforce, a transportation network that gives them easy access to markets and suppliers, abundant energy and water, and convenient and affordable housing for their executives and employees. Lawrence Litvak and Belden Daniels of the Council of State Planning Agencies found that "the real forces which determine whether or not a state is an attractive place to invest are the enormous interregional and international shifts taking place in populations, purchasing power, labor supply, energy and raw materials in real goods markets on a worldwide basis. . . . Profound world economic forces and federal government actions constrain the ability of states to affect economic activity through policy of any kind, let alone capital market ones."[12]

A True Believer in Illinois

Nonetheless, heads in the sand, political leaders remain convinced, despite all the evidence to the contrary, that the old tools of economic development work. Big Jim Thompson, governor of Illinois, was one such true believer. Casting about for solutions to declining smokestack industries, high unemployment, and dozens of distressed areas, Thompson followed the Dukakis model between 1977 and 1983. He inspired the creation of eight state economic development authorities and four Chicago venture capital corporations. His centerpiece was the Illinois Development Finance Authority. Other inducements followed quickly: state loans and subsidies, a stepped up infrastructure construction program, even more tax incentives, and a variety of state-funded training programs.

One of Thompson's critics described the birthpangs of economic development Thompson-style "You've got to keep in mind that a lot of these authorities were created at the time Illinois was coming out of a recession. The recession put the state in such off balance position that they were willing to try any gimmick that came along. Almost any proposal that was offered was accepted."

Among the recipients of Thompson's bounty were Sears Roebuck and Company, the Chrysler Corporation, the Caterpillar Corporation, and Keystone Steel. The Sears case is especially revealing of the desperate measures a state will take to retain a business. In 1988 and 1989 word spread that Sears was going to pull out of the Chicago Loop and look for a cheaper location for its headquarters. Sears hinted that Texas or North Carolina looked especially attractive. That was enough to get the state to twist its laws and offer Sears a seductive package of benefits: a suitable site for relocation in the affluent suburb of Hoffman Estates, 35 miles northwest of Chicago; some $61 million in state and authority money to prepare the site and build highways leading to it; a designation of the town as an enterprise zone to make Sears eligible for tax abatements and other incentives ordinarily reserved to lure businesses to depressed areas; and tax increment financing (TIF), normally a scheme applicable only to companies willing to relocate in the inner cities. For Sears this meant the acquisition of an 800-acre site valued at $100 million. In exchange for this outright gift Sears agreed to pay property taxes on the developed land. Illinois used industrial revenue bonds to buy the land and paid them off with Sears' property taxes.[13]

Furious at the misuse of enterprise zones and tax incentive financing designed for inner cities, 14 black legislators in the Illinois house of representatives tried to block the giveaways for Sears. Their spokesman, Anthony Young from Chicago's west side, called it "a double slap in the face. Sears could have gotten the same kind of incentives in the west side without any legislation. Now anybody who talks about leaving Illinois will be coming for a tax break."

Jay Hedges, director of the Illinois Department of Commerce and Community Affairs that orchestrates economic development in the state, admitted that calling Hoffman Estates a blighted area was "a loose description of blight, a very loose description. We reached into our bag of tricks and offered what we had to close the deal. . . . You don't get one of these projects coming along but once in a decade. Are these just giveaways? No. Our goal is to keep these jobs."

"Our choice was to watch them go or help them stay," argued Jeffrey Johnson, who directs the state's enterprise zone program. He, Hedges, and the governor's staff raised the hobgoblin that the flight of Sears, the largest private employer in the state, would mean the loss of 7,600 jobs, $400 million per year in salaries, and $19 million in taxes.[14]

Whether or not Sears was practicing "industrial blackmail" by playing off one state against another or was serious about its exodus from the state is a moot question. Its tactics worked, and the luscious deal was concluded in the summer of 1989. In the meantime the blighted areas of Chicago designated as enterprise zones remained abandoned and decayed. The state's abuse of programs intended for the inner city hastened the decay.

General Motors proved to be less susceptible to the state's wooing. Despite a basket of tax-free delights offered by the state, GM succumbed to the even greater charms of Tennessee as the ideal location for manufacturing the Saturn car. Some 5,000 jobs were at stake.

Governor Thompson took this as a personal affront and vowed "never again." When the Chrysler Corporation and Mitsubishi were looking for a site for their Diamond Star plant, a joint venture with about 2,400 employees, the governor flew to Japan to sell the attractions of Illinois as did 30 other governors for their states, and, more important, proffered a package of benefits worth about $400 million. Chrysler and Mitsubishi grabbed these giveaways:

- Free land and financing for land improvements
- Construction and improvements of roads
- Construction and remodeling of water and sewage systems
- Exemptions from state and local utility taxes
- Exemptions from state and local sales taxes on building materials, pollution control facilities, and equipment and materials required in the manufacturing process
- Investment tax credits
- Job income tax credits
- Pollution control bonds offered by the Illinois Development Finance Authority

- Designation of the area as an incentive zone
- Job training assistance,[15]

Thriving under such "TLC," the Diamond Star Motors Plant opened in downstate Bloomington Normal in 1985 at a time when Chrysler was showing record profits. The state-local investment cost $40,000 to $50,000 per job in contrast to the usual rule-of-thumb that government investments should not exceed $5,000 per job. As Chrysler's sales tumbled in the late 1980s, the new enterprise began to flounder and the state's investment looked exceedingly shaky. What many critics of the state's largess feared came to pass as many employees were laid off.

The state again became Lady Bountiful when General Electric planned to shut down its factory in Cicero, Illinois, in the 1990s and to spend $160 million to expand its plant in Decatur, Alabama. This time, though, GE rejected the usual welcome wagon full of gifts. It claimed that tax breaks, wages, and productivity had no bearing on the decision. The sole reason for the move was the opportunity to consolidate resources and develop new manufacturing technology. After the decision was already made, GE eagerly negotiated extensive benefits with the state and local governments in Alabama: a state construction loan of $10 million at 2 percent interest; $20 million in tax-exempt industrial revenue bonds issued by the local Industrial Development Authority (IDA) in Decatur; undetermined millions to build roads near the plants; and nearly $1 million to train 700 new employees.[16]

The GE setback was merely a blip in an ever upward spiral of job creation according to the elaborate state bureaucracy that promotes economic development. Puffed with pride, the Illinois Development Finance Authority, with authorization to issue $3.5 billion in industrial revenue bonds, cites the nearly 25,000 jobs it had created or retained since its establishment in 1983. This was merely part of the 200,000 new jobs claimed by all Thompson public authorities and the Department of Commerce and Community Affairs. With dizzying speed they reel off hundreds of triumphs like Belleville Shoe Manufacturing Company, the Laserage Technology Corporation, the University Micro Electronics Center, Zenith Electronics Corporations, and on and on.

Piercing through this fog of self-congratulation, Robert G. Cranson, the auditor general of Illinois, lays out the facts. Over 90 percent of all applications for loans, subsidies, tax incentives, and grants are casually approved. Local industrial development authorities are out of control. No followup exists to see if jobs were actually created while double and triple counting of new jobs takes place. New jobs in one area may be offset by jobs displaced elsewhere. This was sheer heresy to the governor's staff, who castigated Cranson as antieconomic development.[17]

In a major study of economic development in Illinois in 1990, the Illinois Economic and Fiscal Commission (IEFC), the chief research arm of the legislature, shared many of Cranson's views. It disconcerted the Thompson administration by finding that "there is no statistical evidence that business incentives actually create jobs. The presence or absence of such incentives is not a primary influence in a business location decision." IEFC bolstered its case with hard data. From 1969 to 1989 nonagricultural employment growth nationally had climbed 54.3 percent. In Illinois it had risen only 18.3 percent, one-third of the national pace, not enough to keep up with a new crop of job seekers. For the industrial sector producing private goods the record was dismal. Between 1947 and 1989, it had lost about 234,000 jobs in the face of an upward trend for the nation as a whole.

IEFC searched for basic causes that froze job expansion in Illinois. It discovered that Thompson's economic strategy was almost irrelevant. What hit industry hard was its aging plants and equipment, its costly energy requirements, and its inability to cope with the ups and down of the business cycle and foreign competition.[18]

Roger J. Vaughan, an observant monitor of state economies, concluded that Illinois' economic developments took place in spite of government actions and not because of them.[19]

Despite the spate of public authorities, tax breaks, low-interest loans, loan guarantees, grants, land giveaways, and customized roads and sewers for favored firms, Thompson was as impotent as Dukakis in bucking the economic tide. After he left office in 1991, his legacy was billions of dollars of debt, hundreds of millions of dollars of unnecessary expenditures, and few new jobs to show for his efforts.

New York's Quest for Jobs

Mario M. Cuomo outbid all governors in his quest for jobs. State and local economic development authorities flourished as never before with the Urban Development Corporation and the Job Development Authority the linchpins of economic revival. The Port Authority of New York and New Jersey and the Power Authority of New York State also initiated new programs to stimulate the state's economy. Even as the state's multibillion-dollar deficits exploded, the governor added more funds in the budget for grants, loans, subsidies, and appropriations for at least 18 programs designed to create jobs. By 1990–1991 the state's contribution alone reached nearly $100 million for the Urban Development Corporation, the Science and Technology Foundation, the Department of Economic Development, 19 economic development zones, and several regional development corporations. This was quite apart from the billions of dollars raised by state and local public authorities.

To harmonize these scattered efforts, Cuomo appointed as "economic czar" Vincent Tese, a wealthy former trader in commodities. Tese wore four hats: commissioner of economic development, chairman of the Urban Development Corporation, chairman of the Job Development Authority, and chairman of the Science and Technology Foundation, which was supposed to hatch future IBMs, Eastman Kodaks, and Xeroxs. In a grand gesture Tese contributed his salary to charitable organizations and took on his many assignments with zest and belligerence.

After eight years of his war on economic decay, Governor Cuomo boasted, with his usual passionate rhetoric, that his administration had created 1 million jobs. Tese joined him in these claims: "We hardly need apologize for the programs and the results, more than one million new jobs in seven years and hundreds of millions of dollars in investment in poorer communities." For critics who were skeptical about his claims, he had a barbed reply: "As the Governor likes to say any jackass can kick down a barn. It takes good people to build one."[20]

The governor was especially irascible when reporters looked in vain for the new jobs and cited the high unemployment rate in New York State. His standard repartee was that the state's economy would have been far worse without his intervention. Still he couldn't squash some stubborn facts: a loss of 200,000 manufacturing jobs since he had assumed office in 1983; a further loss of 46,000 jobs between 1989 and 1990; and the failure to win back the 247,000 jobs lost in the pre-Cuomo years between 1974 and 1982.[21]

In the recession of 1991 the governor's earlier optimistic message of 1986 suddenly became hollow: "Two years ago, I presented my initial program to rebuild New York. As you can tell from the recovery I have just described, that program has worked. Jobs are up, taxes are down and New York has resumed its place at the leading edge of our nation's economic progress." Confronted later by doubters who had the poor taste to remind him of these inspiring words, he blamed the fiscal and monetary policies of the federal government for the plight of the state. Like any other governor he took the credit for new jobs when times were good and made Washington, D.C., a scapegoat for hard times.

The governor's flagship in economic development was the Urban Development Corporation (UDC). After its default in 1975, UDC abandoned its mission to provide low-cost housing and took refuge in the safer seas of small business promotion, the construction of prisons and convention centers, and the redevelopment of rundown areas like Times Square. So diverse were its activities that it became a conglomerate with several subsidiaries: the Times Square Development Corporation; the Convention Center Development Corporation (jointly with the Triborough Bridge Area Tunnel Authority); the Mortgage Loan Enforcement and Administration Corporation; the Harlem Urban Development Corporation; the Western New York Economic Development Corporation.[22]

In the dark days of UDC's collapse, Governor Hugh L. Carey had appointed Richard Ravitch, a successful real estate developer in New York City, to head the authority. Ravitch restored UDC to solvency with a heavy infusion of state money and a record of partiality to favored contractors and consultants. To prop up UDC's sagging reputation, Governor Cuomo chose William J. Stern as its chairman in 1983. Stern stayed only two years and left in a blaze of self-congratulation. In parting, he stressed that Governor Cuomo had asked him to "transform the UDC from a place noted for its ability to deliver lucrative contracts to a few well-placed New Yorkers to an effective tool for creating jobs and wealth for all New Yorkers. We have accomplished that goal. We have begun more economic development projects, created more jobs, realized more dreams than any of us imagined we could."[23]

Once he was safely out of the combat zone, Stern revealed the truth as he saw it, although it took him two years to arrive at his revelation. He urged the outright abolition of the Urban Development Corporation and the Job Development Authority. This, he claimed, would be an important first step in getting the state out of the business of helping business. "We can never make intelligent decisions on something like that [subsidies]," he argued, citing a number of shaky projects. "Why not let the market decide. This has never been debated, just grown up, willy-nilly."[24]

When Tese presided over UDC, starting in 1985, he focused even more than his predecessors had on economic development. In a stream of interviews and press releases, he gloried in the "brand-new jobs" that UDC had created or the old jobs that had been retained.

Again, the record doesn't support such ballyhoo. Many of the new jobs turned out to be mirages or else jobs that would have materialized without UDC's interventions. UDC construction contracts generated new jobs, but these were short-term in nature.[25] In some touch-and-go situations UDC served as a catalyst in attracting some new firms or retaining and expanding businesses already in New York. But the figures churned out by UDC were characteristically unreliable and inflated.

Even minor triumphs were offset by investments that backfired. In a highly touted move, UDC and its affiliates put together a $17-million loan and subsidy package to lure a $100-million Toshiba–Westinghouse picture tube factory to Horseheads in the depressed Southern Tier of the state. Some 800 jobs were at stake. What UDC didn't foresee was that the new plant would lead directly to the loss of 700 jobs at GE's picture tube plant in Syracuse. Unable to compete with the government-subsidized and technologically advanced Toshiba–Westinghouse factory, GE closed its plant in 1987. Tese was casual about this turn of events and claimed GE intended to close its plant no matter what. "At least those jobs are in New York," he consoled worried citizens in Syracuse. "The bottom line is that project Toshiba-Westinghouse is a winner."[26]

Long on hyperbole, UDC was short on results, and the price of its survival was high. From the time of its near demise in 1975 through 1981 it drained the state of over $500 million billion dollars. During the next 10 years, it again came close to this figure. As late as 1991 the state provided $42 million. Legally, most of the appropriations are repayable, but no such miracle appears to be in sight.

The Job Development Authority (JDA) proudly calls itself "New York State's Economic Development Bank." Few banks are as soft-hearted in approving loans and loan guarantees. Since 1961 the voters have authorized it to issue $600 million in bonds for small businesses and in 1991 raised its bonding capacity to $900 million. This by itself is a rare phenomenon since voters generally have no voice in the finances of most public authorities. Proceeds from the tax-exempt bonds are used for low-interest loans and loan guarantees to companies eager to expand facilities, build new plants, and acquire machinery and equipment. Loan applications to JDA are screened by over 100 nonprofit local development corporations (LDCs) to take local concerns into account.

In its annual glossy report JDA ticks off its success stories. State Comptroller Edward Regan and several investigative reporters are not impressed. Their probes and audits show that most loan recipients fail to create the number of jobs they promised and that JDA rarely validates its job data. The default rate on loans approximates 2 percent, and the tales of failure match those in any other state. After its own investigations, the Albany *Times Union* thundered: "If the JDA is not creating jobs—really creating them and not just granting loans to companies that would have increased its number of employed anyway—it has no value. And it should be dismantled."[27]

Defending JDA's record as a creator of jobs, Robert Dormer, president of JDA, argued: "They [the companies] might be short of their projections, but they're still in many cases higher than their original employment. In other words a guy says he has 100 people working today, he says he's going to have 200 jobs in three years, he's got 150. He's short of his projection, but he's still increased jobs. How do we demonstrate that without the JDA loan, this thing might have happened anyway. That's probably the toughest thing to really get a fix on."[28]

IDAs

Compared to the 155 local industrial authorities (IDAs) in New York State, UDC and JDA are paragons of conservative banking virtues. In the easygoing pre-tax reform days the IDAs dispensed tax-free bond proceeds to any and all comers. On the eve of the Tax Reform Act of 1986 they had issued about $1.2 billion of these bonds. After Congress sharply curtailed the volume of bonds intended for private purposes, bond issuances fell precipitously to a mere $144 million in 1988.

Only slightly taken aback, the IDAs began to sell taxable bonds. In fact in 1988 the volume of taxable bonds was five times the amount of tax-free bonds—$687 million versus $144 million.[29] Knowing a good thing when they saw it, supermarkets, shopping centers, restaurants, real estate developments, and utilities snapped up the bond proceeds with relish. They had quickly learned the well kept secret that the recipients of even the taxable bond proceeds enjoyed numerous state and local tax breaks: no personal income tax on the bond interest; no property taxes; no 8 percent sales taxes on equipment and materials; exemptions from sales taxes on operating expenses; no mortgage recording tax; no federal restrictions on projects; long-term loans; and loopholes on taxes.

Belatedly, the state government in 1991 became aware of the loss of millions of dollars of potential income at a time when it had a record-breaking deficit of over $6 billion. Conceding that he had no firm figures on the losses, James W. Wetzler, commissioner of taxation and finance, complained: "We really do not have an estimate. It might be surprising, but that's really the whole point. Here's a government program conducted through the tax system—a tax expenditure—about which we have no control or not even any knowledge of how much it's being utilized."[30]

The results were bizarre. One supermarket chain, Price Chopper, enjoyed a harvest of IDA funding and tax breaks. Competitive Grand Union stores did not. Through subsidies the state and local governments often favored one competitor against another. Another company, Fagliarone Grimaldi and Associates in Syracuse, acted as an agent of the local IDA and conferred tax benefits on its own suppliers.

Runaway IDAs might be tolerated if they produce jobs. Yet, no one knows how many jobs they have created or saved or, indeed, whether they have created or saved any.[31] What is certain is that many defaults and abuses dog IDAs every step of the way. For example, in 1990 investors in the New York Muni Fund, a money market fund specializing in tax-exempt municipal bonds, learned that the value of their shares had dropped about 7 percent because of defaults by two major retail stores funded by the Niagara Falls IDA. Both had borrowed nearly $14 million from the IDA. Such defaults cover the state.

The entire IDA funding process is "vulnerable to fraud and favoritism" according to the New York State Commission on Government Integrity. In all corners of the state the commission found evidence of conflicts of interest and lack of oversight by IDAs. The Roosevelt Raceway, a once-premier harness track in Hempstead, Long Island, illustrates these abuses. In 1984, a group of investors, the Roosevelt Raceway Associates, obtained a loan of $54 million through the Hempstead Industrial Development Authority. Their avowed purpose was to buy and refurbish the 172-acre race track and restore it to its former glory. In 1988 the track failed and closed, a victim of deliberate neglect by the owners according to the Standard Breed Owners Association. The way was open for the investors to sell the land zoned for industrial use and now valued at $200 million. After repaying the loan, the owners would reap a profit of $150 million. This triggered investigations of misrepresentation and tax fraud by county, state, and federal law enforcement officials. The IDA shrugged off these events and protested that its sole responsibility was to protect the bondholders.[32]

Long Island was the scene of another IDA fiasco. The Nassau County IDA and the Hempstead IDA raised $155 million in tax-exempt bonds for real estate developers to convert Mitchell Field, a county-owned former airport, into a commercial zone. While the developers did not own the land outright, they secured 99-year leases with minimal or no rents. In defiance of conflict of interest laws, the developers, their attorneys, IDA board members, and elected officials worked behind the scenes to advance the project. One board member had a financial interest in the project. Through heavy campaign contributions the developers greased the way for county and town support. In addition to bargain basement rents, the developers benefited from lucrative tax breaks running into millions of dollars. Nassau County District Attorney Denis Dillon launched an investigation in 1989. While he found no evidence of criminality, he documented the many conflicts of interest and other "improprieties."[33]

Across the state in Buffalo, the inspector general of the U.S. Department of Commerce investigated the use of $8.5 million of federal grants awarded to the Erie County IDA. A blistering report in 1989 cited numerous conflicts of interest, evidence of loans to enterprises that did not need them, and unjustifiable writeoffs of loans. The IDA had used some of the federal money to establish a venture capital investment firm and then loaned money to some of the very companies it had invited to fund the investment firm.[34] Aside from the tightening of controls, only a few minor slaps on the wrist followed.

A Look at Some Other States

As befits the Empire State and the Big Apple, everything—including economic development—is larger than life. So is the puffery. Less gargantuan, Massachusetts and Illinois suffer from the same overblown pretensions. Elsewhere in the country the familiar pattern of inflated job claims, unnecessary tax breaks, dubious low-interest loans, and dashed hopes of economic revival reaches into every nook and cranny. Here are some selected state "rap sheets."

California. Governor George Deukmejian (1982–1990), like Governor Ronald Reagan 20 years before him, was an evangelist of economic development. During his administration the state spent some $50 million a year for grants, loans, and loan guarantees to small businesses, high-tech firms, enterprise zones, and foreign trade programs. But the big money came from public authorities, especially local industrial development authorities that can issue both tax-exempt and federally taxable bonds. Unlike other states,

California monitors and approves the issuance of local industrial development bonds through an Industrial Development Financing Advisory Commission in the state treasurer's office. It has had some moderate success in nipping in the bud New York State-style fiascos. But all of these props could not weather the recession of 1990–1991 that in one year resulted in a loss of 100,000 jobs.[35]

Pennsylvania. Pennsylvania, too, has all the artifacts of job development. Like other states it engages in bidding wars to attract industry. Its confrontation with Volkswagen illustrates the hazards of this policy. In its search for a new plant in the United States, VW asked Ohio and Pennsylvania for their best offer. Pennsylvania won with some $71 million in subsidies, including low-interest industrial development bonds and a bundle of tax incentives. The plant started operations in 1978. Only nine years later, in 1987, it closed the facility and eliminated 2,500 jobs.[36] From this chastening experience Pennsylvania and its authorities emerged sadder but not wiser. At the next call to battle they are ready to lose again.

New Jersey. New Jersey's Economic Development Authority (EDA) is the largest in the country, having issued over $8 billion in bonds. With a mission to aid small businesses in distressed cities, it has not overlooked such giants as Exxon and Hoffman LaRoche and utilities with political connections such as the Hackensack Water Company. Conventional bank loans are not appealing when EDA can save a company 2 percent to 3 percent in interest. Since EDA is not responsible for the repayment of the debt, it has been rather casual in approving loans for marginal firms. The result is a high default rate of 4 percent.[37]

In this climate even Donald J. Trump, the flamboyant entrepreneur, does his bit for economic development. Sensitive to the needs of Atlantic City, which had sunk into a morass of poverty, unemployment, crime, and racial tensions, he and fellow promoters spent over $5 billion to build gambling casinos, hotels, and convention facilities. With characteristic modesty he called his flagship casino "Taj Mahal"—familiarly known as "Taj" to more than 7 million patrons. As a quid pro quo for gambling profits, Trump and the other casino owners either had to buy bonds from the New Jersey Casino Reinvestment Development Authority or invest directly in authority projects. The authority was to be the vehicle for the construction and rehabilitation of housing and urban development in Atlantic City. Behind the Trump glitz urban decay never let up. About one-half of the city's population received public assistance. The millions of dollars diverted to the authority had a minimal effect. Some of it fell into the pockets of six mayors and other officials who were charged with corruption.[38]

Missouri. Under the banner of economic development, Missouri like most states had sports stadium fever and created the Jackson County Sports Complex Authority (Kansas City) for its favorite ball teams. No sooner had the authority gotten under way in 1985 with tax-exempt bond issues of over $8 million than it steered hundreds of thousands of dollars of contracts to politically connected law firms, banks, financial advisers, and underwriters. In turn the beneficiaries spread around sizable campaign contributions. An investigation by the *Kansas City Star* disclosed that the beneficiaries either "did nothing" or "did anything of value" or "were available to add what was necessary."[39]

Kentucky. To revive the inner city, Kentucky and 36 other states have created enterprise zones loaded with tax breaks for adventurous entrepreneurs, the latest fad in economic development. Among the most fervent supporters of these public-private ventures are President George Bush, former President Ronald Reagan, and Jack Kemp, secretary of HUD. So far, however, they have not persuaded a skeptical Congress to raise money for the zones. Most of the plans for the enterprise zones are ineffectual and have not led to any meaningful changes in inner-city neighborhoods.[40] This message didn't get through to Kentucky. The largest urban enterprise zone in the United States is in Louisville and covers 47 square miles. Capitalized at over $1 billion, it stretches past the city limits into suburban Jefferson County, straddling several ghettos on the way. Although billed as the savior of the inner city, it has turned out to be a smashing success only for suburbanites.

Ohio. As part of the bag of tricks of economic development, Ohio, along with nearly all the states, is addicted to convention centers and fashionable marketplaces. Public authorities with billions in tax-free bonds are at the center of the action. In Columbus, the Franklin County Convention Facilities Authority is constructing a $94-million convention center scheduled to open in 1992. Rebutting local doubting Thomases, the authority holds out the promise of $2 billion in revenue over the next 10 years—a typical come-on.[41]

Toledo started out with similar glowing predictions in 1984 when it built Portside, a $36-million festival mall owned by the nonprofit Toledo Economic Development Corporation. In 1990 it became a ghost town with barred windows, deserted restaurants, and empty streets as the promised rush of business never materialized. In the wake of the debacle, Mayor John McHugh reflected sadly: "It's been a very expensive learning process; my advice to other cities would be: Don't do it." Even J. Michael Porter, president of the Toledo Area Chamber of Commerce and a leading supporter of Portside, conceded that fantasies rather than hard financial analysis led to Portside. "We were looking for the magic potion that was going to turn the community around and the whole romantic notion of a portside kind of thing really appeared to be a wonderful solution."[42]

Florida. Local public authorities dominate projects for economic development in Florida as they do in most states. One scheme that blew up was the construction in the late 1970s of a 208-acre research center, Innovation Park, in Leon County that was to foster economic ventures between Florida state universities and private firms. The Leon County Research and Development Authority financed the park by selling $15 million of certificates of participation (COPs) to the Allstate Insurance Company. Among the early renters were three state agencies that tested materials, foods, and even the urine of jockeys and horses at Innovation Park. In 1989 a skeptical legislature refused to appropriate money for the leases on the ground that the agencies were not conducting bona fide research and development projects. Immediately the COPs went into default and the public authority and Allstate sued the state, claiming breach of contract. The circuit court ruled against them and reminded them that all lease payments were contingent on legislative appropriations. No appropriations, no rent money. Allstate was left with an empty office building and painful memories of the hazards of buying lease-backed COPs and bonds.[43]

Undoubtedly, economic development authorities and their ever-caring governments will regard the tales of these wayward adventures as one-sided and unfair. In all states they are ready to trot out success stories, hoping that the exceptions will prove the rule while they are in fact bogged down in a quagmire of failure, fiasco, fantasy, and finagling. In World War II they would have been classified as 4-F (unfit for service).

Academics have tended to succumb easily to their puffery, writing hundreds of tomes about the new marvelous tools of economic development. Occasionally, though, they realize with a start that no meaningful evaluation backs up the self-serving claims of public authorities. One perplexed researcher reflected: "Whether it can be concluded that state development policy pays dividends remains to be seen. Such activity can bring immediate political dividends, but it may take years to produce the expected economic dividends."[44]

Promises! Promises! Unable to cope with national and international economic tides and whirlwinds that have destroyed millions of blue-collar jobs, governors and legislatures spend billions of dollars through public authorities to build castles in the air. How much better off their states would be if they concentrated instead on what is do-able: upgrading the infrastructure; investing in training programs for displaced workers; providing business data and technical assistance to small firms that cannot afford them.

These more limited programs make economic sense, but not political sense.

8

Housing Horrors

After roving gangs shot her sixteen-year-old daughter and killed her daughter's best friend, Martha Waddington and her family of five fled the crime-infested and decaying Cabrini–Green public housing project in Chicago. What she found in slumlord-owned housing was even worse. In rapid succession she rented and moved from five different apartments. In one, the plumbing didn't work. In another, the floor boards rotted and paint flaked off the walls. In a third, rats ate the children's clothing. For these amenities she paid about $400 to $500 a month, nearly 10 times the $47.50 monthly rent at Cabrini–Green. As in any public housing project, the rent at Cabrini–Green could not exceed 30 percent of her income.

Now she yearned once again for an apartment in a public housing project. She told the *Chicago Tribune*, which carried a series of articles on public housing in 1986, "I want to get back into public housing because it's cheaper. Paying high rent is taking food out of my kids' mouths. My father said I should never have moved out of the project. I keep hearing people tell me that. And, once I get there I'll be just fine."

She added her name to a waiting list of 20,000 families looking for a vacancy in the 41,000 apartments in 137 projects owned and managed by the Chicago Housing Authority.[1]

Melvina Johnson would gladly give her apartment to Martha Waddington if she could escape the Altgeld Gardens project on Chicago's far south side. In contrast to high-rise Cabrini–Green, Altgeld has pleasant two-story row houses. But it is also the turf of local gang members who have attacked her children and stolen her money. In anger Johnson cried out, "If I had a job I wouldn't be here. This is not a good place to raise kids. There's gangs and stealing cars. Sometimes I'm really afraid for my kids." No longer does she shop at the local supermarket in the development because "the gangs take bags from people and take their checks."[2]

Waddington and Johnson are among 1.4 million families that live in projects owned by over 3,400 independent local public housing authorities in the United States. At least 1 million families are on waiting lists for apartments. And the wait will be long, perhaps years for many families. The chief source of funding for public housing is the federal government, supplemented by minimal aid from some big state and local governments.[3] That is why public housing authorities are closely linked with federal housing programs.

About 400 miles southwest of Chicago, Carla Parott and her five children rent a privately owned house in Columbia, Missouri. She can do this only because the U.S. Department of Housing and Urban Development (HUD) subsidizes the rent and pays the utilities under Section 8 of the federal housing law. But Parott's dream of living in a "real house" has been shattered. Carbon monoxide fumes from a defective furnace poisoned her family. Armies of roaches invaded the house. Shoddy electrical and plumbing systems failed. This didn't faze the owners, who collected more rent than they could in the open market. The Columbia Housing Authority that managed the Section 8 program saw no evil, heard no evil, and did virtually nothing to correct the abuses.[4]

Some 2.7 million families like the Parotts live under the umbrella of the Section 8 Housing Assistance Program and at least 800,000 more are trying to join them. Designed during the Nixon administration in 1974 as a cheap alternative to the construction of public housing and partly as a means of preserving existing housing, Section 8 authorizes the use of rent vouchers and certificates for poor families and gives grants and tax breaks to property owners for the rehabilitation of buildings rented to the poor. Again, federal aid in this program dwarfs the billions of dollars spent by state and local governments in a variety of housing programs.

By virtue of public housing, rent assistance, and other federal programs over 4 million low-income families have found a third-rate home somewhere. When state and local rent-subsidized units are taken into account, the figure climbs by an estimated 300,000.[5] At the center of the action are the local housing authorities and 53 state housing finance authorities and agencies (HFAs). While the HFAs assist poor families, their main clients are low-income and moderate-income families. In their behalf they loan money at below-market interest rates to developers who build multifamily units and to qualified first-time buyers of single-family homes. Over 1.5 million families had benefited from these subsidies by the end of 1988.[6]

A Housing Crisis

Compared to the nation's vast housing needs, authority-run housing programs are but halting steps in the right direction. They don't help the 27 million families, nearly one-third of all families, that huddle together in crowded or substandard apartments. They don't serve the 9 million families, a whopping 11 percent of all families, that spend more than half of their income on rent or the 22 million families, 26 percent of all households, that must squeeze more than 30 percent out of their earnings for rent. Between the two groups well over one-third of all families in the United States spend more money than they can afford on rent. At the same time as rents rise, incomes adjusted for inflation are dropping. By the year 2000, one-third of all households and 70 percent of all households with low incomes will not be able to find adequate affordable housing. This is a conservative estimate. The private market can no longer produce a house or an apartment they can afford. These grim statistics make a mockery of the sanctimonious rhetoric about family values that pours out of Washington, D.C. and state capitals.[7]

At the bottom of the ladder are an estimated 1.5 million to 3 million homeless people. No one knows the precise figure but we do know that most of them lack homes simply because they are poor. Only a minority are alcoholics, drug addicts, or mentally disturbed individuals.[8]

Just when the need for housing is desperate, the supply of existing rental housing is shrinking. According to Harvard University's Joint Center for Housing Studies the nation lost more than 1 million nonsubsidized, privately owned rental units between 1974 and

1987. We can blame it on foreclosures, abandonment, gentrifica-
tion, and the conversion of rental apartments into cooperatives and
condominiums. Moreover, existing public housing is deteriorating.
Worth over $75 billion, most of it is in serious disrepair and requires
an expenditure of $20 billion just to make it habitable. Since 1975
the federal government has spent only $8 billion. To maintain and
modernize the apartments during the next 10 years will cost untold
billions.[9]

The dream of a home of one's own is becoming a mirage. For the
first time since World War II home ownership is slipping steadily.
While about 64 percent of the nation's households still owned some
kind of home in 1990, a decline in home ownership is taking place
at the rate of 2 percent per year. For young householders aged 30 to
34 the decline has been especially dramatic. In 1976, 61 percent of
people in their 30s were proud home owners. By 1987 the figure
had dropped to 52 percent, and it is still heading downwards. At
this rate most young families, unlike their parents, will not be able
to afford a home and will compete for the shrinking supply of rented
apartments.[10]

Even the comfort of subsidized rentals for moderate-income families may fade. Since the 1960s federal programs have provided
low-interest loans and tax breaks to developers who agree to maintain a prescribed ceiling on rents. These policies have produced
some 2 million privately owned and federally subsidized housing
units. During the next 15 years over half of these apartments could
be withdrawn from the market as restrictions limiting their use
expire. At that time building owners will be free to rent to anyone at
any price and displaced tenants will begin a search that will lead to
more costly and less satisfactory apartments.[11] By 1995, another
1.2 million families may lose their apartments as landlords pull out
of the Section 8 program.[12]

This is the depressing environment in which local public housing
authorities and state housing finance authorities operate.

The Backdrop of Public Housing

In 1933, in the very depths of the Great Depression, Franklin Del-
ano Roosevelt, in ringing tones, described a nation where one-third

of the population was ill-housed, ill-fed, and ill-clothed. Nearly 60 years later at least one-third of our people are still ill-housed. Federal and state housing programs for the poor and those with moderate incomes are in tatters, serving only a small fraction of needy families. With high hopes Roosevelt started the first national housing program in 1937. Over 44 years later, beginning in 1981, Ronald Reagan become the first president to savage public housing construction and subsidies. The Bush administration did only marginally better. In 1981 federal aid for new commitments of housing assistance peaked at $30 million. In 1989 it was down to $7.5 billion, a cut of 75 percent. The euphemistically named "The National Affordable Housing Act of 1990" provides additional token aid while burdening states and cities with more housing costs.[13]

The main engines of public housing and subsidized housing—local public housing authorities and state housing finance authorities—are sputtering. In too many cases they are woefully mismanaged and some are prone to unholy and illegal alliances with private developers, contractors, and politicians. The national overseer of public housing, HUD, has been scandal-ridden, and hundreds of housing authorities carry the same stigma. Unguarded, federal and state pools of money for housing have lured the greedy at the expense of the poor.

None of these crippling blows were even dimly foreseen during the Great Depression, when federal, state, and local governments took the first feeble steps to provide housing for the poor and to save existing homes from foreclosure. As Hoovervilles, the instant shantytowns of the 1930s, were springing up around him, President Herbert Hoover preferred words to action. His way out of the housing crisis was to call a Conference on Home Building and Home Ownership in 1931. But he did not heed the prophetic challenge of the conference:

> To those who look upon government operations in the field of housing construction with abhorrence, the challenge is definitely offered. . . . If business, financial, and industrial groups fail to take the task in hand and apply the large sums of capital required and the utmost of planning genius and engineering skill to the problem, it seems likely that American cities will be forced to

turn to European solutions of this problem, through subsidization by the State and municipal treasuries and probably through actual ownership and operation of housing projects by municipal authority. It can hardly be doubted that the next ten years will determine which choice will be made between these alternatives[14]

Vast changes came even sooner than the conference had anticipated. Prodded by Governor Alfred E. Smith, the New York State Legislature was the first to create self-financed local public housing authorities in 1934. Again, the unsung father of public authorities, Julius Henry Cohen, drafted the legislation just as he did with regard to the Power Authority of New York State and the Port Authority of New York and New Jersey.[15]

Without the intervention of the New Deal, the act would have remained a dead letter. In the early 1930s the Public Works Administration (PWA) pressured state legislatures to create local housing authorities, pumped grants and loans to those that went along, and bought tax-exempt bonds issued by the authorities. This was an emergency action under the National Industrial Recovery Act (NIRA). To make the program permanent, Congress approved in 1937 the U.S. Housing Act, the first national action to provide public housing to low-income families. The legislation authorized the secretary of the interior, then Harold Ickes, to channel grants and loans to the housing authorities. The author of the bill was Senator Robert Wagner of New York.[16]

For the impoverished middle classes that had lost their homes or could not afford to buy a home, FDR initiated a series of unprecedented programs run mainly by government corporations (the federal lingo for public authorities). A Home Owners Loan Corporation (HOLC) bought troubled mortgages to stave off foreclosures. A Federal Home Loan Bank System borrowed money from the federal government and lent it to savings and loan associations (S & Ls) and mutual savings banks to provide funds for mortgages. Banks for Cooperatives, part of a Farm Credit System (FCS), lent money to rural banks for housing. At the same time a Federal Savings and Loan Insurance Corporation (FSLIC), destined for a tragic end in 1989, insured deposits in the S & Ls. Similarly, the Federal Deposit Insurance Corporation (FDIC), also virtually bankrupt in the 1990s, insured deposits in commercial banks. To expand the supply of credit for housing, the Federal National Mortgage Association, familiarly known as "Fannie Mac," bought mortgages from banks. It raised money by selling bonds and later by selling stock in the capital markets with the mortgages as security. In 1968 it was privatized and became a government-sponsored enterprise (GSE), federally chartered, federally subsidized in effect, federally coddled, and privately owned.

This was not enough for nervous bankers and investors. To limit their risks a Federal Housing Administration (FHA), now in HUD, insured mortgages. The Government National Mortgage Association (GNMA), housed in HUD and blessed with the nickname of "Ginnie Mae," guaranteed the payment of principal and interest of private securities backed by insured or guaranteed mortgages. With these inducements few banks and developers could resist the New Deal no-lose game.

After this whirlwind beginning, it was downhill all the way. President Harry Truman (1949–1953) kept the faith by persuading Congress to approve the construction of 800,000 low-income apartments that would be owned and managed by local public housing authorities. Ideologically opposed to public housing, the Eisenhower administration (1953–1960) tried to scuttle the Truman program and favored public-private partnerships, with the private sector pocketing the gains and the public sector holding the risks.

With the ascendancy of the Kennedy and Johnson administrations (1961–1969), it looked as if the second spring for public housing had broken out. In 1965 Congress set a 10-year goal for the construction of 26 million housing units with 6 million apartments reserved for low-income and moderate-income families. This proved to be pie in the sky and became an early victim of the Vietnam war. Despite their populist rhetoric, guardians of the New Frontier and the Great Society hankered for public-private partnerships, Eisenhower-style. Soon mortgage insurance superseded direct federal loans and local public housing authorities were encouraged to lease privately owned buildings rather than to expand public housing significantly. To stimulate home ownership, the federal government subsidized interest rates and allowed small down payments. But the core of its housing program was Section 236 of the Housing Act, overflowing with giveaways for private developers. Robert Kuttner, who investigated this latest bonanza to private interests, found that Section 236 gave

> developers government-guaranteed one percent mortgage loans, plus lucrative tax breaks, and in some cases rent subsidies as well. By syndicating the tax shelter, a developer could do a 236 deal literally without putting in a nickel of his own money, and in some cases developers took substantial amounts of money out of the deal before the apartment was even built. Since all the profit was front-loaded, the program did not encourage the developer to hang around and manage the project. Eventually about half million such units were built, and within a few years HUD had repossessed over one-third of them.
>
> In the 1970s, investigating Section 236 buildings that had gone into default, I encountered a charming bit of HUD argot: the phrase "suede shoe boy." HUD people used it to describe the sponsors of failed projects, implying a sleazy developer. I asked a longtime HUD official to define a suede-shoe boy. "I guess," he said wearily, "it's anyone who will do business with HUD." Despite the lavish bribery at taxpayer expense, dealing with HUD was such a nightmare that most of the developers willing to join the club were not worth having.[17]

Once President Richard Nixon assumed office in 1970, he let Section 236 slowly expire. His contribution was the Section 8 rent subsidy program that provided rent certificates to the poor. Landlords who cheered the new program had nothing to lose. The certificates guaranteed the difference between tenants' rent and 30 percent of their income. After five years landlords could expel their tenants and upgrade their apartments for the growing horde of yuppies. Opposed bitterly to public housing, Nixon, nevertheless, provided welcome grants for urban development via the Community Development Block Grants (CDBGs) and the Urban Development Action Grants (UDAGs). He added still another privately owned Government-sponsored enterprise (GSE) to the maze of housing corporations and agencies. This was the Federal Home Loan Mortgage

Corporation ("Freddie Mac"). Like Fannie Mae, Freddie Mac bought mortgages from the banks, pooled and packaged them, and sold securities backed by the mortgages to investors. The banks were thus free to lend even more money for housing.

In a breather before the Reagan administration, President Jimmy Carter (1977–1980), like President Gerald Ford before him, modestly expanded rent subsidies and housing construction. Then came the depredations of President Ronald Reagan. Even Nixon's housing programs proved to be too much for Reagan. Aided and abetted by a supine Congress, he cut out the remnants of public housing construction altogether and shredded rent subsidies. Instead of rent certificates that put money in the hands of landlords, the administration preferred rent vouchers given directly to tenants. The difference was slight.

So-called tax reform in 1986 compounded the carnage. It virtually wiped out existing tax incentives for private real estate developers to build housing for families with moderate incomes. Out the window flew tax deductions for accelerated depreciation, allowable losses, and low ceilings for capital gains. As a substitute, the Reagan administration initiated a new and fairly modest scheme of tax credits for the rehabilitation of housing for low-income groups. This is administered by state and local public housing authorities and is currently the chief federal subsidy for low-cost housing.

Other victims of tax reform were state housing programs for moderate-income groups, managed by HFAs (housing finance authorities/agencies). By capping the amount of tax-exempt housing bonds the HFAs could issue and subjecting many investors to taxes on hitherto tax-free bond interest, the tax reform act crippled mortgage financing for first-time home buyers and developers of low-cost apartments. In 1985, the last year before tax reform, HFAs and other state agencies had issued $37 billion of housing bonds. One year later, the amount dropped to $10.9 billion. By 1990 bond issuances were up to $15.7 billion, but still less than half of the 1985 figure.

What the Reagan administration didn't do by design, it achieved by neglect. Because of token regulation, hundreds of savings and loan associations, the chief providers of home mortgages, toppled, and the Federal Savings and Loan Insurance Corporation (FSLIC) that insured their deposits went bankrupt. This led to the largest bailout by taxpayers in American history.

Plagued by scandals since its creation in 1968, HUD sank to a new low under Samuel R. Pierce, Jr., Reagan's secretary of housing and urban development. In 1989 congressional committees and the General Accounting Office uncovered widespread fraud, waste, abuse, and mismanagement. Shady contracts enriched developers, financial advisers, attorneys, and consultants with Republican connections. Pierce's law firm, Battle Fowler, also benefited from this largess. HUD overrode the opposition of local public housing authorities and its own regional offices to provide grants for marginal projects in which politically influential developers had invested. It failed to supervise hundreds of local housing authorities that were rife with corruption, fraud, and mismanagement. It ventured into privatization by allowing private lenders, without HUD checks, to appraise property and commit the government to mortgage insurance. This practice cost the government at least $3.7 billion in losses. The Federal Housing Administration (FHA), a wing of HUD, suffered losses of over $8 billion because of defaults on the payment of mortgages by homeowners, fraud, and mismanagement.[18]

Long on talk and short on money, the Bush administration eagerly promoted housing programs that were easy on the purse. It attempted to convert public housing into tenant-owned units. Only few tenants with an average family income of about $17,000 in 1990 could afford the modest prices. For all occupants of public housing the average income was slightly over $6,500.[19] The Bush agenda merely used what existed and did not add to the stock of publicly owned apartments except for relatively few pushed through by Congress. Jack Kemp, secretary of HUD, explained his opposition to public housing: "We're not going back into the construction business. The stock of housing in America is vast. I'm not saying it's good. A lot of it is in disrepair." He opted for renovation of existing privately owned housing and continuation of the rent voucher program. "If we're going to subsidize anybody, we should subsidize the poor, the family, the renters, the person in public housing. Our money should get people into housing and not go to a developer who gets a multimillion dollar profit."[20]

Housing Policy Today

Some 55 years after the New Deal, housing programs for the poor and those with moderate incomes are in shambles. Only a trickle of assistance has survived: deteriorated public housing, rent vouchers, and rehabilitation of old and shabby privately owned apartments. In despair state and local governments and public authorities, with minimal federal aid, have raised their own housing budgets and turned to nonprofit corporations and volunteer and community organizations to provide housing for the have-nots. As impressive as these efforts are, they are far too few to be meaningful. A thousand points of light are no substitute for multibillion-dollar housing programs.

If the poor have been left behind, the middle class has benefited although not on the same scale as in the past. In contrast to $15 billion for existing housing programs doled out to the poor every year, the federal government subsidizes the middle class at roughly $45 billion annually by permitting tax deductions of mortgage interest and property taxes for owner-occupied principal and second homes.[21] Through a panoply of government corporations, government-sponsored enterprises (GSEs), and federal agencies, it stands ready to insure and guarantee mortgages, and through a flock of sistern and brethren such as Fannie Mae, Ginnie Mae, Freddie Mac, and Farmer Mac, it buys mortgages and pools them for resale to investors via mortgage-backed securities so that the banks can lend even more money to aspiring home owners. Since World War II nearly 40 million families have managed to have their own home because of the clutch of GSEs and government corporations.[22]

This is the scorecard of the magnitude of the bounty available mainly to middle-class home owners in contrast to the poor clients of public authorities:

Government corporation, GSE, or federal agency	Outstanding debt, mortgage guarantees, and mortgage-backed securities (billions)	Recent losses
FHA (Federal Housing Administration)	$275 (1989)	$ 7 billion
VA (Veterans Administration)	364 (1991)	2.4 billion

Government corporation, GSE, or federal agency	Outstanding debt, mortgage guarantees, and mortgage-backed securities (billions)	Recent losses
GNMA (Government National Mortgage Association— Ginnie Mae)	350 (1989)	1 billion
Farmers' Home Administration	23 (1989)	9 billion
FHLBS (Federal Home Loan Bank System)	117.9 (1989)	

GSEs (government-sponsored enterprises)

FNMA (Federal National Mortgage Association— Fannie Mae)	423.2 (1990)	350 million
FHMLC (Federal Home Loan Mortgage Corporation— Freddie Mac)	344.8 (1990)	
FCS (Farm Credit System: Farm Credit Banks, Banks for Cooperatives; Federal Agricultural Mortgage Corporation—Farmer Mac)	55.2 (1990)	5 billion

Local Housing Authorities

In this labyrinthine maze the state and local public housing authorities and the housing finance authorities struggle to keep housing afloat for the poor and the near poor. Overshadowed by programs that tilt to middle-income families and overlooked by the federal government, they are slowly retreating from what once had been the promised land of low-cost housing. Out of sight and out of control, many authorities have succumbed to the temptations of rivulets of federal, state, and local money, the lure of patronage, contracts, kickbacks, and bribes to political cronies, and costly mismanagement. No state is free from this taint. The few safe-guards that existed were drastically cut when the Reagan administration gave some 600 local housing authorities, about 18 percent of all housing authorities, relative autonomy in running their affairs. This was done under the aegis of the Public Housing Authority Decontrol Program, part of Reagan's deregulation efforts.

As a tribute to their efficiency, 20 housing authorities in New Jersey were deregulated. Two years later Jack F. Kemp, secretary of HUD, invaded the state with a strike force to investigate all of them, also vowing to audit the other 59 authorities in the state. The Passaic Housing Authority (PHA) was the prime target—"the straw that broke decontrol's back," according to Michael B. Javis, his deputy assistant secretary. As evidence of abuses mounted, HUD seized PHA, the third takeover of a housing authority in the United States.[23] HUD had this unusual but rarely used power because of the size of the federal investment in public housing.

Eight miles west of Manhattan, Passaic is a former milltown with a poor, mainly black and Hispanic population. The local government, however, is firmly in the hands of white politicians. To house some 2,000 poor and elderly individuals, the Passaic Housing Authority (PHA) owns and operates Albert Speer Village, described by *Common Cause* in 1990 as a "bleak cluster of eight story brick apartments ringed by pothole streets." For the residents the village is a rotting shell. For Paul Marguglio and his associates it was a money machine. He drew about $250,000 a year for four jobs as executive director, modernization director, contracting officer, and purchasing agent. From 1986 to 1988 his wife Louise received $95,000 after working only one day. His stepson and stepdaughter were also on the payroll. As supplements to the family income, Marguglio enjoyed over $200,000 in kickbacks from grateful landlords who benefited from Section 8 rent supplements, business firms that did business with the authority, and the authority's attorney, August Michaelis, who received about $320,000 in legal fees in 1988.

Marguglio's deputy director, Donald V. Pieri, collected $107,000 a year for four jobs, and minor functionaries did nearly as well. Even Passaic Mayor Joseph Lipari benefited. In return for campaign contributions, he steered business firms to PHA. PHA, in turn, sold five cars worth $65,000 to the city for $1 each. According to federal investigators the top staff of PHA misappropriated about $1.7 million in federal funds, abused credit cards, billed the authority for unnecessary travel expenses, and relaxed on long vacations at the public's expense.

When the investigation revealed that Robert Cantalupo, the maintenance supervisor, provided an air-conditioned room for 40 stray cats, and his wife used laundry money to buy food for the cats, Marguglio defended cat care as a worthy and humanitarian project. After all cats controlled rodents and could be regarded as unpaid employees of PHA. Seeing nothing wrong in setting up an adoption clearing house for cats, he was shocked when a HUD official ordered him to "get rid of the bloody cats."[24]

In the wake of HUD, FBI, and congressional investigations, Marguglio and Michaelis pleaded guilty to felony charges of conspiracy to defraud the government, tax evasion, and lying to Congress. Both faced 10-year sentences. Other staff members also entered guilty pleas. They joined the executive directors of the Perth Amboy, Carteret, and Woodbridge housing authorities who had previously gone to jail. Other executive directors queued up for their turn.

Calling the Passaic and other housing authorities "an ethical swamp of the first variety," U.S. Representative Tom Lantos of California, chairman of a House subcommittee, crystallized the issues that troubled him most: "In addition to learning more about how the Passaic Housing Authority went out of control, we will want to learn from our witnesses if they believe this situation to be an aberration or a national problem and what can be done to prevent future Passaics."[25]

The congressman has his work cut out for him, for he will find Passaics in every state. Ohio has more than its share of shenanigans as is evident in Akron and Cleveland. The Akron Metropolitan Housing Authority (AMHA) appeared to be a model of rectitude and efficiency. It provided homes for thousands of poor and elderly, coasted over obstacles that thwart development in other communities, and aggressively went after every dollar of federal housing funds. So successful had it been in the eyes of HUD that it was touted as a national showcase.

After an eight-month investigation in 1982 and 1983, Dennis McEaneney and John Kostrzewa, reporters of the *Akron Beacon Journal*, found that the AMHA was a cesspool of favoritism, conflicts of interest, and "sweetheart" deals. It turned out that the authority was the personal fiefdom of Herbert Newman, legal counsel and former executive director of AMHA, and David Levey, his successor. A week after the *Beacon Journal* published its series of articles, Newman and Levey resigned and the county prosecutor and HUD started long overdue investigations.

Before joining AMHA, Newman practiced law with Akron attorney Eugene Oestreicher. No sooner had he become executive director than he hired Oestreicher to handle AMHA's legal affairs. Other attorneys in Oestreicher's office were Newman's wife Dianne and Bernard Schneier, a partner of Newman's in seven federally assisted housing projects they had bought. After resigning as executive director, Newman retained his ties to AMHA as legal counsel and consultant, still steering legal business to Oestreicher. Nor did he forget Schneier. When Schneier sold a six-apartment building to an AMHA subsidiary, Newman's consulting contract required him to review his partner's purchase. This cozy arrangement was part of a familiar pattern. While Newman was executive director, Oestreicher and Schneier sold a house, at a handsome profit, to AMHA. Referring to this and similar deals with friends, family, and associates, a HUD official commented wryly: "He likes his friends a little too much. He'll sometimes bend over backwards to help them." But he quickly added that HUD had never unearthed hard evidence of favoritism or wrongdoing.

Newman's ties extended to a small clique of contractors and businessmen. One accounting firm that benefited was Heinick-Slavin. Two partners in that firm are cousins of Lawrence Apple, a vice president of Transcon Builders, which won over $29 million in contracts from AMHA. The other favored contractor was Associated Estates (later known as Adam Construction), which received $68 million in awards. Newman was not fazed by the conviction of Carl Milstein, the head of Associated Estates, for bribery and fraud in a Cuyahoga County public housing project. Milstein's son-in-law reorganized the company, called it Adam Construction, and continued to get the lion's share of AMHA's business. Over a six-year period, these two firms pocketed over 80 percent of all construction contracts.

Other beneficiaries of Newman's included Stuart Willen, a former business partner of Newman, who leased several apartment buildings to AMHA and sold bonds in behalf of another project, and plumbing contractor Stephen Comunale, who was in three partnerships that rented homes to tenants holding AMHA-issued Section 8 rent vouchers and snared several contracts to work on housing projects.

After Newman set the precedent, David Levey followed suit in his tenure as executive director. He continued to give Adam Construction and Transcon preferential treatment while allowing AMHA to loan money to nonprofit organizations in violation of state law. His brother Laurence owned several homes that housed tenants with AMHA rent subsidy certificates. He also placed 51 of his 214 employees in AMHA housing, regardless of eligibility, despite a long list of prior applicants. Before he resigned Levey defended himself against charges of impropriety: "I have never given any member of my family special consideration. I have not used my influence on their behalf and I have not had prior knowledge of their dealings with the authority. I have had no financial gain in any way from their dealings."

No state, city, or federal agency, least of all HUD, had poked into the affairs of the AMHA until the *Beacon Journal* began an investigation.[26]

While not in Newman's class, William E. Lee and John C. Rafferty, Jr., two wealthy Akron businessmen, manipulated the federal rent subsidy program to collect hundreds of thousands of dollars in inflated payments from AMHA according to the *Beacon Journal*. Like many landlords throughout the country they practiced a simple scam. For example, they bought an apartment complex from HUD for $10,000. To inflate the debt and thus the value of the building, Rafferty "sold" his one-half interest in 1983 to Lee for $515,000, but no money actually changed hands. Lee then applied for a Section 8 housing subsidy since he was rehabilitating a building for low-income families. Based on bogus property values, the housing authority paid him a monthly rent subsidy of $351 per apartment instead of the $285 that was more appropriate. John Fitzpatrick, Section 8 director of AMHA, later became a business associate of Lee and Rafferty. When the phoney transactions surfaced, Wayne Calabrese, who doubled as AMHA's outside legal counsel and lawyer for Lee and Rafferty, defended Fitzpatrick. So successful was the Akron operation that Lee and Rafferty tried it in Cleveland and it worked again due to a supervisor in the housing authority who enjoyed their gifts and gratuities.[27]

Especially colorful was Patricia Brisbin's career as a slumlord in Cleveland. A member of the city council, she bought rundown houses in the meanest streets of the city and rented them to the poorest people, collecting hefty federal subsidies via the Cuyahoga Metropolitan Housing Authority (CMHA). She kept one step ahead of prying inspectors, but was later convicted of hiring criminals to burn unprofitable houses so that she could collect insurance money. She did this with impunity while the apathetic CMHA was unaware of the abuse of its own programs. Nothing happened until James Neff, an enterprising reporter of the *Cleveland Plain Dealer*, disclosed Brisbin's take of housing subsidies for "ghost tenants," criminal violations of the housing code along with other landlords, racial harassment, large scale arson, and other scams to defraud the CMHA.

Brisbin pleaded guilty to theft of public money. She was convicted of arson and sentenced to jail for five to 15 years. In the meantime, her fellow slumlords, each with 20 to 30 properties, continued to prey on federal and city programs created to help low-income tenants and home owners.[28]

Annapolis is home not only to the Naval Academy, but also to over 1,100 families who live in 10 projects of the Annapolis Housing Authority. Years of neglect, mismanagement, and cost overruns were finally capped by the indictment in 1988 of Arthur G. Stressel, Jr., the executive director, for fraud, bribery, and racketeering. Among his other peccadilloes were coast-to-coast junkets with authority board members to attend housing conferences. They ran up $65,000 in hotel, restaurant, and bar bills at the expense of the authority. This finally led to investigations by HUD, the FBI, and the U.S. General Accounting Office. Up to that point HUD's monitoring was casual at best.

In the aftermath, the legislature clamped down on the autonomy of local housing authorities, and for the first time since 1937 subjected them to state oversight.[29]

Journeying southward to sunny Florida, the same dreary saga of theft, embezzlement, shoddy management, abuse of authority funds, and shady tieins with private firms unfolds in such havens of retirement as Palm Beach, Clearwater, St. Petersburg, and Orlando. Between the areas of lavish homes, pockets of poverty dot Florida. While the county public housing authorities attempt to deal with them through publicly owned and rent-subsidized housing, too often the chief beneficiaries are real estate developers.

The Palm Beach County Housing Authority, in particular, has had a long and sorry history of abuses of housing programs. Since 1980 two executive directors have faced criminal charges because of theft and embezzlement and a third resigned after being charged with the illegal award of contracts. When Barry Seaman became executive director, his hard-driving management style seemed impressive, but he soon developed what he called a "symbiotic relationship" between the authority and Leased Housing, a private firm that managed public housing projects. Seaman was simultaneously executive director of the authority and president of Leased Housing. Nine other staff members worked for both organizations and, with Seaman, drew pay from both, making frequent out-of-town trips to oversee projects managed by Leased Housing in other cities. Seaman dismissed charges of conflict of interest by pointing to Leased Housing's invaluable role in managing properties. On investigation, HUD disagreed and found 13 of 20 projects substandard. In one project managed by Lease Housing elderly and disabled residents were terrorized by criminals and drug addicts.[30]

David York, chairman of the St. Petersburg Housing Authority Commission, followed a similar path. He maintained business arrangements with real estate investors who received federal money through the authority, giving them up only as charges of conflict of interest mounted. He and his executive director also awarded most contracts to five favored firms.[31]

More serious were Michael Gray's problems as executive director of the Clearwater Housing Authority (CHA). In 1982 he pleaded guilty to misappropriating CHA funds for personal expenses. He was let off lightly with 30 days' imprisonment and three years' probation.[32]

In Orlando, Sam C. Mazzotta, executive director, and two board members manipulated the Orange County Housing Finance Authority to their advantage in 1984 and 1985. Mazzotta owned a company that helped developers get low-cost loans from the authority while as executive director, he approved the loans. The two board members borrowed sizable interest-free sums from the authority. Together they did a better job in steering low-cost loans to developers than in providing rental housing at a reasonable cost, according to the *Orlando Sentinel*. Under fire Mazzotta resigned and the two board members were replaced while the county government went through the motions of tightening controls.[33]

Scattered throughout the Midwest and the Southwest are small and large housing authorities with similar stories. In Newport, Kentucky, a poor city of less than 20,000 inhabitants, the Newport Housing Authority squandered hundreds of thousands of dollars, could not account fully for expenditures from a $3.4-million HUD grant, and, astonishingly, left vacant 190 apartments, one-third of its 574 apartments. At the eleventh hour Jelica Stepp, the executive director, resigned in 1988 and HUD charged into the fray with a long overdue report.[34]

"Mired in an administrative and financial nightmare," according to the *Columbia Missourian*, the Columbia Housing Authority (CHA) in Missouri is no better. It closed its eyes to substandard housing for tenants with rent subsidies; it failed to control rents charged by buccaneering landlords; it perpetuated racial segregation in housing; it misused millions of dollars of federal funds. Although CHA is a relatively small housing authority in a small city, it quickly succumbed to the social problems of big cities. As one resident put it, "public housing is like a city within a city." It became a mecca for criminals with violence, vandalism, and drug addiction an everyday affair.[35]

In Houston, Texas, charges of nepotism and conflicts of interest simmered in the Houston Housing Authority in 1987. Darrell Fitzgerald, an architect, won a contract to rehabilitate two housing projects while his wife, Joy, was deputy executive director of the authority. Dr. Luckett Johnson, a physician, was selected to examine applicants for jobs and employees of the authority injured on the job while his wife Marcia was the authority's general counsel. The *Houston Post* first broke the story in 1987 followed by a HUD investigation. Earl Phillips, the executive director, mixing his metaphors, termed allegations of conflict of interest "sour grapes obviously by someone who tried to stir up the pot." Both husbands quit their jobs.[36]

In Dallas the Housing Authority failed to eradicate racial discrimination and segregation in public housing. It took a federal court order in 1989 to force the authority to provide 100 scattered three-bedroom units of housing as a first step in the settlement of the law suit. Still ahead was the demolition of 2,654 units of 3,500 apartments in a West Dallas housing project to wipe out physical and racial blight.[37]

In the very pit of public housing stands the Chicago Housing Authority (CHA), the second largest in the country after the New York City Housing Authority, the worst-managed according to HUD, and, for years, a magnet for corrupt white and black politicians. Its high-rise slums wall off poor black families, most of them headed by single parents, from the white and small affluent black communities. In 48 reports since 1979 the U.S. General Accounting Office has castigated waste, mismanagement, and uncontrolled expenditures by CHA including deficits running into many millions of dollars, and has painted a doomsday picture of the tall monuments to failure:

> Deteriorating buildings, damaged heating and water systems, broken elevators, and roach and rodent infestation are commonplace at many projects. This situation has resulted from a poorly maintained and aging housing stock. Abusive tenants have also contributed to this situation. The authority estimates that it would need about $1 billion over a 5-year period to upgrade its projects to an acceptable level.
>
> Tenants also live under the constant threat of crime and violence. In 1987 over 16,000 criminal incidents occurred on Authority properties, an 11.5-percent increase over 1986. During this same period, homicides, aggravated assaults, and rape increased about 63 percent.[38]

GAO went on to charge that "over the years CHA has apparently not had the capability and/or desire to operate the authority effectively." To the insiders this meant that under the regimes of Mayors Richard J. Dailey, Jane Byrne, and Harold Washington, CHA was a cesspool of graft, corruption, and patronage. For 20 years Charles Swibel, an appointee of Dailey, was chairman of the authority and manipulated it to serve his private real estate interests and to award contracts to politically connected firms. Only after rare pressure from HUD did Byrne force him out in 1982.

As the first black mayor, Harold Washington did no better. His choice as chairman of the CHA board was Renault Robinson, the first black chairman. One of his early acts was to fire dozens of mechanics and craftsmen so that he could replace them with his own appointees. In the cold winter of 1983 hundreds of elevators, furnaces, and electrical systems failed because of lack of maintenance. Finally, Robinson resigned when HUD threatened a federal takeover of CHA.[39]

Today CHA remains what it has been since the 1960s—a crumbling warehouse for the poor, but under new and somewhat more hopeful leadership.

On the West Coast one can hear the same litany of failure. In 1985 Dianne Feinstein, then mayor of San Francisco, forced the Housing Authority (SFHA) to fire Carl Williams, her own appointee as executive director. SFHA had run up deficits of over $6 million in managing 6,888 apartments in 47 projects and misused $3.8 million in federal subsidies.[40] Four years earlier a jury in Seattle had convicted David Miller, director of the rehabilitation program of the Seattle Housing Authority, of theft, fraud, and kickbacks.[41]

On the East Coast, the Buffalo Municipal Housing Authority (BMHA), one of the oldest in the nation, fostered racial segregation, mismanaged a $65-million building program, and provided jobs for Mayor Griffin's political allies. Only after the *Buffalo News* disclosed what one of its reporters called "hell" did HUD, GAO, and a subcommittee chaired by Senator Daniel Patrick Moynihan investigate BMHA from 1987 to 1991.[42]

In nearby Syracuse, New York, Mayor Lee Alexander chose the New York City law firm of Fisher and Fisher over local attorneys to serve as the city's outside counsel and paid them handsome fees. Influential in the state Democratic party, the Fishers had also contributed generously to Alexander's election campaigns. In 1979, with the mayor's support, they and other investors bought an apartment complex at bargain-basement prices for federally subsidized tenants. Since the mayor controlled the nominally independent Syracuse Housing Authority (SHA), he had no trouble getting SHA to approve the deal. Along the way the Fishers garnered tax breaks, low-interest loans, and heavy subsidies. But HUD balked at this conflict of interest when the Fishers also received subsidies for vacant apartments. In a final charade in 1985, it asked the Housing Authority, Alexander's lapdog, to probe the Fisher story. Nothing came of the investigation except the elimination of subsidies for ghost tenants.[43]

The Boston Housing Authority (BHA) vies with the Chicago Housing Authority for the rare distinction of being the worst housing authority in the nation. Calling it "a housing horror story," Superior Court Judge Paul Garrity placed BHA under his receivership in 1979 and did not relinquish control until 1984. While some improvements had occurred, BHA soon returned to its old ways of bloated budgets, patronage, lack of financial control, and mismanagement. HUD placed BHA on parole by keeping it in 1990 on the "troubled list" of housing authorities.[44]

With eyes riveted on the scandals in HUD, the nation has overlooked equally serious flaws in hundreds of local housing authorities. By itself each authority may not make much of a national splash; taken together, they constitute a national housing tragedy of historic proportions. Not even the many exemplary housing authorities can brake the downward spiral of a failed policy.

To name names, 13 public housing authorities are among the best in the nation: Boulder (Colorado), Denver, Greensboro (North Carolina), Hampton (Virginia), Hartford, Houston, Louisville, Manchester (New Hampshire), Milwaukee, New Berlin (Wisconsin), Norfolk (Virginia), Pierce Count (Washington), and Seattle. They offset only in part the sloppy management in hundreds of housing authorities.[45]

Housing Finance Authorities

If the 3,400 local housing authorities struggle to provide housing for the poor, the state housing finance authorities or housing finance agencies (HFAs), as they are variously called, primarily serve moderate-income families ($30,000 to $40,000 a year). Invented by Governor Rockefeller in 1968, HFAs and their clones and mutations have spread into every state and even into some cities. The core of their program is the sale of tax-exempt mortgage revenue bonds for single-family and multifamily housing. The proceeds then flow to first-time home owners who benefit from low down payments and mortgages with low interest rates; to real estate developers who, in return for tax breaks and mortgages with interest rates 2 percent to 3 percent below conventional rates, agree to construct or renovate apartments at prescribed rents and at controlled profits; and to banks that sell mortgages to the HFAs and recycle the funds to provide more mortgages. From 1981 through 1987 HFAs had issued nearly $50 billion in housing bonds.[46] Today they serve fewer families because of limits in the Tax Reform Act of 1986.

On top of tax reform came the avalanche of federal cuts in housing money. Up to the late 1980s when tax revenues still rolled merrily into state treasuries, HFAs, with the aid of state funds, tried to rescue programs for low-income, moderate-income, and middle-income housing, the elderly, homeless, and handicapped, home and apartment rehabilitation, and energy conservation from the ashes of federal deregulation. Despite the collapse of state resources in the recession of 1990–1991, the salvage operation continues on a smaller scale. From their own funds raised by fees, charges, and investments, HFAs manage to squeeze out a few hundred thousand dollars here and there and occasionally $1 million or $2 million for a variety of modest housing programs with dazzling catchwords. State aid is minimal—less than 1 percent of direct expenditures; local assistance nearly 5 percent. The only significant funds come from the sale of tax-exempt bonds.[47]

Many HFAs also act as surrogates of HUD by monitoring rent subsidies for tenants and tax credits for "mod rehab"—modernization of apartments for families with moderate income.

In comparison to local housing authorities, HFAs are relatively untainted by scandals. In the *Machinery of Greed*, Diana Henriques documents corruption, bribes, kickbacks, embezzlement, political favoritism in contract awards, criminal negligence in management, padded payrolls, and ill-advised investments in at least five HFAs in Rhode Island, New Mexico, Utah, New Jersey, and Illinois in the late 1970s and early 1980s. Then came a series of defaults in New York, Massachusetts, New Jersey, and other states.

Even allowing for such failures, the constraints under which they operate, and murky public-private relations, in the impure world of housing several HFAs in California, New York, Massachusetts, Pennsylvania, Ohio, and Texas turn in a creditable albeit modest performance. Leading all other HFAs in lending activities is the California Housing Finance Agency (CHFA) with outstanding indebtedness of over $3.5 billion for buyers of single-family homes and developers of low-cost, multiunit rental housing. Together with local housing authorities, it produced 11,000 housing units for moderate-income Californians in 1988–1989. Combining these programs with a variety of direct assistance, loans, grants, and veterans' housing programs administered by CHFA and state agencies, California had some $6.5 billion in housing bonds outstanding as of 1991. In addition, the state spends about $1.6 billion annually for housing activities.[48]

On a smaller scale, the Wisconsin Housing and Economic Development Authority (WHEDA) has it all: subsidized rental housing, home improvement, multifamily rental housing, housing for the old, the disabled, and the homeless, rural housing, nonprofit housing, energy conservation. At least 20 programs nibble away at housing needs and each one produces a few hundred homes and apartments annually. The sums are small, but, cumulatively, they are helpful. All told they make only a ripple in a sea of unmet needs.

New York State has pulled out all the stops in housing. Not one but five state housing authorities have borrowed nearly $10 billion to expand the supply of affordable housing for low-income and moderate-income individuals and families, the elderly, and the homeless. The Housing Finance Agency finances low-income and middle-income housing through the sale of tax-exempt bonds. The Urban Development Corporation monitors projects built in the past (it has deserted its commitment to provide new housing). The State of New York Mortgage Agency buys mortgage loans from banks and assists qualified first-time home buyers. The Battery Park City Authority has leveraged surplus revenue to raise $1 billion for housing in New York City. Similarly, Big MAC channels excess revenue into New York City for housing, transportation, and school construction. Although it is hard pressed by $6-billion deficits, the state

government spends about $1.8 billion annually on housing includ-
ing subsidies to state and local housing authorities.

These expensive efforts offset in small part the abandonment of
low-cost housing by the federal government.

Every state HFA runs large and small housing programs as in
California, Wisconsin, and New York. In a more recent development many cities and counties have rushed to the aid of home
buyers and apartment dwellers with moderate incomes by creating
local HFAs, separate from local housing authorities, which issue
tax-exempt bonds. California has dozens of them like the Sacramento Housing and Development Agency. Two large HFAs in
Pennsylvania are the Philadelphia Redevelopment Authority and the
Allegheny County Residential Finance Authority. In Texas, Harris
County established a Housing Finance Corporation and its major
city, Houston, did the same. Other states that have developed tax-
free local home financing are Colorado, Illinois, Louisiana, Kentucky, Tennessee, Oklahoma, and Maryland. So rapidly have local
HFAs proliferated that Nuveen and Co., a large-scale buyer of tax-
exempt bonds for its mutual funds, has alerted investors to the
growing risks of mismanagement and lack of control.[49]

As befits the Big Apple, New York City not only has the biggest
public housing authority in the nation, but also a New York City
Housing Development Corporation for multifamily housing. To
support this program the city collects federal and state subsidies and
raises its own funds. In what it called the most ambitious housing
program in the nation, exceeding other city and state efforts, the
city, in the late 1980s, produced 3,500 subsidized apartments in
formerly abandoned buildings and had 13,000 others under construction as part of a total of 47,000 apartments scheduled for
renovation by the mid-1990s. Despite the cost, it was, like other
state and local programs, woefully inadequate. Soon a struggle for
these scraps of housing developed between the advocates of low-
income housing and the proponents of moderate-income housing.[50]

What's Ahead?

During the last 15 years state and local public authorities and their
parent governments have stepped into the void left by a federal

government that has abandoned its commitment to low-cost housing. Their best efforts, although costly, have turned out to be marginal. At a time when housing needs are as desperate as they were in the 1930s, no fully responsive federal, state, or local help exists.

Unlike Germany, Britain, France, and other countries, public housing is anathema to the policy makers in Washington, D.C. Yet it offers the one hope of providing affordable housing to the poor poor, the poor, the near poor, and the homeless. Despite the havoc wrought by uncontrolled and unaccountable housing authorities, they still have the potential to realize at long last the aims of FDR's social revolution in the 1930s. They can be major instruments in expanding public housing and in salvaging the disappearing stock of decayed private housing without feathering the nests of real estate developers. To do this, they require stiff regulation, leadership, and control not yet forthcoming from federal, state, and local governments.

As for the federal government, the housing menu it offers is a starvation diet. It is not too much for a nation with untapped fiscal and physical resources to provide 10 million low-cost apartments and homes via local and state housing authorities over the next 10 years.

9

The Big Fix

One of the ugliest stretches of elevated urban highways in the United States is a two-mile segment of I93 in Boston that runs between the north end of the city and Callahan Tunnel, the access to Logan Airport. Built in the early 1950s, the road is so congested and dangerous that 190,000 vehicles a day inch along at an accident rate twice the national average. This is the eyesore and bottleneck that the "Big Dig," officially called the Central Artery and Third Tunnel Project, will eliminate during the next 10 years at a cost of $5 billion. As a retirement gift to former House Speaker Thomas P. O'Neill, Jr., the federal government will pick up about 85 percent of the tab and the state the rest.[1]

Rounding out this massive project will be an extension of the Mass Turnpike into the third tunnel, with the Turnpike Authority responsible for the costs, and the expansion of Logan Airport by the Massachusetts Port Authority (Massport). The overall cost of all phases will reach about $10 billion.

Large and small projects such as the Big Dig carpet the country as the nation tries to repair its deteriorating infrastructure. The effect of the Reagan administration's legacy plus that of virtually bankrupt state and local governments was deep and widespread: thousands of miles of dilapidated and congested highways; aging, unsafe bridges; underfunded and run-down mass transit systems; crammed airports; obsolete and inefficient ports; inadequate and deteriorating solid waste and wastewater treatment facilities; insufficient hazardous waste facilities; and substandard drinking water systems.

In the most penetrating review of public works in the history of the country, the National Council on Public Works Improvement in

1988 warned that "a declining infrastructure inevitably will jeopardize the productivity of our economy and our quality of life." To highlight widespread deterioration and obsolescence, it rated all parts of the infrastructure as substandard on a scale from A to D:[2]

Highways	C+
Mass Transit	C−
Airports	B−
Water Resources	B−
Wastewater Treatment	C
Solid Waste Treatment	C−
Hazardous Waste Treatment	D

These were the bitter fruits of years of neglect. From a high of 2.3 percent of the GNP in the 1960s, expenditures for public works tumbled to 1 percent in the 1980s. Federal outlays, in 1984 dollars, peaked at $25 billion in the late 1970s. For state and local government the crest was $34 billion in 1972. Thereafter, expenditures slid steadily in the 1980s.

Repairing the Infrastructure

How much will the Big Fix of the infrastructure cost? The commission's relatively modest estimate is nearly $1 trillion for the last decade of this century, assuming that public spending for public works will more than double the annual rate of $45 billion. Other estimates from specialists range from $1 trillion to $3 trillion.

Where will the money come from? As is customary in the United States, a complex web of financing, similar to the Massachusetts deal, ties in the federal, state, and local governments and public authorities. Where governments fail, public authorities step in. Thus, public authorities own and operate 5,000 miles of toll roads and dozens of bridges. These are the holdings of such authorities as the New Jersey Turnpike, the Indiana Transportation Finance Authority, the Maine Turnpike Authority, and the New York State Thruway Authority.

Mass transit is almost exclusively an authority game, with 236 train and bus systems owned and managed by authorities like the Southeastern Michigan Transportation Authority, the Southeastern

Pennsylvania Transportation Authority (SEPTA), the Chicago Transit Authority, and the San Francisco Bay Area Rapid Transit District (BART).

While public authorities control only 40 percent of the large commercial airports, they command some of the biggest and the best such as the JFK Airport in New York, Logan Airport in Massachusetts, and the San Diego Airport. Public authorities also dominate half of the 106 ports in the country.

The 10 largest public authorities with strategic positions in the infrastructure and with annual revenues ranging between $500 million and $5 billion are the New York City Metropolitan Area Transit Authority (MTA), the Port Authority of New York and New Jersey, the Chicago Regional Transportation Authority, the Washington (D.C.) Metropolitan Area Transit Authority, the Lower Colorado River Authority (Austin, Texas), the Massachusetts Bay Transportation Authority (Boston), the Southeastern Pennsylvania Transportation Authority (Philadelphia), the Southern California Rapid Transit District (Los Angeles), the Southern California Metropolitan Water District (Los Angeles), and the Sacramento Municipal Utility District. Other contenders like the Massachusetts Water Resources Authority are rapidly crowding in for the privilege of being among the Big Ten.

Highways and Bridges

The sharp cuts in highway funds by the Reagan administration and further slashes by the Bush administration in the early 1990s catapulted public authorities into an even more prominent role in highway transportation.

At the heart of the struggle is the funding of about 3.9 million miles of roads and 576,702 bridges in the United States. In this vast network the federal government supports nearly 660,000 miles of interstate, primary, and secondary roads, 22 percent of all roads. These are the main traveled highways. The other roads are mainly unpaved rural roads. Federal aid reaches nearly 275,000 bridges, 48.4 percent of all bridges.

The annual cost of federal highway transportation aid approximates $14 billion to $16 billion—small potatoes compared to the roughly $55 billion spent by state and local governments. Highway and bridge financing comes down to a federal share of 25 percent, a state share of 50 percent, and a local share of 25 percent.[3]

In relation to the needs, highway transportation is grossly underfunded. Nearly 40 percent of the bridges are structurally deficient or functionally obsolete; several have collapsed with a tragic loss of lives. During rush hours over two-thirds of the interstate highway system is choked with slow-moving cars. At least 42 percent of these roads have deteriorated dangerously, yet traffic will double by the end of the century. Just to restore roads and bridges to 1985 standards will cost about $430 billion over 15 years according to conservative estimates of the U.S. Department of Transportation.[4]

As small as the federal share is, the Reagan and Bush administrations cut it even more. Federal aid comes mainly out of a highway trust fund to which all of us contribute about $16 billion a year via taxes on gasoline, diesel fuel, tires and parts, and truck and bus accessories. From this fund dedicated solely to transportation, the federal government by law is supposed to pay 90 percent of the cost of constructing roads and bridges in the interstate system, 75 percent of the cost of all other major highways, and 80 percent of the cost of all other major bridges. The states match the federal share and finance the cost of all other construction as well as the operation and maintenance of roads and bridges. Gasoline taxes and highway user fees support over four-fifths of their costs. Local governments receive federal and state aid for roads and bridges and also raise their own funds through taxes.

Shortly after he assumed office in 1981 President Reagan whittled away at grants for highway and bridge construction. Between 1980 and 1991 federal aid for all forms of transportation dropped almost 20 percent in constant dollars.[5] After peaking at $16 billion in 1965, federal grants for highway transportation sank to $18 billion in 1982 and began the slow climb to $14 billion in 1990, again in constant dollars. Despite hefty balances of $10 billion in the highway trust fund, the Reagan administration refused to allocate all the funds to the states. With the consent of Congress it began to misuse them along with the social security funds to mask the size of the federal deficit. In a Gramm–Rudman–Hollings deficit reduction straitjacket, Congress reluctantly went along with this step.

The Bush administration resolved to shrink the federal role even more. Claiming that the state and local governments were not doing enough, it announced in a 1991 report, *Moving America*, that the time had come to "increase the state and local share of federal-aid projects . . . allow greater use of toll financing on federal-aid highways, reduce federal operating assistance for urban transit."[6] The administration proposed a $89.1-billion highway program, roughly an expenditure of $18 billion a year for 1992 through 1996. This was a nominal increase of about $3 billion a year and far below the amount necessary just to keep up with inflation. As part of the package the administration wanted to slash the federal share from 90 percent to 75 percent for interstate highways and bridges and from 75 percent to 60 percent for other state roads and bridges.[7]

Dismayed governors, mayors, county executives, and public interest groups quickly attacked the new round of proposed cutbacks. Said Governor Mario M. Cuomo of New York, "This plan perpetuates the existing Federal fiscal policies that continually seek to force state and local governments to pick up the slack for proposed Federal cutbacks in domestic programs." Governor Wallace G. Wilkerson of Kentucky agreed: "More and more of the burden is being shifted to the states, and our ability to handle these things is getting less and less and less."[8] Governor James R. Thompson of Illinois proclaimed that the Bush message to the states was "read my lips, raise your taxes."[9]

One defender of the governors was Congressman Beryl Anthony, a member of the House Ways and Means Committee and chairman of the Anthony Commission on Public Finance. Anthony kept hammering away on the double jeopardy inflicted on the states: the Tax Reform Act of 1986 that severely limited their capability to issue tax-exempt bonds for the infrastructure and the reluctance of the federal government to pay its fair share to prop up the nation's crumbling infrastructure. "How in all conscience" he asked, "can we ask state and local governments to do more, while the federal government shrinks from its responsibilities?"[10]

Prodded by Senator Daniel Patrick Moynihan of New York State, the Bush administration in November 1991 agreed to spend $119 billion for highway programs over six years, $12 billion more than it had originally planned (*New York Times,* November 2, 1991).

As a way out of the fiscal bind, the Bush administration dangled before the states the lure of toll financing of federally aided roads. This was a dramatic break with federal law and policy. Since 1916 there had been a flat prohibition against the use of tolls on federally aided highways. Gradually Congress loosened the vise to the point where motorists pay tolls on 2,700 miles of the 44,000 miles of interstate highways. The quid pro quo is the promise of public authorities to lift the tolls once the debts are paid.[11] The British call this the never-never plan.

Once the nose of the federal camel was in the tent, it pushed ahead. In 1987 Congress approved a nine-state pilot program to permit tolls on additional federally aided highways. Under this ploy the federal government pays only 35 percent of project costs instead of 75 percent to 90 percent; the motorist ends up paying three times through user fees, taxes, and tolls. The administration and Congress also cast a benevolent eye on several schemes to privatize roads as in Virginia, Colorado, Illinois, and California. This would be easy on federal and state purses, but tough on motorists' pockets.[12]

With these federal blessings, toll financing took on a new life in the United States. Since 1980 eight state governments have initiated at least 11 new major toll projects or extended existing toll facilities, mainly operated by public authorities. Even more projects are on the drawing board. This is on top of 210 existing toll roads, bridges, and tunnels. Not far behind are dozens of local governments that have created toll-financed road districts in Texas, Montana, California, Iowa, Colorado, New Mexico, New Jersey, and Georgia.

Considering bonded debt, revenues, and expenditures, the following major state highway and bridge authorities top all the others save the Port Authority of New York and New Jersey:[13]

Oklahoma Turnpike Authority
Massachusetts Turnpike Authority
Greater New Orleans Expressway Authority
West Virginia Turnpike Commission
Rhode Island Turnpike and Bridge Authority
Texas Turnpike Authority
Georgia State Tollway Authority
Kansas Turnpike Authority

Illinois State Toll Highway Authority
Indiana Toll Road Commission
Ohio Turnpike Commission
Maine Turnpike Authority
Chesterfield County Toll Road Authority
New Jersey Turnpike Authority
New Jersey Highway Authority
New York State Thruway Authority·
Delaware Transportation Authority
Kentucky Turnpike Authority
Pennsylvania Turnpike Commission
Texas Turnpike Authority
Maryland Transportation Authority
Orlando-Orange County Expressway Authority
Jacksonville Transportation Authority
Richmond Metropolitan Authority
West Virginia Turnpike/Toll Road Commission

The Port Authority of New York and New Jersey remains in a class by itself, with its complex of bridges, tunnels, airports, and port facilities.

Relatively untainted by scandals and defaults that afflict other authorities, transportation authorities have become the cash cows of state and local governments. Long after they pay off their long-term debt, they continue their tolls to finance state highway and other activities. Instead of keeping tolls at the lowest possible levels, they charge what the traffic will bear and divert surpluses to the states, as in Florida, New Jersey, Illinois, and New York. They do this at the instigation of governors and legislatures.

With no income tax, Florida gobbles up tolls as fast as it can generate them to augment its revenue. Sixteen toll roads operate in the state: seven are independent county expressways; seven are county-managed such as Dade County's Miami Airport Expressway, East-West Expressway, and South Dade Expressway; and two, including the premier 321-mile Florida Turnpike, fall within the bailiwick of the State Department of Transportation. Prior to 1969 the Florida State Turnpike Authority owned and operated the turnpike. Then, in a rare move, the state terminated the authority and shifted all its powers to the Department of Transportation.[14]

Early on the state recognized a money machine when it saw one. To make sure that the cash flow never stopped, the legislature continued the tolls even after all indebtedness ceased. With the excess revenue, the state can build even more toll facilities, making the system a self-perpetuating source of funds. In a generous spirit, the legislature extended the same financial bag of tricks to the county authorities. So confusing were these arrangements to the public that there was not a murmur of protest.

New Jersey has long exacted tribute from its three highway authorities: the New Jersey Highway Authority (Garden State Parkway), the New Jersey Expressway Authority (Atlantic City Expressway), and the Turnpike Authority. The authorities transfer $25 million a year to the state so that, together with other funds, it can build and maintain "free" highways. This is an insignificant sum in a state given to multibillion-dollar deficits. Following the Florida example, the state came close in the late 1980s to abolishing the three authorities and shifting the remains to the Department of Transportation, but the legislature rejected the change, preferring to maintain its perquisites of sinecures, patronage, and a free-wheeling lifestyle. Even a proposal to merge the authorities under one super-authority died quickly. In 1991, in a more ambitious gambit, the Florio administration arranged to sell 4.4 miles of Interstate 95 between the George Washington Bridge and the New Jersey Turnpike to the Turnpike Authority for $400 million. The Turnpike Authority would also pick up maintenance costs. Florio's state treasurer Douglas Berman candidly admitted the reason for the sale: "There remains a big hole in the budget. The $400 million sale will help fill that void."

A submissive authority had no qualms about the sale, but doubted that it could charge tolls on its newly acquired road because of federal restrictions. Transportation Commissioner Tom Downs put these doubts to rest, pointing out that Maryland, Kansas, West Virginia, Maine, and Delaware took over sections of interstate highways and imposed tolls on them. This can be done if the state pays back to the federal government the federal share of building the road. A toll-happy national government is unlikely to quibble over the terms of the transfer, now being negotiated.[15]

Governor Mario M. Cuomo uses public authorities to help plug part of his annual budget deficits. The Thruway Authority, which stretches 559 miles from New York City to the Pennsylvania border, towers above all the others as a source of hard cash. By 1996 annual tolls will pour in at a rate of $400 million a year while costs will run only about $300 million. That leaves a $100-million surplus annually for a hard-pressed governor. The extra cash could even amount to $200 million if tolls are raised. Leveraged, this free cash could raise bond issues of more than $1 billion.

Quick to pounce on this bonanza, the governor sold 71 miles of the dilapidated Interstate 84 to the Thruway Authority in 1990, averting annual maintenance expenditures of $10 million and capital costs of at least $113 million for resurfacing, renovation, and the repair of 99 bridges. With the same dexterity he arranged for authority takeover of the Cross-Westchester Expressway at a cost of about $300 million. The financing of these transactions was consistent with several of the governor's other money-raising schemes. Cuomo had sold Attica prison to the Urban Development Corporation (UDC) for $200 million. To acquire it, UDC had to float a bond issue that will cost taxpayers $550 million over 30 years to buy back a prison they had paid for 60 years before. In 1991 the governor was also contemplating a deal to sell 14 office buildings in the state government complex, the State Campus, to the Dormitory Authority. Should this transaction go through, it will compel the taxpayers to buy buildings they thought they had financed in the 1950s.

But the Thruway Authority is a special case. By 1996 it will be debt-free. The toll plazas supposedly will come crashing down and motorists will enjoy a free ride over its entire length. An upset assemblyman, Mark Alan Siegel, who is chairman of the assembly committee on public authorities, warned: "I can tell you this—New York State does not have a sufficient revenue system to meet all its road needs." To continue tolls beyond 1996 would defy federal law and force the state to return to Washington $335 million worth of grants that had been pumped into the authority. This would not be as terrible a burden as it sounds. For a one-time payment of $335 million the Thruway will collect $400 million a year on and on into the indefinite future.[16]

For years the Triborough Bridge and Tunnel Authority of New York City, a Moses creation, had saddled motorists with tolls far greater than operating costs. At the behest of its master, the New York State Metropolitan Transportation Authority, it was diverting the surplus into other projects and mass transportation.[17]

Unchecked by the governor or legislature, the Illinois State Toll Highway Authority operates three toll roads and is now building a fourth, the North-South Tollway. A runaway authority, it sets tolls far in excess of costs in defiance of state law that mandates the lowest possible rates. With a surplus of $237 million in 1988, it began to use the funds for the fourth tollway despite lack of statutory approval. Only the auditor general protested. Not even a hint of chastisement came from the governor or legislature, who apparently did not believe in looking a gift horse in the mouth.[18]

On the whole, transportation authorities are money makers. But even they have left a trail of defaults on the payment of bonds behind them, although not on the same scale as other public authorities. The most notorious were the Calumet Skyway Toll Bridge Authority, now the Chicago Skyway ($110 million), the West Virginia Turnpike Commission ($133 million), and the Chesapeake Bay Bridge and Tunnel Commission ($100 million). Since 1963 the Calumet Skyway has failed to pay the required interest on the bonds and a U.S. district court has stepped in to protect the investments of the bondholders. In the meantime, the City of Chicago covers arrears. Bondholders in the other states lost their investment.

The Texas Turnpike Authority came close to a default in 1978 on the payment of interest on $102 million in bonds. At the last minute a restructuring of the debt averted collapse. Not so fortunate was the MLK Bridge in East St. Louis, which failed in 1974. As late as 1986 a Missouri judge forced bondholders to accept 54 cents on the dollar. Still other defaults on bridge bonds took place in Nebraska and West Virginia.[19]

How much cleaner is the California experience! The home of the first major tax revolt in modern times, it turned around in 1990 when the voters doubled gasoline taxes, loosened expenditure limits, and approved the issuance of over $4 billion in bonds for highway transportation and, to a lesser extent, for mass transportation. This was done openly after vigorous public debate and without the subterfuge of more expensive backdoor financing through public authorities.

Mass Transit

Mass transportation by trains and buses is virtually a public authority monopoly. Under the best of circumstances, it is a deficit operation. The only questions are the size of the deficits and who pays for them. Passengers generally travel at subsidized fares that cover about 36 percent of the annual cost of some $17 billion. The other revenue comes from state and local appropriations and taxes (52 percent), the federal government (6 percent), and investments (6 percent). Even though the federal government is very much a junior partner, it doles out reluctantly every dollar it spends for capital grants and operating assistance under the Urban Mass Transportation Act.

During the 1980s the Reagan and Bush administrations slashed transit funding by one-third, from $4.6 billion (1981) to $3.2 billion (1991). Considering inflation, this was a 50 percent cut. With the help of Congress they froze $4.1 billion earmarked for mass transportation in the Highway Trust Fund. If the Bush administration has its way, further cuts will continue well into the 1990s. In 1991 the administration unveiled a plan to spend $16.3 billion between 1992 and 1996. In current dollars this is a mere 1 percent increase over the previous five years and in inflation-adjusted dollars a calamitous drop of up to 20 percent. For existing capital projects the federal contribution would drop from 80 percent to 60 percent and for new ones from 75 percent to 50 percent, and the administration would eliminate subsidies for maintenance and operation altogether.[20]

Again, under Senator Moynihan's leadership, Congress rejected this by persuading the Bush administration to spend $32 billion for mass transportation over a six-year period—a major increase. The New York Times reported on November 2, 1991 that states would have greater discretion in spending the funds.

The latest changes came none too soon. Major transit systems— all run by public authorities—faced deep financial troubles. One, the Southeastern Pennsylvania Transportation Authority (SEPTA) serving Philadelphia and its suburbs, teetered on bankruptcy. Mired by large deficits, state and local governments were in no position even to maintain previous levels of support. By mid-1991 the outlook was bleak. Several transportation authorities such as Miami's

Metro-Dade Transit Agency curtailed routes while others raised fares. The effect was to cut ridership in public transportation, already at a low point of about 5 percent of all trips.[21]

Bush's transportation secretary, Samuel K. Skinner, former chairman of Chicago's Regional Transit Authority, was unabashed: "Transit systems probably should cut back services," he said. "Most places run service where it's a luxury rather than a necessity." Mass transit is no luxury to New York, where 49.3 percent of the workers rely on public transportation, or to San Francisco, where the figure is over 22 percent; or to Chicago, Skinner's former bailiwick, where public transportation is a must for more than one-fifth of all workers. A spokesman for Skinner's successor at the Chicago Regional Transit Authority estimated that the effect of the Bush–Skinner proposals would be to raise fares up to 20 percent, curtail service at night, and shut down several stations and bus routes.[22]

One of the outstanding managers of transit systems is Louis Gambaccini, general manager of Philadelphia's SEPTA, former secretary of transportation in New Jersey and a senior official in the Port Authority of New York and New Jersey. Embittered by federal cutbacks, he compared the alacrity with which the government rescued the savings and loan associations with its indifference to mass transportation:

> The federal government has committed some $150 billion to $300 billion, depending on whose estimates you choose, over the next 30 years to bail out the savings and loan industry. The lower figure—$150 billion—is three times the total investment at the federal level in transit over the last 25 years, since the Urban Mass Transportation Administration (UMTA) program began. It is half again more than the 30-plus year Interstate Highway System costs, and it is three times the size of the Marshall Plan funding.[23]

SEPTA had a special grievance. In 1983 the federal government sold Conrail after investing millions of dollars in its rehabilitation and pocketed the purchase price of $2 billion. At the same time it unloaded Conrail's obsolete commuter lines in the Philadelphia area on SEPTA. The cost of rehabilitating the equipment and other capital facilities exceeded $2 billion, yet only a dribble of assistance came from the federal government. Unless SEPTA gets $450 million a year for new equipment and major improvements, it will "deteriorate beyond repair within five years." In 1990 it was receiving about $150 million a year. A state government with a budget deficit of nearly $3 billion planned to cut $37 million in aid for SEPTA and the federal government planned another $28-million cut. The City of Philadelphia, which also subsidizes the system, was $10 million behind in its payments. By the middle of 1991 SEPTA was walking a tight rope, facing the prospect of closing down the entire system or perpetuating some of the most dangerous safety hazards in the country.

SEPTA is one of 1,726 transit systems in the nation that serve large and small urban and rural areas. Most are bus systems and only 27 heavy and light rail systems (although the larger systems combine train and bus facilities). About 23 public authorities carry most of the traffic. The 30 largest authorities, including SEPTA, move over 70 percent of all passengers.[24]

The largest mass transit system in the United States—and, for that matter, in the world—is the New York City Transit Authority (TA), which carries one-fourth of all passengers in the nation. In a Rockefeller-blessed shotgun wedding in 1965, TA became one of five subsidiaries of the New York State Metropolitan Transportation Authority (MTA). The other reluctant partners are the Long Island Railroad Company, the Metro-North Commuter Railroad Company, the Triborough Bridge and Tunnel Authority (seven bridges and two tunnels), and the Metropolitan Suburban Bus Authority. All of MTA's mass transit systems carry 2 billion riders a year, almost one-third of all mass transit users in the United States.

Other boosterisms describe this transportation giant. Its network covers 4,000 square miles and encompasses 12 counties in New York and two in Connecticut. Over four-fifths of the people who work in Manhattan use MTA's services every morning. Its train fleet is larger than the combined fleets of all other rapid transit and commuter railroads in the United Sates. Its 10-year (1982–1991) capital improvement program totaled over $16 billion, just about the size of projected federal aid for mass transit from 1992 to 1996. From 1992 through 1996 MTA will need another $11.5 billion according to its latest plan.

MTA also breaks records for the massive subsidies pumped in by the federal, state, and local governments, the Triborough Bridge and Tunnel Authority, and the Municipal Assistance Corporation to keep it alive. To support the capital program, the federal government contributes about one-third of the cost, the state and city about 15 percent, other public authorities nearly 3 percent, bond financing over 39 percent, and a motley array of revenue sources the rest.

For routine operation and maintenance MTA is also a supplicant. Despite high fares, passengers pay only about 40 percent of the cost while heavy state and local subsidies and taxes cover the deficit. As essential as MTA is, it has become a bottomless pit. Ridership is declining and subsidies are increasing, although the 1990–1991 recession acted as a brake. And some 67,000 unionized employees hang on to generous salaries and fringe benefits that consume over 70 cents of each dollar of revenue.

As in housing, mass transit authorities in Chicago and Boston are rife with mismanagement, patronage, corruption, and uncontrolled costs. Nominally independent, the Chicago Transit Authority (CTA) has been the political playground of a succession of mayors. While rumors of their exploits have been the stuff of gossip for many years, it took a six-month investigation of the CTA by the *Chicago Sun-Times* in the latter part of 1987 to unravel a skein of bribery, favoritism in the award of contracts, flagrant disregard of safety, nepotism, exorbitant spending on travel, overpayments— even contractor-financed sex parties for weary executives.

Among the vignettes that emerged from the *Sun-Times* articles was the award of a $38-million diesel oil contract to an obscure oil company that provided substandard fuel and fleeced CTA of $624,000. Only after the newspaper stories did CTA insist on repayment. This forced the company out of business and led to an FBI inquiry into collusion between the company and CTA employees.

An entrepreneurial former official of CTA sold the authority a "miracle graffiti remover" at $23.50 a gallon, three times the price paid by the New York City Transit Authority for a nonmiraculous remover that worked. Even more enterprising was Art Smith, Mayor Washington's appointee to the Police Board. Smith ran bus services for CTA, the board of education, and other city agencies at a contracted cost of $11 million a year. For CTA he transported elderly and disabled individuals. His pickups were late 30 percent to 50 percent of the time, making his service the worst of four private carriers in Chicago. Despite Smith's dismal record and a long list of improprieties, CTA extended his contract and granted him a rate increase.

In violation of safety regulations CTA ran 70 defective trains with broken brake-failure warning systems. Supervisors kept this information from motormen. Despite a rash of car fires that destroyed 14 cars worth over $10 million, CTA failed to order key pieces of equipment that could prevent the fires. It was unable to cope with heavy snowfalls because of the lack of sufficient equipment to keep the electrified third rails free of ice. While the system was deteriorating around them, CTA executives spent $278,000 a year on travel to conferences where they allegedly learned how to manage mass transit systems.

Other typical maneuvers were bribery of employees to win contracts and multimillion-dollar contracts awarded to 20 companies without competitive bidding. More atypical was the *Sun-Times* report of sex parties hosted by Richard Deprizio, president of the V.N. Deprizio Company that won a CTA contract for $13.4 million to build a CTA extension to O'Hare Airport. A week after the newspaper story, Deprizio was murdered Chicago gangland style.[25]

Nothing as sensational as a gangland slaying tarnishes the legend of the Massachusetts Bay Transportation Authority (MBTA, or "the T") in the Boston area—just routine heavy patronage, mismanagement, pilferage, runaway costs, and the iron grip of 20 politically powerful unions. The predictable result is that MBTA is the least efficient and most costly major mass transit system in the country. For a brief spell Governor Michael Dukakis, during his first term, attempted to seize control of the "T" by installing a professional management team that included Robert R. Kiley and David Gunn.

Just when Dukakis' team began to nibble at intractable problems, the incoming governor, Edward J. King, forced them out in 1978. And the old political alliances of the governor, the unions and favored contractors, resumed. Both Kiley and Gunn later assumed top management posts in the Philadelphia and New York City systems. During the second coming of Dukakis from 1983 to 1990, the "T" was virtually untouched and continued to receive a blank check from the state government. Routinely the state covered deficits that approximated $500 million in 1990 and paid debt service on $1.2 billion in bonds issued by the "T."[26]

Barebone but efficient, other mass transit authorities sidestep the perils of Boston and Chicago. In California the authorities hang on with the aid of a fraction of the state motor fuel tax and the sales tax. This keeps the Bay Area Rapid Transit District (BART) in San Francisco, Metro Rail (Southern California Rapid Transit District) in the Los Angeles area, and other California rapid transit districts running. In other parts of the country mass transit systems are struggling with service cuts, fare increases, and shrinking subsidies. So goes the tale of woe of New Jersey Transit, Metropolitan Atlanta Rapid Transit Authority (MARTA), Washington D.C.'s Metropolitan Area Transit Authority (MATA), Metropolitan Transit Authority (MTA) of Harris County, Texas (Houston Area), the Dallas Area Rapid Transit (DART), Greater Cleveland's Rapid Transit Authority (RTA), and the Metro-Dade Transit Agency (Florida).

Because of America's love affair with the automobile and a lukewarm commitment to the infrastructure, mass transit, despite the best efforts of public authorities, is still fairly primitive compared with systems in Europe and Japan. No bullet trains pierce the country as in Japan. No French T.G.V. hurtles between cities at 185 miles per hour. The technology exists and the need is obvious, but the political will is flabby.

Air Travel

High flying is something else again. Some 16,000 U.S. airports speed Americans on their way, far more than those in the rest of the world combined. About one-third or 532 handle commercial aviation. Among these, 72 large and medium-sized airports monopolize 90 percent of all commercial traffic. Twenty-seven, including the "big hub" airports in Atlanta, New York City, Los Angeles, and Dallas–Fort Worth, control about 70 percent of all flights.

Every one of us can claim ownership of one or more of the 532 airports with counties, cities, and public authorities our chosen agents of management. Despite trendy mutterings of privatization, attempts have been bungled as in Albany County, New York, and elsewhere. So the airports remain firmly in the public domain. Cities and counties enjoy a commanding lead in ownership compared with public authorities—60 percent to 40 percent. While control by authorities is steadily creeping up, local governments show no signs of letting go of Hartsfield–Atlanta International Airport, San Francisco International Airport, Los Angeles International Airport, Miami International Airport, Denver–Stapleton Airport, Chicago O'Hare Airport, Philadelphia International Airport, and a few other big ones.[27]

There is every incentive to retain ownership because by and large airports are money makers and not drains on local purses. For some local governments they are a buzzing hive of patronage and for others a prized symbol of boosterism and economic growth. When the going gets rough, the cities can always unload them on public authorities as Boston did with Logan Airport, now in the professional hands of Massport.

For an assortment of local reasons, many cities and counties have turned to public authorities for salvation. There may be regional problems that no one government can surmount; busted budgets; revulsion against cronyism, patronage, and mismanagement; and an uproar against financial skullduggery. Whatever the burning issues that prompted the creation of airport public authorities, the choice has been a good one and has led to smooth and professional operations in contrast to festering problems in several large city-owned or county-owned airports.

Among the cities where public authorities fly high are New York City (JFK and LaGuardia Airports), Newark, Minneapolis—St. Paul, Cincinnati, Seattle—Tacoma, Portland, Oregon, San Diego, Salt Lake City, Tampa, Louisville, Tucson, and dozens of others.

Regardless of the form of ownership, most airports scrape by with enough revenue to meet their operating costs and debt service for billions of dollars of tax-exempt bonds (for example, in 1990 Denver City and County marketed $700 million of airport bonds). Their steady sources of revenue are aircraft landing fees, parking and road tolls, and a percentage of the gross profits of concessionaires. For example, Massport collected some $200 million in revenue from Logan Airport in 1990. Nearly 96 percent came from fees and tolls. If the airports run into hard times, they look to the states or local taxes to bail them out as occurred in Michigan and other states. Normally, though, state help is miniscule except for a handful of state-owned airports such as in Hawaii.

No matter what their needs, airports are not permitted to make a profit. Although airlines can raise their fares at will, federal law restricts airport revenue solely to an amount sufficient to cover operating expenses and debt service. In the Alice-in-Wonderland lexicon of Washington, D.C., this ceiling is called the "reasonableness" rule. Should an airport violate it, federal aid would be jeopardized. Only the airlines are winners and continue to pay low landing fees based on aircraft weight, as they have for the last 50 years. They pull out all stops in opposing special peak-hour takeoff and landing fees, even though these fees could raise revenue for desperately needed expansion and modernization.[28]

For the relief of congestion and the assurance of safety in the crowded skies, airports need at least $25 billion during the next five years and the Federal Aviation Administration (FAA), which controls air traffic, needs another $25 billion ($31 billion by the year 2000). The federal government is the exclusive but reluctant provider of funds for major capital improvements such as runways and the purchase of sophisticated equipment to monitor flights and security. Congress forced it to assume this role by creating the Airport and Airway Trust Fund in 1971. By taxing passengers, air cargo, and general aviation fuel, the government's fund has built up over the years to the point where it began to show weighty surpluses of over $7 billion a year in the Reagan and Bush eras. Rather than allocate these funds to hundreds of approved projects, the president and Congress hung on to them grimly to fudge the size of the federal deficit.

In 1990, the Bush administration belatedly recognized the need for an expenditure of $47 billion over the next five years to upgrade the civil aviation system. But, as in other modes of transportation, it quickly passed most of the bucks to airline users and tried to relieve the federal government of still another obligation. Were its plan adopted, passengers would pay a ticket tax of 10 percent instead of 8 percent. Airlines would pay higher fuel taxes and of course pass on the added costs to passengers. Shippers of air freight would face increased taxes. And the "reasonableness" rule would be shattered, allowing airports for the first time to charge a takeoff fee of up to $3 for each passenger. Should the passenger change planes, the fee for a round-trip ticket could exceed $12. Those airports that elected to impose passenger fees would lose part of their federal grants on the order of 50 cents for every dollar in new fees. Users would pay 85 percent of the cost of the FAA with the government's share dropping from the current 57 percent to 15 percent.

Thus did an administration that had proclaimed itself against new taxes, propose another round of taxes under the disguise of "user fees" that did not come under the ban on taxes.

According to James L. Oberstar, a Minnesota Democrat who chairs the House subcommittee on public works and transportation and tends to muddle his metaphors, "It's a fiscal Trojan horse. It will eat you alive." He vowed to use his influences to commandeer the surplus in the trust fund and to shift most of the costs to the federal government.[29]

James B. Busey, the head of FAA, enunciated the administration's party line: "The users of the national airspace system are not paying their fair share of system costs." His boss, Samuel K. Skinner, secretary of transportation, promised a batch of benefits if only airline users would pay for them.[30] Public authorities and other airport owners eagerly snapped up the proposals. Unfettered by federal controls, they would charge an additional $1 billion a year in airport fees and receive billions in federal grants for airport expansion. For the Port Authority of New York and New Jersey, which was struggling with a $3-billion redevelopment plan for JFK Airport alone, the proposal couldn't have come at a better time. U.S. citizens would be hit again with the national shift from taxes to fees.

Shipping via Port Authorities

As in the air, so by the sea public authorities rule. In fact, some 106 port agencies exist, nearly half under the thumbs of cities and counties as in Los Angeles, San Francisco, and Miami. Modeled after the Port Authority of New York and New Jersey, they were mostly created in the 1920s and 1930s when they took over dilapidated piers and marine terminals owned by railroads and shipping lines. Today they control and manage marine facilities, container ports, marinas, grain terminals, and shipyards. Some function as landlords and merely rent facilities to shippers, passenger lines, and truckers. Others are vigorous day-to-day operators.

The largest port authorities have evolved into conglomerates that run airports, air cargo facilities, mass transit, bridges, ferries, tunnels, bus terminals, industrial parks, finance centers, foreign trade zones, trucking facilities, and telecommunication centers. As such, they have become de facto economic development authorities as well because of the large segment of the infrastructure under their control.[31] Whether people go by land, sea, or air, sooner or later they will be in the hands of one of these multifaceted authorities like Massport, San Diego Unified Port District, Port of Seattle, Port of Portland, the Delaware River Port Authority, the Jacksonville Port Authority, the Port of Oakland, or the Port Authority of New York and New Jersey. It is especially difficult to escape the clutches of the latter with its seven marine terminals, four airports, two heliports, two tunnels, four bridges, two bus terminals, the twin-tower World Trade Center, and the PATH mass transportation system.

Until the 1970s and early 1980s, port authorities on the East Coast, especially in Boston, New York, Philadelphia, Baltimore, and Hampton Road, Virginia, handled most of the general cargo shipped to and from the United States. Most of the trade was with Europe. Then a steady decline began in the Northeast and Midwest ports as the United States became the largest consumer rather than producer of goods. A torrent of goods began to pour in from the Pacific rim countries, nearly all of it passing through the West Coast ports. By the end of the 1980s the value of cargo handled in Los Angeles shot up by 239 percent, in Long Beach by 147 percent, in Tacoma by 685 percent, in Oakland by 71 percent, and in Seattle by 89 percent. At the same time the Port Authority of New York and New Jersey limped along with a 10 percent increase. The only bright spots were authorities in Hampton Roads and Charleston, South Carolina, which began to dominate foreign trade in the Southeast.[32]

Measured in terms of tons of cargo handled, the changes were even more dramatic with the West Coast ports surpassing most of the East Coast, Midwest, and Gulf ports.[33] This hit an especially sensitive nerve since tons of cargo translate into stevedoring and trucking hours and hence employment. Declining cargo coupled with automation such as container ships shrank the number of dock workers in New York from 30,000 in the 1950s to about 4,000 in the early 1990s. In Baltimore, Boston, Philadelphia, and Miami longshoremen also became a dying breed.

In quick reaction to this change of fortune, port authorities along the Atlantic Ocean began to spend hundreds of millions of dollars to modernize and automate their docks and piers. If the 1980s was the era of the Pacific trade, the 1990s, they fervently hoped, would bring the European Community as well as a reviving Latin America to their shores.

Hedging their bets, some of the port authorities on the East Coast began to turn to international air cargo as a salvation. So successful was the Port Authority of New York and New Jersey, in particular, that in 1989 the value of air cargo moving in and out of New York topped cargo shipped by sea by $11 billion.[34]

In the meantime, the East Coast ports competed fiercely among themselves for a declining share of cargo. The Delaware River Port Authority and the Philadelphia Port Corporation were pitted against the Maryland Port Administration (Baltimore) and the Virginia Port Authority (Hampton Roads), while Massport competed against all of them. All of them together confronted the Port Authority of New York and New Jersey.

One of the few booming ports on the East Coast, the Virginia Port Authority, had leaped ahead by combining and modernizing three separate ports and tying them in with road and railroad networks. When the closely related Delaware River Port Authority (New Jersey and Pennsylvania), the South Jersey Port Corporation, and the Philadelphia Port Corporation attempted a merger in 1988, they fell apart in a squabble over control, patronage, and jobs. Congressman Jim Florio, later governor of New Jersey, failed to move them, despite an eloquent plea for unification:

> Unfortunately, our region's port facilities, despite some spectacular individual success stories, are not operating as an integrated system. Our region is in danger of losing the race to other ports. The ports of the Delaware River Valley actually compete for cargo with the ports in Baltimore and Norfolk, yet there is one crucial difference between our ports and theirs. Their ports operate as an integrated whole, under the direction of unified port authorities. In contrast, our ports operate almost as independent

fiefdoms, with each facility seemingly more concerned with taking traffic away from facilities across the river, than competing with ports that are far distant.

At a time when we should be facing up to the challenges and the tough new realities of survival in a global economy, it is unwise, in the long term, for Camden to see Philadelphia as its rival, and vice versa. The result is, individual port facilities are competing with each other for declining cargoes, and not with the real competition in Baltimore, Norfolk, and other places. This internal competition, and the lack of a unifying agency, make it harder to plan and make the necessary improvements that could benefit the entire port region on the Delaware River.[35]

U.S. District Court Judge Stanley S. Brotman in Philadelphia had another view of one of the would-be partners, the Delaware River Port Authority. Raising questions about poor management, fraud, and other improprieties, he called it an "agency run amok."[36]

In the aftermath of the abortive attempt at unification, the South Jersey Port Corporation, long afflicted with mismanagement, defaulted on the payment of its bonds and became a ward of the state. The moribund Philadelphia Port Corporation was replaced by a new authority, the Philadelphia Regional Port Commission.

More so than on the West Coast, the ports on the East Coast have suffered from the stifling embrace of the International Longshoreman's Association (ILA), frequently dominated by corrupt chieftains. For years they controlled the Port of New York and exacted tribute through extortion, bribery, kickbacks, pilferage, and loan sharking. Although invited by the governors of New York and New Jersey to police the ports, the Port Authority preferred the high road of port and economic development. Finally, in 1953, to break the hold of the ILA, both states, with the approval of Congress, created the Waterfront Commission of New York Harbor, another authority, to control crime and oversee labor-management relations. An unprecedented regulatory agency, the commission registers and licenses stevedores, stevedore companies, supervisors, and other waterfront employees, and monitors hiring practices.

At best this is a holding operation. If the stranglehold of the ILA has eased, it is due as much to automation as to policing by the commission. Before the ILA agreed to containerization and other technological changes, it demanded a high price on the entire East Coast: a guaranteed annual wage whether longshoremen worked or not, and preservation of featherbedding in the form of thousands of redundant jobs. Ultimately these demands were a self-defeating last hurrah. High prices for cargo handling forced even more shippers to the West Coast and the number of longshoremen withered steadily.

The same disease set back the Port of Baltimore, where labor problems, crime, and corruption as well as competition from other ports led to a large drop in general cargo handled by the port. An imaginative ILA added still another quirky item to its contract called the "rain clause" by its members and the "Baltimore curse" by everyone else. At the first sign of rain, the longshoremen were free to leave their jobs and still get paid. They cheerfully took up the old refrain, "in every life some rain must fall."[37]

The ports of New York and Baltimore were not the sole offenders. In Florida, the Everglades Port Authority of Fort Lauderdale, the home port of many cruise lines, paid exorbitant fees for bond issues, spent an unnecessary $3 million for overstaffing, contributed to political parties, and bought opera tickets and extravagant gifts for its commissioners. Only an investigation by the *Miami Herald* in 1989 triggered long overdue oversight by the legislature and started the authority on the road to probity.[38]

Nor is small necessarily beautiful. As the Woods Hole, Martha's Vineyard, and Nantucket Steamship Authority plies the pristine waters of Nantucket Sound, few tourists would suspect that its hold is full of rattling skeletons. Although a small line, it ran up over $3 million in cost overruns. At board meetings board members verbally and even physically assaulted each other rather than trying to bring a runaway authority to heel.

Even the prosperity of the West Coast ports did not obscure patronage and corruption at the ports of San Francisco and Los Angeles in the 1970s and early 1980s or the lack of judgment of the Portland Port Authority (Oregon) in authorizing James Locke, a convicted thief, to build a $43.2-million coal export terminal on its property to serve the Japanese market. In 1982 Governor Vic Atiyeh presided over the ground-breaking ceremony. A year later the luckless project collapsed, leading to losses of millions of dollars by the American Guarantee Financial Corporation and the Far

West Savings and Loan Association that Locke had cajoled to underwrite the enterprise. The *Oregonian* pointed out that Locke's record of business failures did not deter his partners.[39]

The Port Authority of New York and New Jersey still remains the goliath among port authorities. None of the others come close: over $6 billion in assets; nearly $1.5 billion in annual revenue; $1.1 billion in operating expenses; outstanding debt of about $3.5 billion; about 9,500 well-paid employees; and an even better paid top staff of 49 executives, each earning $110,000 or more. Nor does any other port authority sport a diversity of functions that besides tunnels, bridges, airports, and mass transportation also include a World Trade Center, industrial parks, a legal center, a telecommunication center, a resource recovery facility, an export zone, and a Fishport.

After a slow and penny-pinching beginning, the Port Authority, under the leadership of Austin Tobin, became an exceedingly profitable nonprofit organization that was able to undertake such far-flung ventures. What made all this possible was the authority's abandonment of its original mission to provide rail transport between New York and New Jersey. That would have been too costly and risky compared to the high-return and low-risk enterprises that the authority preferred. Only after pressure from two Rockefellers—Nelson, the governor, and David, CEO of the Chase Manhattan Bank—did the authority agree in 1962 to take over the bankrupt Hudson and Manhattan Railroad that ran between New Jersey and New York. This became the refurbished Port Authority Trans-Hudson Corporation (PATH). But Tobin insisted upon and got a quid pro quo for his change of heart: a profitable 110-story World Trade Center and a commitment that the authority would no longer venture into unprofitable mass transit operations.[40]

When Tobin resigned in 1972, William J. Ronan, Governor Rockefeller's powerful secretary and alter ego, refused to accept appointment as executive director of the Port Authority. He spelled out his reasons in a letter to the chairman of the selection committee:

> I reluctantly concluded that, with notable exceptions, Port Authority Commissioners appear to assign a higher priority to the bond market than to mass transportation. . . . The Metropolitan

Transportation Authority offers more real opportunities than the Port Authority with all its resources unless there is a clearcut change in its policy and directions.[41]

Once Tobin was out of the way, the authority—under relentless pressure by the governors and legislatures of New York and New Jersey—bought $400 million worth of buses for both states, developed two bus terminals, expanded PATH, aided New Jersey Transit, and planned rail links to JFK and Newark airports. More so than in the past, it began to portray itself as a protector of the regional economy and an active participant in the repair of the infrastructure. In 1991 it claimed credit for some 425,000 jobs in business sectors "anchored" by its investments, 166,000 temporary construction jobs, and 20,000 new jobs. When Peter C. Goldmark, Jr., was executive director from 1977 to 1984, he proposed the creation of a Bank for Regional Development that would receive profits from the World Trade Center and lend the funds to local governments for the construction of sewers, tunnels, and bridges. So far this has not materialized as funds were used for other purposes.[42]

At the peak of its profitability in 1987, the Port Authority launched a five-year, $5.8-billion capital plan to refurbish and expand the airports, the light rail system, and the tunnels. Higher tolls and fares would pay for the improvements. Suddenly in 1989 a shock wave went through the once invincible authority. For the first time surpluses evaporated and it ran up a deficit of $57 million. Among the heavy losers were PATH, the bus terminals, Holland and Lincoln Tunnels, the Newark New Jersey Legal Center, two industrial parks, the Fishport in Brooklyn, and the Teleport. Only another round of toll and fare increases helped. Minimizing economic development projects, the Port Authority is now returning to the basics: airports, bridges, tunnels, the port, and PATH.[43]

So the search for ways and means to shore up the decayed infrastructure via public authorities goes on. If federal and state grants and taxes will not pay for the thousands of projects, fees will unless simmering fee revolts break out in earnest. The burden of paying for government continues to shift to the less advantaged because of the regressive nature of fees.

10

The Big Cleanup

America is awash in waste, toxic poisons, and contaminated water. To clean up the muck would cost at least $500 billion over the next 10 years. Federal, state, and local governments will not or cannot raise such enormous sums. The U.S. Environmental Protection Agency (EPA), which orchestrates the "big cleanup," dispenses advice on a large scale but with very little money. Currently, it proclaims the need for "innovative financing" and "alternative financial mechanisms" among the states. In the gobbledegook of Washington, D.C., this means any system of raising money that does not depend on general taxes, federal grants, and overburdened state and local governments. Once again, it is a call for even more public authorities financed by user fees.

The states needed no prodding by EPA. After all they had already created thousands of authorities to sidestep budget and constitutional booby traps. This time they plunged avidly into a new round of environmental authorities.

Love Canal, Woburn, and the Stringfellow Acid Pits

Few events focused public attention on the need for a massive cleanup of the environment as much as the poisonous cauldrons in Niagara Falls, New York, Woburn, Massachusetts, and Glen Avon, California, seventy-five miles east of Los Angeles.

In the 1890s William Love of Niagara Falls, New York, planned a model town as a sharp contrast to the squalor of his own rapidly industrializing city. His first step was the digging of a canal, promptly named Love Canal, with the aim of siting the new town downstream from the Niagara River. No sooner had he begun than his utopia foundered on the shoals of poor planning and financial distress, leaving behind a six-block pit. Between 1947 and 1952 the Hooker Chemical Corporation, a subsidiary of the Occidental Petroleum Corporation, turned the pit into a waste dump and buried about 22,000 tons of toxic chemicals in it. It then covered the pit with dirt and sold the land for a school and homes with the backyards sitting on top of the old canal bed. No government regulations stood in the way.

By the early 1970s the poisonous chemicals bubbled to the surface in backyards and the school playing field and contaminated water systems. Suddenly the incidence of leukemia, respiratory diseases, and skin disorders reached a new high and, in the late 1970s, hundreds of families abandoned their homes. To ease the blows, the federal and state governments bought their homes at prevailing market prices. After a decade of massive cleanup, the U.S. Environmental Protection Agency (EPA) and New York State announced in 1990 that much of the Love Canal area was safe enough for families to buy 236 abandoned homes at bargain-basement prices. Environmentalists fumed at what they called a dangerous precedent and vowed to sue in the courts to overturn the decision.[1] At the same time liability suits against Occidental continued.

The inhabitants of Woburn, Massachusetts, also found themselves in a fool's paradise. Toxic chemicals dumped behind industrial sites seeped into the local drinking water supply and resulted in excessive cases of leukemia. It may take 10 to 20 years before the full extent of the damage is known in terms of cancer, heart disease, neurological disorders, and reproductive problems.[2] Toxic dumps such as these have become time bombs.

Nor was fate kinder to the residents of Glen Avon, California who suffered from the dumping of 34 million gallons of acids, solvents, and pesticides in the nearby Stringfellow Acid Pits. Just as Love Canal became a symbol of uncontrolled hazardous waste on the East Coast, so did Stringfellow become a bitter issue on the West Coast. Among other factors it led to the jailing of Rita M. Lavelle, former administrator of hazardous waste programs for the EPA for perjury, the firing of Anne McGill Burford, the head of EPA, and the expulsion of twenty other Reagan appointees for misconduct and mismanagement. By the end of 1991 corporate polluters had paid over $34 million in fines. This was just the beginning as other suits claimed damages running to nearly $1 billion.[3]

Hazardous Waste

New Jersey has the dubious record as the state with the largest number of hazardous sites followed closely by Michigan, New York, Pennsylvania, and several other Midwestern states. Including these, Love Canal, and Woburn, the EPA estimates that some 27,000 hazardous sites exist. As the search for environmental poisons continues, the figure may reach 130,000 to 425,000.[4] They have become symbols of a nation that has recklessly, greedily, and thoughtlessly assaulted and degraded its environment.

Along with hazardous waste sites, billions of gallons of wastewater and storm water overflow our sewers daily and foul our rivers, bays, and oceans. Yet only about 7,000 wastewater treatment plants, half the number needed, exist to cope with the flood that engulfs them. "Pure water" has become a myth in many communities as consumers spend millions of dollars on bottled water. Some 59,000 water systems, large and small, struggle against growing odds in complying with federal and state water quality standards and supplying enough water to 220 million people.[5]

America leads the world in the amount of trash it throws away—some 165 million tons a year. Nearly 95 percent ends up in landfills that are rapidly closing because they have reached the limits of their capacity or have contaminated the groundwater below them. At least one-third of the 10,000 municipal solid waste landfills fail to meet federal air and water quality standards.

The time has come for America to pay the cost of a ravaged environment, and the bill for the "big cleanup" is high. By the year 2000 this is what we will have to pay in addition to current costs, according to the most conservative estimates:

	Billions of dollars
Wastewater treatment	$100–120
Drinking water	90–100
Hazardous federal sites (nuclear and other)	150
Other hazardous and solid waste sites	100

As we learn more, the estimate of nearly $500 billion over the next 10 years may be on the low side.

Except for hazardous waste, sewer, water, and solid waste systems have traditionally been a local responsibility with some state aid thrown in by a handful of states. By the 1950s technical and financial problems had overwhelmed local and state governments. At this point the federal government charged into the fray. Over the next 30 years it enacted clean water, clean air, safe drinking water, and environment cleanup laws and issued thousands of regulations to chastened industries and governments. More important, until the era of Reaganomics it was relatively free with its money.

Local governments became the prime beneficiaries especially in building and modernizing wastewater treatment plants and sewer systems. From 1956 to the late 1980s the federal government dispensed about $50 billion in construction grants that covered 75 percent, and at times 95 percent, of the cost of the new projects. Federal aid peaked at $9 billion in 1976. With the advent of the Reagan administration in 1981, it dropped to $4.6 billion, then to $2.4 billion. At the same time the grants paid for only 55 percent of project costs, not the previous 75 percent.

Even this was considered too much by the White House. In 1987 it approved legislation that, on a phased basis, cut out grants altogether, with 1994 the last year for this aid. The federal government provides only one-time seed money to states that set up loan funds for local governments to finance wastewater treatment plants. The states, however, must comply with two conditions. First, they must establish state revolving funds (SRFs), many of them public authorities, as the recipients of the seed money. Second, they must contribute 20 percent of the federal grant that was authorized at $9.6 billion, but quickly fell to less than $2 billion a year. In the future, repayment of the loans by local governments will replenish the SRFs. With this move the federal government washed its hands of wastewater treatment plants. Now state and local governments are on their own.

To assure safe drinking water the federal government saddles the states and cities with regulations and standards. Nothing else. Worst of all, it provides no money for compliance.

From 1978 to 1982 Washington, D.C. doled out token assistance for solid waste recovery systems. It cut even this after 1982. Because of the outcry over Love Canal and similar tragedies, Congress and the administration created a Superfund ranging from $8.4 billion to $11.2 billion by 1996 to clean up hazardous waste sites. The contributors are manufacturers of petroleum and chemical feedstocks, oil companies, the offenders from whom the government recovers some money, and state governments that pay 10 percent of the cost of the cleanup. The biggest polluter of all is the federal government itself, which was slow in raising $150 billion to clean up the massive pollution in its nuclear plants and defense facilities.

The Tax Reform Act hastened the flight of the federal government from its environmental responsibilities just as it had done for the rest of the infrastructure. The act outlawed tax-exempt bonds for pollution control systems in utilities and other industries. It curtailed the volume of these bonds for other environmental projects so long as private firms had more than a 10 percent interest. For all the hoopla about public-private partnerships and privatization, the legislation discouraged joint enterprises to process solid waste, provide water, and operate sewer systems. No longer were enticing tax-saving incentives available such as investment tax credits and accelerated depreciation of plant and equipment. Not even a contract with a municipality for waste processing was a sure thing since the act required renewal of service contracts every five years.

In 1991, at a time when state and local governments were bogged down with a collective deficit of $100 billion and needed help most, the federal government turned its back on them. It spewed out regulations and controls, but no money. The annual cost of complying with federal standards was about $90 billion. State and local governments were unable to raise even half that amount. Senator Peter Domenici of New Mexico and Senator David Boren of Arkansas tried to contain the damage by introducing legislation to authorize tax-exempt bonds for rebuilding the infrastructure including cleanup of the environment, but the Bush administration, loathe to lose any revenue, fought this measure.

Left to muddle through as best they could, state and local governments created more public authorities, while those already in place raised user fees sharply. On the average, home owners and apartment dwellers paid about $500 a year in the late 1980s for sewer, water, and solid waste facilities in contrast to previous bills of some $200. And the end was not in sight. Braving public wrath, several state governments managed to win approval of sizable bond issues for environmental projects. Also, bucking the tide, many states imposed taxes earmarked solely for the infrastructure. Ten enterprising states created bond banks (public authorities) that lent money to fiscally strapped local governments for water and sewer facilities.

All of this helped, but not enough. At this point EPA proposed the use of "alternative financial mechanisms" (AFMs).[6] The National Council on Public Works Improvement was more explicit in calling for the creation of independent authorities:

> One way to ensure that proper rates are established for wastewater services, is to separate the institution that is responsible for sewer service delivery from the general municipal government. Such an arrangement allows the wastewater utility to operate in a more business-like fashion, with control remaining at the local level. An independent authority would be less subject to the political pressures to keep rates low.[7]

In the 1980s the states established yet more public authorities. All states now have revolving funds (SRFs) for wastewater facilities capitalized by federal grants and state matching funds. Most of the SRFs are public authorities that sport such titles as the Ohio Water Development Authority, the Texas Water Development Board, the Virginia Resources Authority, the Pennsylvania Infrastructure Authority, the Kentucky Infrastructure Authority, the Georgia Environmental Facilities Authority, and the Maryland Water Quality Financing Administration. Combining waste and water, the Massachusetts Water Resources Authority has the worst of all possible worlds. Through such authorities as the Delaware Solid Waste Authority, the Connecticut Resources Recovery Authority, and the California Pollution Control Financing Authority, the states have begun to create and finance regional waste disposal and resource recovery systems. Born in adversity, the SRFs and the other environmental authorities have banded together to create the Council of Infrastructure Financing Authorities as their eyes and ears and lobbying right arms in Washington, D.C.[8]

Far more environmental authorities have sprouted at the local and regional levels in addition to the thousands of existing water, conservation, municipal utility, river irrigation, and flood control special districts/public authorities. Skipping randomly across the country, we can spot the South Central Connecticut Regional Water Authority, the Alaska regional development authorities, the East Bay Municipal Utility District in Oakland, California, the Brazos River Authority in Waco, Texas, the New York City Water Finance Authority, and the Northeast Maryland Waste Disposal Authority. This is not to say that the cleanup of the environment is the exclusive domain of public authorities. Many cities and counties continue to hang on to water, wastewater treatment, and solid waste disposal facilities. As their financial crises deepen, however, they will regularly spin off more of them to public authorities.

What occurs under these circumstances is both good and bad. On the positive side many authorities, administered by top-flight professionals, have taken on a task rejected by governments and have done it reasonably well. But the negatives also loom large: manipulation of some public authorities by private interests; patronage and nepotism; looting and chicanery; and gangland connections.

Impure Water

Even pure water has this strain of impurity. The struggle over water rights in the arid parts of the Southwest and the far West has long been part of bloody Americana. In Texas, canny promoters learned in the 1970s that they could gain as much by financial wizardry as by carnage on the range. As permitted by loose laws and even looser regulatory agencies, they created water districts (over 1,000 of them) and issued tax-exempt bonds to finance the construction of water and sewer lines in their real estate developments. Once the homes were sold, the developers pocketed their gains and left districts with an overhang of bonded debt for the next 30 to 40 years. If the home owners were lucky, the county or city annexed the district and assumed the debt burden as Houston, Harris County, and Austin did on several occasions. Otherwise they were stuck with debt because of a decision in which they had no part. Belatedly, the state tightened controls and forced developers to pay at least 30 percent of the cost of wastewater, sewer, and drainage systems.[9]

In bucolic Bucks County, Pennsylvania, greed and conflicts of interest surfaced when the county created the Neshaminy Water Resources Authority (NWRA) to build a water supply system, including a vital component, the Point Pleasant Water diversion project, known locally as the "Pump." From 1984 to 1988 opponents of the Pump controlled NWRA and spent $19 million to fight the project rather than to construct it. They contended there were cheaper ways of supplying water than pumping it out of the Delaware River by constructing the Pump. Lawyers, consultants, and public relations agencies collected much of the boodle.

When a new county administration took control in 1988, it found only $5 million left in NWRA's treasury instead of at least $12 million needed to build the Pump. This piqued the interest of the *Intelligencer-Record* of Doylestown, Pennsylvania. In a seven-part series running from February to March 1988, it reported such choice tidbits as

- A $2.4 million settlement with a general contractor fired for "deficient" work
- A $2.2-million payment to a mainline Philadelphia law firm to fight the Pump in the courts
- Nearly $900,000 in studies designed to prove that an abundant supply of groundwater made the Pump unnecessary
- $450,000 to archaeologists who dug up arrowheads and stone tools near the Pump site with few if any contributions to science
- A bank trustee who disbursed funds contrary to the terms of bond indenture and covenant
- Lucrative consulting contracts with a firm controlled by the NWRA chairman, John H. Elfman, Jr.
- A $100,000 audit by Arthur Young and Company that observed: "No matters came to our attention that caused us to believe that the receipts and disbursements might require adjustment"

• Bucks County taxpayers paying the entire $79.5 million in principal and interest on NWRA's bonds although, legally, it is an independent authority.

For the New York City Municipal Water Finance Authority that deals in hundreds of millions of dollars, the Bucks County affair is small change. Afflicted with the Empire State disease of public authoritis, New York City hived off its far-flung water and sewer systems to the new authority in 1984 in the usual sleight of hand to free its budget of wastewater and sludge and to waltz around the state constitution. This was no piddling transaction since it will cost the authority nearly $9 billion over the next 10 years to improve its systems. By 1991 it collected over $700 million annually in revenue and assured the restless bondholders that its "low" rates would continue to go up. New York City's rates were actually on the low side with an annual charge for single-family residential homes of $220 in 1989 compared with Houston's $509, Boston's $414, and Jacksonville's $461.

In this preemptive strike New York City joined Erie (Buffalo), Monroe (Rochester), Onondaga (Syracuse), Suffolk (Long Island), and Albany counties that also created water authorities.

Massachusetts and California have opted for dramatically different ways of providing water to their citizens. Out of the turmoil of political battles and court orders emerged the Massachusetts Water Resources Authority (MWRA), arguably the most vilified and hated authority in the United States. Had its mission been solely to bring water to the Boston Metropolitan area, it would have been tolerated despite gripes about its high rates. But Governor Dukakis, the courts, and the legislature also saddled it with the cleanup of Boston Harbor and the removal of solid waste. Evenhandedly, MWRA managed to affront not only the 41 communities around the harbor, but also fishermen and Cape Codders who feared the corrosive effect of sewer effluents on productive fishing grounds.

In contrast, Californians have long had a love-hate affair with their State Water Project (SWP). To the amazement of jaded Easterners and Midwesterners, they demonstrated that they could develop one of the largest water systems in the world without creating a public authority. In a mammoth engineering feat the Department of Water Resources pumps water 550 miles from the snow-covered north Sierras to parched southern California. With its maze of pipelines, aqueducts, dams and reservoirs, and hydroelectric plants, SWP is the largest water supply complex among the states. Only the federally owned Bonneville Power Dam, the Grand Coulee Dam, and the Hoover Dam are larger. SWP is the largest single consumer of electricity in the state because of its pumping stations and the 12th largest producer of electricity.

Started in 1960, SWP is the primary or supplementary supplier to two-thirds of the people in the state. It is strictly a wholesaler and sells its water to 30 water districts, mainly public authorities, which also add supplies from regional and local sources. Nature made the north-south water axis inevitable. Nearly three-fourths of the state's population lives in southern California, but three-fourths of the rain and snow falls north of Sacramento. In good years nature may provide an abundant supply of water, but man allocates it. And political man has chosen to give farmers in the Central and Imperial valleys 85 percent of SWP's water to produce one-half of all the fruits and vegetables in the nation. The alfalfa crop alone absorbs more water than the combined water supplies of San Francisco and Los Angeles.

When supplies are reasonably adequate, few conflicts arise between the big farm factories of the south and city dwellers. Now that California has experienced five years of drought, including some of the driest years on record, water wars have begun to rage in the state capital. Envious city folk complained bitterly about the farmers who could flood their fields without restraint while they had to count each toilet flush and car wash. Under pressure, the agriculture lobby reluctantly agreed to take only 50 percent of SWP's supplies. Still water rationing in the cities stiffened until the new allocations could take hold.

Sharp cutbacks in irrigation and/or conservation appear to be the answer. But political parties were hesitant about imposing this draconian measure on water-dependent farmers. Instead they turned to SWP again and suggested that it channel into its system water from the north that now flows into San Francisco Bay. Governor Pete Wilson proposed that farmers be permitted to sell their water rights to cities as part of his drought action plan.[10]

SWP has found its status as a state agency a mixed blessing. While it has a measure of independence because it is self-financed, it chafes under state contract, procurement, and civil service laws. It lacks the flexibility to respond quickly to emergencies, runs into unconscionable delays in acquiring supplies, and pays noncompetitive salaries. As a result, it is losing engineers and hydroelectric workers to private utilities. So far, though, no has seriously proposed that it be converted into a public authority.

Aside from agriculture, SWP's biggest customer is the Metropolitan Water District, which serves 15 million people in five counties: Los Angeles, Orange, Ventura, San Diego, and Riverside. In addition, the district and other public authorities develop whatever supplies they can from groundwater and river water. For example, the Centra Costa Water District planned to spend over $600 million between 1988 and 1992 to give 500,000 people "better stuff coming out of their tap" through a chain of dams and reservoirs. By a 2 to 1 margin the voters approved bond issues for the new projects.

Some 2,000 mini and maxi water districts in the state must comply with 83 national drinking water standards enacted in recent years. EPA enthused: "the country is now at the brink of a new phase, and a new opportunity in water quality management." But it acknowledged mournfully, "It's particularly important that states and local governments understand that federal grant monies to fund basic state programs will be diminishing." Recovering from this admission, it sketched a vision of a new day: "It is also a time of new ideas and creativity in financial thinking. Many states have packaged new ways to fund environmental programs and public-private partnerships have forged new bonds to support joint environmental efforts."[11]

The message in this obscure bureaucratese is clear: more fees; higher fees; more public authorities; and higher prices to privately owned water companies. All this would happen on top of deficits in water systems in 35 states.

The Sewers of America

Holding their noses and clutching their pocketbooks and wallets, Americans don't like to think about the treatment of sewage and wastewater. No longer, however, can they ignore the flood of storm water and industrial, commercial, and human waste. No longer can they ship the sludge that remains from the treatment of wastewater to accommodating landfills, deep oceans, and friendly shores. Instead, Americans have plunged into a debate about some 15,000 aging sewer systems that will cost billions of dollars to be brought up to current standards and needs. They now must struggle with such foreign issues as the primary treatment of sewage that removes 40 percent to 50 percent of the pollutants; secondary treatment that extracts 85 percent; and advanced treatment that will return pure water to our streams. The purer the effluent, the more costly the treatment.

In the past wastewater treatment was a local responsibility. In most places it still is. But the locals alone cannot carry the heavy costs despite higher taxes and fees. With the federal government no longer the fiscal savior, they now turn to the states, private industry, and newly hatched public authorities. Take Columbus, Georgia, a city of 165,000 on the banks of the Chattahoochee River. Under the gun of a state law, it must curb the overflow from its antiquated sewers that pour water with a bacteria count 500 times the state standard into the Chattahoochee. Meeting state standards would cost the city about $135 million, double sewer bills, threaten its bond ratings, and possibly deter industry from settling there. Water Works President Billy Turner cried out in frustration: "I have no idea how we're going to pay for this."[12]

If Turner worked in Tennessee, Utah, New Jersey, Rhode Island, California, or many other states he would find a sympathetic ear and a somewhat more open purse in state capitals. In 1983 over half of Tennessee's 252 municipal sewage plants failed to meet discharge standards and faced a cost of about $2 billion over the next 20 years. At the initiative of Governor Lamar Alexander, now U.S. secretary of education, the legislature agreed to appropriate $14 million annually for wastewater facility construction. While the amount falls short of meeting needs, it represents seed money that, with any luck and higher user fees, may sprout.[13]

Far more money comes from Utah's Wastewater Project, which lends generous sums to local governments and guarantees many of their sewer bonds; Ohio's Water Development Authority, which finances wastewater, water, and solid waste facilities; New Jersey's Wastewater Treatment Trust, which provides loans at benevolent rates to projects on its priority list; the West Virginia Water Development Authority, which does the same; the Kentucky Pollution Abatement Authority, which coaxes local governments with loans if they raise fees; and the California Clean Water Bond Fund, which offers grants and loans with low interest rates to sewage-clogged communities.[14]

As alternatives to municipal operation of sewage plants, local governments are increasingly embracing public authorities and private firms. Chicago and 51 other municipalities created the Metropolitan Reclamation District, which is digging 109 miles of tunnels at an estimated cost of nearly $3 billion to store 1.3 billion gallons of storm water before releasing it to sewage treatment plants. Leo R. DiVito, the district's chief engineer, argues that a total job is far better than piecemeal reconstruction. "If you take it one piece at a time, then you're going to live with it forever," he warns. "You don't get instant gratification. You've got to do the whole thing and you've got to stick with it. Don't forget we went to the moon in 10 years."[15]

On a smaller scale but still a relatively complex project, the Valley Forge Sewer Authority in Pennsylvania serves eight neighboring communities. Without federal help, it couldn't have started. Now that it's on its own it is wrestling with chronic problems of high costs and low fees. In New Jersey, California, and Texas MUDs are the vogue. These are municipal utility districts such as the Cape May County Municipal Utilities District (New Jersey), which processes the sewage of 16 local governments, or the Sacramento Municipal Utility District.

After wavering between city-operated and public authority-operated sewer and water systems, Houston combined them both in 1988 to improve their efficiency and effectiveness and also to avoid future $500,000 fines for violations of the state water pollution laws. Overnight the Coast Water Authority (San Jacinto River) and the Trinity River Authority became part of a consolidated system with an outstanding debt of about $1.6 billion and plans to increase the fees of 1.9 million citizens to pay for the debt.[16]

At every opportunity EPA and the White House trumpet "public-private partnerships" and "privatization" as a major solution to financing wastewater treatment plants. So far the gospel has not reached much of the heartland or the hinterland of America, but the EPA has not given up. It promotes the use of a "Self-Help Guide to Local Governments" to induce them to consider such variants of public-private ventures as contract services, developer financing, turnkey facilities (a private firm builds a sewer plant and turns it over to the locality), and full privatization financed with equity capital and assured a profitable rate of return. EPA pounces on every shred of evidence of such schemes, and promotes them as models for private operation of waste disposal systems. One of its ardent supporters urged the creation of a SWAT team (Sewer and Water Action Team) to promote privatization.[17]

Trashing About

If America is drowning in liquid waste, it is also being buried in solid trash. It generates "over 4.5 billion pounds of garbage a year, more trash than any other nation in the world," according to the National Solid Waste Management Association.[18] Municipalities pay over four-fifths of the costs of waste disposal and are frantically searching for ways to slough off the jetsam of a throwaway society. Landfills are not only running out of space, but many filter toxic chemicals into groundwater supplies. The federal government broadcasts warnings, standards, and mandates, but offers no money.

Hard-pressed local governments debate the alternatives of municipal operations with skyrocketing fees, the creation of public authorities, or privatization of the collection, processing, recycling, burning, conversion to electricity, and disposal of waste. The latter is now a $20-billion industry with such corporate giants as Waste Management and Browning Ferris extracting handsome profits from the debris of the nation.[19] Nor have local mafias and their allies in government overlooked gold in those hills of garbage as they monopolize trash collection in many cities.

Variants of these schemes are popping out all over the country. Some seem to be working; others are failing.

One bright spot is the Delaware Solid Waste Authority, the first statewide authority to manage waste disposal. It has proven to be both environmentally safe and cost-effective. It recycles waste of an astonishing 70 percent of the state's population, an achievement more in line with that of several European countries and Japan than with the United States. From all corners of the globe, waste-watchers trek to Delaware to note firsthand how the authority converted 40 substandard landfills into four state-of-the-art solid waste facilities. It manages to charge fair fees and turn a modest profit while it relies on private contractors to process the waste, limiting its own role to financing and oversight. Some of the ingredients of the authority's success are the small size of the state and the support of large corporations such as Dupont.

In nearby Maryland, the Northeast Maryland Waste Disposal Authority develops and finances resource recovery and other solid waste facilities in a four-county area with a population of nearly 2 million. It disposes of roughly 1 ton per person a year, close to the national average, and incinerates 70 percent of its waste in contrast to a national average of 5 percent. Unlike the Delaware Authority, it has little clout to carry on its program and depends on the gentle art of persuasion to lure hesitant communities into its net.[20]

This regional approach with public authorities as the engines of change is spreading to all corners of the nation. In Utah the Davis County Solid Waste Management and Energy Recovery Special Services District burns the trash of 12 communities north of Salt Lake City. It owns the mass-burn plant, but contracts with a private firm to operate it. Similarly, the Southeastern Public Service Authority of Virginia operates 10 transfer stations, two landfills, and an incinerator plant in behalf of six cities and two counties. In an unusual bistate arrangement the Sullivan County, New Hampshire Regional Refuse Disposal District joined the Vermont Southern Windsor/Windham counties' Solid Waste Management District in contracting with a privately owned and operated waste-to-energy facility.[21]

The Port Authority of New York and New Jersey financed a $230-million resource recovery project in Newark, New Jersey, to burn about 2,300 tons of garbage daily and convert it into electricity. A private plant, American Ref-Fuel Company, a subsidiary of Browning Ferris Industries, Inc. and Air Products and Chemicals Inc., designed, constructed, and now operates the facility. The Port

Authority took the public-private route on the heels of the apparent success of other Ref-Fuel projects in Bergen County (New Jersey), Hempstead (New York), Houston (Texas), and Lehigh County (Pennsylvania). No final verdict is in on the garbage-energy connection.

None of these pioneering ventures would have taken place without PURPA—the federal Public Utilities Regulatory Policy Act. PURPA forces investor-owned utilities to buy electricity from qualified cogenerators, small power facilities, and solid waste resource recovery plants.

Propelled by the same energy, the Connecticut Resources Recovery Authority (CRRA) triggered waste-to-electricity systems in Hartford, Bridgeport, and other communities in the state. The Rhode Island Solid Waste Management Corporation (a public authority) is also trying to energize the state with garbage. Few other state governments are as active in this area. They advise and regulate, but give the local governments the responsibility of developing facilities. Some states like New York and Maine hold out incentives to foster waste-to-ergs complexes, but give little followup support.

Waste disposal can be especially smelly when it falls into the hands of shady operators in MUDs, other public authorities, local governments, and marginal businesses that thrive on garbage. Take the case of the Allegheny County Sanitary Authority (ALCOSAN), the largest solid waste-processing system in the Pittsburgh area, which serves 78 communities and 1 million residents. On June 15, 1987, James Creeham resigned as executive director after County Comptroller Frank J. Lucchino released a report documenting what he called a "pattern of abuse at the agency." The comptroller also called for the resignations of authority board members Eugene "Jeep" DePasquale and James O'Malley because of their milking of authority funds. Some months earlier board member James Bull quit after charges that he sold jobs at the authority and misused travel funds.

In coverage of the authority that began September 1986 and ended October 1987 the *Pittsburgh Press* spelled out bribery, payroll abuse, patronage, shoddy management, lucrative contracts to companies with political ties, violations of public disclosure laws, and questionable campaign contributions. In the words of its managing editor, "it cracked through the obscurity of a public authority to document the abuses of public trust possible within these hidden governments."

Thanks to the *Pittsburgh Press* and Comptroller Lucchino, these highlights—and lowlights—startled the jaded public:

- More than two-thirds of ALCOSAN's legal fees of about $600,000 between 1982 and 1986 went to Governor Robert P. Casey's law firm, Dilworth, Paxson, Kalish, and Kauffman of Philadelphia. Creehan had been Casey's assistant when Casey was auditor general.
- Creehan had personally contributed handsomely to Casey's gubernatorial campaign, including a $20,000 loan that he never satisfactorily explained.
- Contrary to authority policy and state policy, ALCOSAN issued at least 15 no-bid contracts to Creehan's friends and business associates. Creehan skirted bidding requirements by splitting large-scale purchases into segments of less than $4,000. Nor did ALCOSAN use competitive bidding when it obtained $2.2 million in insurance coverage from a friend of Creehan and a brother of board member James O'Malley.
- The Spiniello Construction Company graciously and without charge filled and graded a site owned by Creehan. Indeed it was grateful because as a member of the Pittsburgh Water and Sewer Authority Board, Creehan had voted in favor of an award of $16 million in contracts to Spiniello. When the *Pittsburgh Press* revealed this exchange of favors, Creehan finally decided to pay Spiniello.
- A California company headed by Ralph J. Maffi, a former neighbor and political supporter of O'Malley, won a $101,000 no-bid contract for several small engineering projects. It turned out that Maffi had falsified his credentials and was not a professional electrical engineer.
- A grand jury heard testimony that board member James E. Bulls had sold jobs. It also indicted Donald B. McCune, an authority employee, for extorting money from business firms.

- ALCOSAN became a dumping ground for political cronies of board members and Creehan.

- Creehan's private ventures showcd an entrepreneurial spirit that was not squashed by his position as executive director: loans from firms that later received authority business; the acquisition of eight tax-delinquent properties that the city refused to sell to other potential buyers; his profitable real estate dealings with Ronald Schmeiser, Pittsburgh's finance director; and an $80,000 mortgage loan from Slovak Savings and Loan Association that later became a depository for authority funds.

- ALCOSAN ranked first among Allegheny County and Pittsburgh agencies in the bond fees it paid to favored lawyers. The authority paid twice the legal bills of the city or county for bond issues of comparable size. To spread its bounty around, it retained three bond counsel, at one time including the law firm of state senate Democratic leader Edward Zemprelli that also handled bond issues of the Pennsylvania Turnpike Commission.

- To find out how the rest of the world was handling solid waste, board members Eugene De Pasquale, Joseph Stanek, James O'Malley, James Bulls, and Edward Stevens became extraordinary globetrotters. With travel expenses of over $32,000, De Pasquale topped them all. His overseas trips included conferences in Vienna, Munich, Rome, and Athens.

De Pasquale fumed at these revelations. He called them "garbage."

Despite all this, ALCOSAN does not stand alone as a symbol of a public environmental authority run amok. Its counterparts range throughout the country.

Privatization, too, has its hazards. With great hoopla, Vicon Recovery Systems, Inc., backed by the Industrial Bank of Japan, built a plant in 1987 to convert waste into energy in the Rutland, Vermont area. Designed to burn 240 tons of trash a day, the plant was touted as being capable of incinerating the waste of 60 Vermont communities. Nine months after opening the company went bankrupt because of mismanagement and its failure to get approval of high rates for electricity from the Vermont Public Service Board.

The Japanese bank was left in the lurch with a loss of $33 million as were other creditors with total losses of $6 million. Especially hard hit were the Vermonters who now had to scramble to dispose of their garbage and couldn't agree on how to do it.[22]

Vermonters had to face up to the same issues that were troubling the rest of the country. Buy the plant? No, said the voters, who turned down a bond issue by a large majority. Invite another company to take over the plant? Only Hudson Valley Environmental Inc. of Greenwich, Connecticut, was interested, providing it could burn medical waste from other parts of the East Coast. The Vermonters quickly rejected this option. Continue to burn waste? Definitely not, argued the environmentalists, who preferred recycling. In this clash of views, many of the towns began shipping their waste to an incinerator in Claremont, New Hampshire, where the spirit of free enterprise reigns relatively unchecked.

An even sadder tale is unfolding in McDowell County, West Virginia, one of the poorest and most economically depressed counties in Appalachia. To turn the county around, the inhabitants welcomed a proposal from Capels Resources Inc. of Philadelphia to develop mammoth landfills for out-of-state trash. Hoping that the project would convert waste into jobs, Mayor Martha Moore of Welch, one of the cities in the county, said somewhat apologetically, "If we weren't so economically depressed, we might not be so elated about it. But we're looking beyond that. We're looking at it as a stepping stone to the future."

This was unacceptable to the West Virginia Environmental Council. Norm Streestra, a member of the council, lashed out saying, "They have basically prostituted themselves into accepting trash as some sort of road to economic development."

The line was now drawn. Deserted by steel companies and coal mine operators that had pockmarked a once beautiful countryside and polluted the streams, and forgotten by a state government that built no roads and provided no help for water and sewer plants, McDowell County, sadly, saw garbage as the only alternative to a slow and painful decay.[23]

In importing trash, the county would join largely rural states like Kentucky, Alabama, Louisiana, and Indiana, which in 1989 accepted 5.5 million tons of solid waste from New Jersey and 2.4

million from New York. This is proving to be too much for many of their citizens who are now beginning protests that may develop into full-scale garbage wars in the 1990s. Several states are also beginning to erect legal barriers against the import of trash, hoping that the courts will not find these an unconstitutional interference with interstate commerce.

Islip, Long Island, is still feeling the sting of its rejection by Southern states and Caribbean countries that refused to accept its garbage. The crisis came in 1987 when the town landfill ran out of space for commercial trash. Town officials loaded a barge with 3,200 tons of waste and sent it on a journey to parts unknown. Like the *Flying Dutchman* the barge sailed to port after port, only to be turned away. After a 6,000-mile voyage, Brooklyn, New York, alone accepted the spurned trash for burning. Then, it sent the ashes home to Islip for a proper burial. After this lesson, the town built a $55-million resource recovery plant, composted leaves and yard wastes, and recycled 30,000 tons of trash annually.[24]

Toxic Wastes

Toxic wastes remain an unrelieved horror. Eleven years after the Superfund got underway in 1980, only 63 of the 1,300 hazardous sites on EPA's priority list have been cleaned up. Nothing has been done with the 700 sites next in line and the thousands of sites yet to be included on the list. Yet the modest steps taken so far have cost $11.2 billion.

In report after report the U.S. General Accounting Office has documented serious delays in EPA's programs of identifying, regulating, and reporting hazardous wastes.[25] Less tactful, *Barron's* called the Superfund a super flop. It reminded its readers that in the early days of the Reagan administration, Rita Lavelle, the first Superfund administrator, went to jail for lying to Congress about her ties to a major polluter in California. Congressional pressure forced Anne M. Burford to resign as EPA administrator when she failed to turn over subpoenaed documents to committees. When William K. Reilly became the administrator in 1988, he acknowledged the mess of mismanagement and slipshod expenditure control he had inherited.[26]

In the meantime, American manufacturing firms churn out 250 million tons of toxic, corrosive, ignitable, and explosive wastes annually. They manage to treat 96 percent of this mixture at the source. It's the critical 4 percent that must be disposed of safely to avoid more Love Canals.[27]

Despite the tragedy of Love Canal corporate America has not yet learned its lessons. As late as 1991, the Aluminum Company of America paid a $7.5-million fine for violating hazardous waste laws at its plant in Massena, New York. This was the largest criminal penalty levied against a company for such offenses. Among its violations, it dumped PCB-contaminated soil on its property, then shipped 33 railroad cars full of contaminants to Alabama, labeling the poisons "nonhazardous." It illegally disposed of acids and caustic solutions by pouring them into wastewater pipes leading to the Grasse River.

Charles R. Boots, the mayor of the Village of Massena, had mixed feelings about the violations. While he deplored the pollution, he reminded his listeners that Alcoa was the largest employer in the area and without Alcoa there wouldn't have been a Massena in the first place.

In paying the unprecedented fine, Alcoa joined the United Technologies Corporation of Connecticut that had previously paid $3 million and Eastman Kodak that had paid $1 million for an array of environmental offenses. Other investigations of possible violations focused on multibillion-dollar corporations like General Motors, General Electric, Reynolds Metal Company, Exxon (apart from the Valdez spill), Dupont, B. F. Goodrich, and Weyerhauser.[28]

Nothing has befouled our lakes, rivers, and streams more than industrial toxic wastes, acid rain, agricultural fertilizers, and pesticides. Nearly 19,000 of the nation's waterways are severely polluted and thousands of beaches close each year because of these hazards (2,400 in 10 states alone in 1989 and 1990). Lake Erie hovers between death and life. Forty-one sites in Lake Michigan are biologically dead. Of these one of the worst is Indiana Harbor and Canal in Indiana, where millions of cubic yards of toxic muck rest on the bottom. Other depositories of poisonous slime in the Great Lakes are Saginaw Bay (Michigan), Waukegan and Sheboygan harbors (Wisconsin), Ashtabula River (Ohio), and Buffalo River (New

York). So far obvious solutions like a regional hazardous waste authority have eluded the competing states and Canada. An International Joint Commission that monitors the lakes in behalf of the United States and Canada tut-tuts with alarm, but is impotent.

The fate of the once Great Lakes is shared by Oregon's Tualatin River, the South Umpqua River, and nine other bodies of water; many segments of the Mississippi; the Hudson River in New York; the Rouge River in Michigan; and hundreds of once pristine waterways that have become the sewers of America. The Rouge River meanders 126 miles through southeastern Michigan and flows into the Detroit River, which then brings its waters to Lake Erie. On the way 168 communities and their manufacturing firms pour a witches' brew of arsenic, chromium, mercury, PCB, and lead into the river without treatment.[29] So far regulation has proved to be futile.

One of the worst offenders in failing to clean up hazardous waste is the federal government. As a legacy of the cold war, it deposited millions of tons of nuclear and other toxic wastes in oceans, rivers, landfills, shallow ditches, and waste pits. It continues to generate 250 million metric tons of poisons a year not only in the Defense and Energy Departments, but also in research laboratories, parks, forests, and other governmental agencies. At the very least, the U.S. government must spend $150 billion to comply with federal and state environmental laws. It is beginning to dole out a few billion dollars here and there.[30]

The Congressional Office of Technology Assessment estimates that the cleanup of private and public poisoned dumps will cost about $500 billion over the next few decades, just about the amount of the bailout of the defunct S&Ls. Year by year the environmental bill is going up and by 1994 will reach $200 billion, twice the cost in 1989.[31]

This is too much for the largest corporations in America; they are beginning to fight back. While now acknowledging their role in the pollution of landfills and waterways, they claim that their fellow culprits are cities, school districts, and small businesses that dump garbage in the same landfills. Consequently, these groups should pay their fair share of the cost. At stake are billions of dollars. In Monterey Park, California, alone the cleanup of a 200-acre toxic dump would cost $600 million to $800 million. When EPA sued

Shell, Exxon, Chevron, McDonnell Douglas, and 60 other companies for these amounts, the corporations immediately filed countersuits against 29 cities that also used the landfill. Should they win, one city, Alhambra, a suburb of Los Angeles, will be liable for a payment of $20 million to $30 million over the next decade. This is a cost its $50-million annual budget cannot absorb.

In 10 other states corporations are employing the same tactics and forcing cities to make an agonizing choice between settlement or high legal fees to defend themselves against corporate attacks. Utica, New York, its surrounding 41 towns and school districts, and over 400 small business owners settled. They agreed to pay $1.8 million while Chesebrough-Pond's USA and Special Metals Corporation that sued them would pay $7.2 million to clean up a landfill near Utica. Other cities chose to fight. In Killingworth, Connecticut, one of 24 towns sued by the Upjohn Company, General Electric, Atlantic Richfield, and Goodrich, the selectmen decided to take on the corporate giants. So far it has spent $45,000 out of its annual $1.6-million budget to avoid a liability of $1 million. If the 24 towns lose, it will cost them over $50 million to purify two landfills.

These are the unintended consequences of the federal toxic waste control laws aimed at corporate polluters. A lawyer defending the New Hartford Central School District in upstate New York complained bitterly, "They're fighting it because they didn't do anything wrong. Dick and Jane's school lunch isn't hazardous." Another lawyer in the State of Washington argued the reverse position in behalf of his industrial clients: "If Joe's Pizzeria sent hazardous material to a dump site, they're just as liable as Chevron." Joe's pizzas may not sit well on some stomachs, but, according to satisfied customers, are hardly considered hazardous.[32]

Less than 1 percent of municipal waste is hazardous. Yet corporate lawyers have found enough loopholes in the loosely drawn Superfund Act to try to shift part of the blame and costs to hard-pressed local governments and momma and poppa stores. Blasting the law suits as a ruse "designed to make Superfund a joke," 86 cities formed American Communities for Cleanup Equity to lobby for amendments to the Superfund law.

Between law suits and other mounting costs for purifying toxic sites, states and cities are taxing themselves heavily and, in the main, turning to hundreds of private firms, large and small, to treat their poisonous garbage. This, too, has its costs. Investors want a handsome return on their shares to compensate them for a risky business. This of course means even higher fees. Liability is elusive no matter who processes waste. And private companies and governments may find they are stuck with multimillion-dollar liability suits emerging from the most unexpected corners. The siting of a hazardous waste plant is a burning issue in all states and often holds up the best-laid plans. Regionalization of toxic treatment plants is an obvious solution in most parts of the country. Yet private firms by themselves cannot easily form intergovernmental ventures although they have started in a small way. Finally, the Tax Reform Act of 1986 curbs the amount of tax-exempt bonds that can be sold for a privately owned hazardous waste processing facility.

For these reasons the states are groping for a public solution to a public menace. Once again the use of public authorities looms as a way out of their dilemma, but it will not be easy. For example, 12 states, including New York, banded together to create an ambitious regional toxic waste program. In October 1989 New York State pulled out of the cooperative venture, claiming that the other states were shipping more hazardous trash to New York than New York was exporting to them. Environmental Conservation Commissioner Thomas C. Jorling reported that New York collected 50,000 tons from the New England states, but sent only 13,000 to them. "We could not allow the entire Northeast to continue to plan for utilizing New York's landfill—disposal capacity," he explained.

Michael Brown, director of safe waste management in Massachusetts, affirmed that his state was a net exporter of waste. But he boasted triumphantly that it was far ahead of New York in reducing the volume of toxic waste.[33]

Is this the beginning of the hazardous waste war of the states? It remains to be seen. In the meantime the Province of Ontario in Canada is setting an example for the contentious states. It created a public authority, the Ontario Waste Management Corporation, to operate regional waste treatment facilities. By all accounts it is doing well. So has the City of Rotterdam in the Netherlands, which established AVR, a public corporation, to incinerate waste. So has

France with six River Basin Finance Agencies that finance the shipment of waste to technologically advanced facilities. Denmark and Sweden have created public corporations to operate regional collection stations and treatment plants.

The states are on the verge of following these models. In a failsafe policy, Florida, Georgia, Kansas, North Carolina, Washington, Utah, and Oregon plan to operate their own plants if private mechanisms for disposing of hazardous waste fail. Displaying a continued faith in the private sector, Arizona and Minnesota bought land for waste disposal plants and leased it to private firms. Maryland built a state-of-the art landfill for toxic waste only to have it fail when it lost its largest single corporate customer.[34]

In their quest for pure drinking water, pure streams, lakes, and rivers, pure air, and undefiled land, the states face almost intractable fiscal and political hazards. They can no longer count on the federal government, and turning waste disposal over to the private sector has had mixed results. On the one hand evidence of corruption, scandals, and pollution mounts up. On the other, some ventures have turned out to be successful. Pelted by a fractious public, state and local governments cannot foot a bill running into billions of dollars. Public authorities can be a boon or a bane. So like characters in a Pirandello play, the states keep looking for an author who will provide the script.

11

Power to the People

When electricity first lit the dark streets of America in the 1890s, publicly owned, nonprofit power systems generated and distributed much of the power. In short order, though, newly created private utilities leaped ahead and dominated the market. In a never-ending battle between public and private power, this is still the situation today. Two hundred and sixty-five private utilities sell electricity to three-fourths of the households in the United States. Left with a one-fourth share are 2,054 public power systems, mainly public authorities, and 949 nonprofit rural electric cooperatives.[1]

Most public power authorities are small. But the few giants among them are notable for their size, their low rates, and their positive impact on local economies: the Sacramento Municipal Utility District (SMUD), the Intermountain Power Agency in Utah and California, the Municipal Electric Authority of Georgia, the Power Authority of the State of New York (PASNY), the Salt River Project in Arizona, the Puerto Rico Electric Authority, and the Los Angeles Department of Water and Power.

The power authorities generally stand out in comparison with public authorities in other fields and, for that matter, with private utilities because of their low cost and efficient operations. Nevertheless, several authorities have been plagued with policy and management problems as they entered the nuclear age. Some have forgotten that their main allegiance is to the public and not to private interests. Many continue to battle with private utilities for a greater share of the market. Their stories illuminate the play of power politics.

Perhaps few events in generating power have riveted the public's attention so much as the near nuclear catastrophe of Three Mile

Island in Pennsylvania, the Chernobyl tragedy in the Soviet Union, the shutdown of two nuclear plants by WHOOPS in the State of Washington, the dismantling of the $5.5-billion Shoreham nuclear plant owned by the Long Island Lighting Company (LILCO) in Suffolk County, Long Island, and the last-minute decision to operate the Seabrook nuclear plant owned by the Public Service Company in New Hampshire.

Sheer mismanagement led to the collapse of WHOOPS. On the other hand, the Shoreham and Seabrook troubles resulted directly from the opposition of Governors Cuomo and Dukakis, respectively. Both feared that, in a major mishap, local communities would not be able to cope with a nuclear fallout from the plants. In the controversies surrounding Shoreham and Seabrook, public authorities were major participants.

Governor Cuomo Takes On Shoreham

When Cuomo first campaigned for the governorship in 1982, he gave no clue that he would become a vigorous foe of LILCO and Shoreham. During the campaign he voiced no opposition to Shoreham, which was nearly ready to provide electricity to LILCO's 1 million customers on Long Island. Shoreham was not a sudden happening. It had been under construction for 22 years.

Cuomo's public position on Shoreham shifted from neutral to reverse when Suffolk County Executive Peter Cohalan and the county legislature refused to consider an evacuation plan in the event of a nuclear disaster. Under federal law and regulations, such a plan was required before a nuclear plant could open even if the Federal Nuclear Regulatory Commission (FNRC) had certified the safety of the plant. In effect, this meant that each local government enjoyed a veto power over nuclear plants; by refusing to act on an evacuation plan, the plant could be kept out of operation.

To the relief of many Long Islanders, and especially the residents of Suffolk County, the county government exercised this veto power over the opposition of the federal government. The public scorned LILCO. Its rates were among the highest in the nation, second only to Con Ed in New York City, and its reputation for poor service was notorious. The prospect of entrusting nuclear power to this ruthless and mismanaged company alarmed many citizens. Even after an improvement in management, the hostility continued to mount. Antinuclear activists fanned the opposition by citing the difficulty of escaping from a nuclear fallout on a long and narrow island with just two congested east-west roads.

Convinced that the opponents of Shoreham had legitimate grievances, Cuomo vowed to kill the plant after it was completed in 1984. His chosen instrument for this task was a new public authority—the Long Island Power Authority (LIPA) created in 1986. A bitterly divided legislature authorized LIPA to buy LILCO and to terminate Shoreham with one unusual proviso: No legislative approval for these acts would be needed. The legislature gave up its fundamental lawmaking powers in order to let Cuomo take the heat alone.

During the first skirmish between LIPA and LILCO, LIPA offered to buy LILCO for $7.4 billion, New York State's version of the nationalization of a private firm. LILCO rejected the offer and William J. Catacosinos, the new and highly respected CEO of LILCO, condemned LIPA's offer. "It is though an arsonist set torch to your house so that he could buy it at a fire sale," he charged. Governor Cuomo shrugged off the analogy and warned, "There is life after LILCO."[2]

Then he tightened the noose. His allies in the county government continued the impasse on the evacuation plan while he appointed two new members of the Power Authority of the State of New York (PASNY). Their votes would give the board a majority in favor of having PASNY play a key role in dismantling the nuclear plant. Cuomo promised the residents of Long Island that he would assure their safety and keep the cost of electricity down, scorning threats of federal intervention. Challenging the Department of Energy and the Federal Nuclear Regulatory Commission, he stated, "We will never agree to allow Shoreham to operate."[3]

In May 1988 LILCO capitulated and sued for peace on fairly favorable terms. In return for a token $1 sale of the nuclear plant and its commitment to pay dismantling costs, LILCO got assurances for rate increases of at least 5 percent for each of the next 10 years and for heavy federal and state tax deductions for its losses.

This meant that it would not have to pay federal taxes for a decade or more.[4]

Blustering his way through the rate increases that he sought to minimize, Governor Cuomo raised the red flag even after the peace treaty had been signed:

> I don't trust LILCO. Why should I? . . . Would I suspect that they might get cute with the agreement? Absolutely. Do I suspect that they might go to politicians down there . . . and say, "Don't worry, we'll help you [mothball the plant]?" Yeah, they could do that.
>
> If I catch them we'll do everything we can legally to make them pay for it. Any way they can be punished for it they will be punished. . . . LILCO will have a strong incentive to operate efficiently and with sensitivity to its customers' needs, knowing that otherwise LIPA, at any time, may attempt to convert the company to public ownership.[5]

In several rearguard actions the Bush administration sought to stave off the closing of Shoreham, seeking relief in the U.S. Supreme Court as late as 1991. The efforts were too late, however, and Shoreham joined the more than 100 nuclear plants across the United States that had been cancelled.[6]

Reflecting the wide local support of Governor Cuomo's policy, Frank R. Jones, the Republican supervisor of the Town of Islip in Suffolk County, cheered the governor. "The Governor has to get high marks. He came into a situation that was politically dangerous and he caused the momentum to go against LILCO."[7]

Predictably, the nuclear energy industry called it "a bad agreement for the nation as a whole." The energy industry generally dismissed the Shoreham affair as "an eccentric political situation." More objective supporters of Shoreham, including six Nobel Prize laureates, mourned the destruction of a plant that had met the highest federal standards. Some newspapers questioned the inconsistency of the governor's position. For years PASNY's Indian Point nuclear plant and the neighboring Brookhaven National Laboratories had operated routinely in New York State without a murmur from the governor. Only Shoreham raised "unique issues of public safety for him."[8]

Whether or not one agrees with Cuomo in dismantling a costly nuclear plant on the verge of operations, two public authorities were critical of his actions: the Long Island Power Authority (LIPA) with an authorization to issue tax-exempt bonds and, if necessary, buy LILCO, and the Power Authority of the State of New York (PASNY), the agent for decommissioning the plant.

The *New York Times* castigated both Governor Cuomo and Governor Michael Dukakis of Massachusetts for having "exaggerated the dangers of nuclear power, while spurning those of climatic warning. . . . It's leaders like Governors Dukakis and Cuomo who obstruct the one kind of baseload power plant that produces no greenhouse gases. In the crowded annals of human folly the sagas of Seabrook and Shoreham will surely rate a space."[9]

Dukakis Takes On Seabrook

In his battle against Seabrook Dukakis also had to contend with a public authority, the Massachusetts Municipal Wholesale Electric Company (MMWEC), which distributed electricity to 36 publicly owned utilities, mainly in Massachusetts. The Public Service Co. of New Hampshire, an investor-owned utility, built the Seabrook nuclear plant near the Massachusetts border and readied it for operation in 1986. Ten years earlier, in 1976, MMWEC had purchased an 11.6 percent share of Seabrook by issuing over $1 billion in tax-exempt bonds.

From the start Governor Dukakis fought Seabrook with the support of many Massachusetts residents. Conversely, officials in New Hampshire were Seabrook's staunchest backers.

Once the plant was ready, Governor Dukakis refused to approve an evacuation plan for six Massachusetts communities within 10 miles of Seabrook. His position was similar to that of Governor Cuomo's:

Seabrook, N.H., has the largest summer beach population within four miles of any nuclear plant area. There are only two,

two-lane roads leading from the plant. There are inadequate shelters. I have a responsibility to protect people who live in the six Massachusetts towns in the Seabrook evacuation planning zone.

Because we have found no safe way to evacuate people in case of accident, this plant poses a major threat to our health and safety, and I cannot in good conscience support it.[10]

Effectively stymied, the Public Service Company hemorrhaged slowly, lost over $2 billion, and finally went bankrupt. And MMWEC stood to lose its $1-billion investment. Immediately one of the major bond-rating agencies suspended its bond rating, putting MMWEC on the threshold of default with only a chancy prospect of a bailout by a deficit-ridden state government. In an uncanny replay of the WHOOPS fiasco in the State of Washington, the MMWEC board invoked the take-or-pay contracts with its members, the publicly owned utilities, and asked them to pay their share of the debt service. In a series of legal maneuvers and court actions the Supreme Judicial Court of Massachusetts reaffirmed the validity of the take-or-pay contracts. Conversely, the Vermont Supreme Court invalidated them for publicly owned power systems in Vermont that were part of MMWEC's network.

What is startling about the controversy was the insulation of MMWEC from public control. Despite Dukakis' opposition to Seabrook, he could not prevent the authority from investing $1 billion in the plant. This was a case of public policy flying in opposite directions at great expense because of an autonomous public authority.

Evacuation plan or not, federal regulators, supported by New Hampshire, stepped into the controversy in March 1990 and granted an operating license to Seabrook. With the plant about to go online and the prospect of revenues instead of losses ahead, the bankrupt Public Service Company planned to merge with a utility giant, Northeast Utilities. Seabrook became the 113th licensed nuclear power reactor in the nation.

A second major victim of Seabrook's troubles was the consumer-owned New Hampshire Electric Cooperative, which had a 2.2 percent interest in Seabrook. After defaulting on $255 million in debt largely for Seabrook, the cooperative went bankrupt. It had borrowed its stake in Seabrook from the U.S. Rural Electrification Administration, which agreed to stretch out the repayment of the debt until the end of bankruptcy.[11]

The Beginnings of Public Power

The alphabet stew of the public authorities that we have encountered so far in this chapter (WHOOPS, PASNY, LIPA, MMWEC, the Cooperative) has its roots in the latter part of the nineteenth century. So do the other 2,049 public power systems.

As early as the 1890s fierce debates raged throughout the country on the issue of public versus private control of the newly developed resource of electricity. Small-town America opted for municipally owned electric systems. In the first two decades of the twentieth century major cities such as Seattle, Los Angeles, Phoenix, Cleveland, Kansas City, and Tallahassee decided that they, too, preferred low-cost, nonprofit power. One of the firmest supporters of public control of the new resource was President Theodore Roosevelt (1901–1909), who championed governmental development of the nation's rivers to provide cheap hydroelectric power. Prodded by Roosevelt, Congress approved the Reclamation Act of 1906, authorizing construction of a hydroelectric dam and power plant on the Salt River in Arizona and giving municipally owned power systems preference over private systems in the purchase of surplus hydropower from federal irrigation projects.[12]

Fearing that the potential for huge profits might slip through their fingers, private utilities in the regulation-free 1920s attacked public power as a threat to democracy and proceeded to acquire as many electric systems as possible through mergers and consolidation. By 1926 16 holding companies controlled about 85 percent of the nation's supplies of electricity. Their economic and political clout reached into every state capital, county courthouse, and city hall. They virtually wiped out competition, rigged rates, discredited opponents, and bribed those they could not intimidate. In disgust, Pennsylvania Governor Gifford Pinchot, an advocate of public power and a close friend of Theodore Roosevelt, warned that "nothing like this gigantic monopoly has ever appeared in the history of the world."[13]

Another Roosevelt, FDR, continued the battle against the "power trust." As governor of New York State he preached the "undeniable" right of public ownership of electric power as a "birchrod in the cupboard" to protect consumers against abuse. Under his leadership a fractious legislature created the Power Authority of the State of New York (PASNY) in 1931 to harness the hydroelectric potential of the St. Lawrence River and eventually the Niagara River. Within four years other states followed his lead by establishing the South Carolina Public Service Authority, the Grand River Dam Authority (Oklahoma), and the Lower Colorado River Authority (Texas).

As a presidential candidate in 1932, FDR was unequivocal in his support of public power: "Where a community, a city, or a district, is not satisfied with the service rendered or the rates charged by the private utility, it has the undeniable right as one of the functions of government to set up its own governmentally owned and operated service."[14]

Once in office FDR embarked on a course that would change the lights of America. In 1933 after a no-holds-barred struggle between public and corporate adversaries, Congress created the Tennessee Valley Authority (TVA), which provided low-cost power to 110 municipal utilities and 50 rural cooperatives in the Southeast. By law, publicly owned systems had preference in buying electricity from TVA. In 1935 the Roosevelt administration set up the Rural Electrification Administration (REA) to lend money at low rates to rural cooperatives for the generation, transmission, and distribution of electricity. Next, the administration established the Bonneville Power Administration (BPA) to develop hydropower from the Bonneville dams on the Columbia River in the Pacific Northwest. This project was followed by federal dams and power plants on the Colorado and Missouri rivers.

Taunting his opponents, FDR claimed that these projects would provide "forever a national yardstick to prevent extortion against the public and encourage the wider use of that servant of the people—electric power."[15]

A further setback for private utilities came with the passage of the Public Utility Holding Company Act of 1935. This legislation broke up many of the private conglomerates, gave the new Securities and Exchange Commission (SEC) power to monitor the holding companies, and authorized the Federal Power Commission (now the Federal Energy Regulatory Commission) to regulate interstate wholesale electric power rates.

This was FDR's public power legacy. It spelled the end of deregulation and resulted in the near destruction of monopolies. To protect consumers, it intensified competition between public and private systems so as to lower rates. It led to an expansion of public power, including federally owned systems that produce over 8 percent of the power in the nation. FDR's Power Authority of the State of New York (PASNY) became the model for TVA and other public power authorities and government corporations.

PASNY Reverses Course

Started as an heir to the two Roosevelts, PASNY, the biggest public power agency outside the federal government, became the light that flickered. The legislation creating PASNY in 1931 was crystal clear in giving preference in the allocation of St. Lawrence power to publicly owned utilities and rural electric cooperatives:

> In the development of hydroelectric power . . . such projects shall be considered primarily as for the benefit of the people of the state as a whole and particularly the domestic and rural consumers to whom the power can economically be made available, and accordingly that sale to and use by industry shall be a secondary purpose to permit domestic and rural use at the lowest possible rates.

Twenty-two years later in 1953 the St. Lawrence project finally began followed by the Niagara project in 1957. When they were completed, private utilities and industrial firms rather than publicly owned utilities gobbled up over three-fourths of the power. Consumers never enjoyed the intended low rates based solely on PASNY's costs. Contrary to its original purpose, PASNY blocked the access of publicly owned utilities to publicly owned power.

This is how it happened.

For over two decades the federal government stalled on signing a treaty with Canada for the joint harnessing of the St. Lawrence River because several obstacles stood in the way. One complication was that the St. Lawrence Seaway had to be developed in tandem with dams for hydroelectric power. Fearful of increased competition, ports along the East Coast fought and succeeded in delaying the construction of the seaway and, indirectly, the dams. Also senior officials in the Roosevelt and Truman administrations preferred federal rather than state control of St. Lawrence power. Thomas E. Dewey, then governor of New York State, led the opposition against them. The impasse was finally broken when New York State agreed to share some of the power with nearby states.

In selecting a chairman of the authority, Governor Dewey wavered between John E. Burton, his highly respected budget director who would likely have followed the letter of the law, and Robert Moses who was still at the height of his power. Moses won and exacted as his price for accepting the chairmanship the right to recommend the four other members of the board. Immediately Moses and his allies scuttled the preference clauses in the legislation as unprofitable and allocated most of the power to firms like Alcoa and General Motors and to private utilities. To lock in this power grab, they approved 29-year contracts that effectively shut out municipally owned utilities. PASNY had issued 50-year tax-exempt bonds to finance the projects, but, as revenue exceeded forecasts, it retired the bonds prematurely. Instead of taking advantage of lower debt service to cut power rates, it ploughed the surplus into nuclear plants and other ventures.[16]

The same pattern occurred in the development of hydropower on the Niagara River. In approving the Niagara Redevelopment Act in 1957, Congress required PASNY to "give preference and priority to public bodies and nonprofit cooperatives within economic transmission distances." This stricture applied to at least half of Niagara's power, but quickly became a dead letter. All of the succeeding governors—Harriman, Rockefeller, Carey, and Cuomo—abetted the takeover of public power by private interests. They rationalized their flouting of the law by arguing that low-cost power was the key to economic development, especially in the western part of the state. Hence, to attract, keep, or expand industry, preference in the allocation of power should go to private firms and utilities.[17]

After years of passive resistance, the municipally owned utilities struck back in 1978 by asking the Federal Energy Regulatory Commission (FERC) to divert Niagara power from private utilities to public utilities. This was at a time when Moses' 29-year contracts were coming to an end. FERC found that PASNY had acted arbitrarily in selling preference power to private utilities for 29 years while failing to meet the needs of "preference customers." It ordered PASNY to terminate contracts with private utilities five years earlier than scheduled in order to free power for public systems. In 1984 the U.S. Court of Appeals upheld the FERC ruling, but allowed PASNY to use St. Lawrence hydropower to meet, in part, the needs of publicly owned utilities.

PASNY once again displayed its bias toward private utilities by taking over, at peak prices, two failed power plants of Consolidated Edison (Con Ed). For years investor-owned Con Ed, which served the New York City metropolitan area, had experienced frequent breakdowns because of obsolete equipment; yet public opposition prevented it from constructing new plants. After the Arab oil embargo of 1974, high oil prices brought Con Ed to the verge of bankruptcy, forcing the utility to cut dividends and seek higher power rates.

Malcolm Wilson, who had succeeded Nelson Rockefeller as governor, the legislative leaders, and the Public Service Commission, the utility regulatory agency, faced three choices: take over Con Ed completely and merge it with PASNY; approve insufferably high rates; or bail out Con Ed. They opted for the latter and had PASNY, at a cost of $500 million, take over Con Ed's coal-fired plant in New York City and a nuclear plant at Indian Point, 35 miles from New York City. PASNY issued additional bonds for this purpose. In addition, modernization and completion of the plants would cost another $500 million. Con Ed promptly restored the dividends and rejoiced at its coup. According to Jack Newfield, an investigative reporter who followed the Con Ed affair closely, PASNY could have bought the entire company for $500 million at prevailing stock prices and, as a nonprofit public authority, lowered rates.[18]

Having started out with two massive hydroelectric plants, PASNY now owns two nuclear plants, a coal-burning plant, a pumped storage plant, and two small hydro facilities. With assets of about $6 billion, it provides as a wholesaler one-third of the electricity in the state, mainly through private utilities. Still the state is short of cheap and abundant power. While industrial firms and consumers in the western part of the state benefit from low-cost hydropower, their counterparts in Long Island, in Westchester County, and in the New York City metropolitan area pay the highest rates in the nation because they rely mainly on costly coal-burning and nuclear plants. To appease them, PASNY is importing relatively cheap hydroelectricity from Hydro Quebec and Hydro Ontario, two public authorities. It has also built a cable under Long Island Sound to bring more power to the often short-changed citizens of Long Island.[19]

Furious squabbles persist despite the self-praise of Chairman Richard Flynn of PASNY: "We're a good example of government at its best. We're one of the greatest advantages New York has."[20]

Two state legislators took a less rosy view. William Hoyt of Buffalo, chairman of the Assembly Energy Committee, admitted he was leery of PASNY: "Authorities make me nervous. They're chartered by the legislature and commissioned by the governor, but they're out of reach of the average citizen or legislator. The Public Service Commission has no oversight of the power authority. They seem to be untouchable."

Assemblyman Daniel Feldman of Brooklyn ascribed imperial ambitions to PASNY: "These people view themselves as Roman emperors. They're not answerable to the legislature and they lead a lifestyle that meets their imperial needs." Feldman's pique resulted from the high salaries, chauffeur-driven cars, and expensive travel in PASNY.

Backed by the governors, PASNY kept most of the cheap hydropower in western New York while downstate legislators complained of discrimination. Viewing itself as the keystone of economic development, PASNY preferred to allocate power to industrial firms while giving short shrift to consumers. Exempt from state regulation and governors' vetoes, it doubled the rates for residential and farm customers.[21] Even then, rates were still relatively low in western New York.

PASNY strayed so far from its original mission that in 1985 a bipartisan coalition of state assembly members introduced a bill authorizing the state to buy seven privately owned utilities as the foundation for a statewide public power grid. Thomas F. Barraga, one of the key movers, laid out the issue bluntly: "The Power

Authority of the State of New York, the agency responsible for producing and distributing cheap power has failed to live up to its obligations." Were his plan to be adopted, he forecast savings of $1 billion a year, lower rates, and more efficient operations.[22] All available data supported his claims, but he got nowhere. Control over PASNY still eludes the legislature.

Since World War II consumers of public power have paid less for electricity than customers of private utilities—about 21 percent less in 1988 for home owners and apartment dwellers and 6 percent less for industrial and commercial firms. Administrative costs for publicly owned systems have also run consistently below overhead costs of private utilities. Citing recent major studies, John D. Donahue of the Kennedy School of Government at Harvard University emphasized that "no study even hints at superior private efficiency. . . . Many researchers have looked at the power industry to assess differences between public and private management. The evidence broadly contradicts the common presumption that private utilities will operate more efficiently than their public counterparts."[23] The main difference is that public systems don't worry about dividends and greater margins of profit for investors.

Despite their lower rates publicly owned electric utilities contribute proportionately more to state and local governments than do private companies, mainly through payments in lieu of taxes and contributions. During 1988 public power systems paid an average of 6.1 percent of electric operating revenues to state and local governments compared to 5.9 percent for private utilities.[24]

Notwithstanding the advantages of public power, the return to the PASNY of FDR's vision was not about to happen on Cuomo's watch, even though he had threatened a takeover of the private Long Island Lighting Company (LILCO). His focus, like that of his predecessors, was more on public power for industry and private utilities, and less on power for publicly owned utilities. Nor was the Republican-dominated state senate likely to support public power at a time when privatization was trendy.

PASNY is one of the larger nonprofit publicly owned electric utilities. Some 454 of these exist and account for 86 percent of public power. Together with the smaller publicly owned utilities and cooperatives they compete with private utilities for a greater share of the market. As they approach the year 2000 they have two options: continue to battle the investor-owned utilities for access to a larger market, or, considering political realities, enter into a public-private partnership. They have been doing some of each.

California's Power Problems

Few public electric authorities are as scrappy as the California authorities: the Northern California Power Agency (NCPA), the Sacramento Municipal Utility District (SMUD), and the M-S-R Public Power Agency (Modesto Irrigation District, Santa Clara, Redding). To maintain and expand their power base they are regularly locked in combat with the giant private utility, Pacific Gas and Electric, and a hostile federal government. Especially notorious is the "quad seven" case, so-called because E-7777 was the docket number in a federal proceeding. In the early 1970s NCPA petitioned the Federal Power Commission, FPC (the predecessor of FERC—the Federal Energy Regulatory Commission) for access to hydroprojects of Pacific Gas and Electric (PG&E). For 20 years FPC-FERC did nothing. Then in 1991 it dismissed the complaint about "PG&E's anticompetitive behavior" and suggested that NCPA file another complaint. NCPA had no choice but to comply, but enlarged its complaint to include "the commission's will to act."[25]

NCPA lost again in the 1980s when, with other public authorities and cities, it tried to prevent a grab of federal rivers and lands, worth about $100 billion, by PG&E and a coalition of other large private utilities. In 1920, Congress had given these utilities the right to build 162 dams and sell power from the rivers. It required no payments from the utilities, but attached one condition to this arrangement: The rights would end in 50 years and, unless Congress renewed them, the private utilities would have to put their dams out for bid at fair compensation. Public power systems like NCPA would have statutory preference in bidding for hydropower.

As the leases began to expire, PG&E waged a massive public relations campaign to keep the public resources in private hands. It lined up 27 members of Congress, including Barbara Boxer of Marin County, and 143 cities, counties, and towns in support of its position and used its influence to shut out proponents of public power from hearings in city halls. The PG&E pitch was that Californians enjoyed some of the lowest electric rates in the nation because of the federal leases. Why, then, change an arrangement that benefited everyone, especially the profitable PG&E? Although public power advocates fought back and urged Congress to retain the public preference clause of the 1920 legislation, they were stymied. Not even the prospect of demonstrated lower rates by nonprofit publicly owned utilities swayed a state beguiled by PG&E's one-liner: "Help prevent the hydro takeover."

In frustration Roger Fontes, a manager of NCPA, told the *San Francisco Bay Guardian*, which carried a series of articles headlined as "They're Stealing Our Rivers," "I think a lot of these cities passed the resolution without considering the other side. About the only times we have been able to make a presentation is when we have heard about the resolutions by chance. PG and E has an entire public relation team working on this."[26]

PG&E tactics worked. After a passionate debate between advocates of public versus private power with the then Representative Albert Gore of Tennessee a crusader for publicly owned power, Congress passed the Electric Consumer Protection Act of 1986 that gave publicly owned power systems preference in the original licensing of hydropower dams, but not in the relicensing of the dams. It would be up to the Federal Energy Regulation Commission (FERC) to determine in relicensing whether a public or private utility best served the public interest. Virtually nothing changed as a result of the legislation.

Notwithstanding these setbacks, several aggressive public authorities in California and nearby states have banded together to expand publicly owned power. The $5-billion Intermountain Power Agency (IPA) is the creation of six southern California cities (Los Angeles, Anaheim, Riverside, Pasadena, Burbank, and Glendale) and 29 public power suppliers in Utah. Most of the power goes to California. IPA joined forces with the $1.1-billion Southern California Public Power Authority (SCPPA) to build a transmission line linking the northern and southern segments of southern California. Constructed at a cost significantly below estimates and completed ahead of schedule, the projects of IPA and SCPPA are not only financially stable, but operate above expectations and consistently produce low-cost power.[27]

With annual revenue of nearly $600 million, the Sacramento Municipal Utility District (SMUD) serves 435,000 customers oil-fired, hydro, nuclear, and geothermal power. It is also concentrating on smaller plants that extract methane gas from landfills, convert waste into energy, produce steam from wastewater, tap Canadian hydropower, and exploit windpower. Arguing for more diversity, S. David Freeman, the general manager of SMUD, stated, "Smaller is smarter. Big plants get big troubles. . . . My job is not to go to Vegas and roll dice. . . . Enlightened thinking is certainly leaning toward placing an extra value on renewables."[28]

Although smaller than SMUD, M-S-R Public Power Agency is just as aggressive in producing low-cost power. In a complex arrangement with two private utilities, the Tucson Electric Power Co. and Public Service of New Mexico, it has a large ownership interest in plants of both companies and is also co-owner of a coal-fired electric generating plant. As part of a diversification program to lessen its dependence on PG&E, Santa Clara gets 35 percent of M-S-R's power. It also has links with three other public authorities: the Northern California Power Agency, the Central California Power Agency, and the Transmission Agency of Northern California.[29]

Wheeling and Dealing

Private utilities can choke the growth of publicly owned power plants by blocking access to 80 percent of the 614,000 miles of high-voltage transmission lines in the nation. The other 20 percent is owned by the federal government. Access to the private power network is vital because it gives public authorities an opportunity to buy and sell surplus electricity economically in the wholesale power market—a practice called "wheeling." In an interview with *City and State* magazine, Philip Edwards, a senior vice president of Standard and Poor's, punned: "The have nots [the public authorities] are using leverage to gain access to transmission systems so that they can wheel and deal in the wholesale power market."[30]

For years the Federal Energy Regulatory Commission (FERC) claimed that it lacked regulatory powers and could not force the private utilities to open access to their lines even though this would intensify competition. Finally, under pressure from a public authority, the Utah Associated Municipal Power System (UAMPS), FERC yielded and in 1989 made access a condition for approving a merger between two private utilities: the Utah Power and Light Co. (UPLC) and the Pacific Power and Light Co. Pacific Power agreed to permit publicly owned utilities to use part of their excess transmission capacity and to build additional transmission lines for power pooling.

After this unexpected victory, Alene Bentley, a representative of UAMPS, stated candidly, "We have been trying for several years to get Utah Power and Light to wheel for us. We felt like we had exhausted every avenue available. . . . We spent $1.7 million in hearings and lobbying the state legislature to order UPLC to wheel for us."[31]

With this precedent behind it, it looked as if FERC would exact similar conditions for the pending merger of San Diego Gas and Electric Company and Southern California Edison Company on the West Coast and Northeast Utilities and the bankrupt Public Service Company of New Hampshire on the East Coast. Both mergers are still pending. Quickening the pace of joint access, the Wisconsin legislature in 1989 required public and private utilities to share existing and future power facilities in the state.

Joint Action Agencies

Those publicly owned utilities that collaborate extensively with private utilities as well as other public power systems dub themselves "joint action agencies." Scattered throughout the country, 63 such agencies have entered into complex forms of ownership and power supply contracts with private and public utilities. The Piedmont Municipal Power Agency in South Carolina typifies this new breed of organization. With a 25 percent share in the nuclear plants of the private Duke Power Company, it transmits power to 10 municipalities. Its strength is the strength of 10. However, should one of the cities default on its payments to Piedmont, the other nine cities would be liable for the entire debt. So far the public authority has been financially stable and provides power at wholesale rates below those of other power suppliers in the state.[32]

Marching through Georgia, the Municipal Electric Authority of Georgia is a joint owner, albeit a junior partner, with the Georgia Power Company, of four nuclear and four coal-fired plants together with 1,123 miles of transmission facilities. It provides electricity to residents of 48 cities and collects annual revenues of over $500 million. Other large joint power agencies with revenues of $100 million to $500 million are the Southern California Public Power Authority, the Platte River Power Authority in Colorado, the Florida Municipal Power Agency, the Indiana Municipal Power Agency, the Massachusetts Municipal Wholesale Electric Company, the North Carolina Eastern Municipal Power Agency No. 1, the Texas Municipal Power Agency, the Intermountain Power Agency in Utah, and the Washington Public Power Supply System.[33] In the wings are 52 smaller joint public authorities that are rapidly growing as an alternative to "pure" public and private utilities.

Among the comers are the Lower Colorado River Authority that sells electricity wholesale to 42 municipalities and rural cooperatives in central Texas and the South Columbia Basin Irrigation District in the State of Washington that provides hydropower to Seattle and Tacoma.

The biggest if not the best among the public power systems, whether joint or monolithic, are four with annual revenues (1989) of $1 billion to $1.8 billion: the Salt River Project in Arizona, the Power Authority of the State of New York, the Puerto Rico Electric Power Authority, and the Los Angeles Department of Water and Power, the largest city-owned utility in the United States. In comparison with private utilities, however, they are of only middling size. Of 265 private power companies, 42 earn $1 billion or more in revenue. The giants among them top the rest of the world: Pacific Gas and Electric Co., with operating revenues of $9.1 billion in 1989; Southern California Edison Co., $6.5 billion; Public Service Electric and Gas Co. in New Jersey, $4.6 billion; Consolidated Edison Co. in New York, $5.6 billion; Duke Power Co., $3.6 billion; Georgia Power Co., $4 billion; Commonwealth Edison Co. in Illinois, $5.8 billion; Texas Utilities Electric Co., $4.3 billion; Virginia Electric and Power Co., $3.5 billion.[34]

Dominating three-fourths of the market, the investor-owned electric utilities fear no competition from public power authorities. When they are challenged, as in California and New York, they can generally rely on compliant officials, legislators, intensive lobbying, and easy-going regulatory bodies to protect their interests. Few publicly owned authorities of the kind favored by Presidents Theodore Roosevelt and Franklin D. Roosevelt exist to act as a brake on rates charged by private utilities. In a win-win situation the private utilities are also pleased to have public authorities bail them out at the consumers' expense as the Power Authority of New York did for the Consolidated Edison Company.

"Cash Cows"

Publicly owned utilities may not be as rich and powerful as their private counterparts, but, like some other kinds of public authorities, they are rapidly becoming the "cash cows" of local governments. Nearly all pay taxes or tax equivalents to state and local governments. They are money makers in contrast to mass transit authorities, which require heavy subsidies, and sewer and water authorities, which barely break even. Frequently, in many small cities, they make the differences between deficits and small operating surpluses.

As fiscally hard-pressed governments cast about for funds, short of tax and fee increases, they eye longingly the surpluses of public power authorities. In 1991 the American Public Power Association, which represents the interests of publicly owned systems, alerted its members to this latest threat:

> Government may look at the local public utility as the cash cow to finance the new responsibilities. Prudent surpluses, set aside to fund maintenance activities or upgrades, may be tempting targets for local politicians looking for cash. Public power then faces the job of convincing the local community not to kill this goose that lays golden eggs, by showing that spending those surpluses recklessly will result in deteriorating performance, higher costs, and rate increases. . . . In these circumstances, public power systems may have to resist attempts to force transfer of unreasonable portions of utility revenues to city general funds. The immediate problem of a fiscal squeeze may blind political leaders to the long-term foolishness of diverting revenues needed for the maintenance of the utility. In a more extreme form, such pressures can lead to calls for sale of the utility as a source of quick cash. Either

course amounts to cannibalizing an existing, productive asset in order to pay current operating expenses. In most cases, the superior value of the productive asset can be easily demonstrated. However, it cannot be assumed that the citizen owners will understand this without its having to be explained.[35]

In 1985 Governor Arch A. Moore, Jr., of West Virginia thought a public power authority might be one solution to the severe economic problems of his state. When private utilities shunned the use of polluting high-sulphur coal in West Virginia in favor of low-sulphur coal from other states, he persuaded the legislature to create the coal-burning West Virginia Electric Generation Authority. Far more important than pollution was the promise he dangled before the voters of two plants that would burn 5 million tons of impure West Virginia coal and put 3,500 miners back to work. Over the opposition of environmentalists the authority started one power plant in Morgantown in 1989.[36]

Like other public authorities, the power authorities were hemmed in by Congress in the Tax Reform Act of 1986. The act cut back their use of "private purpose" tax-exempt bond financing, thereby cramping their ability to start joint ventures with private utilities. Prior to the tax changes public power systems had issued about 29 percent of all municipal bonds. In 1990 their share dwindled to 4.1 percent.[37]

Despite an unfriendly federal government and needy state and local governments, public power authorities are in excellent financial shape even though their share of the market is limited. In contrast to many private utilities they are efficient, innovative, and better positioned to keep rates down. Whether they stay that way and grow depends more on ideology and future FDRs than on hard-headed measures of performance.

Public Authorities Join the Welfare State

From schoolhouses to universities, from clinics to hospitals, from nursing homes to retirement centers, from juvenile facilities to jails, public authorities have made their imprint on the United States. They have become firm pillars and bankers of the welfare state. Thanks to the miracle of tax-exempt bond financing, they have poured billions of dollars into thousands of projects that state and local governments or their constituents have been unwilling or unable to support. In 1990 health care and education facilities and programs consumed 38 percent of the $128 billion of tax-exempt bonds that were issued. With housing bonds the figure goes up by more than half.[1] It's been relatively easy sailing for the health, education, and welfare authorities, since tax reform scarred them less than it did other public authorities.

But the results have been mixed. In the main, like other public authorities, they have been cunning means of circumventing state constitutions and budget controls. That aside, many of their accomplishments are visible and impressive. Others are monuments to profligacy absent any controls.

Public Authorities and Long-Term Care

Included on any list of failures are many of the public authorities that financed nursing homes and retirement havens, a $40-billion growth industry for our graying population. When they aren't

bogged down by sheer mismanagement, they are prey to unscrupulous promoters who have milked them of hundreds of millions of dollars. Between 1980 and 1989 the default rate for bonds
issued for retirement centers was an astonishing 20 percent. This
compares with a 1 percent default rate for industrial development
and hospital bonds. In 1988 65 bond issues for nursing homes
totaling $750 million were in some stage of default.[2] As the long-
term care industry continues to mushroom, it will seek even more
tax-free financing.

In a study of retirement centers in 1990, the U.S. General Accounting Office recounted some horror tales of their failings. To
protect the guilty it identified them by case study project number
and not by name. This is what happened to the hapless residents and
investors who selected "project number 2."

In 1981, somewhere in the South or the Midwest where most of
the failures occurred, a nonprofit organization issued $53.2 million
in tax-exempt bonds (through a public authority) to acquire and
renovate a 460-unit apartment complex for the elderly. In December
1983, 14 months after the financing, the project defaulted on the
payment of the bonds. Its occupancy rate was .2 percent. It ran out
of money for construction and found that the promised market had
not materialized. Out of the ruins investors managed to salvage 52
cents of each dollar. The few residents who were there could not
recoup their entrance fees fully. Only brokerage houses and banks
profited.

Residents and investors who chose "project number 6" experienced a similar fate. In 1980 the nonprofit corporation issued $12.2
million in tax-exempt bonds for a combined nursing home and
retirement center. In 1987 the project defaulted on the payment of
principal and interest even though its occupancy rate was 73 percent. The usual villains emerged out of the debris: the use of a
marketing company that had never marketed a retirement center;
cost overruns; poor projections of needs; uneven cash flow; and
unrated bonds. In 1988 the bond trustee, with the approval of a state
court, sold the facility to a for-profit organization for $5.8 million.
Bondholders managed to retrieve 56 cents for each dollar invested.

Nor did residents and investors in "project number 7" fare any
better. In 1982 the unnamed nonprofit corporation had $20.5 mil-

lion in unrated tax-exempt bonds issued in its behalf to develop a combined health care and retirement center. Failure and defaults followed in 1985. In a court-approved reorganization plan bondholders got an unrated bond valued at $3,500 for each $5,000 bond they had bought plus some cash. New management salvaged the project, which is currently operating as a nonprofit retirement center with an occupancy rate of 94 percent.

GAO mildly observed that the "facilities were prone to weak financial structures, inexperienced developers, and overestimated market projections."[3] Not a word about promoters who dazzled local officials and boards of nonprofit corporations with the wonders of tax-exempt bond financing. Not a word about the lack of state oversight. Not a word about public authorities that issued suspect "nonrecourse" bonds for which they were not liable. Of course, the bonds had higher interest rates because of their risky nature. That led careless investors to buy them.

GAO did not cover the far from anonymous Pike County Building Commission in Kentucky that sold over $5 million of tax-exempt bonds in 1979 to build a 120-bed nursing home. Pike County committed itself to lease the facility and to pay debt service as well as part of the operation and maintenance costs. In 1986 the project was complete except for one major flaw. It lacked a heating and cooling plant. The visionary members of the commission had been persuaded to rely on an expensive, high-tech coal gasification system that never worked. To build a more conventional heating and cooling plant at this point would be too expensive.

The frustrated county cancelled its lease and the voters by a 2 to 1 margin turned down a proposal to issue GO bonds to refund the 1979 bonds. Just when the project was on the verge of default the state stepped in and forced the county to pay debt service for the unused facility. To underscore its determination, it withheld state aid from the county in 1984 until it resumed lease payments. It spelled out its position in unmistakable terms: "Default in payment of such bonds by the County under its lease of the facility from the commission, is contrary to public interest in that it will impair the County's credit rating, may similarly affect the credit of all other Kentucky counties . . . and may also affect the credit rating of the state itself."

To stay in the good graces of Wall Street the county reluctantly pays debt service year after year for an unopened nursing home while it looks for a private operator, not a public authority, to bail it out.[4]

Hospital Authorities

Compared to the nation's 6,438 hospitals, many of them ailing, the financial woes of retirement centers and nursing homes are relatively insignificant.[5] About 53.5 percent of the hospitals are private nonprofit institutions; 28.7 percent state and local government general, mental health, and teaching hospitals; and only 17.8 percent private for-profit facilities. This means that governments and nonprofit corporations own over four-fifths of all hospitals. With few checks, they are free to resort to tax-exempt bond financing to construct their facilities. And they do this at a rapid clip, having sold nearly $16 billion in bonds in 1989 and nearly $14 billion in 1990. Because of tax changes they never again reached 1985's record of $34 billion.[6]

Standing ready to raise money for them are state and local public authorities. Nearly every state has at least one authority eager to finance hospital construction. Depending on how one counts them, New York State has five. In 1990 the Wisconsin Health and Education Facilities Authority sold $71 million in bonds for a local general acute care hospital. The New Jersey Health Care Facilities Financing Authority sold bonds for a $60.3-million hospital. The California Health Facilities Financing Authority raised $92.3 million for a children's hospital and $70.6 million for an acute care facility. Also active were the Michigan State Hospital Finance Authority, the Illinois Health Facilities Authority, the North Carolina Medical Care Commission, the Oklahoma Industries Authority, the Mississippi Hospital Equipment Financing Authority, the Massachusetts Health and Education Finance Authority, and the Louisiana Public Facilities Authority.

Topping all other state public authorities in the amount of bonds issued was the New York State Housing Finance Agency, which sold $553 million in bonds for New York City's public hospital system. This was the largest health care bond sale on record, surpassing a previous high by the Delaware Economic Development Authority that in 1985 had issued $500 million in health care bonds.[7]

At the local level about 1,300 hospital and health districts and other public authorities are eager to finance the construction of hospitals and clinics. Texas boasts 140 hospital districts, Georgia 107, Pennsylvania 58 and Washington 40. Like their state counterparts they did a brisk business in 1990. In Pennsylvania the Allegheny County Hospital Development Authority issued $127.5 million in bonds for a general acute care facility. In Knox County, Tennessee, the Health, Education and Housing Facilities Board raised $140.5 million for a hospital. The Lubbock Health Facilities Development Corporation in Texas issued $100 million in bonds for a general hospital. The Harris County Hospital District (Houston area) sold $224 million in bonds for hospital equipment. Trying to meet the needs of the Twin Cities, the Minneapolis–St. Paul Housing and Redevelopment Authority issued $160.6 million in bonds for a general acute care hospital.[8]

No public authorities that raise funds for hospitals are as complex, elusive, and difficult to track as New York State's web of intertwining authorities. All are products of the proliferation of authorities in the Rockefeller days. A Facilities Development Corporation (FDC) finances through tax-exempt bonds the construction and rehabilitation of health and mental health facilities for state agencies, municipalities, and voluntary nonprofit corporations. It has recently added local prisons and municipal buildings to its portfolio. Almost indistinguishable from FDC is the Medical Care Facilities Finance Agency, which specializes in marketing bonds for mental health services facilities, municipal hospitals and nursing homes, nonprofit hospital corporations, and nonprofit residential health care facilities. It also makes insured mortgage loans to these institutions.

For strategic, political, and financial reasons the state administration also turns to the Housing Finance Agency (HFA) and the Dormitory Authority (DA) to finance hospital and nursing home construction although this activity is remote from original missions of these authorities. With outstanding debt of about $9 billion in 1990, the DA channels about 10 percent of its resources to health care facilities. It has also become one of Governor Cuomo's most dependable money machines. To free money in HFA for the administration's use in offsetting its budget deficits, DA issued over $3 billion in bonds in 1990–1991. This made it possible for DA to take over debt that HFA had assumed in behalf of the State University of New York, leaving HFA with luscious cash reserves set aside for repayment of the original debt. This the governor promptly preempted with the legislature's eager consent. DA also cheerfully contributes $2.5 million a year to the state government as payment for scattered state services.

Other state and local public authorities join the Big Four in financing health care facilities. In this fiscal maze it is nearly impossible for outsiders to piece together the expenditures and debt for medical and nursing centers. That's precisely the point—to keep everyone except a few insiders in the dark.

So far the government medical empire is in no danger of fiscal collapse. Like other health institutions it gets the overwhelming part of its revenues from Medicaid and Medicare and a smaller portion from third-party insurance plans and patients' fees. Despite the many cost controls imposed by the federal government and insurance companies, it gets by handily. As in other states, however, independent, nonprofit hospitals have a harder time. They contend with low occupancy rates, competition from outpatient clinics, and cuts in reimbursement.

This is not to say that the public authorities spend their money wisely—especially when they are under the thumb of zealous governors such as Rockefeller. Rockefeller's answer to crime was to try to sweep drug addicts off the streets by placing them in narcotic addiction control facilities built by a public authority. This turned out to be a $250-million folly. His mental health experts persuaded him to spend $1 billion for new 1,000-bed units in mental hospitals also financed by a public authority. Under an ill-conceived deinstitutionalization program, the administration promptly emptied the shiny new buildings and turned the patients over to local communities that were not ready or willing to receive them. At long last many of the mentally ill and the senile have begun to drift back to their erstwhile homes.

Like several other states, Massachusetts combines the financing of health and education institutions in one public authority: the Health and Education Finance Authority (HEFA), which rolled up over $4.5 billion in debt for its clients by 1990. To stay in business HEFA goes its wary way and is not a team player. When the state health-planning agency decided that the City of Lowell needed two and not the three hospitals the city had requested, Lowell turned to HEFA, which promptly loaned it $20 million to build an unnecessary hospital. In a desperate fiscal plight, the city is now paying off the debt. At the same time HEFA was fending off attacks from hungry public authorities such as the Massachusetts Industrial Finance Authority (MIFA) and university-building authorities that were trying to lure HEFA's potential clients.

Hospital financing is also a big business in California with its 479 independent hospitals, the largest number in any state. Two public authorities are the chief financiers: the Health Facilities Financing Authority (HFFA) and the Health Facility Construction Loan Insurance Program (housed in the State Health and Welfare Agency). For example, HFFA raised over $400 million for the nonprofit Catholic Health Care West, a 3,159-bed hospital in Burlingame. The Merritt Peralta Medical Center in Oakland also benefited with $79 million in loans as did the Sutter Community Hospitals in Sacramento with a $157-million loan. Cities and hospital districts cover what HHFA does not by issuing hospital revenue bonds. Because of fierce competition from health maintenance organizations (HMOs) and preferred provider organizations (PPOs), which offer discounted rates for long-term contracts, some of the hospitals are financially shaky. Their plight has deepened even more because of state Medicaid payments (Med-Cal) that cover only about two-thirds of the costs of treating Med-Cal patients. By 1988 13 hospitals had closed and more are nearing their end. Why HFFA should continue pumping money into clear losers with very little hope of survival remains an intriguing question in California.

The Health Facility Construction Loan Insurance Program (Cal-Insurance) insures bonded debt for health facilities just as commercial bond insurers like AMBAC and MBIA do. Such "credit enhancement" is designed to lower interest rates because of the superior quality of insured tax-exempt bonds. By 1989 Cal-Insurance had insured over $2 billion in tax-exempt bonds for 138 projects. The bond market doesn't share California's enthusiasm for Cal-Insurance and exacts somewhat higher interest rates for its hospital bonds than bonds insured by commercial carriers. So far the difference is slight since the state unconditionally guarantees the insured bonds and stands ready to bail out hospitals that fail to pay interest on their insured debt.[9] The constitutionality of this program has not been challenged.

Education Authorities

Education authorities outdistance health authorities by a wide margin and sprout by the thousands in every corner of the nation. As with most public authorities, it's difficult to get a precise fix on their numbers because of the hazy enumeration system of the U.S. Bureau of the Census. According to the latest census figures, 707 school-building authorities exist in the nation. Yet Pennsylvania alone reports that 738 local education authorities are thriving, having issued $5.2 billion in tax-exempt bonds to build 754 schoolhouses.

Education authorities come in two sizes and forms. One is the very large cluster of state and local education building authorities that sell bonds to construct elementary, high school, and university buildings. The other type issues, guarantees, and services student loans for higher education. They have a common trait and that is their ingenuity in skirting around constitutional restrictions.

Since the early 1940s Pennsylvania authorities have been pioneers in the fine art of constitutional evasion, having been the first to develop the lease-purchase plan discussed in Chapter 2. They sell bonds to buy land and construct school buildings. Then they "lease" the buildings to school districts and municipalities that are not legally free to borrow on a grand scale. Year by year the school districts pay rent under a lease-purchase plan and eventually own the buildings. Pronounced good-as-gold by a state Supreme Court that looked the other way, the lease-backed scheme spread like wildfire.

Other states quickly hastened to follow the Pennsylvania beacon. Kentucky broke its constitutional shackles by creating a School Facilities Construction Commission to finance and construct school buildings and vocational education facilities. So did Virginia with its Public School Authority. The same was true of the Chicago Public Building Commission, Indiana's Merrillville Multi-School Building Corporation, Louisiana's Public Facilities Authority, Michigan's School Bond Loan Fund, and on and on.

In 1989, New York City, the city with the biggest problems, predictably established the biggest school-building authority in the nation—the School Construction Authority (SCA). SCA is chartered to finance and oversee $3.6 billion in school construction by 1994. While handling this challenge, SCA is trying to fend off bid rigging and labor racketeering that plague nearly all city construction projects. In an uncharacteristically defiant gesture, it banned 52 construction companies from bidding on school projects. One was a company headed by Alvin Benjamin, a large developer of over 50 public housing projects. Two of Benjamin's key employees had been convicted of bribery. Also on the blacklist was Ralph Arred, the Democratic party leader in Yonkers, whose electrical contracting company in the Bronx had failed to disclose its bankruptcy in 1986. Hungry for their share of the multibillion-dollar bonanza, some shady contractors were busy setting up respectable fronts while SCA was busy trying to pierce through the facade. Off to a rocky start, SCA did not help too much. It ousted its first president and was bogged down in mismanagement.[10]

California has its own version of constitution-bending, lease-backed financing for schools. A school district cannot issue general obligation bonds for construction without getting the approval of two-thirds of the voters. To bypass this irritating technicality, the districts with the connivance of the state, engage in lease financing that requires no referendum. To begin, the districts sell certificates of participation (COPs) to investors to acquire land and construct buildings. Then the state reimburses the districts through the California State School Lease-Purchase Program and funds the construction of the projects. Finally, it rents the facilities to the districts under a long-term lease.

Two spoilers have disrupted this complex scheme to evade the laws and the constitution. Laboring under a nearly $15-billion deficit in 1991, the state was slow in reimbursing the school districts. In fact, it was behind some $3 billion in payments. The districts had to issue even more COPs to keep their projects afloat. Under heavy fiscal pressures themselves, this additional burden has brought some districts to the brink of bankruptcy and one past the brink. In a case with national repercussions, the Richmond District, 25 miles east of San Francisco and the 15th largest of the state's 1,100 school districts, declared bankruptcy. It was the first urban school district in recent history to take this desperate step.

In the same plight as Richmond are five other districts that may go under. Should this occur, the six may default on about $34 million in COPs and tax-exempt bonds. This leaves the state with two options. It can either bail out the districts, as one county court has mandated, or allow them to sink into bankruptcy. The latter route will leave investors without any recourse whatsoever because state law bars them from evicting their nonpaying school tenants.

Unhappy with his choices, Governor Pete Wilson complained that the judge's order to bail out Richmond "sets a terrible precedent that will allow a district to spend itself into bankruptcy and then without concern for the fact, look to the State to provide more money."[11]

This is the result of devious means of financing of school construction.

What school building authorities can do, state university construction authorities can do bigger, better, and, with any luck, more safely. They have demonstrated this since the early 1950s by embarking on a record-breaking spending spree using lease financing. Nearly every state leans on an authority like the Pennsylvania Higher Education Authority or the New Hampshire Higher Education and Health Facilities Authority to provide dormitories, academic buildings, performing arts centers, and athletic complexes for their college-bound youngsters.

One authority was not enough for Massachusetts or New York State, each of which has four higher education building authorities. These four play interchangeable roles. When one encounters political and fiscal roadblocks, the others are pleased to get the business, while the colleges are in the fortuitous position of playing one off against the other for the best deal. In the end, the taxpayers and the students pay for all the deals.

First in the nation in tax-exempt bond financing for public and private nonprofit colleges and universities, the New York State Dormitory Authority has an outstanding debt of about $9 billion. Its name is a misnomer since it spends more money on hundreds of academic facilities than on dormitories. The DA's annual expenditures for construction total nearly $600 million, placing it among the top 10 governmental construction agencies in the nation and making it the darling of the higher education world and, of course, Wall Street.

Up to now the shadow of default has not fallen on higher education building authorities. Only Lassen County Community College in California had its come-uppance in 1986 when it defaulted on $7 million in COPs used for a waste-to-energy cogenerating plant that failed. When investors insisted on repayment, the college declared bankruptcy, leaving them with the unpalatable recourse of repossessing a project that no one wanted.[12]

To guard against such defaults a new federal government-sponsored enterprise stepped into the breach in 1986. Like other GSEs it has an affectionate nickname—"Connie Lee" (College Construction Loan Insurance Association). A mixed ownership corporation with public and private representation on the board, Connie Lee can, for profit, buy, sell, and insure the debt of higher education institutions for plant and equipment. Starting in a small way, it primarily provides bond insurance for construction bonds issued by colleges and universities.

Unlike higher education building authorities, higher education loan authorities live on the razor's edge of default. For all the good they do in broadening access to a college education by lending money for undergraduate and graduate programs, their record is replete with defaults running at the rate of $2 billion a year, indefensible guarantees of loans, and funding of marginal private trade schools. This time, though, the federal government and not a state is the big loser.

The federal government is central to an operation that guaranteed or subsidized nearly $18 billion in loans for 9.7 million students in 1990. It does this through seven major programs, of which the most important is the so-called Stafford Loan Program (named after a congressman as a ticket to immortality). The entire operation rests on a bewildering and expensive public and private bureaucracy.

A student starts the loan machinery whirling by applying to one of 12,000 lenders for a loan. The lender can be a friendly bank; a shaky savings and loans association; a credit union; one of 54 state public authorities like the California Student Loan Corporation, the Nebraska Higher Education Loan Program, and the Pennsylvania Higher Education Assistance Corporation; and one of several regional nonprofit loan-marketing corporations chartered by the states. By the end of 1989 these lenders—most of them small—held about $50 billion in outstanding loans. Twenty-five lenders with 54 percent of the loans dominated the market. The top 10 were the Student Loan Marketing Association (Sallie Mae), Citibank, Chase Manhattan, Chemical Bank, Marine Midland, Manufacturer's Hanover Trust Company, three state public authorities, and the New England Education Loan Marketing Corporation (Nellie Mae).

The lenders have nothing to lose. The federal government guarantees their loans against borrowers' death, disability, and bankruptcy. Through state guarantee agencies—mainly public authorities—it protects them against defaults. The public authorities pay the defaulted amount to the lenders and, in turn, are reimbursed by the federal government. The lenders get tidy fees from students and the federal government. The government also pays them the difference between the below-market interest rates charged to the students and prevailing interest rates plus some profit. For example, an undergraduate student who can demonstrate financial need can borrow up to $17,250 and a graduate student $54,750. While they attend school, the students make no payments whatsoever. After they graduate or leave, they pay 8 percent during the first four years and 10 percent thereafter.[13]

Lest the banks and other lenders tie up too much of their cash in long-term student loans, the federal government has still another safety valve. In 1972 it created the Student Loan Marketing Association (Sallie Mae), a privately owned and federally chartered government-sponsored enterprise, to buy guaranteed loans from the lenders and also to lend them money so as to enlarge the pool of student loans. Sallie Mae raises funds in the bond market at low interest rates because it is a GSE and uses the proceeds to buy the guaranteed student loans. To the pleasure of investors, who own about 199 million shares of Sallie Mae's stock, it enjoys a hefty profit derived from the spread between interest it collects on the loans and the cost of borrowed funds. In 1990 it held $19.2 billion, or nearly one-third of all outstanding loans.[14]

Its success soon brought competitors into the secondary market for student loans. Joining Sallie Mae in avidly snapping up loans from the originating lenders are commercial banks, regional non-profit corporations such as the New England Education Loan Marketing Corporation, and public authorities such as the Colorado Student Obligation Loan Authority, the Pennsylvania Higher Education Assistance Agency, the California Student Loan Finance Corporation, the Indiana Secondary Market for Education Loans Inc., the Nebraska Higher Education Loan Program, Inc., the Virginia Educational Loan Authority, and the Kentucky Higher Education Student Loan Corporation.

No matter where one turns in this labyrinthine maze, state and local public authorities in every state are heavily engaged in the brisk action. They make loans, guarantee them, insure them, service them, and buy loans from other lenders. To raise money they issue tax-exempt bonds and even taxable bonds. For example, in 1990 the Michigan Higher Education Student Loan Authority and the Arkansas Student Loan Authority each went to market with a $50-million bond issue. The Nebraska Higher Education Loan Program, Inc. topped them with a $122.5-million issue. Until the Tax Reform Act of 1986 the authorities could build up profitable reserves and earn tidy sums by investing unused bond proceeds. Like other public authorities they came under the axe of Congress and, as a result of the tax changes, the volume of tax-exempt bonds they can issue now has a statutory ceiling.

In their zeal to create public authorities for higher education loans, the states anointed them with an unusual dose of autonomy. Some of the authorities used this independence to escape the clutches of their founders. This was especially true of the Wisconsin Higher Education Corporation (WHEC) and the New England Student Loan Marketing Association (Nellie Mae).

Like most authorities WHEC was a contrivance to evade the Wisconsin constitution. The legislature established it in 1967 as a private nonprofit corporation to guarantee and service higher education loans. Successful from the start, WHEC guaranteed and serviced over $2 billion in loans. To the chagrin of the legislature, as WHEC prospered it escaped all the controls over personnel, procurement, and construction that shackled state agencies. Determined to bring this upstart to heel, the legislature approved a bill in 1985 that, among other things, would remove the president and board of directors of WHEC, curtail their functions, and subject it to legislative control. Governor Anthony S. Earl promptly vetoed the bill with language that raised hackles in the legislature:

> These sections subject the Wisconsin Higher Education Corporation (WHEC) to certain provisions of state law that ordinarily apply only to governmental bodies. Also, the WHEC Board is restructured by these provisions to consist of gubernatorial appointees and legislators. The chief executive officer of WHEC would also be a gubernatorial appointee.
>
> WHEC is a private not-for-profit corporation organized under chapter 181 of the Wisconsin Statutes to provide for a guaranteed student loan (GSL) program. The WHEC Board includes four members elected by the gubernatorially-appointed Higher Educational Aids Board. This current governance structure is sufficient for public accountability in the GSL program, and I have therefore vetoed the legislative changes that unduly interfere in the governance and operations of a private corporation.[15]

Just as quickly as the governor acted, the legislature overrode the veto. WHEC sued in the lower court of the state and asked the court to declare the legislation unconstitutional and to enjoin the legislature from scuttling the corporation. The court sided with WHEC and, in effect, lectured the legislature that it could not renege on a deal it had made 20 years before. After some minor compromises with WHEC, the legislature leaders decided not to appeal the case to higher courts. So WHEC still rides high, thumbing its collective nose at its makers.

Two Massachusetts public authorities created in 1981 have also won the war of independence. The Massachusetts Education Loan Authority (MELA) issues tax-exempt bonds to buy from lenders student loans that are not federally guaranteed. Nellie Mae (New England Loan Marketing Corporation) guarantees loans and also buys guaranteed loans from lenders in Massachusctts and New Hampshire to free up capital for more loans. In an abortive attempt to rein in runaway authorities, the legislature in 1990 asked the Dukakis administration to provide some minimal data on authority revenues, expenditures, and debt. Nellie Mae's reply to the administration's query was almost contemptuous. On January 23, 1990, Lawrence W. O'Toole, president of Nellie Mae, sent this curt letter to L. Edward Lashman Jr., secretary of the executive office for administration and finance:

> I am in receipt of your letter of January 19th requesting information required of state financing authorities. As I indicated in my letter to you in January, 1989 on this same subject, I believe that we are included on a list of state financing authorities in error.
>
> The New England Education Loan Marketing Corporation is a private non-profit corporation. It receives no funding from the Commonwealth and issues debt in its own name without any claim or pledge of the credit of the Commonwealth or on any revenue stream derived from the Commonwealth.
>
> Thus, any information on Nellie Mae finances would prove to distort the actual financial reporting required by Chapter 240. I hope this clarifies our status and that the records of Administration and Finance can be corrected to delete The New England Education Loan Marketing Corporation from your listing of state financing authorities.

MELA provided only some worthless token data, equally contemptuous of the legislature's request.

Now many student loan authorities and other agencies that process loans are under a cloud of default and delinquency. From 1983 to 1989 defaults in guaranteed loans shot up 352 percent and reached over $2 billion a year. This is just the beginning. Two federally chartered nonprofit organizations that guaranteed loans in several states had a default rate of nearly 46 percent: the Higher Education Assistance Foundation (HEAF) and the United Student Aid Funds Inc. (USAF). Following at a distance were higher education loan authorities in California, New York, and Pennsylvania with a combined rate in defaults (in terms of dollars) of over 21 percent. The remaining 33 percent of defaults were sprinkled over the other 47 states.

HEAF was the worst. It is the largest single guarantor of student loans ($8.8 billion) and also "the highest payer of default claims to lenders." What led to its troubles and the declining fortunes of state loan authorities were loans to students attending proprietary schools.[16]

This is a sordid tale that is just beginning to unfold. In May 1991 a subcommittee headed by Senator Sam Nunn of Georgia found "fraud and abuse at every level" of the higher education loan programs, "particularly in the area of proprietary schools." It reported that "many of the schools were more interested in collecting financial aid checks than in education" and scorned oversight by the U.S. Department of Education as "dismal."[17] With equal justice it could also indict state education departments, higher education loan authorities, banks, and higher education accrediting agencies that have "fostered fraud on a wholesale level" because they "won't police the system."

These are the biting words of Dan Hedges, a legal services lawyer in Charleston, West Virginia, who filed a suit against lenders and guarantee agencies in behalf of a client, George Leeson, and 2,000 other students who had attended Northwestern Business College, an unscrupulous private, profit-hungry trade school. Taken in by the "college's" advertisement for a law enforcement course that all but guaranteed a job as a police officer, Leeson enrolled in the course and found that the school, without consulting him, had taken out a loan of about $3,000 in his behalf from a local bank.

As the *New York Times* reports the story, "Mr. Leeson said the school had promised him expense money, a weapon's permit and a chance to ride in police cars. Instead, his teachers kept quitting and the course did not even include books. Then, about halfway through the yearlong course, he arrived at school one night to find it padlocked for good. All he had to show for his efforts was his unpaid student loan."[18]

A sympathetic federal judge ruled that Leeson should not repay the loan and pointed a finger at the banks that disavowed responsibility. The banks, in turn, did some finger pointing of their own at guarantee agencies and federal and state education departments.

Similar suits are under way in California, Kentucky, New Jersey, and Texas. California has two particularly scandalous examples. The California Student Loan Finance Corporation (CSLFC), a public authority, issued about $1 billion in tax-exempt bonds in the 1980s and used the proceeds to buy student loans from banks. To service the loans it unwisely retained United Education and Software (UES), termed by *Barron's* "a small but infamous company," that processed student loans and ran a chain of vocational schools. UES had caused losses of millions of dollars in several banks because of "improper" servicing of loans. This time UES triggered losses ranging between $450 million and $650 million, the biggest financial loss in the history of the student loan program. The federal government refused to pick up the tab for the defaulted loans because of the violations of its guidelines by UES. This left CSLFC's bondholders with little prospect of repayment and CSLFC with public exposure of its poor judgment.

In the legal brouhaha that ensued and still goes on, the bondholders sued Bank America, the trustee of the bonds. Japanese banks that had issued letters of credit to CSLFC to improve its bond rating agreed to pay the bondholders. But they also sued Bank America to recover their losses. The bank hinted that it might sue Peat Marwick Main and Co., the auditing firm for UES and CSLFC. Professing innocence, UES blamed computer glitches for the losses, intimating that IBM might be the culprit.

Joe McCormick, executive director of the Texas Guaranteed Student Loan Corporation, was sympathetic to the plight of his California counterpart. According to *Barron's*, he even found some grounds for optimism in the untidy mess: "I don't see the sky falling yet. I'm glad that the department [U.S. Department of Education] took a firm position on enforcing its rules and regulations. And although I sympathized with Bank America's plight, it's time everyone accepts their proper role and responsibility in carrying out this program."

Lawrence O'Toole, president of Nellie Mae in Massachusetts, also saw some good coming out of the debacle: "Secondary-market makers are warning banks that they will not buy loans made to students attending vocational schools with high default rates. The banks, in turn, are turning down loans from high-risk institutions."[19]

Another California scandal revolved around the First Independent Trust Co. (FITCO), which loaned over $1 billion to students, most of it to those attending trade schools. So sloppy was FITCO in processing the loans and so remiss in transmitting funds to the U.S. Department of Education that the State Banking Department closed it for good in May 1990. Still up in the air was the validity of loans guaranteed against default.[20]

To the credit of the Bush administration, it proposed in 1991 a dismantling of the entire expensive and buck-passing loan bureaucracy that serves the lenders more than the students. Instead of borrowing from banks and state financing authorities students would deal exclusively with colleges that would get their funds directly from the federal government. In one deft move, at considerable savings to taxpayers, the proposal would bypass banks, other lending agencies, and public and private corporations that service loans. It would probably deal a fatal blow to Sallie Mae, Nellie Mae, and state public authorities that, with handsome profits, create a secondary market by buying loans from lenders. Led by the banks, the large student loan bureaucracies fiercely opposed the proposal. Whether Congress has the political will to take on these interest groups remains one of the leading issues of the early 1990s.

Robert D. Reischauer, a highly respected economist and director of the Congressional Budget Office, also floated an idea whose time may yet come. Again, sidestepping the banks and other lenders, students would repay the loans through "slightly higher payroll taxes in their working years" deducted from their paychecks.[21] Should the two proposals be enacted, the 54 state higher education financing authorities would come to a quick end.

Correction Facilities

When it comes to financing jails, public authorities are becoming indispensable. With crime one of the fast growth industries in the nation, they are busily financing the building of jails to house 260 of every 100,000 Americans incarcerated for a year or more. Try as they might, they, with the states and local governments, are a long way from meeting the need for nearly 42,000 new cells a year. In the first half of 1989 only 1,800 new cells had opened to welcome the army of prisoners. This rate of construction is not enough for the courts that have ordered more than two-thirds of the states to end overcrowding in prisons and jails.[22]

In the meantime, flouting nearly every state constitution, public authorities do what they can to stem the tide. Led by the California Statewide Community Development Authority, the New York State Urban Development Corporation, the West Virginia State Building Commission, the Alabama Judicial Building Authority, the Michigan Municipal Bond Authority, and the Texas Public Finance Authority, they are floating tax-exempt bonds to wall in the offenders.

Because of the shortcomings of government, a private corrections industry has begun to flourish. The Corrections Corporation of America (CCA) is the largest private prison operator with nearly 4,000 cells in Florida, Tennessee, Texas, and New Mexico. The states pay CCA the operating costs plus some healthy profits. In 1985 Lamar Alexander, then governor of Tennessee and now secretary of the U.S. Department of Education in the Bush administration, upset the prison bureaucracy by proposing (unsuccessfully) that CCA take over the entire corrections system in the state. Incidentally, his wife was a shareholder in the corporation. Close behind CCA is the Wackenhut Corporation, which runs seven corrections facilities and sees a bright future for private entrepreneurs. Its two fears are the opposition of strong corrections unions and civil libertarians who are wary of prisons for profit.[23] So far the experience with privatization is too meager to be adequately evaluated.

Still More

As their latest venture since joining the welfare state, public authorities have reached out to children and youthful offenders. In 1986 Palm Beach County in Florida created a special taxing district for juvenile services. The citizens had no objection to additional taxes for a service they welcomed. "The true benefit of special taxing districts is making children's services impervious to political whim," argues Jack Levine, head of the nonprofit Florida Center for

Children and Youth. With this classic defense of public authorities/special districts, other Florida counties decided that they too could establish special districts for children just as they create districts for water, sewers, and mass transportation. California, Ohio, Oregon, Minnesota, and Texas also like the idea and appear to be ready to welcome this latest brand of public authority.[24]

Also closely intertwined with the welfare state are state and local building authorities that thrive in every state. While their primary goal is to erect government buildings and other public facilities, they are more than willing to lend a hand and an open purse to hospitals, campuses, and jails. None can equal the New York State Urban Development Corporation (UDC), a conglomerate that among its many functions has raised hundreds of millions of dollars to finance the construction of welfare-related facilities. But that's New York. While other state public authorities may not be in the same megaclass, they are still prospering, notably the Texas Public Building Authority, the Texas Public Finance Authority, the Alabama Building Renovation Finance Authority, the Rhode Island Building Authority, and the Ohio Building Authority.

Protecting the poor, the aged, and the hard-pressed middle classes means big business for public authorities. Notwithstanding state constitutions, the authorities are avidly financing retirement homes, schools, universities, hospitals, jails, and youth centers. So have they become pillars of the welfare state.

13

Reclaiming the
Shadow Government

On the eve of the twenty-first century, state and local governments are in shambles and disarray. They have abdicated many of their most important responsibilities and turned them over to more than 35,000 frequently autonomous public authorities/special districts/ government corporations. No matter which label is used, these independent bodies have become the backdoor government, the invisible government, the shadow government.

Their ascendancy signifies a breakdown in the American system of government. Instead of accountable and visible elected officials, we now have undemocratic public authorities insulated from voter control. Instead of clear-cut centers of responsibility, we sink in a swamp of buck-passing agencies. Instead of control over the public purse by voters and their representatives, we find public authorities running up more debt than all state and local governments combined. Instead of complying with constitutional taboos on revenues, expenditures, and debt, elected officials deliberately flout them.

This is not a conspiracy. No evil men and women have concocted these schemes. The creators were fairly reputable governors, mayors, and legislators who found themselves hemmed in by a system they had not made. For all their campaign promises they were impotent to deal with pressing and complex problems of housing, education, health, economic development, transportation, the environment, and crime. Restrictive constitutions, outmoded budget and accounting systems, and nay-saying taxpayers blocked their aspirations. As they saw it, the only way out of the dilemma was to flout the rules of the game and to bypass the voters. For them the creation of public authorities was a reasonable way to meet pressing public needs.

This has been their course over the last 70 years. What they could not reach through the front door, they achieved through the back door. The chosen vehicles for their machinations were self-financed public authorities. As Annmarie Hauck Walsh, a long-time observer of public authorities, reminds us: "Authorities have not usurped power. Elected officials have failed to exercise it."[1]

At any point the courts could have scotched the stratagems to give the people what they needed and wanted but refused to pay for. But they, too, were reluctant to stymie elected officials determined to find shelter for the poor, hospitals for the ailing, schools and colleges for the young, and cell blocks for criminals. Under fierce political pressure, they connived in sidestepping state constitutions. These acts by a supposedly independent judiciary were hardly moments of glory.

In the end, the honorable men and women in the courts, the legislatures, and governors' chairs, through a tacit if not overt conspiracy, overruled the constitutions. They have much to answer for. In their zeal to demolish what they regarded as outmoded institutions and constitutions, they opened a Pandora's box of runaway and wayward governments.

By now the litany of their failures is all too clear, but bears repeating: an uncontrolled debt burden of over $500 billion; monumental spending sprees, both good and bad; laundering of money from various sources to con and confuse the voters; burdening the poor with regressive fees; bailing out bankrupt and failed authorities; opening the way to corruption, patronage, and pork barrels; subverting statutory missions of authorities by sanctioning new and dubious ventures; lifting checks, balances, and controls from public authorities; deceiving voters by making budgets look smaller while shifting costs to public authorities; and failing to monitor the performance and costs of authorities.

This is what happened to the Passaics among housing authorities, the WHOOPSes among power authorities, the UDCs among economic development authorities, the ALCOSANs among environmental authorities, the "T"s among transportation authorities, and the CSLFCs among health and education authorities—and hundreds more.

Especially disturbing, the elected officials opened the doors of public authorities to the rich and powerful while excluding the general public. The insiders are the banks, Wall Street firms, and politically connected law firms, contractors, real estate developers, and unions. The outsiders of course are the snubbed voters. In this climate unelected heads of public authorities such as Robert Moses and Felix Rohatyn outrivaled governors and mayors in the exercise of power.

Still, it would be a mistake to tar and feather all the states for these failings. Several like Wisconsin and California (except at the local level) have avoided many of the excesses. At the other extreme are reckless adventurers like New York, Pennsylvania, Illinois, Massachusetts, and Texas, which used authorities for improper purposes and failed to provide adequate accountability. It would also be a mistake to play down the solid achievements of many authorities even though the price has been high fiscally and politically. They filled a vacuum left by elected officials who abdicated their responsibilities and produced schools, universities, hospitals, housing, power systems, transportation networks, and water and sewer plants. They dealt with regional problems that respected no political boundaries. They often provided a flexible organization to respond to consumer demands and market trends.

The social and economic turmoil that gave rise to public authorities is still with us. So are the public authorities, many of them bloated with money and power and continuing to multiply at a rapid rate. How can we arrest this disintegration of government? How can we reclaim government for the people?

One way to begin is to turn to the source of many of the problems—the constitutions themselves. Most are hopelessly outmoded and contain constraints to control borrowing that are relics of the nineteenth century. They reflect a deep distrust of elected officials and of representative government, demonstrating a touching faith in simple constitutional formulas to deal with the fiscal, economic, and social turbulence of society.

The hard fact is that the constitutional restrictions have not controlled the pursestrings. The evidence on this score is overwhelming. If they worked, there would be little need for devices such as public authorities to get around them. If they were enforced, governments would be paralyzed in the face of overwhelming needs. A tough constitutional clause is no substitute for a hospital bed, a schoolhouse, or a cell block.

That leaves voters with two options. One is to continue the hypocrisy of constitutional provisions that are dead letters. The other is to scuttle them and eliminate requirements for voter referenda, debt limits, and other shackles. Citizens would have to count on a responsible, representative government to do the job.

In one fell swoop the lifting of obsolete constitutional controls would strengthen representative government. It would wipe out the need for thousands of shell authorities that are nothing but schemes to raise money outside of the constitution. It would result in disbanding much of the army of bond counsel, financial advisers, and bond underwriters that, at astronomical fees, specialize in ways to bypass constitutions. (Many of them, however, would still be busily engaged in crafting honest-to-goodness general obligation and revenue bonds.) It would save billions of dollars by eradicating a large sector of the invisible government. It would end much of the dissembling and deception that deepen the public's mistrust of government.

The uproar at this proposal by some is predictable. There are those who regard any attempts to excise constitutional restrictions on borrowing as shocking and irresponsible. So deep-rooted is the distrust of elected officials that the proponents of control want more and not fewer built-in chains. Under no circumstances do they want to give governments a free hand with big money.

This abiding faith in constitutional fetters continues even in the face of their obvious failure. As a result, movements to limit borrowing, taxing, and spending abound throughout the land. Some are led by demagogues, others by bewildered citizens baffled by the complexity and unresponsiveness of government. In addition to Proposition 13 in California and Initiative 2 1/2 in Massachusetts, they have also been successful in imposing constitutional and statutory caps on spending and taxing in 22 states. Their latest exploits are a limit on the terms of legislators in California, Colorado, and Oklahoma, and a campaign to try the same in other states including Washington.

John Burick, a leader of the antilegislative revolt in Washington, makes no bones about the aims of his group, called Limit: "This is a mainstream effort to regain control of government, and it has a full head of momentum."

Public interest groups such as Common Cause and the League of Women Voters are trying to stem this new populism. Margaret Colony of the League of Women Voters spelled out the league's concerns: "We know the political process is not working well and is not very responsive to the average citizen. But this type of measure is so drastic that it would only compound the problem. And it takes away people's choices. If you want somebody out of office, vote 'em out."[2]

None of these caveats will diminish the fervor of those in search of easy answers, but a countervailing force exists. In many states voters are slowly beginning to learn the futility and the negative consequences of facile solutions. Ten states have dropped constitutional requirements for voter referenda. Nevertheless, the results are mixed. Even without severe controls over borrowing, Illinois and Massachusetts are no better than they were before. In fact they have more rather than fewer authorities used as gimmicks to make state budgets look smaller than they are. On the other hand, Wisconsin, also among the 10, has achieved more open representative government. At least the process of stripping constitutions of their barnacles is under way.

The faster constitutional change takes place, the sooner states will get rid of phony authorities that are mere transmission belts to pass money through the back door. Still, thousands of bona fide authorities will remain. They actually construct, manage, and operate large and small-scale facilities and systems. Should they go?

Yes and no. Where authorities are merely ploys to deceive voters as to the size of the budget, they should go—and go fast. Voters are beginning to lose patience with this all-too-common scenario: A city in financial distress spins off its water and sewer systems to a new authority. Presto! Overnight the budget shrinks and the mayor boasts about lower taxes. In the meantime, the authority charges high fees for services once covered by the budget. When voters get around to adding all the figures, they find they are paying more than they did before the switch, especially if they are poor. Such bait-and-switch public authorities are deliberate contrivances to obfuscate the citizens. Their functions belong in the general government from whence they came.

Nor should the states hang on to authorities because they are supposedly more efficient and businesslike than the state and local bureaucracies. Contrary to widespread myths, they are on the whole no more effective than regular governmental agencies running comparable programs. Some authorities are paragons of superb management, while others are mediocre, corrupt, patronage-ridden, self-serving organizations. Some are no better than traditional state and local agencies rife with wrongdoing and abuse of power. Few public authorities match the excellence of some state agencies such as the California State Water Project housed in the Department of Water Resources or the Albuquerque Joint Water and Sewer System in New Mexico or the Florida Turnpike that is part of the Department of Transportation or the Los Angeles Department of Water and Power, or Oregon's veterans' housing agency. Conversely, few general government agencies come close to the outstanding management of such public authorities as the Port Authority of New York and New Jersey, the Sacramento Municipal Utility District (SMUD), the Wisconsin Housing and Economic Development Authority (WHEDA), the Delaware Solid Waste Authority, the Massachusetts Port Authority, and the Georgia Power Authority, to cite but a few.

Whether an authority or a general government agency can best operate a major program depends on the political culture in each state. Given indifferent, hidebound, and inflexible governments, a public authority may be the only means of getting the job done. Given a responsible government, most authorities may be redundant.

Sweeping generalizations will not do. Each state should examine its public authorities on a case-by-case basis with the burden of proof for continued existence placed squarely on the authority. Where authorities duplicate each other as in economic development, health, education, and construction, they should be consolidated or eliminated. Where they cannot survive without heavy subsidies, they could, in most instances, be folded into the general government, ending the fiction that they are self-sustaining, independent authorities. Where authorities have outlived their usefulness as in student loan and economic development programs, they could be early candidates for termination.

What should be the fate of all other public authorites, especially the thousands of power, housing, environmental, and transportation authorities that are among oldest in the nation? To discard them would be to throw the baby out with the bath water. Despite the failings of many, they do a creditable job overall with some power and port authorities being models of sterling management. Unlike housing and transportation authorities, they tend to be self-sufficient and churn out surpluses. By design, the housing and transportation authorities will continue to be losers and, to stay alive, will require regular infusions of cash. Nevertheless, their corporate structure, their flexibility, and their quick response to changing public needs give them an edge over systems locked up in a state and city bureaucracy.

Public authorities appropriately are indispensable in attacking interstate, interregional, and intraregional problems that transcend outmoded political boundaries. No viable substitute exists for the Port Authority of New York and New Jersey, the Texas Housing Agency, the Bay Area Rapid Transit, the Delaware Solid Waste Authority, the Arizona Salt River Project, and hundreds like them that vault over jurisdictional walls fashioned in the eighteenth century.

Through such winnowing of the chaff from the wheat the states can substantially cut public authorities down to size and end up with a manageable number. The price of survival of those that are left should be a return to responsible and accountable government. This is easier said than done. One of the puzzles of our age is how to achieve a delicate balance between desirable autonomy and flexibility on the one hand, and accountability and control on the other. How do we bring public authorities under the wing of general government without gutting them? How do we pull together the scattered and loose fragments of government without smothering them in layers of bureaucracy?

Fortunately, experience points the way. Several states, the federal government, and some foreign governments have developed workable mechanisms of overseeing public authorities: the governor's veto power as in New Jersey; central agencies to monitor debt as in Texas, Kentucky, and California; special units in budget offices to oversee authority budgets as in New York; performance contracts between governments and public corporations as in France; full-scale audits of public authorities as in Illinois; the federal Government Corporation Control Act of 1945 that sets up criteria for the creation of government corporations and requires them to submit business type budgets to the president; and restrictions on the number of authorities as in Wisconsin. What's needed is a framework of accountability and control that incorporates the best of these features and spells out the relationships between governments and their authorities. At a minimum, the framework could take this form:

Sunset and sunrise. Insert a sunset clause in the legislation creating each public authority. This means that at the end of five or 10 years the authority would automatically expire unless, after extensive public hearings, the governor and the legislature give it another lease on life. No instant miracles will occur. But the process would force into the open the festering issues that surround authorities as well as their strong points.

Who's boss? Remove all doubt that the governor of the state or the mayor of the city is the boss. Give these officials the clear power to appoint a majority of authority board members during their term of office. This should blow away any fuzziness as to who is in charge and end buck passing.

Let the sun shine in. Throw light on the dark recesses of public authorities. Incorporate their budgets (at least in summary form) in state and municipal budgets for all to see, but distinguish carefully between those that are tax financed and those that are supported by user fees. Force elected leaders to take a stand on the budget. This should not mean petty and niggling controls that disgrace the budget process in every part of the nation. Rather, there should be only a straight up-or-down and take-it-or-leave it vote on the policies, revenues, expenditures, and debt of public authorities.

The gun behind the door. Give governors untrammeled veto power over the actions of public authorities. The Port Authority of New York and New Jersey has thrived despite this constraint. Governor Jim Florio of New Jersey has used the veto power to both thrash and cajole public authorities.

Tell them what to do. Strip the basic statutes governing authorities of any doubletalk and ambiguity with regard to their mission. Spell out clearly what they should be doing and the expected results. Set up checkpoints to end adventuring and empire building outside of their legal jurisdiction.

A deal is a deal. As part of their contract, public authorities should explicitly lay out their targets for the year. At the end of the year, they should report on their success or failure in meeting their goals. The point is to keep their feet to the fire—always.

Minding the money store. Set up in one place in government an agency that would manage and monitor all debt, including the debt of public authorities. This could be the central budget office or a special office of debt management.

Lifting the burden from the poor. Highlight the regressive and oppressive fees of public authorities that hit the poor especially hard. Either give them rebates through the tax system or get the general taxpayers to shoulder the cost of many authority operations.

Following the rules of the road. Compel authorities to follow the rules on staffing, pay, purchasing, contracts, and construction. If the restrictions are petty and self-defeating, change them for everyone. But don't let two governments exist side by side—one free of so-called red tape and the other choked by it. In the extreme when all else fails, exempt some authorities from the rules only if they can make a convincing case for special treatment.

Revealing the secrets of the board room. Require an open review by governors and mayors of bond issues, prospectuses, and bond covenants of public authorities. Force these officials to take a stand on new debt and to explain their yeas and nays. This should go a long way in eliminating backdoor financing and private deals between authorities and bond underwriters.

Creating a level playing field. Competitive bidding by bond underwriters for bond issues should be a "must." End the charade of behind-the-scenes negotiated deals with favored brokerage houses.

Sharpening the teeth of the watchdogs. Rather than perfunctory checks on public authorities, insist on a nonstop independent audit of their performance and operations. The audit reports should be easily accessible to the press and the public.

Freedom of information. Open the minutes, books, and records of authorities to public scrutiny, even if it hurts.

Neither glossy nor flossy be. Annual reports should reveal results and costs and should not be self-serving, expensive extravaganzas.

A searchlight on subsidies. Collect all the scattered information on subsidies to public authorities and put it in one place, preferably the budget. Let the searchlight focus on the annual bailout of many public authorities.

None of these proposals are unrealistic. Somewhere in the great laboratory of American states each one is operational and, where it is in effect, it has brought prodigal authorities back to their parent governments without tying them up in straitjackets. But hardly enough of the proposed changes have taken root.

When change comes, it will be slow, incremental, evolutionary. No instant panaceas will emerge. It took 70 years to tear American governments apart. It may take 10 to 20 years to make them whole again.

The agenda for change is daunting. It means major surgery on constitutions and statutes. It means bitter confrontations with private interests that feed at the public trough. It means a new and constructive relationship between general government and public authorities that will keep representative government preeminent and yet give public authorities the flexibility and corporate structure they need. Above all, change calls for a leadership not yet in sight and a constituency still to be born.

Were the proposals adopted, they would not end all political manipulation, corruption, patronage, and special dealing. Politicians will always try to beat the system for short-term gains. By forcing their maneuvers into the open, however, the changes may act as a brake.

A new framework of accountability may even revive a dormant press that, with the exception of a handful of stubborn investigative reporters, is barely aware of the existence of the shadow government. Only when a scandal breaks does the press suddenly awaken. The proposed flow of information may induce continuing coverage of one of the big stories in the nation.

If eternal vigilance is the price of liberty, it is also the price of a strong and responsible representative government. Some of the proposed controls over public authorities may sharpen such vigilance.

No matter what is done, the specter of an unresponsive and unyielding federal government will continue to hover over state and local governments. By cutting federal aid and slowly dissolving the ties that bind it to the states, the national government has forced state and local governments, fearful of tax revolts, to resort to subterfuges like public authorities to finance their operations. So long as the federal government abandons its domestic priorities, these actions will continue and lead to a further disintegration of American governments.

SELECT BIBLIOGRAPHY

American Banker—*The Bond Buyer. 1989, 1990, 1991 Yearbooks*. New York: Thomson, 1989, 1990, 1991.

Caro, Robert H. *The Power Broker*. New York: Alfred A. Knopf, 1974.

Cohen, Natalie R. *Municipal Default Patterns*. New York: Enhance Reinsurance, 1988.

Feldman, Roger D., Richard Mudge, and Kenneth I. Rubin. *Financing Infrastructure Tools for the Future*. New York: Executive Enterprise, 1988.

Henriques, Diana B. *The Machinery of Greed*. Lexington, Mass.: Lexington Books, 1986.

Katz, Harvey. *Shadow on the Alamo*. New York: Doubleday, 1972.

Leigland, James, and Robert Lamb. *WPP$$: Who Is to Blame for the WPPSS Disaster*. Cambridge, Mass.: Ballinger, 1986.

McClelland, Peter D., and Alan L. Magdovitz. *Crisis in the Making: The Political Economy of New York State Since 1945*. New York: Cambridge University Press, 1981.

National Council on Public Works Improvement. *Fragile Foundations: A Report on America's Public Works*. Washington, D.C., 1988.

Newfield, Jack. *Abuse of Power*. New York: Viking, 1977.

Seidman, Harold, and Robert Gilmour. *Politics, Position and Power: From the Positive to the Regulatory State*, 4th ed. New York: Oxford University Press, 1986.

Smith, Robert G. *Ad-Hoc Governments*. Beverly Hills: Sage, 1974.

———. *Public Authorities in Urban Areas*. Washington, D.C.: National Association of Counties Research Foundation, 1967.

Walsh, Annmarie Hauck. *The Public's Business*. Cambridge, Mass.: MIT 1978.

NOTES

Chapter 1: The Rise of the Shadow Government

1. Paul Glastris, "The Government Debt Racket," *Washington Monthly*, February 1985.

2. Jack Newfield, *Abuse of Power* (New York: Viking, 1977).

3. Suggested by James Leigland, Martin School of Public Administration, University of Kentucky.

4. Luther Gulick, *Tax Review*, November 1947.

5. *City and State*, March 12, 1990.

6. *Boston Globe*, October 24, 1989.

7. Natalie R. Cohen, *Municipal Default Patterns* (New York: Enhance Reinsurance, 1988).

8. John Strahanich, "Inside the Invisible Government," *Boston Magazine*, October 1989.

9. For much of this information I am indebted to Jameson W. Doig, Woodrow Wilson School, Princeton University. Especially useful was his paper "Public Authorities: Tensions Between Entrepreneurship and Accountability," delivered at the annual meeting of the American Political Science Association, New Orleans, August 31, 1985.

10. Cited by Robert G. Smith, *Ad-Hoc Governments* (Beverly Hills: Sage, 1974).

11. Ibid.

12. David C. Perry, State University of New York, Buffalo, provided background materials on Robert Moses. Also helpful is Jon J. Lines, Ellen L. Parker, and David C. Perry, "Building the Twentieth Century Public Works Machine: Robert Moses and the Public Authority," Nelson A. Rockefeller Institute of Government, State University of New York, Fall 1986. The definitive story of Moses is, of course, Robert A. Caro, *The Power Broker* (New York: Alfred A. Knopf, 1974).

13. John K. Galbraith, *The Affluent Society* (Boston: Houghton-Mifflin, 1958).

Chapter 2: Always a Borrower or a Lender Be

1. Merl M. Hackbart and James Leigland, "State Debt Management Policy: A National Survey," *Public Budgeting and Finance*, Spring 1990.

2. *Albany Times Union*, November 31, 1990.

3. John C. Nuveen and Co., Inc., "Florida Leasing in the 1990s" (Chicago, October 1991).

4. Moody's Investment Service, *Municipal Issues*, March 1989.

5. Ben Weberman, column in *Forbes*, November 17, 1989.

6. Apogee Research, *Performance Report on the Nation's Public Works* (Washington, D.C.: National Council on Public Works Improvement, 1987).

7. Ben Weberman, column in *Forbes*, April 17, 1989.

8. *Sacramento Bee*, April 15, 1990.

9. Harvey Katz, *Shadow on the Alamo* (New York: Doubleday, 1972).

10. *Municipal Default Patterns*.

11. *Boston Globe*, October 24, 1989.

12. Ben Weberman, column in *Forbes*, November 23, 1990.

13. Letters to *Barron's*, November 19, 1990.

14. The Bond Buyer, *1991 Yearbook* (New York, 1991).

15. Ibid.

Chapter 3: A Fate Worse Than Debt

1. Office of Applied Energy Studies, Washington State University, *Final Report to the Washington State Legislature* (Olympia, 1982).

2. Howard Gleckman, "WPPSS: From Dream to Default," *The Bond Buyer* (1984).

3. *Chemical Bank* v. *WPPSS et al.*, 99 Wash. 2d 772 (1983).

4. See Howard Gleckman, "WPPSS: From Dream to Default," *The Bond Buyer*, 1984; James Leigland and Robert Lamb, *WPP$$: Who Is to Blame for the WPPSS Disaster* (Cambridge, Mass.: Ballinger, 1986); *The Bond Buyer, 1989 Yearbook* (New York, 1989); *Bond Investors' Letter*, various issues 1990, 1991; *New York Times*, July 11, 1988; September 13, 1989; Fitch Investors Service, Inc., "Washington Public Power Supply System," August 11, 1989; Harold E. Rogers, Jr., "What Went Wrong with WPPSS?" *Municipal Finance Journal*, Winter 1984.

5. Robert M. Bleiberg, "Fool Me Twice," *Barron's*, August 21, 1989.

6. Gleckman, "From Dream to Default."

7. New York State Moreland Act Commission on the Urban Development Corporation and Other State Financing Agencies, *Restoring Credit and Confi-*

dence, Report to the Governor (Albany, N.Y., March 1976); Peter D. McClelland and Alan L. Magdowitz, *Crisis in the Making* (New York: Cambridge University Press, 1981).

8. Timothy B. Clark, "The Rapid Rise and Fall of UDC," *Empire State Report*, April 1975.

9. *Abuse of Power*.

10. *Restoring Credit and Confidence*.

11. *Abuse of Power*.

12. Ibid.

13. Ibid.

14. *New York Times*, March 3, 1990.

15. General Court of Massachusetts, Senate Ways and Means Committee, *State Funding for the MBTA: The Silent Crisis* (Boston, 1986).

16. "The MBTA: What's Gone Wrong," *Boston Globe*, December 14–24, 1979.

17. *Boston Globe*, October 25, 1989.

18. General Court of Massachusetts, Senate Ways and Means Committee, *State Authorities: The Fourth Branch of Government* (Boston, 1985).

19. *New York Times*, February 13, 23, 26, September 20, December 12, 1990; January 9, 1991.

20. *Report and Recommendations of the State Commission of Investigation on County and Local Sewerage and Utility Districts* (Trenton, 1983).

21. *Municipal Default Patterns*.

22. Matthew Schifrin, "The Moynihan Ripoff," *Forbes*, December 11, 1989.

Chapter 4: Who's Minding the Store?

1. Annemarie Hauck Walsh, New York State Legislature, Commission on Economy and Efficiency in Government, *Hearing*, (Albany, 1982). Walsh explores issues of accountability and autonomy in her book, *The Public's Business* (Cambridge, Mass.: MIT, 1978).

2. *Restoring Credit and Confidence*.

3. New York State Senate Committee on Investigations and Taxation, *Millions at Risk* (Albany, 1983).

4. *Newsday*, June 12, 1986.

5. New York State Assembly Committee on Public Authorities and Corporations, *Report* (Albany, January 1987).

6. City Club of New York, February 6, 1987.

7. New York State Commission on Integrity in Government, *Underground Government* (Albany, 1990).

8. Colorado Legislative Council, Committee on Accountability of Government Authorities, *Report* (Denver, 1986).

9. Auditor General of Illinois, *Feasibility of Consolidating State Revenue Bond Agencies* (Springfield, 1989).

10. State of Washington Senate, *Report* (Olympia, 1980).

11. *WPP$$.*

12. *State Authorities: The Fourth Branch of Government.*

13. Massachusetts Ways and Means Committee, *State Authorities: Public Finances and Public Responsibility* (Boston, 1989).

14. *Boston Globe*, October 23, 1989.

15. *County and Local Sewerage and Utility Authorities.*

16. Diana B. Henriques, *The Machinery of Greed* (Lexington, Mass.: Lexington Books, 1986).

17. *Newark Star Ledger*, March 14, 1989.

18. Ibid.

19. Ibid.

20. *City and State*, March 12, 1990.

21. Ibid.

22. Virginia M. Perrenod, *Special Districts: Special Purposes* (College Station: Texas A&M University Press, 1984); *Shadow of the Alamo.*

23. Ibid.

Chapter 5: The Law Be Damned!

1. *Montano* v. *Gabaldon*, 766 P2d 132 (New Mexico, 1989).

2. *Texas Building Authority* v. *Jim Mattox, Attorney General of Texas*, 686 S.W. 2d 924 (Texas, 1981).

3. *State Ex Rel Warren* v. *Nusbaum*, 208 N.W. 2d 780 (1973).

4. *MBTA* v. *Boston Safe Deposit and Trust Co. et al.*, 205 N.E. 2d 546 (1965).

5. *State of Flordia* v. *The School Board of Sarasota County*, Docket No. 74794, April 26, 1990.

6. *New York State Coalition for Criminal Justice* v. *Coughlin*, 103 A.D. 2d 401, 479 NYS 850 (1984).

7. William J. Quirk and Louis Wein, "A Short Constitutional History of Entities Commonly Known as Authorities," *Cornell Law Review*, April 1971.

8. *Wein* v. *City of New York et al.*, 36 N.Y. 2d. (1975).

9. *Wein* v. *State of New York*, 39 N.Y. 2d 136 (1978); *Wein* v. *Levitt*, 42 N.Y. 2d 300 (1977).

10. *Matter of Fuchsberg*, 426 N.Y. 2d 639 (1977).

11. *Robertson* v. *Zimmerman*, 218 N.Y. 52 (1935).

12. *Comereski* v. *City of Elmira*, 125 N.E. 2d 241 (1951).

13. *Plumbing, Heating, Piping Contractors Association* v. *New York State Thruway*, 185 N.Y.S. 2d 534 (1961).

14. *Purcell* v. *Regan*, 510 N.Y.S. 2d 772 (1975).

15. *Matter of Russell* v. *Jones Beach State Parkway Authority*, 363 N.Y.S. 2d 428 (1975).

16. *Patterson* v. *Carey*, 370 N.Y.S. 2d 783 (1975).

17. *Credit Markets*, July 24, 1989.

18. *Smith* v. *Levitt*, 355 N.Y.S. 2d 687 (1971).

19. *Wein* v. *State of New York*, 383 N.Y.S. 2d 238 (1975).

20. *Chemical Bank* v. *WPPSS et al.*, 99 Wash. 2d 772 (1983).

21. *In re Washington Public Power Supply System Litigation* 720 F. supp., D.C. Arizona, September 15, 1989.

22. *New Jersey Turnpike Authority* v. *Parsons*, 69 A 2d 875 (1949).

23. *Behnke* v. *N.J. Highway Authority*, 97 A 2d 647 (1953).

24. *Safeway Trails et al.* v. *Kervick et al.*, 197 A 2d 366 (1964).

25. *Bituminous Products Co.* v. *New Jersey Turnpike Authority*, 92 A 2d 836 (1963).

26. *Newark* v. *New Jersey Turnpike Authority*, 81 A 2d 705 (1951).

27. *State of New Jersey* v. *Daquino*, 152 A 2d 377 (1959).

28. *Broadway National Bank of Bayonne* v. *Parking Authority*, 183 A 2d 873 (1962).

29. *Dean* v. *Kuchel*, 218 P. 2d 521 (1950).

30. *Board of State Harbor Commission for San Francisco* v. *Dean*, 258 P. 2d 590 (1953).

31. *Gude* v. *City of Lakewood, Colorado*, 636 P. 2d 69 (1981).

32. *People* v. *Chicago Transit Authority*, 392 ILL 77 (1945).

33. *Bates* v. *Board of Education, Allendale Community Consolidated School District*, No. 17, Docket 68681 (1989).

34. Memorandum, May 5, 1982.

35. New Jersey Superior Court, Law Division, Atlantic County, Docket No. L-01163-18, October 22, 1988.

36. *Hartman* v. *Aurora Sanitary District*, 23 ILL. 2d 109 (1961).

37. John Atkins, "The Municipality and Its Public Authorities," *Local Government Law*, Winter 1983.

38. *U.S. Trust Co. of New York* v. *New Jersey*, 69 N.J. 253, 353 A 2d 614 (1976); 431 U.S. 1 (1977).

39. *New York Times*, April 28, 1977, cited by John I. Kraft, Thomas Lotkith, and Bryan G. Petkanies, "Accommodating the Rights of Bondholders and State Public Purposes," *Tulane Law Review*, Vol. 55, 1981.

40. *New York Times*, May 26, 1977, cited in Kraft et al.

41. *Automobile Club of New York* v. *Port Authority of New York and New Jersey*, F2 407 (2nd CR 1989); *New York Times*, May 15, 1990.

42. *Flushing National Bank* v. *Municipal Assistance Corporation et al.*, 40 N.Y. 2d 731 (1976).

43. *Quirk* v. *Municipal Assistance Corporation*, N.Y.S. 2d 842 (1977).

44. *Opinion of the Justices*, 356 MASS 775 (1966).

45. *Massachusetts Port Authority* v. *Treasurer et al.*, 352 MASS 775 (1967).

46. *New Bedford* v. *New Bedford, Woods Hole, Martha's Vineyard, and Nantucket Steamship Authority*, 336 MASS 651 (1958).

47. *WHEC et al.* v. *Donald J. Hanaway et al.*, Circuit Court Branch 12, 85 CV 5745 (1985); *Wisconsin State Journal*, November 17, 1987.

48. Harold Seidman and Robert Gilman, *Politics, Position and Power*, 4th ed. (New York: Oxford University Press, 1986).

Chapter 6: The Public Authority Sweepstakes: Winners and Losers

1. *The Bond Buyer, 1991 Yearbook*.

2. U.S. General Accounting Office, *Tax Policy: Tax Exempt Bond Issuance Costs* (Washington, D.C., 1989).

3. State of California Senate Office of Research, *Report to the State Senate on the State Treasurer* (Sacramento, 1988).

4. Texas Bond Review Board, *Annual Report, 1988* (Austin, 1989).

5. *The Bond Buyer, 1991 Yearbook*.

6. *The State Treasurer*.

7. Ibid.

8. Diana B. Henriques, "Let the Sun Shine on Municipal Bonds," *New York Times*, March 3, 1991.

9. Penelope Lemov, "For Municipal Bonds It's Not a Plain Vanilla Anymore," *Governing*, June 1990.

10. *Boston Globe*, October 23, 1989.

11. *Credit Markets*, January 9, 1989.

12. Lemov, "Municipal Bonds."

13. *Chicago Sun Times*, November 2, 1983.

14. *The Bond Buyer*, May 1985.

15. Frank Lynn, "Dinkin and Holtzman Contributors Handling City Bonds," *New York Times*, July 6, 1990.

16. Lemov, "Municipal Bonds."

17. *The Bond Buyer, 1989 Yearbook.*

18. Ben Weberman, "A Better Break for Investors," *Forbes*, September 3, 1990.

19. *The Bond Buyer, 1989 and 1991 Yearbooks.*

20. Matthew Schifrin, "Take the $70 Million and Run," *Forbes*, April 11, 1988.

21. *The Bond Buyer, 1989 Yearbook.*

22. *The Bond Buyer, 1991 Yearbook.*

23. *Defaulted Bonds Newsletter*, January 1991.

24. Leigland and Lamb, *WPP$$.*

25. Penelope Lemov, "Bond Lawyers Given Limit on Fees," *Governing*, July 1990.

26. *Albany Times Union*, September 17, 1987.

27. *Albany Times Union*, August 29, 1987.

28. *The Bond Buyer, 1991 Yearbook.*

29. Herman L. Boschken, *Strategic Design and Organizational Change: Pacific Rim Seaports in Transition* (Tuscaloosa: University of Alabama Press, 1988).

30. U.S. Bureau of the Census, *Government Finances 1988–89* (Washington, D.C.: Department of Commerce, 1990).

31. U.S. Bureau of the Census, *Finances of Special Districts, 1987 Census of Governments* (Washington, D.C., 1990).

32. Joseph M. Giglio, Chairman, National Council on Public Works Improvement, "Fixing up America," interview, *Barron's*, November 6, 1989.

33. John Strahanich, "Inside the Shadow Government," *Boston Magazine*, October 1989.

34. Penelope Lemov, "User Fees," *Governing*, March 1989.

35. Massachusetts Taxpayers Foundation, "A Description of an Initiative Petition with Significant Fiscal Impact" (Boston, January 1990).

36. James Lyons, "Tax Cutting Initiatives," *Forbes*, November 12, 1990.

37. *New York Times*, February 26, 1991.

Chapter 7: Bucking the Economic Tide

1. Ronald F. Ferguson and Helen F. Ladd, "Economic Performance and Economic Development Policy in Massachusetts" (Cambridge: John F. Kennedy, School of Government, Harvard University, 1986); David Shribman, "Governor Dukakis' Role in the Economic Turnaround in Massachusetts Draws Questions," *Policy*, July 21, 1987.

2. Illinois Economic and Fiscal Commission, *Report to the General Assembly on Economic Development* (Springfield, 1990).

3. U.S. General Accounting Office, *Small Business Loans* (Washington, D.C., 1988).

4. *The Bond Buyer, 1989 Yearbook.*

5. Glastris, "Government Debt Racket."

6. *Municipal Default Patterns.*

7. Dennis Zimmerman, *The Volume Cap for Tax-Exempt Private-Activity Bonds* (Washington, D.C.: Advisory Commission on Intergovernmental Relations, 1990).

8. *The Bond Buyer, 1990 Yearbook.*

9. Marianne K. Clarke, *Revitalizing State Economies* (Washington, D.C.: National Governors' Association, 1986).

10. Roger Wilson, *State Business Incentives to Economic Growth: Are They Effective?* (Lexington, Ky.: Council of State Governments, 1988).

11. John Herbers, "A Third Wave of Economic Development," *Governing*, June 1990.

12. Lawrence Litvak and Belden Daniels, *Innovation Development Finance* (Washington, D.C.: Council of State Planning Agencies, 1976).

13. Illinois, *Economic Development.*

14. Isabel Wilkerson, "What Illinois Gave to Keep Sears," *New York Times*, August 22, 1989.

15. Illinois, *Economic Development.*

16. *State Business Incentives.*

17. Office of the Auditor General, *Economic Development Progress*, (Springfield, Ill., 1989).

18. Illinois, *Economic Development.*

19. Roger J. Vaughan, "False Maps and New Prosperity: Illinois' Economic Failure," in Ray S. Wehrle, *Economic Development in Illinois* (Illinois Issues, 1986).

20. Letter to the *New York Times*, November 1, 1990.

21. *New York Times*, January 24, 1991; *Albany Times Union*, October 24, 1990.

22. Anne Marie Walsh and James Leigland, "The Authority $24 Billion Debt and Still Growing," *Empire State Report*, July 1983.

23. *The Bond Buyer*, 1987.

24. *White Plains Reporter Dispatch*, February 24, 1987.

25. "The Authority $24 Billion Debt."

26. Gannett News Service, February 21, 1987.

27. *Albany Times Union*, November 16, 1989; March 6, 1990.

28. *Albany Times Union*, October 15, 1989.

29. New York State Legislative Commission on State—Local Relations, *Local Industrial Development Agencies*, 1989.

30. *Albany Times Union*, April 1, 1991.

31. *Albany Times Union*, April 15, 1991.

32. *Underground Government*; *New York Times*, May 3, 1991.

33. *Underground Government*.

34. Ibid.

35. *New York Times*, August 12, 1991.

36. *State Business Incentives*.

37. *Governing*, July 1990.

38. *New York Times*, April 15, 1990.

39. *Kansas City Star*, May 12, 1988.

40. *Los Angeles Times*, December 17, 1990; Eleanor Chelimsky, "Enterprise Zones" (Washington, D.C.: U.S. General Accounting Office, 1989).

41. *New York Times*, February 24, March 26, 1991.

42. *Governing*, August 20, 1990.

43. John C. Nuveen and Co., Inc., "The Risks and Rewards of Non-Appropriation Out Clauses" (Chicago, June 1990).

44. De Lysa Burnier, "State Economic Development Policy: A Decade of Activity," *Public Administration Review*, March/April 1991.

Chapter 8: Housing Horrors

1. U.S. General Accounting Office, *Public Housing: Chicago Housing Authority* (Washington, D.C., June 1990).

2. *Chicago Tribune*, series of 1986 articles.

3. Letter from Mary K. Nenno, associate director for policy development, National Association of Housing and Redevelopment Officials (NAHRO), September 13, 1991; Mark L. Matulef, "This Is Public Housing," *Journal of Housing*, September/October 1987.

4. Charles Finnie, "Public Housing Crisis," *Columbia Missourian*, June 5, 1988.

5. Nenno letter.

6. Mary K. Nenno, *Housing and Community Development* (Washington, D.C.: NAHRO, 1989).

7. Robert Kuttner, "Bad Housekeeping," *New Republic*, April 25, 1988.

8. U.S. General Accounting Office, *Housing and Urban Development Issues* (Washington, D.C., 1988); Congressional Budget Office, *Current Housing Problems and Possible Federal Responses* (Washington, D.C., 1988).

9. *Housing and Urban Development Issues*.

10. "Bad Housekeeping."

11. *Housing and Urban Development Issues*.

12. Mary K. Nenno, "State and Local Governments: New Initiatives in Low-Income Housing Preservation," *Housing Policy Debate*, Vol. 2, Issue 2, 1991.

13. Mary K. Nenno, "Federal Financing and Beyond: Housing and Community Development in the 1990s" (Washington, D.C.: NAHRO, 1991).

14. "50 Years of Housing Legislation," *Journal of Housing*, September/October 1987.

15. Gerald Fetner, "Public Power and Professional Responsibility," *American Journal of Legal History*, Vol. 21, 1977.

16. Harold A. McDougall, "Affordable Housing for the 1990s," *Journal of Law Reform*, Spring 1987.

17. "Bad Housekeeping."

18. U.S. General Accounting Office, "HUD Reforms," June 12, 1991; *New York Times*, February 18, 1990; May 19, 1991.

19. *New York Times*, February 18, 1991.

20. *New York Times*, February 5, 1990.

21. Congressional Budget Office, *The Effects of Tax Reform on Tax Expenditures* (Washington, D.C., 1988).

22. Congressional Budget Office, *Controlling the Risks of Government-Sponsored Enterprises* (Washington, D.C., 1991).

23. *New York Times*, February 7, 1990.

24. Peter Overby, *Common Cause*, May/June 1990.

25. *North Jersey Herald and News*, series of articles from January to March 1990; *New York Times*, February 18, 1990.

26. *Akron Beacon Journal*, series of articles in 1982 and 1983.

27. *Cleveland Plain Dealer*, April–December 1987.

28. James Neff, "Playing the Housing Game," *Cleveland Plain Dealer*, series of articles in April, November, December 1987.

29. U.S. General Accounting Office, *HUD Oversight of the Annapolis Housing Authority* (Washington, D.C., 1988).

30. *Palm Beach Post*, August 29, December 26, 1988.

31. *St. Petersburgh Times*, January 7, 13, 1984; January 23, 1986.

32. *Clearwater Sun*, July 19, 23, 28, 1981.

33. *Orlando Sentinel*, articles in December 1984; and January, March, May, June, August, October 1985.

34. *North Jersey Herald and News*, March 10, 1990.

35. Greg Paeth, "Rebuilding the Housing Authority," *Kentucky Post*, April 24, 26, 1986.

36. *Columbia Missourian*, June 5, 12, 1988.

37. *Houston Post*, May 15, July 9, 1987.

38. U.S. General Accounting Office, *Public Housing: Dallas Housing Authority* (Washington, D.C., 1989).

39. U.S. General Accounting Office, *Public Housing: Chicago Housing Authority* (Washington, D.C., 1986).

40. *Chicago Tribune*, series of articles 1983–1987; *New York Times*, April 17, 1990.

41. *The Bond Buyer*, March 4, 1985; February 26, 1987.

42. *Seattle Post Intelligence*, February 13, March 13, May 16, July 1, 1980.

43. *Buffalo News*, July 19, 20, 1987; U.S. General Accounting Office, *Public Housing: Buffalo Municipal Housing Authority* (Washington, D.C., 1991).

44. *Syracuse Herald Journal*, April 21, 24, May 17, 1985.

45. *Boston Globe*, November 18, 1990.

46. Mary K. Nenno, *Housing and Community Development: Maturing Functions of State and Local Government* (Washington, D.C.: NAHRO, 1989).

47. "New Initiatives in Low Income Housing Preservation."

48. Office of California Budget Analyst, *The 1990–91 Budget* (Sacramento, 1990).

49. John C. Nuveen and Co., Inc., "Tax Exempt Local Single Family Housing" (Chicago, 1989).

50. *New York Times*, March 18, 1990.

Chapter 9: The Big Fix

1. Mary B. W. Tabor, "Highway Project May Bring Boston to a Standstill," *New York Times*, June 6, 1991.

2. National Council on Public Works Improvement, *Fragile Foundations: A Report on America's Public Works*, Final Report to the President and Congress (Washington, D.C., 1988).

3. U.S. Department of Transportation, *Highway Statistics 1988* (Washington, D.C., 1989); U.S. General Accounting Office, *Transportation Infrastructure* (Washington, D.C., 1989).

4. Kenneth M. Mead, "Transportation Infrastructure," statement before the Committee on Environment and Public Works, U.S. Senate (Washington, D.C.: GAO, 1991).

5. *Albany Times Union*, March 21, 1991.

6. David Broder, column in *Boston Globe*, March 11, 1991.

7. GAO, *Transportation Infrastructure*.

8. *New York Times*, March 9, 1990.

9. Broder column.

10. *Public Administration Times*, May 1, 1990; Anthony Commission on Public Finance, *Preserving the Federal-State-Local Partnership: The Role of Tax Exempt Financing* (Washington, D.C., 1989).

11. Congressional Budget Office, *Toll Financing* (Washington, D.C., 1988).

12. *Transportation Infrastructure*.

13. Institute of Public Administration, *Special Districts and Public Authorities in Public Works Provision* (Washington, D.C.: National Council on Public Works Improvement, 1987).

14. U.S. General Accounting Office, *Toll Roads in the States* (Washington, D.C., 1989).

15. *New York Times*, May 3, 1991.

16. *Albany Times Union*, November 15, 1990.

17. *Transportation Infrastructure*.

18. State of Illinois, Office of Auditor General, *Illinois State Toll Highways* (Springfield, Ill., 1988).

19. John C. Nuveen and Co., Inc., "The Chicago Skyway" (Chicago, 1986); *Municipal Default Patterns*.

20. Testimony by Kenneth M. Mead before House Committee on Public Works and Transportation (Washington, D.C.: GAO, 1991); *1989 Transit Fact Book* (Washington, D.C.: American Public Transit Association, 1989).

21. *New York Times*, April 16, 1991.

22. Ibid.

23. *Transportation Infrastructure*.

24. *1989 Transit Fact Book*.

25. *Chicago Sun Times*, various stories in the latter part of 1987.

26. *Boston Globe*, occasional series on MBTA in 1978 and 1987.

27. Joseph S. Revis and Curtis Tarnoff, *Intermodal Transportation* (Washington, D.C.: National Council on Public Works Improvement, 1987); Apogee Research, *A Consolidated Performance Report on the Nation's Public Works* (Washington, D.C.: National Council on Public Works Improvement, 1987).

28. Steven A. Morrison, "Helping Airports Take Off," *New York Times*, March 16, 1990.

29. *New York Times*, March 20, 1990.

30. U.S. Department of Transportation, Press Release, March 14, 1991.

31. *Special Districts and Public Authorities*.

32. *New York Times*, June 12, 1990.

33. American Association of Port Authorities, *1988 Finance Survey* (Alexandria, Va., 1989).

34. *New York Times*, June 12, 1990.

35. *Hearing*, Subcommittee of the New Jersey Senate Independent Authorities Committee, March 4, 1986.

36. *Philadelphia Inquirer*, May 24, 1988.

37. Kathleen Sylvester, "The Wreck of the Port of Baltimore," *Governing*, July 1990.

38. *The Bond Buyer, 1989 Yearbook*.

39. "A Terminal Case," a series published March 4–9, 1984, in the *Oregonian*.

40. Anne Marie Walsh and James Leigland, "The Only Planning Game in Town," *Empire State Reports*, May 1983.

41. *New York Times*, May 31, 1972.

42. *New York Times*, February 3, 1991; *The Bond Buyer*, June 21, 1984.

43. *New York Times*, November 22, 1991.

Chapter 10: The Big Cleanup

1. Philip Shabecoff, "Government Says Abandoned Love Canal Homes Are Safe," *New York Times*, May 15, 1990.

2. Apogee Research, *Hazardous Waste Management* (Washington, D.C.: National Council on Public Works Improvement, 1987).

3. *New York Times,* December 24, 1991.

4. U.S. General Accounting Office, *Superfund* (Washington, D.C., 1987).

5. Congressional Budget Office, *Municipal Water Supply* (Washington, D.C., 1987).

6. EPA, *The Challenge of Meeting Environmental Responsibilities* (Washington, D.C., 1988); EPA, *State Use of Alternative Financing Mechanisms in Environmental Programs* (Washington, D.C., 1988); Roger D. Feldman, Richard Mudge, and Kenneth J. Rubin, *Financing Infrastructure Tools for the Future* (New York: Executive Enterprise, 1988).

7. Apogee Research, *Wastewater Management* (Washington, D.C.: National Council on Public Works Improvement, 1987).

8. George F. Ames, "Role of the State Infrastructure Financing Agencies in the 1990's" (Washington, D.C.: Council of Infrastructure Financing Authorities, 1990).

9. Virginia M. Perrenod, *Special Districts: Special Purposes* (College Station: Texas A&M University Press, 1984).

10. *New York Times*, February 10, 1991; Peter Passell, "Economic Scene," *New York Times*, February 27, 1991.

11. EPA, *Paying for Cleaner Water* (Washington, D.C., 1988).

12. Ken Edelstein, "Expensive Solutions for Aging Sewers," *Governing*, February 1991.

13. EPA, *Wastewater Technical Assistance* (Washington, D.C., 1988).

14. Apogee Research, *Wastewater Management.*

15. "Expensive Solutions for Aging Sewers."

16. John C. Nuveen and Co., Inc., "The 1988 Consolidation of Houston's Water and Sewer Systems" (Chicago, 1989).

17. EPA, "Proceedings of the National Leadership Conference on Building a Public-Private Partnership," (Washington, D.C., 1989).

18. *Public Administration Times*, July 1990.

19. *New York Times*, February 26, 1991.

20. R. U. Beck and Associates, *Solid Waste* (Washington, D.C.: National Council on Public Works Improvement, 1987).

21. Ibid.

22. *New York Times*, August 27, 1988; December 20, 1989.

23. Mark Paxton, "County Accepts Trash for Jobs and Clean Water," Associated Press report in *Cape Cod Times*, July 14, 1991.

24. *New York Times*, October 23, 1988.

25. U.S. General Accounting Office, *Hazardous Waste* (Washington, D.C., 1988).

26. Shirley Hobbs Scheibla, "Messy Cleanup," *Barron's*, December 18, 1989.

27. *New York Times*, July 18, 1991.

28. *New York Times*, July 12, 1991.

29. U.S. General Accounting Office, *Water Pollution* (Washington, D.C., 1988, 1989); *New York Times*, April 15, July 29, 1991.

30. Congressional Budget Office, *Federal Liabilities Under Hazardous Waste Laws* (Washington, D.C., 1990).

31. *Barron's*, December 18, 1989.

32. Keith Schneider, "Industries and Towns Clash over Who Pays to Tackle Toxic Waste," *New York Times*, July 18, 1991.

33. *New York Times*, October 18, 1989.

34. Apogee Research, *Hazardous Waste Management*.

Chapter 11: Power to the People

1. American Public Power Association, *Public Power: Annual Statistical Issue* (Washington, D.C.: January/February 1991).

2. *Barron's*, October 30, 1989.

3. *Long Island News*, September 8, 1989.

4. *New York Times*, May 27, 1988.

5. *Long Island News*, September 8, 1989.

6. *New York Times*, May 27, 1988.

7. Ibid.

8. *Barron's*, October 30, 1989.

9. "Clean Power's Strong Enemies," *New York Times*, March 14, 1990.

10. Letter to the *New York Times*, March 30, 1991.

11. *Public Power Weekly*, May 13, 1991.

12. American Public Power Association, *Public Power in America: A History* (Washington, D.C., 1990).

13. Ibid.

14. Campaign speech in Portland, Oregon, June 1932.

15. *Public Power in America*.

16. Richard H. Longshore, "The Power Authority of The State of New

York: Accountability and Public Policy" (Ph.D. thesis, Syracuse University, 1981).

17. Michael K. Heiman, *Quiet Evolution* (New York: Praeger, 1988); Roscoe C. Martin, *Water for New York* (Syracuse: Syracuse University Press, 1961).

18. *Abuse of Power*.

19. *White Plains Reporter Dispatch*, February 25, 1987.

20. Ibid.

21. Karen DeWitt, "How Much Power?" *Empire State Report*, April 1987.

22. *Long Island News*, July 10, 1985.

23. John D. Donahue, *The Privatization Decision* (New York: Basic Books, 1989).

24. Ibid.

25. *Public Power Weekly*, May 13, 1991.

26. *San Francisco Bay Guardian*, January 18–24, 1984.

27. John C. Nuveen and Co., Inc., "Tax Exempt Electric Power Suppliers" (Chicago, 1988).

28. *Public Power Weekly*, July 15, 1991.

29. John C. Nuveen and Co., Inc., "M-S-R Public Power Agency" (Chicago, 1988).

30. *City and State*, March 12, 1990.

31. Ibid.

32. John C. Nuveen and Co., Inc., "Piedmont Municipal Power Agency—South Carolina" (Chicago, 1987).

33. *Public Power: Annual Statistical Issue*, 1991.

34. U.S. Department of Energy, *Financial Statistics of Selected Investor-Owned Electric Utilities 1989* (Washington, D.C., 1989); *Financial Statistics of Selected Publicly Owned Electric Utilities 1989* (Washington, D.C., 1989).

35. American Public Power Association, *Project 2000* (Washington, D.C.).

36. *The Bond Buyer*, March 8, 1985; *Credit Markets*, October 2, 1989.

37. *The Bond Buyer, 1991 Yearbook*.

Chapter 12: Public Authorities Join the Welfare State

1. *The Bond Buyer, 1991 Yearbook*.

2. U.S. General Accounting Office, *Tax Exempt Bonds* (Washington, D.C., 1991).

3. Ibid.

4. John C. Nuveen and Co., Inc., "COPs and Lease-Backed Bonds in Major Leasing States" (Chicago, 1991).

5. U.S. General Accounting Office, *Nonprofit Hospitals* (Washington, D.C., 1990).

6. *The Bond Buyer*.

7. Ibid.

8. Ibid.

9. John C. Nuveen and Co., Inc., *Tax Exempt Hospital Financing— California* (Chicago, 1989).

10. *New York Times*, August 27, September 7, 1991.

11. John W. Illyes, "California School COPs and Bonds after Richmond" (Chicago: John Nuveen, 1991).

12. "COPs and Lease-Backed Bonds."

13. Franklin Frazier, "Financial Problems in the Stafford Student Loan Program" (Washington, D.C.: U.S. General Accounting Office, 1990).

14. *Barron's*, July 30, 1990.

15. Memorandum vetoing sections of 1985–86 budget bill, July 7, 1985.

16. "Financial Problems in the Stafford Student Loan Program."

17. Jason D. Parle, "Banks May Be Held Liable for Bad Student Loans," *New York Times,* July 15, 1991.

18. Ibid.

19. Jaye Scholl, "Default Line," *Barron's*, May 13, 1989.

20. U.S. General Accounting Office, *Student Loan Lenders* (Washington, D.C., 1990).

21. Robert Pear, "Administration Seeking to Bypass Banks in Student Loan Program," *New York Times*, January 7, 1991.

22. Eric J. Savitz, "Pros and Cons: The Jury Is Still Out on Private Prisons," *Barron's*, November 6, 1989.

23. Ibid.

24. *Wall Street Journal*, June 29, 1988.

Chapter 13: Reclaiming the Shadow Government

1. *Public Forum on Public Authorities: Government Savior or Government Substitute?* (Princeton: Woodrow Wilson School of Public and International Affairs, Princeton University, 1982).

2. *New York Times*, September 23, 1991.

INDEX

Abrams, Robert, 71
Advance refunding, 56–57
Air travel, 235–38
Airport and Airway Trust Fund, 237
Akron Metropolitan Housing Authority (AMHA), 207–10
Alexander, Lamar, 256
Alexander, Lee, 214–15
Alioto, Joseph, 161–62
Allegheny County Sanitary Authority (ALCOSAN), 260–62
Alter, Edward, 147
American Municipal Bond Assurance Corporation, 54
American Public Power Association, 288–89
Anderson, Barbara, 165 66
Anderson, Warren, 93
Anthony, Beryl, 224
Arbitrage, 59, 86
Arred, Ralph, 298
Assembly Committee on Public Authorities, 97
Atiyeh, Victor, 102, 242

Barraga, Thomas F., 281–82
Bay Area Rapid Transit (BART), 32
Bear, Stearns, 153
Benjamin, Alvin, 298
Bentley, Alene, 286
Berman, Douglas C., 88
Beverly Enterprises, 91
"Big Dig," 106, 172, 220
Big MAC, 8, 17, 80–82, 114, 136, 137
Bodman, Roger, 87
Bond
  callable date of, 56
  counsel, 154–59
  covenant, 134–38
  general obligation (GO), 19
  junk, 53
  maturity date of, 56
  "moral obligation," 4–5, 19, 46–48
  "no worry," 4–5

premature redemption of, 56–57
private purpose, 58
public purpose, 58
rating of, 4, 52–56, 159–60
revenue, 19, 38–39
tax allocation, 48–50
tax reform effects on, 57–62
taxable, 62
underwriters of, 142–54
Bond Investors Association, 89
Bonneville Power Administration (BPA), 10, 64–65, 66–67, 68, 70, 71, 102, 277
Bonsall, Mark, 149
Boot, Charles R., 265
Boren, David, 249
Borrowing, state restrictions on, 35–37
Boston Globe, 104–6
Boston Magazine, 106
Boston Transit Commission, 24
Boxer, Barbara, 283
Bradley, Tom, 162
Brisbin, Patricia, 210
Broder, David, 168
Brotman, Stanley S., 241
Brown, Michael, 268
Bruce, Douglas, 166
Buchanan and Co., 151–52
Bulger, William, 102, 104, 105
Bulls, James E., 260, 261
Burford, Anne McGill, 246, 264
Burick, John, 314
Burton, John E., 279
Busey, James B., 238
Bush, George, 2, 3, 8, 191
Bush administration, 2, 33, 174–75, 198, 223, 224–25, 230
Byrne, Brendan T., 135, 136
Byrne, Jane M., 149, 213–14

Calabrese, Wayne, 209–10
California, 10, 14, 189–90
  borrowing restrictions in, 36

California (*Continued*)
  education authorities in, 298–99
  hospital authorities in, 296–97
  and lease-purchase plans, 42
  and moral obligation bonds, 47–48
  power problems in, 283–85
  Supreme Court of, 131–32
  and tax increment financing, 48
California Housing Finance Agency, 17
Cantalupo, Robert, 207
Carey, Hugh L. , 41, 78–79, 80, 81, 95, 127, 136, 184
Carter, Jimmy, 202
Casey, Robert P., 110, 261
Catacosinos, William J., 272
Certificates of participation (COPs), 44–46
Chicago Housing Authority (CHA), 213–14
Chicago Transit Authority (CTA), 132, 233–34
Citizens for Limited Taxation (CLT), 165–66
City Club of New York, 97–98
Clarke, Marianne K., 177
Cohalan, Peter, 271
Cohen, Claire, 92
Cohen, Julius Henry, 25, 26, 199
Colony, Margaret, 314
Colorado
  and oversight of public authorities, 98–99
  Supreme Court of, 132
Columbia Valley Authority (CVA), 65
Committee on Independent Governmental Authorities, 99
Commodity Credit Corporation (CCC), 27
Common Cause, 314
Comunale, Stephen, 209
Conable, Barber, Jr., 81
Correction facilities, 307–8
Corrections Corporation of America (CCA), 308
Coyle, Stephen, 83
Cranson, Robert G., 9, 38, 100, 182
Creehan, James, 260, 261
Cuomo, Mario M., 41, 79, 81, 88, 96, 97, 110, 113–14, 156, 158, 166, 183–87, 224, 227–28
  and Shoreham, 271–74

Daniels, Belden, 178
Defense Plant Corporation, 30
Deficit Reduction Act (DEFRA) of 1984, 58
Delaware Solid Waste Authority, 258–59
De Pasquale, Eugene, 262
Deprezio, Richard, 234
Deukmejian, George, 189
Dewey, Thomas E., 27, 279
Dinkins, David N., 151
Di Vito, Leo R., 257
Domenici, Peter, 249
Donahue, John D., 282
Dormer, Robert, 186–87

Dormitory Authority (DA—New York State), 6, 47, 95–96, 300
Downs, Tom, 227
Dukakis, Michael S., 8–9, 61, 83, 102, 105, 114–15, 138, 156, 234, 274
  and Boston Harbor, 8–9
  and the Massachusetts miracle, 168–73
  and Seabrook, 274–76
Dunham, Richard L., 77

E. F. Hutton, 153–54
Earl, Anthony S., 138–39, 303
Economic development apparatus, state-level, 173–78
Economic Revitalization Fund of Pennsylvania, 18
Education authorities, 297–307
Edwards, Philip, 285
Ehrlichman, John, 77
Eisenhower, Dwight D., 3
Emergency Financial Control Board (EFCB), 80
Emergency Moratorium Act, 137
Environment, cleanup of, 245–69
Environmental Protection Agency (EPA), 245, 246, 247, 250, 255, 257, 258, 264, 266
Esser, Jeffrey, 112

Faith Evangelistic Mission Corporation. *See* First Humanics
Farm Mortgage Corporation (FMC), 27
Federal Energy Regulatory Commission (FERC), 285, 286
Federal Deposit Insurance Corporation (FDIC), 2, 27
Federal Highway Corporation, 3
Federal Home Loan Mortgage Corporation ("Freddie Mac"), 201–2
Federal Housing Administration (FHA), 27, 200
Federal Housing and Urban Development Act of 1968, 74
Federal National Mortgage Association ("Fannie Mae"), 3
Federal Savings and Loan Insurance Corporation (FSLIC), 1–2, 27
Feinstein, Dianne, 214
Feldman, Daniel, 281
Ferber, Mark S., 147–48, 159
Ferrara, Kenneth J., 55
Finance Guaranty Insurance Company (FGIC), 54
First Humanics, 90–91
Fitch Investment Service, 52, 159
Fitzgerald, Darrell, 212
Fitzgerald, Joy, 212
Fitzpatrick, John, 209
Florida, 192
  borrowing restrictions in, 36
  and lease-purchase plans, 42–43
  Supreme Court of, 121–22

Florio, Jim, 88–89, 109–11, 114, 166, 240–41, 317
Flynn, Raymond, 147
Flynn, Richard, 281
Fontes, Roger, 284
Ford, Gerald R., 5, 81
Fratto, Anthony, 149–50
Fratto, Joseph M., 149–50
Freeman, David, 285
Fuchsberg, Jacob D., 126

Galbraith, John Kenneth, 34
Gambaccini, Louis, 231
Garrity, Paul, 215
Giglio, Joseph M., 87, 92
Gleckman, Howard, 69, 72
Golden, Harrison J., 151
Goldmark, Peter C., Jr., 80, 81, 125, 244
Gore, Albert, 284
Government corporations. *See* Public authorities
Government National Mortgage Association (GNMA; "Ginnie Mae"), 27, 200
Gray, Michael, 211
Great Society, the, 32
Green, Jeff, 149
Grossman, Hyman, 51
Gulick, Luther, 14
Gunn, David, 234

Hanford Nuclear Reservation (HNR), 64, 65, 66
Hazardous waste, 247–51
Hedges, Dan, 305
Hedges, Jay, 179
Henriques, Diana B., 107–8, 216
Herbers, John, 177–78
Higher Education Facilities Authority (HEFA), 61
Highway transportation, 222–29
Hoadley, Frank, 149
Holtzman, Elizabeth, 151
Home Owners Loan Corporation (HOLC), 27
Hoover, Herbert, 198–99
Hospital authorities, 293–97
Housing Finance Agency (HFA—New York State), 6, 42, 73, 76
Housing finance agencies (HFAs), 215–18
Hoyt, William, 281
Hughes, Richard J., 108

Ickes, Harold, 199
Illinois, 9, 14
  and oversight of public authorities, 100–101
  Supreme Court of, 132–34
  and tax increment financing, 48–49
Illinois Economic and Fiscal Commission (IEFC), 182
Industrial authorities (IDAs), 187–89
Initiative 2 1/2, 37, 49, 313

International Longshoreman's Association (ILA), 241–42

Jackson, Henry M., 65, 66
Javis, Michael B., 206
Job Development Authority (JDA), 186–87
Johnson, Jeffrey, 180
Johnson, Luckett, 212
Johnson, Lyndon B., 32
Johnson, Marcia, 212
Johnston, Lemon, 152
Jones, Frank R., 273
Jorling, Thomas C., 268

Katz, Harvey, 50, 112
Kean, Thomas, 40, 86–87
Keefe, Frank, 106
Kemp, Jack F., 191, 203, 206
Kennedy, John F., 64, 65, 66
Kentucky, 191
Kheel, Theodore, 136
Kiley, Robert, R., 234
King, Edward J., 83, 234
Koch, Edward, 7–8, 82
Koenan, Austin V., 148, 149, 151, 159
Koppel, Oliver, 97
Kostrzewa, John, 207–8
Kuttner, Robert, 201

Laird, Melvin, 81
Lantos, Tom, 207
Lashman, L. Edward, 304
Lavelle, Rita M., 246, 264
Lawrence, Barbara L., 87
League of Women Voters, 97, 314
Lease-purchase plans, 39–43
Lee, William E., 209–10
Leeson, George, 305–6
Lefkowitz, Louis, 76
Letters of credit (LOCs), 55
Levey, David, 208, 209
Levine, Jack, 308–9
Levitt, Arthur, 94
Levy, Paul, 21, 53
Lindsay, John V., 74, 75
Lipari, Joseph, 206
Litvak, Lawrence, 178
Locke, James, 242–43
Logue, Edward J., 75–77, 79, 94
Long-term care facilities, 290–93
Love Canal, 245–46
Loveys, Frank A., 87, 88
Lucchino, Frank J., 260

McCormick, Joe, 306
McCune, Donald B., 261
McEaneney, Dennis, 207–8
McGovern, Patricia, 102–4

McHugh, John, 192
Maffi, Ralph J., 261
Magnuson, Warren, 65
Marguglio, Louise, 206
Marguglio, Paul, 206, 207
Marshall, Alton G., 5, 74–75, 79, 94
Massachusetts
 and bond ratings, 54
 hospital authorities in, 295–96
 and moral obligation bonds, 47
 and oversight of public authorities, 102–6
 public authorities in, 169–70
 Supreme Court of, 137–38
 and tax increment financing, 49
Massachusetts Bay Transportation Authority
 (MBTA), 32, 47, 82–84, 103, 121, 167,
 234–35
Massachusetts Convention Center Authority,
 103, 170
Massachusetts Housing Finance Agency
 (MHFA), 84–85, 103
Massachusetts Industrial Financing Authority
 (MIFA), 61, 62, 169–71
Massachusetts Water Resources Authority
 (MWRA), 8–9, 49, 106, 147, 172, 253
Mass transit, 230–35
Matthews and Wright, 152–53
Mattox, Jim, 119
Mazzotta, Sam C., 211–12
Mental Health Facilities Construction Fund
 (New York State), 6, 42
Mercer County Improvement Authority, 41
Metropolitan Atlanta Rapid Transit Authority
 (MARTA), 32
Metropolitan Transit Authority (MTA—
 Houston), 32
Metropolitan Transportation Authority (MTA—
 New York State), 6, 29, 127, 139, 167
Michaelis, August, 206, 207
Miller, David, 214
Milstein, Carl, 208
Missouri, 191
Mitchell, George, 2
Mitchell, John A., 4–5, 46, 155
Moody's Investment Service, 4, 43, 52, 159
Moore, Arch A., Jr., 289
Moore, Martha, 263
Moreland Act Commission, 95, 97–98
Mortgage Subsidy Bond Act of 1980, 58
Moses, Robert, 25, 27, 28–30, 75, 87, 134,
 279
Moss, Robert S., 76–77
Moynihan, Daniel Patrick, 60, 214, 224, 230
Mudge, Rose et al., 155, 156
Municipal Assistance Corporation. See Big
 MAC

Municipal Bond Investors Assurance (MBIA),
 54
Municipal Electric Authority of Georgia, 17
Municipal Securities Rulemaking Board
 (MSRB), 117, 146–47
Municipal Water Finance Authority (New York
 City), 8

New Jersey, 11, 190–91
 and lease-purchase plans, 40–41
 and oversight of public authorities, 106–11
 Supreme Court of, 130–31
New Jersey Building Authority, 40–41
New Jersey Economic Development Authority,
 17, 41
New Jersey State Department of Community
 Affairs, 108, 109
New Jersey Turnpike Authority, 85–89, 130–31
New Jersey Wastewater Treatment Trust, 18
Newman, Herbert, 208
New Mexico, Supreme Court of, 118–19
New York City
 education authorities in, 298
 and Edward Koch, 7–8
 and UDC, 79–80
New York City Transit Authority (TA), 232
New York State
 borrowing restrictions in, 35–36
 Court of Appeals in, 122–28
 hospital authorities in, 293–95
 and lease-purchase plans, 41–42
 and moral obligation bonds, 46–47
 and Nelson A. Rockefeller, 3–7
 and UDC, 93–98
New York State Commission on Government
 Integrity, 98, 188
New York State Metropolitan Transportation
 Authority (MTA), 32, 139, 232–33
New York State Power Authority, 6, 24, 26–27
Newfield, Jack, 280
Nixon, Richard M., 4, 77, 201
Nunn, Sam, 305
Nusbaum, Joseph, 120
Nuveen, 43

Oberstar, James L., 238
Oestreicher, Eugene, 208
Ohio, 191–92
O'Malley, James, 262
O'Toole, Lawrence W., 304, 306–7

Pacific Gas and Electric (PG&E), 283–84
Pennsylvania, 11, 190
 education authorities in, 297
 and lease-purchase plans, 40
Perrenod, Virginia M., 112

Perry, David, 38
Phillips, Earl, 212–13
Pierce, Samuel R., Jr., 203
Pieri, Donald V., 206
Pinchot, Gifford, 276
"Politics of debt," 37–38
Port of New Orleans, 24
Port authorities, 238–44
Port Authority of New York and New Jersey,
    24–27, 135–36, 158, 166, 243–44
Port Authority Trans-Hudson Corporation
    (PATH), 136, 243–44
Porter, J. Michael, 192
Power Authority of the State of New York
    (PASNY), 29, 272, 277, 278–83
Project Finance Agency, 79
Proposition 13, 10, 37, 42, 44, 47, 48, 163,
    313
Public authorities
    accountability and control framework for,
        317–18
    in Africa, 17
    autonomy of, 138–40
    budgets of, 19–20
    in Canada, 17
    as cash cows, 113–15, 288–89
    characteristics of, 15–16
    and the courts, 118–40
    debt of, 17, 18–21
    definition of, 13–14
    fees of, 162–67
    fifth wave of, 33–34
    first wave of, 27–30
    fourth wave of, 32–33
    in France, 17
    in Germany, 17
    in Great Britain, 17
    history of, 22–27
    and infrastructure repair, 221–22
    in Italy, 17
    in Japan, 17
    local, 11–13
    number of, 13–17
    as off-budget, 2, 3, 4, 5–6
    oversight of, 92–117
    and public housing, 194–219
    rise of, 1–34
    second wave of, 30
    and social programs, 50–52
    in South America, 17
    terms describing, 13
    third wave of, 30–32
    ubiquity of, 11–12
    and utilities, 270–89
    and the welfare state, 290–309
Public Authority Control Board (PACB), 95, 98

Public Securities Association, 55
Public Utilities Regulatory Policy Act (PURPA),
    260
Public Works Administration (PWA), 28, 199

Rafferty, John C., Jr., 209–10
Raine, Alden S., 168
Ravitch, Richard, 184
Reagan, Ronald, 32, 57, 191, 198, 202
Reagan administration, 1, 33, 174–75, 202,
    206, 223, 230
Reaganomics, 33
Reconstruction Finance Corporation (RFC), 27,
    30
Regan, Edward V., 151, 186
Reilly, William K., 264
Reischauer, Robert D., 307
Resolution Trust Corporation (RTC), 2
Robinson, Renault, 214
Rockefeller, David, 78, 243
Rockefeller, Laurence, 29
Rockefeller, Nelson A., 3–7, 29–30, 41, 73,
    74, 75–76, 77, 94, 139, 215, 243, 295
Rohatyn, Felix G., 80–82, 147
Romer, Ray, 99
Ronan, William J., 29–30, 243–44
Roosevelt, Franklin D., 26, 27–28, 30, 65,
    197–98, 277
Roosevelt, Theodore, 276
Rostenkowski, Dan, 60
Ruth, Heather L., 55

Salvucci, Frederick P., 83, 104
Sargent, Francis, 83
Savings and loan associations (S&Ls), bailout
    of, 1–3
Schifrin, Matthew, 91
School Construction Authority (New York City),
    8
Schmeiser, Ronald, 262
Schneier, Bernard, 208
Seaman, Barry, 211
Securities Exchange Commission (SEC), 71–72,
    117
Seidman, Harold, 140
Shannon, John, 165
Shirey, John, 165
Siegel, Mark Alan, 228
Simon, William, 81
Skerry, Richard A., Jr., 62
Skinner, Samuel K., 231, 238
Smith, Alfred E., 25, 26, 199
Smith, Art, 233–34
Smith, Jim, 147
Solid Waste Disposal Authority of Delaware, 18
South Carolina v. *Baker*, 60

Southern Pennsylvania Transportation Authority (SEPTA), 230, 231–32
Special districts. *See* Public authorities
Spellman, John, 102
Stabilization Reserve Corporation (SRC), 124–25
Standard and Poor's, 4, 52, 159
Stanek, Joseph, 262
State of New Jersey Commission of Investigation (SCI), 89, 107, 108
State of New York Mortgage Agency (SONYMA), 73
State revolving funds (SRFs), 250–51
State University Construction Fund (New York State), 6, 42
State Water Project (SWP), 253–55
Steingut, Stanley, 93–94
Stennis, John Hampton, 158
Stepp, Jelica, 212
Stern, William J., 96, 184–85
Stevens, Edward, 262
Strahinich, John, 106, 164
Streestra, Norm, 263
Stressel, Arthur G., Jr., 210
Stringfellow Acid Pits, 246
Student Loan Marketing Association ("Sallie Mae"), 301–2
Sullivan, Joseph "Bo," 85–88
Superfund, 249, 264, 267
Sutcliffe, Lee F., 90–91
Swibel, Charles, 214

Tax Equity and Fiscal Responsibility Act (TEFRA) of 1982, 58
Tax increment financing (TIF), 48–50, 59
Tax Reform Act of 1986, 19, 58–61, 63, 86, 90, 142, 144, 173, 176–77, 224, 249, 268, 289
Taylor, Christopher, 147
Tennessee Valley Authority (TVA), 24, 27–28, 64–65, 277
Tese, Vincent, 183, 185–86
Texas
   borrowing restrictions in, 35
   and lease-purchase plans, 42
   Supreme Court of, 119–20
   and tax increment financing, 49–50
Thompson, James C. ("Big Jim"), 9, 100, 178–82
Tobin, Austin I., 26, 243–44
Toxic wastes, 264–69
Trash, disposal of, 258–64
Triborough Bridge and Tunnel Authority (TBTA), 29, 47, 139, 228–29
Truman, Harry S., 27, 200

Trump, Donald J., 133, 190–91
Turner, Billy, 256

Unrah, Jesse, 116, 146
Urban Development Corporation (UDC—New York State), 6, 41, 72–79, 93–95, 114, 122–24, 127–28, 184–86, 228, 309
U.S. Bureau of the Census, 13–15, 163
   misclassification of public agencies and, 14
U.S. Department of Housing and Urban Development (HUD), 195, 198, 201, 203, 206, 207, 208, 209, 210, 211, 212, 213, 214, 215

Vaughan, Roger J., 182

Wagner, Robert, 199
Wall Street
   and bond issues, 6
   response to WHOOPS, 67, 68, 72
Walsh, Annemarie Hauck, 93, 311
Washington, Harold, 149, 214
Washington Public Power Supply System (WPPSS). *See* WHOOPS
Washington State, 10
   and oversight of public authorities, 101–2
   public utility districts (PUDs) in, 65–66, 69
Wastewater treatment, 255–58
Water, cleanup of, 251–55
Weberman, Ben, 45
Wein, Louis E., 125–26
Wetzler, James W., 187
Whalen, Thomas, 160–61
White, Kevin, 105
Whitehead, Bruce H., 91
Whitley, Douglas L., 101, 112, 141
WHOOPS, 10, 63–72, 101–2, 128–29
Wilkerson, Wallace G., 224
Willen, Stuart, 208–9
Williams, Carl, 214
Wilson, Malcolm, 77, 78, 280
Wilson, Pete, 254, 299
Wilson, Roger, 177
Wisconsin
   and lease-purchase plans, 39–40
   Supreme Court of, 120–21
Wisconsin Higher Education Corporation (WHEC), 138–39, 302–3
Woods, George D., 75–76
Wulf, Henry, 15

York, David, 211
Yorty, Samuel, 162
Young, Anthony, 179

Zandlo, Carol, 90
Zemprelli, Edward, 262